68

A TIME OF WAR

JAMES GOULD COZZENS

A TIME OF WAR

Air Force Diaries and
Pentagon Memos, 1943-45

Edited by Matthew J. Bruccoli

Columbia, S.C. & Bloomfield Hills, Mich.
Bruccoli Clark
1984

INTRODUCTION

James Gould Cozzens entered the Air Force in the summer of 1942; he was thirty-nine and the author of ten published novels. Since a distinction of his fiction is an unmatched ability to treat a profession and its life with convincing familiarity, it was inevitable that his service experiences would require a novel. It was less certain that *Guard of Honor* (New York: Harcourt, Brace, 1948), a work that, as he remarked, "pleads the army's case," would prove to be the best American novel to come out of World War II—despite its stateside setting and absence of heroics.

When *Guard of Honor* was about to be published in London, Cozzens wrote to his English editor:

What I wanted to write about here, the essence of the thing to be said, the point of it all, what I felt to be the important meaning of this particular human experience, was its immensity and its immense complexity.

This feeling had grown on me as my so-called military service drew on and I began slowly to realize that through no fault (or indeed merit) of my own I was being shown the Army Air Forces on a scale and in a way that was really incredible. I was coming to know about, I had to know about, more of its innumerable phases than anyone with real command duties would ever have time to know. Not many officers, and I would guess not any, had reason or opportunity to fly into and look over such a number of air fields and installations of a variety quite unbelievable. With the exception of the CG himself, in whose office I was at the end working, I don't think anyone had occasion to sit down with and listen to so many of the air generals. I know that no other one person read, as I had to read every morning, yesterday's activity reports from all the Air Staff sections along with the CG's in-and-out log, the messages from and to the commanders in all combat theatres. This, I can tell you, while serving no good purpose toward winning the war, was an experience; and though I did not see how I could stand it much longer I felt at least that writer's excitement of coming to understand things I would want to tell other people about.

With my head full of all this, I could see I faced a tough technical problem. I wanted to show that real (as I now saw it) meaning of the whole business, the peculiar effects of the interaction of innumerable individuals functioning in ways at once determined by and determining the functioning of innumerable others—all in the common and in every case nearly helpless involvement in what had ceased to be just an "organization" (I think it ceased to be that when it grew past the point where one directing head could keep the whole in mind) and became if not an organism with life and purposes of its own, at least an entity, like a crowd. As in a packed crowd, nobody from the CG down could really move unless somebody else moved; and if he moved, still somebody else had to move too. Thus nobody had a real choice any more; the CG could only do what the capacities of those under him enabled him to do; those under him by steps through the whole chain of command could only do (short of trying to quit; which for physical or mental reasons hardly anyone found feasible) what orders said was to be done.[1]

Remarkable as *Guard of Honor* is as a work of literature, equally remarkable are the documents of the novelist's Air Force service—the official reports and private records he compiled from his coign of vantage. His diaries and memos augment the history books, filling in the published accounts of the "immense complexity" through which the war was waged. This is what happened at the top command level as perceived by a privileged outsider supremely skilled in the techniques of observation.

Cozzens attended Air Force Officers Training School in Miami during August and September 1942. He was commissioned a first lieutenant and assigned to the Training Literature Section of the Training Aids Directorate (TAD) at Gravelly Point, Washington, D. C., as a writer of manuals and reports. On 6 October 1942 he began keeping a detailed typed diary—which ran to 380 single-spaced pages—with the idea that his service experiences would provide material for a novel. TAD was relocated at Orlando, Florida, in November 1942 and then at 1 Park Avenue, New York City, in May 1943. Cozzens was promoted to captain in August 1943. In October he was reassigned to the Office of Special Projects, Office of Technical Information (later the Office of Information Services) at Air Forces Headquarters in the Pentagon Building, Washington, D. C.

He later described the OIS in *Morning Noon and Night* (New York: Harcourt, Brace & World, 1968):

If you supposed, as you reasonably might, that its function was to give out information, you would be much mistaken. What little 'information' it handled was highly classified, prepared for and only available to the offices of the Chief of Air Staff and the Commanding General. From the daily activity reports that all Air Staff sections were directed to send him, and from the Top Secret In and Out Log which he had been cleared to read, one officer [Cozzens] compiled a regular memorandum. Known familiarly as the Scandal Sheet, it called attention to any developments anywhere in the Air Force that could, coming to light, make for unfavorable publicity, harm the AAF. Alerted this way, the high command would not be taken unprepared, could have plans ready to minimize the damage as far as possible if the newspapers picked the business up. While the office did a few odd jobs like this, its principal work was composing speeches for the C. G. and writing articles that he would sign. There was enough of such writing work (by special favor one or another of the Assistant Chiefs of Air Staff was occasionally served) to keep fairly busy five officers in civilian life professional writers, published authors. . . . (p. 300)

Introduction

Writing for General H. H. Arnold (the Commanding General, who was referred to by the Air Staff as "Mr. A.") and General Barney Giles (the Chief of Air Staff) dismayed Cozzens; nonetheless, he understood their qualifications for their jobs:

There's nothing the matter with Gen Giles except that he is, like Mr A, illiterate; something which is habitually made too much of by people who do a lot of reading or writing. Either is really a drawback in the strictly practical affair of getting an army together and fighting with it. Everything you do starts chains of irrelevant ideas (derived from reading and extended by attempting to express in words shades of meaning). I have a pet theory that one of the reasons that we are winning the war is that, markedly in the German case, and relatively in the Japanese case, the generals who oppose us have a high proportion of intellectuals. They waste their time weighing complex factors and looking beyond the immediate objective and while they ponder, their simple and single minded opponents take them for all they have. It is what Hitler meant when he spoke of military idiots. Mr A, like his Chief of Staff, seem to me really dumb—their ideas all absurd and infantile, their crotchets cheap and tiresome. . . . But the fact remains that, by being what he is, Mr A performed the impossible in building the air force; and Gen Giles who acts as what might be called his general manager, by being what he is, keeps it going.[2]

By January 1945 Cozzens had freed himself from speech-writing chores by taking over the press briefings and by enlarging his memos:

As for Mr A, except for an occasional delicate letter or telegram I do nothing for him any more—a decision I arrived at all of a sudden last spring on the occasion of the WAC parade at Bolling Field when he edited my text. I could not help seeing that there was no sense in trying to help him. I think the specific turning point was when he insisted on changing my line: We want you with us when we win, into: We want you with us when we march through Berlin to Tokyo. I just couldn't stand it any longer, so I set about developing my memorandum or gossip service and when the 'indoctrination' conferences were set up, froze onto them. It is now understood that I have no time to write any speeches, so whoever does them, it won't be I. On this basis, I get along quite contentedly, besides improving my mind by the considerable exertions I am put to every day to digest or analyze what the Air Staff is up to, as shown in their twenty-odd activity reports. This makes me very well informed indeed and I find it full of interest. I daresay the set-up is obscure to you, and I don't know whether I can make it clear. There is Mr A on top, and then there is Lt Gen Giles . . . who is both Deputy Commanding General and Chief of Air Staff. As C/AS, he has four brigadier generals as his deputies (Owens, Timberlake, Norstadt, and (until last week) Smith, now replaced by Hood.) Our organization is a so-called exempt organization—that is, not under any of the Assistant Chiefs of the Air Staff (not to be confused with Deputy Chiefs, who are Gen Giles' executives, while the Assistant Chiefs head staff sections—Intelligence; Training; Materiel & Services; Operations, Commitments and Requirements; Personnel, and so on). Our Col Rex Smith . . . reports directly to Mr A (instead, as would be the case of every other Hq office, to one of the Assistant Chiefs). What we are supposed to be doing is advising Mr A and Gen Giles (number 1 and number 2 in command) on 'policy' in matters which involve the AAF's relations to the public. The object of the conferences, for instance, is to sell the newspaper people in an informal way those ideas and attitudes about AAF organization and operations that we would like them to have. We have been quite successful, thanks largely to Gen Smith's gifts (and no doubt it part, to my clear, well-written and well-argued texts). It is a hot way to spend a war, but I daresay it is as useful as anything else I could do.[3]

Cozzens found the seed for *Guard of Honor* while preparing memos on the protest against segregated officers clubs by Negro officers at Freeman Field, Indiana, in 1945. (The setting for his novel was Ocanara, Florida, based on Orlando.) The diaries and memos published here obviously establish background for *Guard of Honor*. But *A Time of War* has not been published to provide a gloss on the novel. The chief worth and wider application of this material is that it provides a unique inside view of the air war by a highly intelligent, keenly observant, civilian-in-uniform granted temporary access to the highest command levels.

When he was finishing *Guard of Honor* in 1947 Cozzens asked General Hume Peabody, under whom he had served at the School of Applied Tactics in Orlando, to vet the novel. Cozzens's letter reveals the loyal-alumnus feeling he had developed for the Air Force and his respect for the professional soldiers as professionals:

In fact, it is a real if slight embarrassment for me to find that I had to depart from a venerable tradition among writers. I know that any writer, caught by the mil. ser. is expected, as soon as he gets shut of it to fearlessly expose the corruption and inefficiency, and not to shrink from getting square with any high placed lugs who had him at a temporary disadvantage. It is awkward to have to say that, after seeing about all there was to see in the AAF, I am for, rather than against, the mil. ser.

This could be sheer ignorance; but of course I don't think so. During many months in Washington one of my jobs, sordid but interesting, was to prepare a daily burn-this report digesting information supplied me confidentially by all the AC/AS offices on what was going wrong. I think it unlikely than any one person in the Air Force was more fully and regularly advised of the scandals, misadventures and dirty deals which here and there enlivened the record. On reflection, none of it seems to me important compared to the remarkable work of a remarkable number of able and devoted men.

I will not say that everyone impressed me highly, or that I approved of everything. Another of my jobs involved sitting down with the visiting brass as soon as it got in and tactfully (I thought) shaping its expressions of opinion so that no one would be shooting his face off at variance with the current line projected by "an AAF spokesman". When this involved telling someone like Kenney or young Curtis LeMay what he did not know he thought, it could be rugged. I don't mean that they were examples of what failed to impress me. I have seldom been more impressed by anyone than by LeMay who once put his chest against mine, my back being against the wall of General Fred Smith's office and said, confusing me with General Eaker, I suppose, that whoever fixed up this idea ought to be socked. At any rate, I saw and listened to a lot; and it led me occasionally to believe I could make better decisions than some I saw the CG and two successive Chiefs of Air Staff making in non-tactical matters. Even in tactical matters I sometimes disagreed with them. By the end of 1944 I was ready, whenever called on, to make important changes. The man I would have appointed CG was Orvil Anderson and the man I would have appointed Chief of Air Staff was you.[4]

When *Guard of Honor* was ready, Cozzens wrote to General Peabody explaining how the military characters had been invented by a process of amalgamation:

I think perhaps I should add one thing—a matter usually classified Top Secret in this trade; but I feel sure you have had experience in safeguarding classified material. All prudent writers publically maintain that their characters are completely original and in no way resemble anyone on earth—quite often I must admit they seem to have a point there, too. But in fact I am sure most writers when they see their character see someone a good deal like someone they have seen sometime. Quite often I think it is a kind of composite. You will find in the ms. two regular army air force general officers and I will confess to you that General Beal, as he moved in my mind was in appearance difficult to distinguish from Lauris Norstad, while in speech and attitude he certainly reminded me of Freddy Smith. Similarly, General Nichols kept looking a lot like General Kuter while his observations were, some of them, not too far from some I have heard General Vandenberg make. You no doubt know all these men and perhaps you know one or more of them very well. I know them well only in the sense that I spent a lot of time looking at them and listening to them. Since, I don't have to say, no portrait is intended, I thought I would ask you, if you noticed any detail of the private life or military career of my generals which seemed uniquely or peculiarly true to you with respect to any of those four you might happen to know well to tell me and I will change it. It would only be so by chance; but I have been surprised before this to find that the chance is not quite as remote as you would expect. When you know a person's face and talk and start inventing a 'story' to suit them, what you decide fits best is sometimes better than that—it's perfect, it really happened to them. This can be awkward for everyone![5]

Although Cozzens did not compile his Air Force diaries with the intention of publication, by 1965 he began considering the idea of publishing them: "talk of the new 'forms' of the novel makes me note that perhaps under the title of: *A Time of War* a book could be put together from my own diaries in the service and the stuff in my Pentagon 'memoranda' with comment on what I did not write then, or what I see today."[6] A list in one of his notepads provides other possible titles: "A Posture of Defence," "Order of Battle," "Forlorn Hope," "The News from Home," "The Fighting Man," "Coign of Vantage," "The Passing Show."[7] Cozzens did not act on this plan; but on 2 January 1976 he asked if I would be interested in publishing a limited edition of his OIS memos: "It has been suggested to me that here was a real picture of top echelon war workings. Since they were in no way official documents the Air Inspector advised me to remove our section file (so they'd never go into Defence Dept. archives). . . ." I indicated my eagerness to undertake the project, and on the tenth he wrote me:

. . . you'll see I really mentioned the memoranda to try to change my churlish image of refusing everybody everything. So I'm now obliged to make sure that problems (added to the length) exist. I feel no security problem would arise, yes; but the fact remains that some items may *not* be clear, and certainly at least a few names of those the Air Inspector gave me note of as misbehaving would need to be blanked. . . . You'd be right in seeing you'd got a unique piece of work—nothing in all the published war stuff is like it; nothing tells any person interested what war-waging at Top Echelon was like, uncolored by self-serving of most General Officer's Memoirs, or by naked & dead hate-that-officer sheer ignorance of never having been there.

As Cozzens reconsidered his offer, he began looking for a way out. When I reported that since the memos were stamped SECRET, they would have to be officially declassified, he wrote in evident relief on 29 January:

Alas, alas, & My God, that 'clearing with Air Force' will have to stop the plan dead for the time being, and I can't blame Connections I'll leave nameless for thinking I must be losing my mind if I'd supposed anything else. There's only one person left alive who ever saw the memo's you might say professionally & I'd meant to check with him, sure that would work. Thank God again I didn't. Did I know nothing of the congressional Church-Pike rat pack leaving nothing undone to wreck 'security'? Didn't I get the point that until the Ellsberg case (merely nol prosed) gets its quietus, and with it the aiding-and-abetting now scared to death Wash Post-NY Times which would use anything to justify itself—in short, until all that's cleared up we must not only stay out of print but forget those papers even exist. This won't last forever; so, if you like, simply file the copy you have away in obscurity, and if future use becomes possible, it can be all yours.*

Concerned that he had let me down, Cozzens wrote on 22 February:

Your quick willingness to undertake so special a job and your solid plan for its treatment fusses me into wanting to explain my dumbness about security and timing better. The mentioned one person now left alive who knew of the memos is Robert Lovett, the then-Secretary of War for Air. What he was like you'll find, I think justly shown, impersonally in *Guard of H*, p. 57; and more personally, based, that is, on reportings to him at his Executive

---

*The memos were declassified on 28 August 1980 by the Director of Records Declassification Division, General Services Administration, National Archives and Records Services.

Officer's request (though in my case the having anything to do with my being on the CG's staff wasn't so) in *MN&N* [*Morning Noon and Night*] pp 303-07 & pp 389-91. At that time I never knew my memos had ever gone to him. I only learned it years later, 1952, I think when unexpectedly we met once more at Harvard Commencement in a coincidence of both being among those given honorary degrees. Time (like Love?) can level rank and therefore, making cordial small talk on the steps of Widener with his old AAF sidekick, he mentioned them—where were they? I explained the Air Inspector had privately told me, since they were unofficial and no regulation covered them, I'd be smart to lift them from the files while I could. He said: Good; he'd read many of them; pretty soon they could be cleared and he hoped I thought of publishing them. That of course was what I had in mind. . . .

During 1977-78 he discussed with William Jovanovich, his publisher, a plan for editing the Air Force diaries; but Cozzens's death on 9 August 1978 terminated the project.

EDITORIAL PLAN

The Air Force diaries preceding Cozzens's assignment to the Pentagon have been omitted; 76 of his 189 memos have been intercalated with the Pentagon diaries. These diary entries have been edited to remove personal material (such as shopping trips with his wife and office gossip) as well as most of the fairly frequent entries that "We did nothing all day." Deletions are indicated by spaced periods. Certain names in the diaries have been changed to avoid causing possible embarrassment to survivors. The policy on generals—most of whom are now dead—was difficult to set. On the basis that generals are historical figures, their names have been allowed to stand in the diaries. Although Cozzens describes some of the generals he served under as deficient in intelligence, he nonetheless recognizes that they are loyal soldiers who would never knowingly jeopardize the war effort.

The editorial policy has been conservative to preserve the immediacy and informality of the diaries: Cozzens's occasional inconsistencies and his idiosyncratic use of the semicolon have been retained. The only silent emendations in the diaries—except for name changes—are obvious spelling or punctuation corrections. Acronyms and abbreviations are expanded within brackets at their first appearance, and a few words have been supplied in brackets. The diaries have been footnoted, but not the memos; however, the diaries frequently clarify the memo material.

Since the memos have been reproduced in facsimile, names have been blanked—as Cozzens suggested to me—where the material might damage reputations or otherwise cause pain. But if the memo events were reported in the newspapers, the names have been allowed to stand. Cozzens found most people antipathetic: yet he was not malicious, and his intention was not defamatory. In 1970 Cozzens replied to an officer-scholar who had expressed interest in his OIS memos: "About that scandal sheet I think perhaps I should say the important thing seems to me (I being in probably the best position in the AAF to know) that even when collected, concentrated and edited to leave out anything good the stink of scandal never was much of a stink. Some hundreds of individuals were in various ways remiss or worse and that's what I tell about but they form no sample of the some hundred thousands who, if not always competently and intelligently, did (whatever the spate of sorehead postwar novels gives one to understand) a pretty good best they could in re. your school's duty-honor-country."[8] Much of the distinctive character of this material derives from Cozzens's point of view on the events and figures he observed: the perspective of a reclusive writer removed from his comfortable isolation and thrust into a complex military organization, performing duties that involved contact with hundreds of people. James Gould Cozzens did not enjoy the thirty-nine-month interruption; yet it generated "that writer's excitement of coming to understand things I would want to tell other people about."

NOTES

[1]To Kenneth Potter, n.d. CC, Princeton University Library.

[2]To Bertha Cozzens, 13 November 1944. Princeton University Library.

[3]To Bertha Cozzens, 29 January 1945. Princeton University Library.

[4]29 September 1947. CC, Princeton University Library.

[5]n.d. CC, Princeton University Library.

[6]Williamstown Notebooks, 10 January 1966. Princeton University Library.

[7]Princeton University Library.

[8]To Major Vogel, 27 September 1970.

ACKNOWLEDGMENTS

Once again, I am pleased to acknowledge my large debts to the staff of the Department of Special Collections, Princeton University Library: Prof. Richard Ludwig, Jean Preston, Charles Greene, Ann Van Arsdale, Barbara Taylor. G. E. Hasselwander and R. Cargill Hall at the Albert F. Simpson Historical Research Center, Maxwell Air Force Base, provided crucial assistance. Edward Newhouse, Jo H. and Mary Chamberlin, and Margaret McNamee provided eye-witness accounts. Meredith Walker and Catherine Coleman typed and retyped. Judith Baughman participated in every step of the final editing of this volume. Heather Barker and Michael Mullen checked and fetched. The Inter-Library Loan staff at the Thomas Cooper Library, University of South Carolina, was—as always—splendid: Harriet Oglesbee, Lori Finger, Susan Bradley, and Beth Woodard. Prof. George Haimbaugh, University of South Carolina School of Law, provided legal counsel.

I am obligated to these people: Prof. W. R. Anderson, C. E. Frazer Clark, Cary C. Conn, Karin Crine, William H. Cunliffe, Capt. Rick P. DuCharme, Joyce L. Eakin, James N. Eastman, William Emerson, Philip A. Farris, Maj. James A. Grimshaw, Jr., Marilla B. Guptil, William Jovanovich, Col. Frederick T. Kiley, Nellie M. Law, Lt. Col. Henry F. Lippincott, Jr., Jack H. Mooney, Lt. Col. John H. Napier, III, James A. Parrish, Jr., David Schoem, Mary Shaffer, Vernon Sternberg, Senator Strom Thurmond, Maj. John Vermillion, Daniel Wickenden, Robert Woolf. The Office of Air Force History was consistently helpful.

I am fortunate to be at the University of South Carolina, and I am grateful for the support of Prof. George Geckle, Chairman of the English Department.

A TIME OF WAR

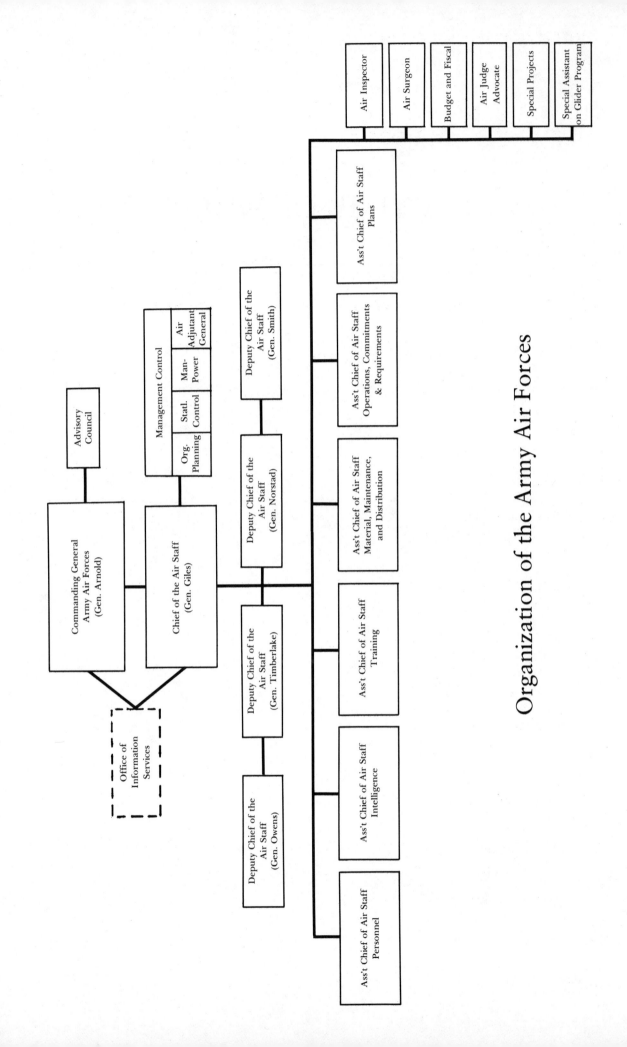

Organization of the Army Air Forces

Advisory Council

Commanding General
Army Air Forces
(Gen. Arnold)

Office of
Information
Services

Management Control

Org. Planning	Statl. Control	Man-Power	Air Adjutant General

Chief of the Air Staff
(Gen. Giles)

Deputy Chief of the Air Staff
(Gen. Owens)

Deputy Chief of the Air Staff
(Gen. Timberlake)

Deputy Chief of the Air Staff
(Gen. Norstad)

Deputy Chief of the Air Staff
(Gen. Smith)

Ass't Chief of Air Staff
Personnel

Ass't Chief of Air Staff
Intelligence

Ass't Chief of Air Staff
Training

Ass't Chief of Air Staff
Material, Maintenance,
and Distribution

Ass't Chief of Air Staff
Operations, Commitments
& Requirements

Ass't Chief of Air Staff
Plans

Air Inspector

Air Surgeon

Budget and Fiscal

Air Judge Advocate

Special Projects

Special Assistant
on Glider Program

In about 9 and to the office[1] where I was flabbergasted by the news that I had been ordered out, neither me nor Col Pardy consulted, to the Office of Technical Information in Washington. I learned it somewhat awkwardly, breezing into our backroom and exchanging banter with Bernard and Callicut, and when I got ready wandering out to speak to Chambers about the *Air Crew* matter.[2] I thought his expression somewhat odd, but laid it to harassment and began at once to ask where Ray and Roach were and what we'd better do. He said they were in Atlantic City and would be back Monday. I said, well in that event there was probably little we could do until then. He said; By the way, you know you aren't here any more, don't you? Afterwards I could see that he must strongly have suspected that I knew very well, having in fact arranged it myself. I said; For God's sake, no what is this? He did not know either. I beat it up to see Col Skeele who said Pardy was in Washington and had squawked, and been told it was at Gen Arnold's personal direction and there was nothing to do, the orders were cut and I was already transferred. I went up then to see Col Straubel at *Air Force*.[3] . . . The idea seemed to be that I would join the people who were trying to write Gen Arnold's reports and so on. He put a call through to Capt, now it seemed Major, Carr and he proved affable enough, even going so far as to say that he thought I would like it better than I sounded as if I did. He said he would phone me tomorrow about whether I could finish the *Fortune* thing or not.[4] He would talk to the General. It disconcerted me a good deal—I kept having that feeling; they can't do that to me; but plainly they could and they had, and there was after all nothing I could say but yes sir. Around the office everyone seemed to regard me with acute envy, and even awe—in Mike Gould's phrase, it was, they thought, God's own job.

. . . My orders came, showing an assignment to something called the Office of Special Projects in the Office of Technical Information. I still did not like it— meaning, I suppose, that I did not like all the damn nuisance; going to Washington, finding a hole to live in, leaving a pleasant apartment, upsetting S's[5] work and so on—which is to say I would like to fight the war not only in safety but in solid comfort. On my 66-1 card,[6] which was delivered over to me I was touched to see that my superiors had given me two Superiors, probably evidence that they did not engineer the change any more than I did.

Monday 1 November 1943

. . . I called Maj Carr's office from Union Station, had lunch, and turned up at 3C124[7] about one. It seemed to be three rooms with a few people scattered through them. A Major Jo Chamberlin[8] whose name I thought I recalled from the weeklies was at one desk and received me kindly, even going so far as to give me a pep talk on the pleasures of working there—I suppose I looked baffled or sulky or something. Major Carr came in finally, very busy in manner and no doubt in fact—thin and pink-cheeked with a little sandy moustache. He too at once set about being kind and encouraging, explaining privileges and perquisites and how one could work to suit oneself. The rest of the set-up was a Lt Reeves[9] said to be a pulp writer and Lt Newhouse[10] who used to write for the *New Yorker*—I felt as if I had joined a literary sideshow. . . .

Tuesday 2 November 1943

Sure enough I was instantly given TD [temporary duty] orders back to New York, suggesting that the Major spoke the truth. I employed myself writing a piece for the Gen to put in some Marine Corps 168th anniversary book and Carr received it with, apparently, pleasure. Lunch with Chamberlin and Newhouse, both great talkers. Newhouse said with satisfaction that there was no army crap about this set-up. I could see how much our viewpoints differed, since I though; more's the pity. It all seems to be easier to take when there is. If I have to do this kind of thing I'd rather do it saying yessir and obeying orders and coming in on time. . . . I caught the 8 pm train to New York—it dumped me in about 1, well worn.

Wednesday 3 November 1943

Into the office where Chambers was talking to Capt Kusner from Ft Worth about the *Air Crew* stuff. He seemed much relieved to see me. Up to *Fortune* where Bill Vogel was in full of enthusiasm. . . . We had a talk with Del Paine and Bill Furth,[11] Del eventually deciding that Vogel would do a rough draft. . . .

Friday 5 November 1943

. . . We conferred most of the afternoon on the *Air Crew* business. . . . It seemed vaguely decided that it might be worth trying a separate publication—I was in a way glad to be out of it; or at least it reminded me that TAD [Training Aids Division] was not exactly the paradise I had come to look back on it as.

2

Monday 8 November 1943

. . . Out to the Pentagon while S continued to look around. Major Carr shook hands with me and said he was glad to see me back, but I saw him no more as apparently the General was after him due to almost being unable to get hold of Newhouse and Chamberlin yesterday afternoon when he had wished abruptly to go over changes in his report with them. I did not know whether this might affect the alleged free and easy life or not and so perhaps my commuting to NY. Carr had not come back by three so I took Chamberlin's advice and left, representing myself as having many things to do. S had hunted in vain all day and decided we might as well take the Parkfairfax[12] thing, if and when. . . . The day seemed depressing, but I could remember the same or even stronger sensations in the same place more than a year ago when I first came in and was doing nothing at Gravelly Point[13] and so I could presume it would pass.

Tuesday 9 November 1943

. . . Over to lunch at the airport with Bert Moore[14] who was a good deal sunk himself with a cold and the loss of more men from ATC [Air Transport Command]. Lt Newhouse proved to be living at the Parkfairfax business and he suggested that I'd better freeze onto it if I was going to. I drove out after lunch and by firmly saying to one of the young ladies that I was in Gen Arnold's office and might have to work all hours got myself an application approved for something called 1513 Mt Eagle Place in a building called 951—one of the duplexes with two bedrooms at $82. . . . Newhouse also took occasion to tell me, with the help of his corrected report, a few things about the General, who seems to be in simplest terms an old bastard, given to hogging credit, and very mean and dangerous to those he dislikes. I had been looking at his extraordinary illiterate books, *Army Flyer* and *Winged Victory* written with Gen Eaker, and clearly their own unassisted work. It seemed plain that he had a taste for fancy, obscure and usually meaningless language so I could see probable trouble of all kinds ahead.

Wednesday 10 November 1943

. . . nothing to do at the office, Carr being again up to his neck, so I did not press him. As a matter of deep military secrecy it developed that the Gen was going overseas somewhere and Chamberlin and Newhouse, both elated at the to-me-repulsive idea, were going to have to fly after in a day or so with the corrected report so any last touches could be given it and they could then fly back with it. . . .

Thursday 11 November 1943

. . . It was announced that Major Haddock[15] was taking over Carr's job—in some

3

way obscure to me Haddock was connected with the outfit a year or so ago, but he has been for two days silent and inoffensive around the office so I trusted he might allow matters to go on—that is, me to go to New York. . . .

Friday 12 November 1943

. . . Over to 1 Park Avenue with some dope for Chambers who seemed glad to get it, but I had in fact nothing to do there, so I went on up to *Fortune.* I talked to Vogel on the telephone, he being home writing, and there seemed no reason to interrupt that, either, so I arranged to see him next week when he would have the draft done. The effect was to disconcert me with a sense of time on my hands—I had no real business here and I was certainly not going back to Washington until I was due there Monday. During the afternoon I did what I could to figure out whether I could write anything of my own, but could not seem to think of much, at least in terms of say, a short story. S suggested that maybe I might like to see whether I really wanted to write the long-ago abandoned civil war book and I gave that some time, looking over my notes—they all seemed to me rather unreal and artificial, as though I were writing through my hat and I could see that if I tried it at all it would have to be from some new angle of approach, and that I could not think of out of hand—but I thought I might keep thinking. I can foresee a lot of delays and waste time in this business and it would help if I did have something.

Saturday 13 November 1943

. . . I tried in the pm to get started on a short story and did better than I expected.

Sunday 14 November 1943

. . . Working on my so-called story in the morning. I found it a pleasure to write but I had no more idea than usual where I was going. . . .

Monday 15 November 1943

To Washington on the 8.30 train. . . . Out to 3C128 where Haddock received me cordially so I soon felt better about him. He seemed sensible and amiable and at the same time shrewd, in the sense of sizing a situation up and seeing what was doing. He questioned me closely on the *Fortune* business, not plainly with any desire to mix in or take over but simply to get straight in his own mind what the people he was commanding were doing. He also gave me the General's Christmas message to do, and a piece for some publication on the 40th anniversary of the Wright brothers' flight.*

*See Appendix.

A Time of War

Tuesday 16 November 1943

Major Haddock took me to see Major Dempsey, who seems to be the General's real & principal private assassin, in the morning. He had an office on D ring with red leather and so on, and made himself very affable—a fleshy genial person of the type best calculated to put my back up; but I soon sensed what I thought was the fact that he was dangerous, and refrained from blurting out, as I had more than half planned, that I didn't like this and wanted to go back to *Air Force* in New York—that is, he was telling me I was just the man for the job and it occurred to me in time that he might not brook contradiction well. Bill Vogel flew in in the afternoon with a cold and part of his ms which, while in fluent Fortunese, was fairly sorry. . . .

Wednesday 17 November 1943

I had put in for my orders for tomorrow, but Miss Kelly told me that the Major wanted to see me—this proved to be a suggestion, rather than order or request, that could I manage not to go until Monday. Newhouse was going overseas to take the corrected report to the General at the very hush-hush rendezvous where presumably the president and everyone else will be—I found I was supporting with relative ease a first rate military secret and other people were going here and there, so I said sure and asked Miss Kelly for orders for Monday instead. I managed to get the Christmas thing done, and not actually without pleasure, since I felt, viewing his previous works, that I had a chance to clean matters up some. Newhouse asked me out to his place where I had some conversation about literature and a drink of rum and met his wife, a pleasant young-looking girl—he, I found, was about ten years younger than I am, but being partly bald and partly gray I had not realized it—nor that he was Hungarian and had known no English fifteen years ago—a nice tribute to the talent for languages they must have, since he writes well and certainly speaks with no accent. . . .

Thursday 18 November 1943

Busy with the General's Wright piece and in the afternoon I turned in that with the Christmas message. Haddock seemed favorably impressed, and I thought myself they weren't bad. . . . I did not seem to do much of anything but it was all vaguely exhausting.

Friday 19 November 1943

Col Straubel turned up today and reproached me warmly with my Christmas message, which it seemed had made a great hit—just the right note of corn, I suppose—and so, he said made it impossible for him ever to get me away. However, it seemed a kind of compliment, and since I had in fact tried, I was pleased. . . .

A Time of War

Monday 22 November 1943

. . . Up to *Fortune* where it was clear that Del did not very much like Vogel's draft, though I could see him, with calculation, refraining from rocking the boat. As nearly as I could judge he and I were still of the same mind about what it ought to have in it. . . .

Wednesday 24 November 1943

Up to work at *Fortune* all day, somewhat enlivened or interrupted by Barbara White's animadversions on Gen Patton, who indeed was taking a licking, and a disagreeably self-righteous sounding one, all around.[16] Though everything I knew about him suggested that he was indeed a detestable heel, I soon found myself arguing that he had probably been a good deal more provoked than the plainly biased stories admitted. I don't know why I take such pleasure in disagreeing with everybody.

Monday 29 November 1943

. . . To the Pentagon where Lt Roach turned up almost immediately (I got in at 8.30), and he was followed by a pleasant nervous Capt Sailors, another navigator with the usual hundred missions (with a little experience you could probably tell how many missions by the degree of nervousness) from the 9th Air Force. They had the *AC* [*Air Crew*] bulletin copy, prepared by Gantz and not too hot, for me to take to Lt Col Lowe in A2 [Intelligence]. I had had dealings with him before on the Ft Worth figures—he is a short, alert looking man with a small dark moustache, a round high forehead and a pleasant intelligent sallow face. He promised to get it cleared for security, but he soon telephoned me and said that Col Besse of *AFGIB* [*Air Force General Information Bulletin*] wanted to see me. It developed that he was against the separate publication and seemed to have ways of making sure that Management Control would also be against it. Since, technically, it was no longer any of my business, I found myself on a spot, with, naturally, no help from Sailors or Roach—they just sat patiently on my neck and waited for me to fix. Col Lowe finally telephoned Col Pardy, who said to do it any way they wanted. The way they wanted was to have Capt Girvin publish it as a standing feature in *AFGIB*, pictures and all, and they would make available enough copies for Ft Worth. We then telephoned Ft Worth and checked that, and everything seemed to be settled. However, Col Straubel of *Air Force* was in our office, and he at once pricked his ears up and hit the ceiling over why *AFGIB* should have it instead of *Air Force*—relations between the publications seem less than good. He took me in at once to see Col Lowe, who soothed him down. One result was that I got nothing done on the *Fortune* matter. . . .

A Time of War

Wednesday 1 December 1943

At the *Fortune* business most of the day, so I was glad to go to the Air Room at 3 to hear Gen Alexander on the 8th Air Force—he was exquisitely boring, but at least a hundred chicken cols sat stolidly in row after row in front of me. They had a few good shots in a too-long film made up of stuff taken on missions—sticks of bombs exploding in pattern on a very sharp and clear countryside. I soon sneaked out. Haddock in distraction asked me when I was coming back because it seemed the Gen, who ought to be back next week, had to accept the Collier Trophy[17] in a few well-chosen words and he had no one to do it but me.

Friday 3 December 1943

. . . Up to *Fortune* where Vogel seemed bright about the article—I could not think why. I had eight new pages, very bad, to load in and had pretty well cut up his copy, and planned a few more inserts. He said he would get it all together somehow. . . .

Saturday 4 December 1943

Up to *Fortune* and working in Bill Furth's office where I got the rest of the inserts finished. . . . Plainly the whole thing still smelled but I thought it might do to send out for coordination.

Monday 6 December 1943

To Washington on the 8.30 train. At the office Newhouse was back from Cairo and Teheran with a copy of the Gen's report with a furious scrawled note on the last page: I will not sign this; but in fact he had; the note resulting, it seemed, from his objection to an end Gen Bissell[18] tacked on, and fury at Newhouse when, having written an end himself, Newhouse said the Gen's end was somewhat bombastic. I don't know whether Newhouse improved the story or not, but it was good. . . .

Tuesday 7 December 1943

Haddock asked me to see what I could cook up in case the Gen wanted to make a speech at Kitty Hawk on Dec 17th, but I could not seem to get much interested in it. . . .

Wednesday 8 December 1943

Major Haddock spent most of the day resisting efforts to move us into less exclusive quarters and apparently succeeded. Copies of the *Fortune* piece came in to many people but not to me so I managed to get a copy from Virginia Kimball at the Bowen Bldg in Washington where there was an office with *Fortune*'s name on the door. She is a fairly plain forthright and business-like little wench with, clearly, an understandable great yen to keep in good with a certain Capt Parker in WD [War Department] review, he being a quick way to clear things if she in return would play ball with him. What he wanted ball-playing on seemed to be Guston's drawings. There were some shots of men carrying ammunition belts looped over their shoulders—as indeed, everyone does carry them—but they were trying to discourage the practise and though it was not a point of security exactly, asked her to have that struck out. She agreed. I thought it was preposterous, but I could see their point. What amused me was Kimball's alacrity to please on a point which she could rightly feel was after all a minor one. I daresay she would fight like the devil for anything that really mattered. On the other hand it seemed to me the War Department's problem, if they wanted to keep men from carrying ammunition that way (with danger of jamming clips), not *Fortune*'s.

Thursday 9 December 1943

In the morning it was again stated that they—somebody around Gen Bissell—were intent on moving us out of our highly desirable (they had not struck me that way) offices and putting us like most people in a large open space. Major Haddock was resisting very strongly, representing that the important and even temperamental work his writers did required seclusion and privacy. This view eventually prevailed. I was working more or less on the possible speech the Gen might need if he got back in time and if he decided he wanted to go to Kitty Hawk on the 17th.

Friday 10 December 1943

Col Pool summoned me up on the *Fortune* ms and I had some conversation with a rather consciously dashing Major Fonda who with swears and twirls of his moustache none-the-less showed that he had really read the thing with pains. He had a number of suggestions or corrections, all, it seemed to me reasonable. . . . In the pm up to the 5th floor auditorium where we were joined by Secty Stimson,[19] doddering in with a Lt Gen and a marine orderly sergeant in full dress to see the uncut pictures of the Marines landing at Tarawa. They were in color and included the usual amount of camera ham, but also some impressive shots—even terrible; such as a long one from a bobbing landing boat in which the am-tracs, scattered over the water ahead kept suddenly going up here and there in puffs of flame as the Jap fire got them; and telephoto lens shots of the first contingents huddled against the lee of the wharf. The camera men had taken care to include many shots of bloated and disfigured dead, including one with no face clearly picked with considerable care for colors. The shot held it for practically a minute at close quarters, and it was not hard to imagine the satisfaction whoever took it felt as he evened things up for the recent doubtless severe damage to his own nerves.

A Time of War

Monday 13 December 1943

. . . To *Fortune* where everyone seemed reasonably happy about the piece. . . .

Tuesday 14 December 1943

In to 1 Park where I discovered that, as I suspected, Col Pardy did not know he was holding the bag on the curve-of-pursuit gadget whose photograph was going to go on the cover but he seemed ready enough to take the responsibility of declassifying it and Waterman sent a corporal up with it at noon. I was busy most of the day writing the text for a box to describe it and a diagram of position sighting which I found not the easiest thing in the world to state simply.

Wednesday 15 December 1943

We finally got a last draft, or Bill finally did, in to the typists—certainly a good bit of a prose mess, but there seemed to be nothing to be done. As fast as I got a few pages cleaned up, Bill by dint of cutting and rewriting, which he does with great speed and energy, would have a new text for that part and the new text it would be discovered later was what the typists got. About that time I saw the box introducing it and realized with relief that they were not saying I wrote it, but merely that it was produced with my aid and collaboration. This was such a load off my mind or I guess conscience that I thought I might as well stop struggling. Over to the Barclay at 5 to have a drink with Bill and his Miss D'Atree, who is a good researcher—a thin, in fact almost emaciated dark girl with active or animated eyes and I understand Communist principles—a point that always interests me, when you can't, as you almost invariably can, see at first glance, the thing wrong with them from which the fundamental discontent from which the will to believe such nonsense comes. In her I could not spot the one thing, so it is probably a case of a curious and intricate combination of things which would take more study than I had time for in an hour.

Friday 17 December 1943

Into the office, where the speech matter was all right because the Gen, due to a snow storm south, could not have got to Kitty Hawk even if he wanted to go; but hell began immediately to pop in connection with a Capt Rogers of Gen Harper's A3 [Operations and Training Office] who was exercised over the curve-of-pursuit and position-sighting business, maintaining the Japs at least did not know about either. I found this extremely hard to believe, perhaps because he is a plump-faced, soft-eyed young man who seemed very unlikely to know anything about it. A good deal of telephoning and fussing followed. . . .

Saturday 18 December 1943

Haddock told me the Gen needed a new Christmas message, this time to the halt and maimed. Considering the wonderful way he and Bissell had managed with a few magnificently inept phrases at crucial points to gum up the other one I was not too encouraged. Virginia Kimball came over about the *Fortune* matter and I had to report to her that there was no soap on the position sighting. Meanwhile a Col Lord had pointed out that the cover gadget came from the Navy and was it clear with them? I telephoned Col Pardy, who did not know it came from the Navy and asked me to get in touch with their liaison officer. After seven or eight calls I located a Lt Allen Browne in PRO [Public Relations Office] over there and got the photograph over to him.

Monday 20 December 1943

. . . The Navy came through by way of a Commander Raborn with the news that the gadget certainly might not be used on the cover of anything, and, I gathered from a Major Keyhoe, what the hell? However, that may have been just the marine corps in the major, for Raborn called me himself soon after and was very pleasant and reasonable. In fact he made me think he was probably right so I told Kimball so—she seemed to feel that I was perhaps betraying her, but I said I would call New York, where Del Paine took it quite calmly. . . .

Tuesday 21 December 1943

. . . Seemingly Gen Bissell did want his piece for *Aerosphere* on Air Intelligence[20] (which I had hoped was forgotten) so I had to stir myself on that, and on writing it seemed to me a pointless letter for the Gen's signature to a Group Captain Seabrook, recently on some New Zealand mission. I did not know why the hell the Gen's secty couldn't write it. Gantz and Hudson and Tamon, and Capt Sailors who came down late last night were in to be taken to Bolling Field where they were having a show of the new army planes—forty or fifty officers moving with a loud speaker truck in the wind down a long stretch of the ramp from feature to feature. They had the PX4OK, which is very beautiful, and the new 63 which seems to be a larger 39, and the 61, the new night fighter, which is a little grotesque but unbelievably grim. We were shown the new modified A20s and the B25 mounting the 75 cal cannon, which you have to see to believe, and the B29, roped off for a hundred feet all around with guards patroling the ropes. You could not tell much, except that once you have seen it the B17, which it resembles on a larger scale, no longer looks in correct proportion. In to have a drink with them, and Hudson left on the 6 pm train. I told him I hoped he would make Col Pardy realize that I had done the next thing to saving his neck by taking up the Navy matter instead of just saying; Col Pardy cleared it; it must be ok.

A Time of War

Wednesday 22 December 1943

Still working at getting some material for Bissell's piece and it is hard to get, since I begin to believe Air Intelligence has in fact nothing special to do with changes in aircraft design and tactics, the slant which was to fit it into *Aerosphere* and so get the Gen a full page photograph there.

Thursday 23 December 1943

The *Fortune* thing got actually and finally finished—that is, Kimball sent over a photostat of a wind drift indicator which TAD had apparently sent them as a substitute for the curve of pursuit gadget and Col Lowe instructed review to stamp that and stamp the proof. A Lt Vanta did so. Bitterly cold in the eve. To Union Station where the trains were all late, and the place packed. I had a bottle of beer with two young and exhausted Engineer 2nd Lts, just in from Ft Belvoir where they had been having a 6 weeks course—a hostess came up and asked me while I was brooding on my beer if I minded their joining me. They had red wind-burned faces and looked dead, beginning at once to wolf ham and eggs. One of them asked me suddenly if I could tell him how to get into the Air Force. They then both began to talk explaining that they had been transferred from the Quartermaster without warning and given the works down at the Engineers' school where, it seemed plain, they follow that fatuous false analogy; ie. if exercise will make a man's muscles grow, plenty of exercise for those muscles he is going to have to use to fight is indicated in training. Good & true. They then observe that endurance is also very important; therefore give a man plenty of training in sleeping on the ground, going without food, being exposed to the weather. I am fairly sure that men who, while they get progressively harder and harder exercise, are fed well, allowed to get enough sound sleep and protected from unnecessary exposure will prove to have more endurance when they need it than those who were 'trained' to have it. . . .

Friday 24 December 1943

. . . Up to OC&R [Operations, Commitments and Requirements] to see a Col Summerfelt, a stocky young former West Point football player (I heard) who laboriously picked over what I told him about Bissell's piece and visibly racked his brains. Finally he got a Major Elder, who got out some modification files. While not uninteresting, they proved to be not much to the point. We did little in the pm but sit around waiting on the Gen's eggnog party at 5.15. The Gen himself received at the door in an obvious holiday mood—he proved to be rosy faced and white-haired and a good deal less tough-looking than I expected. The narrow red carpeted conference room was crowded with other generals and colonels and their secretaries, a group of very coy gay girls who were presently singing or screaming Off we go into the wild

11

blue etc and then Christmas carols. The Gen regarded them with the chin-chucking or perhaps even bottom-pinching beam characteristic, I have begun to realize, of the old and great. There were two punchbowls full of something with plenty of rye in it at ends of the polished table. It took us half an hour to get out.

Monday 27 December 1943

I was still trying to get some stuff for Bissell's *Aerosphere* piece from various people who knew nothing about it. Newhouse said perhaps sensibly that I would get over that—just make it up yourself and if they find it's wrong, let them prove it by finding the right people. . . .

Wednesday 29 December 1943

I finally went ahead and wrote the *Aerosphere* nonsense anyway, figuring that the general idea was to make an excuse to publish Gen Bissell's picture rather than to enlighten the reader. . . .

Thursday 30 December 1943

The *Aerosphere* thing finally got off my hands and I started on a speech for the Gen to make at the Los Angeles coliseum. . . .*

Friday 31 December 1943

Finished the Gen's speech, which I could not help feeling was much too good for him, but I expect he will manage to louse it up—perhaps properly. I think that business is partly that he has to make some ill-advised changes in order to feel that it isn't being written for him—somebody is doing the rough work and he is then putting it into final shape, so it is really his own after all. . . . At noon Gerald Carter, a waiter from Harvey's, brought over his boy (known as Fitzgerald C) a corporal just out of the quartermasters school and telephoned up to me. I had listened to him about it a few times in there but hardly expected him. The kid was on furlough with orders to Jefferson Barracks and wanted a chance to take exams for aviation cadet training. He proved to be an intelligent, slight, very black kid with a couple of years of college and his father, rather affectingly, having got him an education, was almost frantic to see that he got a chance. I said I'd see what I could do, which I think disappointed him, because I daresay he expected I could just take him upstairs and give him 2nd lt's bars and wings.

Saturday 1 January 1944

We had little to do, as almost everyone else had a hangover and I could not get far

*See Appendix.

12

with Fitzgerald Carter's affair. At 2 oclock Haddock said Dempsey thought the speech was all right so I might as well go home, so I did.

Monday 3 January 1944

. . . There was still nothing to do, so I bestirred myself about Fitzgerald, going first to Lowe and from him to Col Pool in Gen Harper's office, who did little; but Col Ryan came in and said I should see Col Hopwood up in personnel, and there to my astonishment a Lt Col took me to a major, neither of whose names I got, and damned if they didn't (perhaps because I had said I was from Gen Arnold's office) say they could and would notify the CO at Jefferson Barracks that the boy was to be given a chance to take the exams and held there until the results came in—an interesting example, I guess, of what you can do if you bother people enough. Up to see Seversky's *Victory Through Air Power* in the afternoon—very highly colored—in company with some Hollywood majors Reeves knew. Lowe told me in the pm that Bissell 'liked' the *Aerosphere* thing, but he had a text, and sure enough, the usual few senseless sentences had been thrown or crammed into it. I honestly think the man is mad. . . .

Tuesday 4 January 1944

The Gen duly loused my speech up a little—the peculiar changes that have nothing to do with the sense, but simply make sentences more awkward or ungrammatical, baffle you; but I could see I might as well reconcile myself to being baffled. In the pm Haddock suddenly threw on me a secret report by something called a Committee of Historians, apparently a foible of Mr A's* which had taken nine of them 7 weeks @ $25 dollars a day to write a 'disinterested' description of the state of Germany. The idea was that I could make a digest of the 56 pages and write a covering letter to the President explaining how bright Mr A was to think of it. As there was nothing in it not in all the newspapers it seemed hard. However down came a WAC [Women's Army Corps] lt named McCarthy, a brisk brassy haired faintly tough little girl who had been taking coats and getting pencils for the committee, and some after five, a Major Monaghan, a solid and swearing former professor from I think Yale from the BPR [Bureau of Public Relations], who had been chairman, just in from NY. . . .

Wednesday 5 January 1944

. . . Major Monaghan turned up fairly soon . . . and I went in with him and Haddock to take the stuff to General White. He was a lean faced but ruddy man with cropped wavy hair and an air of great precision; reasonably young-looking, though with command pilot's wings and a retread ribbon, among a few others. I thought he

*For security reasons Gen. Arnold was referred to by his aides and staff as "Mr. A."

13

seemed reasonable and went to write out the letter from the Gen to the President, from, or away from, a draft of Monaghan's.* The obvious point seemed to be to capitalize the fact that the Profs found nothing by saying it was interesting to note that it coincided with the findings by and large of intelligence; so we did that, and brought it back. Gen W had suggested shifting around the parts of the summary but said he left it to Haddock's judgment—a gingerly point since Haddock had no time yet to determine whether White, as of this morning in Bissell's job, meant by that that he really should judge, or that he should get smart and adopt the Gen's opinion. Haddock shifted the military angle to the front and, I thought rather encouragingly, White said; Against your better judgment? with a tone and expression that seemed to suggest a rudimentary sense of humor. . . .

Thursday 6 January 1944

. . . Haddock brought in a request from a WAC Major Baughman that maybe the Gen would like to make a short new picture praising the WACs in place of one he had made. Haddock arranged to have it put on in a 5th floor projection room for us, a business somewhat perplexed by the presence of a wholly unexplained major general of the ASF [Army Service Forces], a vast red faced man with white hair and re-tread ribbons, and a chicken col with the staff badge. He did not seem to know why we were seeing it nor even why he was. The picture was fairly awkward, though instructive to me, since it showed plainly that Mr A was among the world's worst speakers and you could see that any speech written for him simply went down the drain. However, I judged we might do better than that, so Haddock, with the usual signs of the executive's relief at having somebody make a few decisions, decided we (or I) would; so I went and saw Janet Varn to collect what 'literature' they had and then to a Lt Lee, a little earnest librarian-like creature, who seemed to be PRO [public relations officer] in the "Director's" office. Col Hobby[21] was away, which I was sorry for, as I thought I would just go in and see what she was like in the process. . . .

Friday 7 January 1944

With the Gen away there was a sort of general lull in the work and nobody else in the office was doing anything, but I thought I might as well press the WAC matter, if not too hard. Lt Lee had been down at 2 to see a Major Rice, a middle aged Georgia woman who was making free with Col Hobby's general's-style office with the mahogany and carpet and stand of colors. I called her Ma'am assiduously which, somewhat to my surprise, visibly went down very well. She too was earnest in a

*See Appendix.

broad-faced and broad-bottomed way—I don't know just where or how it differs from male earnestness, of which there is plenty around, too—it is just as, or even more, fervent; but at the same time it has a peculiar pedantic or non-practical quality—almost, perhaps earnestness for earnestness' sake. As executive officer I could not help suspecting that she ran headquarters like a family or household so that everyone stood in a personal relationship to everyone else—Lt Lee called her Ma'am, all right; she called Lt Lee Pat. The situation was roughly that of the Dean of Women to the girls, which is essentially different than the masculine relationship of rank and command.

Saturday 8 January 1944

Haddock fetched me in a request to write a letter from the Gen to Mr Johnson, president of Boeing on the occasion, to me at least appalling, of his being selected as Seattle's leading citizen for 1943. It developed by consultation with a man named Kinkaid, who seemed to be a sort of PRO for the company, that the Gen & he were great pals, and that furthermore Mr J (to be addressed as Dear Phil) did not know of the project and was to be taken by delightful surprise (supposing the Gen was willing to sign it). I managed to put together six or seven lines in a hell-fellows tone. Haddock said he was afraid that it would be just what Mr A wanted. I went up at 2 to a projection room on the 5th floor where they put on for me alone (I could not help feeling somewhat important) the Paramount film Lt Lee sent over called *Women at War*, a technicolor number about the WACs considerably loused up with comic interludes and drama but with sufficient scenes of life & work to make me think that if I were to speak my honest mind I would be advising any girl to skip the business and stay home.

Monday 10 January 1944

A Capt Fait over at ATC was supposed to give me some anecdotes about the good services of the Wacs for our supposed project but she called up and confessed herself unable to find any; so it seemed easiest to let the whole project ride. Meanwhile the Military District of Washington seemed by the papers to be having trouble over an attempt to reclassify a WAC lt named Wight; and so, full of unprofessional interest, I did what I could to horn in on that, though without success since the hearing was put off—still it was amazing how much business and how many telephone calls evolved out of it, showing what you could do with strictly factitious stuff if you put your heart to it. . . .

Tuesday 11 January 1944

The work today was a letter inviting a Brazilian Air General named Gomes to come up and look around and so increase the mutual understanding between our two great nations. . . .

Wednesday 12 January 1944

I supplemented the Gen's letter to Dear Phil with a telegram to be read at the banquet, which took lots of time as it seemed almost impossible to find fifty words to say on so excruciating an occasion. The case of the Wac Lt Wight was still more in the papers so, being idle, I renewed my efforts to find out about it and successfully enough heard some from Capt Treadwell, a demure and anxious little number up in Baughman's office. Emboldened then, I tried a direct assault on a Capt Coleman (male) in the MDW [Military District of Washington] office; but was soon glad to beat a retreat as he was not giving without authorization and I feared that the Col commanding, in whose office he was, might come in at any moment and demand to know just where I came in and what I meant by my easy references to Gen Arnold. We went up with Haddock then to see a film done by the Office of Strategic Services for showing to 'industrial workers' on the state of the war, and to my amazement it was good, simple, sensible, well-arranged and effective with some remarks by Secty Patterson[22] which made me regret Mr A all the more, since you could do something for a man who looked and spoke like that. However, I daresay something is cooking, since it developed through various back passages that Major Haddock had been passed over on his certainly well-merited promotion—strongly suggesting that someone was against this office and in the clash of influences his friends had come out second best. Anyone could see that the not impossible next step was abolition of the whole thing unless new steps could be taken and new pressures placed, so I might soon be looking for a job.

Thursday 13 January 1944

We had an idle day, perhaps mostly because Haddock was engaged in reconnoitering his position, or possibly that of Col Lord, a curious twirp in A2 who might have had a hand in whatever was going on. I began to see that it was infinitely, or nearly so, complicated; since into it from different angles, and reacting in different ways, would come Gen Giles, the Chief of Staff; a General Hall, a deputy; two other deputy BGs, one I think called Vandervere; Col Donnell; Major Dempsey. . . ; General White, as our nominal CO; Cols Lord and Lowe under him; and somewhat antagonistic to each other, with possible side influences from Col Westlake of PRO, and who could tell who else. Haddock seemed easy and unflustered and I am prepared to believe he is something of a tactician himself. I think the essence of the thing is to do the jockeying for position without ever appealing to Gen Arnold himself and the object, I really believe, is less power & position than a struggle to

16

prevent arbitrary interference with whatever jobs the several individuals are responsible for. . . .

Friday 14 January 1944

We were again mostly idle, while Haddock again saw people, I thought with gathering confidence. He seemed even ready to expostulate with Mr A about the utterances in Wichita on the 8th Air Force's Tuesday mission.[23] Indeed, from the reports in the Air Room it seemed that he had it a little wrong since there were in fact less than 700 bombers, and worse, most of them had not been able to get onto the German plants represented as out of order for months—which, in any event, he couldn't possibly have known when he made the assertion. On the whole, it didn't strike me as making very much difference since few people would bother to keep any careful tab and except for the men actually involved, the public knew all it needed to know when given the fact that we had lost quite a lot (59) bombers and hoped we had done some damage. If the Gen gave the wrong percentage and claimed more than was in fact done, what of it?

Saturday 15 January 1944

. . . Haddock after a kind of conference, he lying on his back on the table in our room, decided we might use the Nat Geographic speech* to get the Gen out of his vagarious statements on the Oschersleben mission, etc so I was able to get started telephoning endless people to track that down—that is, what he really said, and then what the facts really were. The last, a Capt Caldwell of Intelligence did not expect to know until Monday and he doubted if anyone would ever know what had been accomplished at Brunswick since the RAF was over it in force last night—a curious, if quite reasonable, thought.

Monday 17 January 1944

A Lt Neel, a very earnest, somewhat short and wide but well featured little Wac came down at Capt Treadwell's direction to see me about the Gen's piece if any, with much sir-ing; but we did not get any farther forward. Gerald Carter called me up and reported in agitation that his boy seemed to have been side-tracked at Jefferson Barracks and investigation soon showed that he had been. . . .

Tuesday 18 January 1944

Somewhat to my surprise, the Carter matter, when put up to Major Dempsey moved him enough to make him say he would go to bat for it—thus forcing me to revise my

*See Appendix.

opinion of him—Haddock had told me there would be no harm in asking him but he doubted if I'd get anywhere. Fooling with the WAC business in the form of a talk with a Lt Col Crump up in Major Cowling's office—another Hollywood officer, but not such a bad one. He said sensibly that the form would have to depend on the distribution—who did we think was going to show it? I had not thought of that.

Wednesday 19 January 1944

Over to Gravelly Point where I picked up Capt Fait, a big wholesome easy-spoken WAC Captain from California who went down with me to Hangar 6, the Port of Embarkation; where, up a number of steel stairs, she introduced me to a Col Collins, the CO, who greatly praised the work of the Wacs there, saying that many people coming in were a little apprehensive about the sea trip and psychologically some bright and cheerful girls worked well—which I could imagine. Haddock was much engaged on points of policy and some serious thought about what should be done to respond to a very biting editorial in the *NY Herald Trib*[24] on the Gen's shooting-his-face-off habit, so it was hard to get his ear on my various small businesses—Gardner Hudson had telephoned from New York in the morning to see if we could get him a few lines from the Gen on non-commissioned officers to put on the back of a pamphlet they were getting out on the duties of such. I could write the lines all right, but I had to get it approved. I could see the nuisance of being an executive, or in a position to have to make decisions. It is hard for me to believe that the Power & Glory could be much of a compensation.

Thursday 20 January 1944

. . . Haddock turned up, very indignant with a piece with a suspense [deadline] sheet dated for tomorrow and a blue to-be-done-at-once card, which was a statement from General Arnold to be read by Gen Hunter to a meeting of the Institute of Aeronautical Sciences. It had elected him an honorary fellow. What irked Haddock was that it had all begun three weeks ago; but somebody forgot to put it through. All I had to do was get together a thousand words saying how important aeronautical scientists were and that by noon tomorrow. The truth is, I don't really mind; there is a sort of amusement in seeing if it was possible. . . .

Friday 21 January 1944

. . . In the afternoon all hell broke loose in a confused way over some representations by Col Du Bose, the TC [Training Command] liaison man in Gen Harper's office, that the *Fortune* figures, which I thought all long dead and buried, and indeed probably to be published within a week, were a gross violation of security and Gen Yount certainly would not approve and what the hell. I was kept running and

18

answering telephones all afternoon and did not at the end know the score—not that I could be court-martialed, since Lt Col Lowe had approved it; but I did not know whether I had let him in for trouble or not—I couldn't help remembering that he had damn near let the gunnery diagrams and so on go by, and what a hell of a stink that would surely have made.

Saturday 22 January 1944

We got a new slant on the National Geographic speech which the Gen seemed to want to make genuinely geographic; and, besides, his various newspaper breaks and the attending editorial comment made fixing him up a job beyond any low-powered lecture. I began to get together stuff from Base Services and the Air Engineer and ATC on bases in all countries. Meanwhile we put in a memorandum on the Air Wac matter to see if the Gen could be persuaded to let the movies show him taking a personal interest in them, say at Hangar 6. . . .

Sunday 23 January 1944

On as duty officer. Nothing happened and no one called except Gen Vandenberg's secty to tell me he wouldn't be in. I had asked because Haddock told me he might want to talk to me about the *Fortune* figures. Lowe was in and he seemed disposed to take the rap if any, to my surprise saying that he had been new then; he would know now that some of the brass hats had to be let in on things that were none of their business. . . .

Monday 24 January 1944

Over to the National Geographic Society, a building in what, I imagine, is a 1910 marriage of richness with dignity and talked upstairs with Mr Southerland, a black headed manly public relations type about the Gen's speech. Mr S, though he kept saying they would be glad to hear anything because of the honor and the Gen's gifts as a speaker, obviously did not want any scenes in many lands, but rather the low down on what the Air Forces was up to in Europe. When I got back there was a note to say that Mr A would see me at three, which he duly did. He looked pink and clean with his thin white hair very clean too and a sort of narrow-eyed twinkling expression (Newhouse afterwards remarked somewhat drily; "Makes a good first impression, doesn't he?" The answer is, yes he does). It soon developed that he did not want to speak on geography either, but on bomber mission tactics, which someone had likened, to his pleasure, to football tactics. Since it seemed to me we might work into this some sort of repair and recovery of his criticized statements it was all right with me. Dempsey seemed more doubtful—he came in silently in the middle, just in time to have the Gen say that he and Cozzens weren't going to speak

19

on what Dempsey wanted. He made some counter representations, but the Gen was having none and swept us out saying that he would take it up with me again Thursday. We then went into Dempsey's office where Lt Col Crump came and joined with us and Col Barber, I think,—he shares the office—in some discussion. They wanted to know how the bomber tactics came up, and I said that I had asked him what he would like to speak on. This brought about an exchange of glances that seemed to imply that I had a good deal to learn; but they did not seem put out. Crump was there to figure the motion picture angle—the Gen said flatly he wanted them to go out smiling and asked if there were any laughs in *Target Germany*, *Pantelleria*, or *Earthquakers*, the pictures to be shown. It seemed not, so it was up to Crump to find something—they finally decided on some so-called blow-ups; pieces of action not intended for the camera. Back in the office I could see Haddock, too, thought that I did not know much about doing things the easy way. I could see the point but I still wanted to try. At this point the *Fortune* business clarified itself awkwardly—the figures on hours flown per fatal accident were being held unsuitable for publication—God alone could figure out why—and Lowe was indeed holding the bag due to my business of having him have everything stamped. Lt Col Gilder was in, very busy clearing himself, while protesting that he wanted to share the rap if any, a peculiar and not very agreeable piece of squirming. . . .

Tuesday 25 January 1944

Most of the morning up in 5E229 looking at the pictures for the Gen's speech. I did not find out until after lunch that, as I suspected yesterday, 'they' did not like the Gen's choice of subject and from what I could get out of Haddock, Dempsey did not like my 'part' in it. Perhaps he credited me with being smarter than I am, but I could see that my first impression about him was probably right—I mean, a mean and dangerous man; and I suppose I should watch my step and get smart and realize that when I say I don't want anything from him, anything includes trouble. Haddock, much harassed, showed a few marks of the trimmer—just a hint of that fine sense of balance which looks before it leaps—that is, there was no sense in getting my back up, because I had my uses; but if I did not come right around—coming around is the easiest thing I do. I suppose I can't imagine how exasperating I had succeeded in making myself—whether by design, whether by stupidity. The working theory is that the Gen had better lie low and let his various contradictions and overstatements be forgotten, and I can see how wise it is, without, however, losing the vague feeling that I could talk him out of them.

Wednesday 26 January 1944

Dempsey and Barber put in a memo to the old man and it came back with the note

No Comment which was interpreted to mean that he was not taking their suggestion that he change his subject. I set about seeing what I could do along the indicated lines and checking on the Schweinfurt charts so that the Gen could demonstrate bombing tactics from them. There was still an unease—that is, I gathered Dempsey still thought he could bring him around to talk on something else. It occurred to me that a good solution might be to let him say what he wanted to say and confine our efforts to seeing that he said it as well as possible; but I realized that it was not in harmony with the feeling of the moment—a sort of my god how can we keep him from saying what he wants to say. . . .

Thursday 27 January 1944

I did up a few versions of introductory remarks with much checking to avoid issues of controversy, but they did not get around to showing it to the Gen. . . .

Friday 28 January 1944

We got to see Mr A in some strength at 11 and he was performing fine, hitting the desk so we all jumped—that is Dempsey, Col Westlake, Haddock, Major Dame and me, and it was finally decided to do the tactics but with some new charts—I ventured to show him the Schweinfurt ones and he said with pardonable testiness that I didn't have to show him a plotting chart, he'd seen them before. A raw-boned rather pleasant Col Humphrey, formerly with the 8th Air Force, and about to go back, set about making up some charts with me through the afternoon and indeed early evening. . . .

Saturday 29 January 1944

With Col Humphrey putting in a few additional details on the charts and then getting them lettered by the draftsman and then getting them photostated by Mr Albright, all the while making up under some pressure an outline. This George [Haddock] and I revised a few times and had typed by six oclock. He seemed in fairly good spirits, perhaps because his promotion came through around noon, and he even told Dempsey on the phone that he thought this, meaning the speech, was going to be good. Since Mr A had gone it seemed that we would have to come in tomorrow and administer it to him.

Sunday 30 January 1944

In at ten where Haddock soon appeared and told me and Chamberlin, who was duty officer, that apparently there had been a considerable upset and it looked as though some Lt Col called Rex Smith, a product of *Newsweek* and the *Chicago Sun*, was going to take over PRO stuff and he, George, was not going to hold the bag and did not expect to stay. Chamberlin was inclined to discount it, feeling that George would fight and might avert the arrangement, he having averted others. The question was, was he sick of scrambling for the privilege of having, in the ordinary phrase, his ass eaten off. If so, I could see we might easily all fly apart and I might easily be out of here as fast as I came in—I did not know just where, since Straubel would probably be out of *Air Force* too—to make room for some pal of this Smith's. On the whole I could see that I'd better not try to do anything except watch and do what they told me when they told me, thus sparing myself exertion almost certain to be vain. However, I could see that, with Haddock out of it, I would have no patience at all with the present job—by his attitude and character he made it just barely possible. . . .

Monday 31 January 1944

What was to become of us did not get any plainer but Haddock appeared, without saying that he was, somewhat less likely to give in. I took the Gen's or more properly Col Humphrey's maps over to Lt Lee, a slight unmilitary chap with a moustache, at the Archives to be made into lantern slides. The Gen's secty had called me at 8.15 to say that she had the outline with no comment except that Mr A wanted the text quickly. After lunch Major Dame called up to say he had a lovely film called *25 Missions* in, and would like that to be used. I went up to see it with a few Hollywood colonels and Gilder for A2. It was in fact, good; indeed, too good, since it presented all the material I was writing for Mr A to read with his slides in a much clearer and better form. As I had most of his stuff written I thought it would be better not to use it as the customers probably wanted to see Arnold some at any rate, and we had little time to argue about another subject for him. George presented this view to Dempsey who was to see it tomorrow and presumably decide. One agreeable alternative was that Mr A might just say nothing, or a paragraph or two to let them look at him, and then put the pictures on.

Tuesday 1 February 1944

The slides for Mr A came over but when we put them on in the Air Room little or nothing could be seen twenty feet away so we had to hand them back to a Lt Miller in the map making section who reinforced the points. Southerland and two NGS [National Geographic Society] civilians turned up in the morning and we had a kind of conference in Dempsey's office over such details as whether the Gen would return to the stage when the pictures were over and stand to attention while they played the national anthem, a business Dempsey turned down promptly. I got a draft of his remarks to go with the slides done and Haddock and I revised it until well after six.

Wednesday 2 February 1944

I went over the remarks a few more times, but Mr A did not get to see them, so hell is presumably put off until tomorrow. Col [Rex] Smith was in during the afternoon, a square-faced reddish blondish fellow of no very formidable appearance. Going up to projection room 2 to see the revised slides afterwards with George, he said that it seemed to be going through all right and he had taken the opportunity to tell Smith what was wrong—about his probably holding the bag, so I gathered he thought of trying it—perhaps partly because he saw that we all wanted him to, but he remarked that being a Lt Col was unhandy now, because if it didn't work he would have trouble getting out—they could move a major much easier; a Lt Col had to have a command of sorts. I didn't quite follow, since there are thousands of Lt Cols around—it must be the most overgrown and swollen rank in the army—but it looked as though he had made up his mind and so for a while at least we would go on undisturbed.

Thursday 3 February 1944

The Gen finally got around to looking at his speech which he did not seem much pleased about. We had had a scramble all day getting the slides and so on, which we finally projected about noon in the SC main auditorium to the amazement of forty or more females gathered to see a For Women Only film on the dangers of venereal disease. No explanation was offered them about the Gen's lantern slides—we just darkened the place, put the six on and then left. Haddock was in a long time seeing the General and trying to argue him out of his five minute comic. . . .

Friday 4 February 1944

The Gen had indeed made a mess of the speech, a sort of free-hand, and as far as you could see aimless or idiotic tampering with grammar and some of the more important statements, but in spite of his complaints most of it was as written. We went in at 3 to Constitution Hall, an impressive cavern where he stood up us and the Geographic people for an hour. He came in then very jolly and smiling and saw the slides and spoke a paragraph for the loud speakers—the beaming blue eye is I suppose half an act and half real. He soon left and we went back and got the text of the speech which I brought out to his red brick and tasteless house on the post at Ft Myer—I was amused to note the names of big shots on the steps of the rambling old shacks.

Saturday 5 February 1944

Reports came in . . . that the Gen did pretty badly, being flustered with his slides and losing his place a few times so I expected to hear soon that I at least was fired. Up at 9 to see Lt Col Baughman on the WAC business—she is just back from her excursion with Hobby—a compact square-featured woman with a weathered face and a brisk eye who said she used to be a newspaper reporter herself. We went over the somewhat limited field and she seemed to have sense of sorts. Watching her and listening to her I could see or thought I could that her patriotism while very deep and genuine was probably (and whose isn't?) not quite disinterested—or at least admixed with the social service worker's pleasure in pushing people briskly around for their own good. I thought of it particularly because she was a little late and Capt Varn was obliged to entertain me for ten minutes, somewhat ill at ease but earnest and so giving the probably-correct impression that she was at this desk in this uniform because she thought she ought to be, not because she had been mentally alert enough to see and take the chance to have the psychological time of her life. I then composed a letter to a Mrs Feldstein explaining on Mr A's behalf that the interests of security had made it impossible for her husband to say goodbye to her before he went overseas. . . .

Monday 7 February 1944

Haddock took me down to see Lt Col Barber in the morning on the idea that we could get up a 'prologue' for the pretty good film *25 Missions*—some technicolor stuff of the Memphis Belle over Wilhelmshaven on its last trip. The hitch was that Hq didn't want any last trip business—no 25 missions and you can come home. Since the picture was built around that idea the order was large. Barber, who is a neat gray intelligent looking man seemed a trifle less intelligent when he came to the problem, and it even occurred to me that that look and that mild calm manner covered a considerable lack of sense—or maybe he merely felt that anything Mr A wanted done would have to be done anyway, so why discuss the means? Haddock became rather short, but we duly took it back and I got together a few paragraphs begging the principal question, I thought fairly well.* Haddock said; Fine; we'll put it away for a few days and then show it to them as the fruit of our prolonged labor.

Tuesday 8 February 1944

I began to work languidly on the WAC matter and got as far as fixing up a date with Lt Col Crump on the movie end and Capt Varn (who however she may sign herself, it seems is called Caroline rather than Janet) when Haddock came in with new business and I was obliged to call it off and run up to see Gen Craig in OC&R—he however went out to the airport by his private door without ever seeing me and I had only a few words with a bald-headed Col McKee or Gee who thought I would get what material I needed—it was for some remarks Friday to a graduating class of

*See Appendix.

WASPs [Women's Air Service Pilots] at Sweetwater—from Jacqueline Cochran's office, as Director of Woman Pilots. She was to be out until 4, or, as in fact it proved, until a good deal later; so I unearthed Capt Varn and found Col Crump and we worked out a picture, assisted by a Major Frank Lloyd, asserted to be a top-notch director. He seemed to feel that he could manage what we had in mind if I would write him a script. Miss Cochran got in a little after five and I went around and was taken aback to get many apologies and several references to me as sir, the last thing I expected from what I presumed would be a self-important jerk, what with her position and her past as a celebrated flyer. She proved to be well-featured with a pile of curly blonde hair, wearing a blue uniform with brass insignia and headquarters buttons though no shoulder bars, being in fact a civilian. She showed me with pride a round blue hat with miniature officer's hat-device on it, and talked quite a lot of unaffected sense with a simple and natural play of expression and much earnestness. When I got back somewhat after six Haddock said: Did you think she was a good guy; and I could only reply, yes.

Wednesday 9 February 1944

I got the piece done for Gen Craig in the morning and brought it in to Miss Cochran who was again very affable, screwing up her brows and widening her wide brown eyes, and perhaps I should say smelling simply delicious with something like Tabu or My Sin. She wanted more emphasis on reading tech orders and not stunting so I put that in and took it up to Craig who this time made room for me. He is a tall young man with an amiable dish-face with a few freckles and a tight ripple in part of his cropped hair of no special color. He acted at loss, and so I took a firm hand with him and got it out intact with merely the somewhat ill-advised suggestion that maybe something should be said about how they had been leading a sheltered life at Sweetwater and now would be on their own. I brought this right down to Miss Cochran who clenched her hands and widened her eyes and said it wasn't so; they had been trained to be on their own. We compromised on a few vague sentences as she was embarrassed to receive while we talked a telephone call from South Plains, Texas to say that Col Olsen had concluded that women did not have the physical strength to tow gliders in a C60—which I believed, having heard Col Olsen myself on the subject. She had made a point of the fact that her girls were doing this so she was understandably a little fussed coming back to face me. I still thought she was all right, though Newhouse . . . insisted she was a smooth article and an accomplished schemer and generally not to trust.

Thursday 10 February 1944

Down early to get Gen Surles to pass on Gen Craig's remarks in review and out to

Hangar 6 to go on with the WAC business. Capt Varn had told me a Lt Sykora was in temporary charge so I picked her up at Gravelly—a small, fairly neat blondish girl who soon developed the fact that actually the Wacs did very little there. However, she and a couple of other small lts on duty rallied somewhat and we saw Col Collins who made us a speech lasting a long time . . . but he agreed that some Wacs could get on the ditching demonstration business for the benefit of the picture. Back and took the completed speech up to the Gen and Miss C—she was entranced by the large type typing and asked anxiously if she could get the use of the machine when she had another speech herself—I said with authority that if she would send up a typist, probably yes. After that we had a long conference with Col Barber and Maj Dame and Col Wyler,[25] an extraordinary stocky little fellow, who discussed mainly aesthetics in defense of making no changes in *25 Missions*, which was apparently his work. I was interested to see that most of the constructive work was quietly done by Haddock who kept everyone to the point gently. Dempsey incidentally at last got around to the matter of Fitzgerald Carter and sure enough showed me, and signed, a directive to the CO at Jefferson Barracks from This Hdq requesting action; so I guess the kid will get his chance after all. The point seems somewhat blunted by my own suspicion that he couldn't possibly get through the examinations, and if he could, probably wouldn't get anywhere since openings are few in the flying training program as far as Negroes are concerned. . . .

Friday 11 February 1944

. . . I got on slowly with the WAC business, with plenty of calls from them and even a visit from Capt Varn, but I found it tough going—everything I wrote in what I imagined might be a script form seemed absurd and when I got down to it I didn't seem to know much of anything. Some of the latter I fixed up in a long and labored conversation with a Lt Col Hewett in Air AGO [Office of the Adjutant General] about the precise ceremony of the Gen's reception. He was bald, deaf, and graying and seemed to have great difficulty in understanding the situation; but eventually we worked out a procedure. At five Lt Col Wyler came in still fussing about the phrases in his picture and we were long delayed in straightening him out.

Saturday 12 February 1944

. . . To Hangar 6 and some talk with a Capt Jones of the North Atlantic Wing on the ditching procedure business—he showed me a rubber raft set up with a sail and all the equipment spread out. . . . M[26] sent me a wire to say that Percy had died today in Canada following the customary operation for the customary cancer of the liver—which seemed very hard both on him and Mary, but on the other hand the inkling of an idea keeps crossing my mind: viz. that a person who gets to die quite suddenly in his early forties is fortunate & happy—he has got everything good out of life he could and is now spared a myriad unpleasantnesses.

Monday 14 February 1944

Up to see a Lt Col Prewitt in Col Bubb's mp [motion picture] outfit, it developing that neither Crump nor Lloyd would be available for the film. He had much rippling near-white hair and I heard from Reeves that in Hollywood and elsewhere he was known as the marcelled bum and reputed to be a great lover. He seemed quite sensible to me, though I did notice him licking his lips lightly when I brought in Capt Varn for him to decide whether or not she would do as one of the WAC officers for the film. He seemed to think yes. I thought he might like to do the casting, but apparently (it is wonderful how hard it is to know) he found a trace of disparagement in my implication that he could or would find time to look over a lot of females and it developed that Varn and I and Lt Col Baughman had better make the choice, which he would veto if we chose too badly. I had then some fuss with Major Williams in newsreels, who wanted (I judged for private reasons) the newsreels themselves to make the pictures. This was plainly impossible as we had to make it our way though to their specifications. I could see he had the ordinary jealousy of power and seemed to feel he might be by-passed somehow—I didn't know enough about it to see just how—so he maintained flatly first that it would be contrary to AR [Army Regulations] to have us make it and give it free to the newsreels. Then he seemed to change his mind and decide that it might be done—I guess because he realized I might report his statement somewhere higher up and presumably it was not true. He then professed himself only anxious to help and I professed myself as only anxious to help and we both said after all we obeyed orders and didn't make decisions so I drew up a memorandum for Haddock—who was meanwhile, and not without satisfaction, though he decorously restrained it, looking at a scandalous feature in the NY *Sunday Mirror* magazine which went into Lt Col Rex Smith with pictures and slurs over his supposed gadding about and impending divorce. It looked as though he would as a result be found not quite fitted for overseeing our section. Haddock said; Honest to God I had nothing to do with this.

Tuesday 15 February 1944

Over with Caroline Varn to Hangar 6 where a Lt Dwight put on a briefing for us and four honest-to-God overseas passengers who, I saw, were going to be sorely disappointed when they discovered that Varn wasn't on the ship after all. The speech was not noteworthy except for the somewhat baffled observation about the equipment; "And here—" holding it up "—is a copy of the New Testament." I

27

spent the afternoon trying to cast it together as a script and the result seemed to sound both silly and awkward.

Wednesday 16 February 1944

I went on with the script. . . . Dempsey called up and said [Fitzgerald] Carter's affair had gone through, which I decided was a triumph.

Thursday 17 February 1944

. . . Over to Gravelly Pt with Col Prewitt at 10 where we proceeded with our 'casting' and I could see that indeed the Lt Col's mostly white wave of hair and (it seemed to me) somewhat conscious suave manner just about persuaded Major May (who is not beautiful and whose own hair is gray) that he was as charming as anything she had ever seen. I ought to say that whatever his reputation, I found him very pleasant and agreeable, and what he said seemed sensible. We were there some time while Lt Sykora sent for people they thought might do and engaged them ostensibly on other business while the Col looked them over. Back to the Pentagon and I got the script finished and up to Lt Col Baughman who complimented me on it. Thereafter we ran into trouble when I took down a fresh copy to Major Williams. He was agreeable, too, and repeated his proposition that we were both caught in the middle, but he now seemed sure that the newsreels wouldn't touch it if Prewitt's people made it—they, the newsreels, would make it themselves; or we could set it up as a short if the War Activities Board would take it as a trailer—a matter Col Westlake would have to take up with somebody named Griffiths. . . . Whether because of the *NY Mirror* piece or not, Rex Smith, Haddock remarked, had not yet got his Piece of Paper, and he Haddock had an idea he wasn't going to get it.

Friday 18 February 1944

Up to see Prewitt in the morning with a copy of my script and it developed that the matter of a short might not be so easy since to his knowledge there was about to be made a short on plain, not air, Wacs at Randolph Field and would the WAB [War Activities Board] want two shorts on Wacs—ans. No. I took it to Haddock who was much more engaged over a conference to decide something about *Air Force* and he was at it most of the afternoon, returning in apparent triumph. . . .

Saturday 19 February 1944

. . . I got still another typing of the Wac script done and up to Baughman's office. There was nothing else doing. . . .

Monday 21 February 1944

We had nothing to do. . . . In the morning Lt Neel brought me in a copy of the script I had left with Major Newberry who had two sensible suggestions about modifying my remarks for Mr A—it will take me a long time, and maybe I never will be able to, on my own, see statements from so many sides that I can anticipate certain objections and so correct myself, or I daresay, even better, say it unexceptionally the first time. At any rate, I can see it when somebody shows me. After that nobody had anything and George seemed disinclined to push the thing with Westlake. Varn called me shortly to find out if I could find out who had got an officer of theirs in dutch in California by giving her an order signed Arnold which told her to parade her Wacs in LA, but without letting the Hq of the 4th Air Force know, so the Hq was sore as a pup. I called up Dempsey, who seemed to bristle faintly at first, probably wondering if, after the Carter episode I had appointed myself general fixer (an office I expect he occupies himself), but he seemed satisfied soon that that was not the case and said with some grimness that a certain Lt Col Wells had been taking a lot on himself lately and he would see that proper action was taken. I spent most of the day reading Shakespeare. Very late our former Major Hartwell appeared, very cordial, with the 7th Air Force patch in brilliance on his shoulder, and a good tan. He had come back to get more staff for his PRO outfit, a feat that seemed to show he was selling himself to someone—presumably Gen Hale. He asked me if I wanted to go out and I said no.

Tuesday 22 February 1944

There was nothing to do all day. To dinner with Major Windrom and he took me to the Shoreham where the Tennessee Society or something was having a party, a dense mass of honey chile dialect girls and women and numerous politicians, one of whom, a representative, said to me that any friend of Guy's was a friend of his and shook hands with me while at the same time patting me on the back, a performance which I had heretofore regarded as purely imaginary. In fact, they all seemed very pleasant but it was a little long.

Wednesday 23 February 1944

. . . We had again nothing to do all day. Gerald [Carter] called me in the afternoon to say that his boy had indeed been transferred and given the examinations and duly flunked them—a business that I suspected was done very brusquely and expeditiously in a spirit of some annoyance at this headquarters. . . .

Thursday 24 February 1944

. . . With Haddock to Secty Patterson's news conference in the morning. He read, very slow, and deliberately a long and somewhat empty statement of this and that with a series of incredible mispronunciations of German names. He also chewed gum but he has a good presence and face, weathered, limberly wide-mouthed, with wrinkles of the experienced-looking sort. They asked him a number of questions, most of which he parried; though he said, while not speaking for the War Department, he personally felt selective service after the war would be necessary. He then decided that that was off the record, since, he said, nobody cared about his personal opinion. Some correspondent said zealously, 'I challenge that, Mr Secretary'; so everybody laughed. Otherwise there was nothing to do. . . . The Rex Smith business seems to have folded up and a new deal included some Col Boberg being chief of administrative matters for AC/AS [Assistant Chief/Air Staff] Intelligence. He was judged unlikely to make trouble as he told George he knew nothing about this business and counted on him to handle it. At four I was given a letter to answer—to tell a Street & Smith pub that the Gen was too busy with the war to write something for them. That was really the only work I did this week and I suppose it took from seven to ten minutes. . . .

Friday 25 February 1944

Nothing to do all day—a matter everyone seems to like. Newhouse remarked that he supposed that what worried me was that I thought very few Japanese air officers at this stage of the war sat around all morning with their feet on the desk reading Shakespeare. . . . Col Prewitt explained to me earlier that now he and Col Bubb thought that maybe the WAC matter should be newsreel, but in any event it all hung on Westlake who was still unready to do anything. . . .

Saturday 26 February 1944

Rainy with nothing to do all day though a lot of people drifted in. . . . Our organization seemed to have been given a few additional touches to Haddock's satisfaction and it was confirmed that Rex Smith was definitely out—showing after all how exactly right Chamberlin was when he refused to take the matter seriously in the first place.

Sunday 27 February 1944

. . . On as duty officer and George Haddock soon turned up to attend a sudden conference with Mr A. The problem, I learned later, was that Mr A was dissatisfied with the 'press' the AAF [Army Air Forces] was getting—seemingly nothing would content him short of full page headlines saying AAF Fighting Whole War By Self; but I was interested to guess that his real trouble is that in 1942 he solved plenty of problems, when the people who were supposed to know told him something was impossible, by saying vehemently; Well do it anyway; and have it done in thirty days. Since, more often than not, it worked—though probably he never could figure out how they did it himself— he now applies it always and in all directions. The hitch is that then all the elements were under his control and had to obey his orders. This is not the case with newspapers, who are a good deal more likely to get their backs up if overbearingly instructed in how to present news. Specifically, he wanted something done about getting the emphasis changed from bomber losses to destruction allegedly accomplished, and his solution was to withhold the losses. Any such policy suddenly applied at this stage would seem certain to have the most unfortunate effects; but he wanted it done anyway. . . .

Monday 28 February 1944

Nothing to do all day. Westlake was supposed to be in Florida so I could not advance the WAC matter and George was mostly out on I suppose more of the same business. He came and sat around our room, sitting on desks, tossing things in the air and catching them and saying that he thought we might be put in directly under Gen Vandenberg, but he himself did not want to work for Mr A because he had no sense. . . .

Thursday 2 March 1944

Still nothing to do, though I realize that things are again going on in the background with George out seeing people and other people coming in about some intricate continued maneuvering for position. . . .

Friday 3 March 1944

. . . There was still nothing to do, which is wearing—I suppose in time I might learn to occupy myself like Newhouse or Chamberlin in writing letters or private manuscripts but I never seem to feel like it and so just spend my time with my feet on the desk reading Shakespeare. . . . About four George turned up plainly much annoyed about something. He asked me to go down to the Summary Section and see if they had anything on an alleged daylight raid by the 8th on Berlin. A captain there declined to show it to me so I had to go and get Col Lowe—this over (the mission had started all right but been snafued by weather) I gathered from him that he had been reassigned, presumably explaining part of George's annoyance—but I can't help noticing that whatever happens to other people, his own position improves if anything.

Saturday 4 March 1944

. . . There was again nothing to do, though George came in and asked me to stand by, he thought there was going to be. However, he was again in and out in conferences with everyone and by five thirty it had not turned up—what it appeared to be was a series of memoranda which it would be our function to 'study' and make recommendations on for the new Public Relations Board having to do with projected books or motion pictures. Someone held them up somewhere so it was decided that they could wait until Monday.

Monday 6 March 1944

. . . George produced in the morning two bound mss., one an 'original story' by Alvah Bessie called "Objective—Burma" and the other a script covering the first third of it which MGM was interested in making.[27] The idea was to figure out whether MGM ought to have AAF cooperation in making it, a point to be taken up by the new AAF Public Relations Board tomorrow. I checked as well as I could with a Lt Col Ross, Airborne Officer for the AGF [Army Ground Forces] Staff, and he thought some changes in represented SOP [standard operating procedure] of the paratroopers were necessary but it looked as if it might do. I was interested to see how drastically and in fact how efficiently the script deviated from the 'original story'—an object lesson in sticking to the point and stressing what was interesting in place of what merely interested the author. We had also another from MGM, a story synopsis which aimed to make clear to the public the desperate perils, the anxieties and longings to be through with it supposed to fill all crew members in the 8th Air Force—which I can partly believe, but it was hard to figure out how a Capt Meredith, with whom I had dealt before on the WAC matter in the Air Force Group, BPR, had figured out that it would do if they just took out anything about 25 missions. It was the last thing anyone would want to do at the moment and you could guess he had confused possible truth and possible dramatic values with expediency. The speech Col Smith was supposed to write for the Gen proved a frost and Newhouse, very indignant, at least superficially, was expected to supply a new one by tomorrow. I thought he did not mind the outrageous demand as much as he said he did, as though perhaps he had an eye to the advantages of being known to be able to do the impossible—and of course it really wasn't too impossible.

Tuesday 7 March 1944

Tomorrow was said to be the anniversary of the present set-up of the Air Forces two years ago so it was to be celebrated by a meeting in which Mr A would show himself to two hundred some AAF Hq personnel who had missed seeing him during that time.* The idea seemed terrible, but that was not in question—we had to fix up a lot

---

*See Appendix.

of incidental stuff for General Giles and him and introductions for the numerous COs of air forces and commands who were also to be there and this kept everyone busy. . . .

Wednesday 8 March 1944

We had a good busy day—it is wonderful how my spirits lift once I am frowning over nonsense and figuring out answers and answering telephones even when it is hard to say what the purpose of it all is. . . .

Thursday 9 March 1944

. . . Most of the afternoon working with George to clean up the junk on his desk as I had told him, still glad to be busy, that I would act as his administrative assistant until he got someone else. We had in rapid succession a proposed Air Corps song—a ms score, which Miss Kane competently took in to a piano in the officers cafeteria, played over, and reported was a re-timed version of a U of Mich football song; a 5th Air Force proposed press release on how a friend of Gen Kenney's provided a lot of costly watches which were nicely engraved for presentation to worthy ground crew men out there—I said, no; if the Gen wanted to be good to them, good; but no press releases implying that private enterprise could reward military virtue, in which George gratefully concurred; some dope about the B24 for somebody in the Treasury to use with some bond advertising to be signed Arnold; a message to the Legion of Valor also from Mr A; a memorandum to Mr Lovett[28] asking him if he would have his photograph taken in colors to go on the cover of the mag *Wings*, and so on. In to have a lobster at the Occidental early and to Brentano's . . . where I stocked myself with Everyman's Bishop Burnet's *History*; Latimer's *Sermons*; *Memoirs of Col Hutchinson*; Locke on *Civil Government*; Reynolds' *Discourses*; Fox's *Journal*; the *Memoirs of Sir Thomas Buxton*, and Goldsmith's *Citizen of the World*—a collection I thought I would note, being just picked at random as stuff that for one reason or another I thought I was fairly sure to want to read. . . .

Friday 10 March 1944

On with the same, including such matters as how about an alleged 'Col' Andrews who had been interesting the big plane manufacturers in a book which they would buy pages in because he was a friend of Mr A's; a case, from the file, rather interesting and curious, as the Air Inspector's men had not turned up anything amounting to impersonating an officer, nor any evidence that he was misrepresenting the project or planning to make money out of it—the only misrepresentation seemed to be that he was a friend of Arnold's and all the brass hats. We notified the Air Inspector to notify by letter all manufacturers that this Hq knew nothing about him and had no interest in his project. There was a lot more stuff taking less time, but considerably more interesting to deal with than Mr A's speeches. I found that my morale continued to be enormously improved and thought to myself that I would freeze on to this if George would let me. . . .

Saturday 11 March 1944

. . . I came in with my pad at 8.30 as the assiduous assistant and did the mail with the Col. We had it all finished by ten with a little stack of things I could take care of—leaving George, I could see, at certainly novel loose ends and the thought crossed my mind that it might be possible to overdo this, because, whether he knows it or not, he, too, probably likes to be very busy. I went up to confront a Capt Warlick in OC&R Emergency Rescue with an adverse decision on a proposed *Air Force* article and found myself telling him about Our Policy, which I forthwith checked, because it certainly seemed to hint that my real interest was in being a busybody and officious to boot. . . .

Monday 13 March 1944

We had an idle day, George being very busy getting together an 'agenda' for the PRO board meeting tomorrow. He said he would like to take me, and then changed his mind and said he couldn't because some of the others might then start bringing people and if it got any bigger nothing would be done. . . .

Tuesday 14 March 1944

George's PRO board meeting was put off until tomorrow so we remained in relatively suspended animation though I spent some time in getting Chester Kerr to find out for me where the Vera Brittain piece on not bombing Germany was really first published—he reported late that it was in a pacifist pub in England called *Fellowship* for March—in case some reply other than the thousand screams already uttered was to be given. Late, too, George decided that a couple of minor generals could have a paragraph or so in some speeches of theirs, but we would not unlimber Mr A. He said he thought it was a hangover from the days when professional soldiers did the fighting and civilians did not have to mess into the business; I said I thought it was a hangover from the teachings of Our Lord Jesus Christ, which caused him two minutes later to come in and say, What the hell are you giving me? I was astonished to see that, though no believing or practising Christian himself, he had a background from a Baptist minister pappy, which made it give him a turn. I had meant it, however true, as a joke. He seemed enough reassured to leave it to me to prepare a passage for inserting in prospective speeches by Gen Hunter and somebody else. . . . Newhouse told me that Brendan Gill was about to be drafted so I called

Gardner Hudson and told him that he might use the man, if they needed any writers. He thought they might. From Newhouse's concern in the matter I began to realize that I might have missed something in never having been an enlisted man or got my bars through OCS [Officers Candidate School]—that is, it might be just possible that the army, which seems to me pretty much all right, justly and reasonably run, could look different if you had been with no previous aptitude thrust into the ranks and set to whatever a 1st Sgt chose to set you to.

Thursday 16 March 1944

The board continued debating, among other things, I gathered, the matter of what the newspapers should say about the bombing missions and George sent me first with a verbal request and then with an R&R [routing & record sheet] which I hastily composed to a Lt Col Bright in the readjusted European section to get material to try to draw up a table or something of what had in fact been happening since 20 Feb in the bombing of Germany. Bright, who had a European theatre ribbon with a few clusters or stars on it, was very suspicious, because, I soon saw, he thought it was being implied that Mr A was not getting proper information from his part of A2. I soothed him as well as I could, but he kept the There-is-More-to-this-than-Meets-the-Eye expression and walked me around to somebody in Analysis who took the R&R and said he would let me know. I reported this back to George who reached for the telephone and then said, abandoning it; hell, let them do it their way, what do you say? . . .

Friday 17 March 1944

. . . I passed the morning composing with consultations an answer to a jerk named Peters who seemed to have made a mess of Brewster for the Navy and now chose to send around a packet of self-vindicating letters and explanations with the apparent idea that Mr A would respond that he was hardly used. . . .

Saturday 18 March 1944

All day on the bombing charts which were not uninteresting. George came in in the afternoon and reported that, after all, he believed Rex Smith was taking over. Chamberlin who had been all week in Wright Field seemed to think it was one more of the same, and it was true that no 'paper' was yet forthcoming, but I thought that George must be, as he said he was, more and more willing to find an out and let this Smith try getting his ears knocked down. Gerald Carter called me about noon to say that he was in Senator Wheeler's[29] office—a matter he had mentioned to me before—and the senator would like to have luncheon with me, any day, any time. It seemed mysterious that the senator did not say so himself but I thought I would not mind seeing so great a curiosity and agreed to Monday at 12.30. I mentioned it to George then and he easily put his finger on it—the senator probably hoped that I might be willing to make some possibly useful political statements about the Negro's hard times in the army. He suggested I call Dempsey who said by all means to have luncheon with him, since it would be supposed my superiors had shut me up if I didn't, but I'd better be prepared for some leading questions which I'd also better be prepared not merely not to answer, but also to see that I said nothing that implied I did not answer because the Army would not let me.

Monday 20 March 1944

. . . In the morning our prospective Col Smith and a chicken col and another lt col came in and surveyed us, asking if all desks were occupied, seeming to show that it was going through. In to the capitol at 12.30 where a blonde girl in the Interstate Commerce room on the 3rd floor said Senator Wheeler was on the floor and ran me across the hall expeditiously to sit in the gallery. A great many of the people attending, the pages crouched in a disorderly way on the steps, the clerks, a couple of senators, and I thought Vice-President Wallace, were all chewing gum while a bumbling fellow with a mess of hair and his back to me was sounding off on FCC [Federal Communications Commission]. Presently the blonde came back and brought me in to the senator's office where a smooth number, exactly in Dempsey's style, called Carney was waiting. After ten minutes or so—Gerald had meanwhile appeared, put a table cloth on what appeared to be a poker table, and begun to distribute fairly fancy food—the senator entered. He proved to be large featured, with a reddish tone to parts of his skin, wearing glasses, shambling slightly, and easy, affable, and to all intents I could see, unaffected, sharp, sensibly spoken. Gerald whisked some cocktails out of an electric refrigerator that looked like a filing case and gave us a good lunch. Since I was prepared for machinations I was somewhat taken aback to find that the senator admired my work and apparently had had me brought around for no other reason. He talked well, easily, and frankly in a strictly non-oratorical way, expressed concern about where we would be after the war if we did not pay as much attention to our interests as England and Russia paid to theirs, did not take up the Army or the Negro question—except to ask if it was true, as he believed, that provision had been made to train Negro pilots. His man Carney held his tongue, but in an easy non-obsequious way, putting in an intelligent word when it seemed appropriate. Gerald improved the hour by producing his second son, Martin, 17, who had his card in the AAF cadet reserve, a self-possessed, intelligent looking and pleasant youth, a good deal brighter, I should think, than Fitzgerald, supporting with composure and good humor even his father's surely disconcerting suggestion that he say what he had to say to the captain fast, because the capt and the senator were busy. What he said was that he wondered if he could postpone getting in a semester because he was ahead of his class but wanted to graduate with them. I told him I was afraid not. Afterwards we kept on talking until 2.30 when I withdrew, thinking well of the senator rather than not.

Tuesday 21 March 1944

. . . I went on with the bombing summary , getting to some of the results, which was instructive in a way, since it was plain that little or nothing was the result or usual result of any hundred or so tons of bombs on a target that was small enough so that when you missed you just missed and didn't hit something else by a mistake. . . . Lunch with George who was certainly supporting well his promotion from Chief to Deputy Chief, but he said while stirring up the filthy food; I goddam well am not pleased. Reeves spent the afternoon playing with Miss Johnson and I spent it putting more figures on my bombing sheets until four when George came back and asked me for 5 minutes for the Gen to the press club to follow a showing of the *Memphis Belle*.*

Wednesday 22 March 1944

At the Gen's five-minutes, which I finally got together and which the board late in the afternoon decided would do with a couple of changes. . . .

Thursday 23 March 1944

I made my revisions on the Gen's remarks and spent much of the afternoon in Mr Lovett's office, George asking me to watch the taking of the color photograph of him for *Wings* mag. The Assistant Secretary is a lank, half-bald fellow—he kept saying to me and the photographer, an earnest fellow with an accent named Houston, that he took a bad picture. It still surprises me to see those in high station so naturally self-conscious or naive. I was in by his 4 foot globe as his stand-in, and after he had slicked his hair, adjusted his finely checked black and white tie, and got his handkerchief well out of his blue serge pocket, Mr L kept saying why not photograph me instead. However, he submitted with reasonable grace though we had a hard time as the photographer kept telling him to chat easily and naturally with me; not the easiest thing in the world. He has a big-nosed, good, lean face, and very nice manners; so we took him against his globe and against his white secty's flag and looking up brightly from work on his desk. . . .

*See Appendix.

Friday 24 March 1944

. . . Capt Meredith came up in the morning to inquire about the WAC matter—seemingly, while we waited on who was going to ask Mr A, they also suspended the other project—the one to be made at Randolph—in case it might conflict; or maybe because Col Bubb and Prewitt and his gang were lazy or otherwise engaged and that would serve as an explanation. Meredith had simply stopped in, saying, though he'd often spoken to me, he'd never seen me. I thought this was an engaging social amenity, and for lack of other material, mentioned the WAC matter, which was the last we had been engaged on, and so heard the story of the suspended action. He had been seeing George on another matter, so I took him back, and George thereon called Dempsey, set me to doing at once a memo for Mr A, and took it over himself. It seemed to me a sort of classic example of how things get to be done and get to be not-done—nobody has thought about the WAC business at all for a month, and yet the same thing could clearly have been done any day of the month. . . .

Saturday 25 March 1944

There was nothing to do, as it appeared that Mr A (a military secret) had departed for one could guess where on short notice though still planning to be back for the Press Club. Taking everything together one might guess that they could be going ashore around the first of April. At something after four George came in waving a paper which proved to be a much belated and mislaid matter of some remarks for the graduation exercises of an AAF Staff School class next Monday at 11. General White had been selected to do the remarking and I could see that George was anxious to agree, though grumbling, that it could be done as a favor to White—just in case he decided to and could get out from under Smith and wanted to work over there. However, the fact that he thus had a personal interest, I could see gave him rather engaging pause—that is, he hovered without committing himself and I think if I had said, hell, no, it was impossible on such short notice, he would with perfect grace have told White so. Naturally I said; sure, we could do it, giving a good example, I suppose, of the truth that you can in fact catch more flies with honey than with vinegar.

Sunday 26 March 1944

In to the office in the morning and got out six pages, including to my surprise what Gen White thought he would like, a humorous touch.* I took it down to George who was lounging with Lt Col Barber on the red leather there and he said I would get the Distinguished Writing About Flying Cross and could go home. . . .

*See Appendix.

Monday 27 March 1944

Gen White seemed content with his speech, so we heard no more of that. To my surprise, the WAC matter also duly came through and Mr A said he would make it. That was fine, but Lt Col Delaney suddenly gummed the works in BPR with the news that Hangar 6 had been restricted straight from Gen Marshall's office, and there would be no photographs or goings-on there. I had a harassed conference with Col Baughman and Caroline Varn and a Major Ludwigsen up there and we thought we might shift it to Bolling if the newsreels would agree, the slant this time being How the AAF meets the manpower shortage. It was hard to handle because a Lt Toole in Williams' office (with Delaney's assistance—he is a fleshy, pig-headed, pig-faced fellow I could not seem to like too well) was determined to stand between us and me and the newsreels—I could see their point, but how could we know what to prepare if we did not know what the newsreels would take?—making it awkward. Or was it my fault that ATC and Col Collins at Hangar 6 didn't know they were restricted? George Bradshaw[30] turned up from Italy, so the office did little work. He proved to be a brown haired boy with an Adam's apple and a beak-like good face and a uniform which he seemed to have slept in since he went over last November. . . .

Tuesday 28 March 1944

Col Delaney wanted a memo from me in the morning about the Wac business, which I thought was a form of stalling; but sure enough in the course of the afternoon they fixed it for the General Thursday. I kept running around and answering the telephone since we had some changes—Mr A's Miss Adkins called to say the Gen thought he would have lunch at Bolling and do it at 2, when we had fixed it at 3, and would I fix the lunch. This I got Dempsey to do. George seemed quite ill at noon, disturbing us all, and went home—I suppose it was a tribute any man could plume himself on, the consternation you could see everywhere at the notion that he might be going to have more stomach trouble in a big way. Col Smith had me over in the afternoon late to Gen Vandenberg's office where he was sitting with the Gen's flags and got off some highly confused suggestions about a cable—very affably, but you could see in an instant how lost we would be without Haddock, because I could only answer yes sir and trust George would be in in the morning. . . .

Wednesday 29 March 1944

. . . To Bolling at 10 with a WAC Lt Anderson from Capt Meredith's BPR section. She was a somewhat blowsy blonde girl, born, I learned, in 1907 when she challenged some remark of mine about what things were like when you got to be my age, with signs of a sense of humor and supposedly some experience with newsreels. .

39

Major Gray, a neat little youth, the Bolling PRO, had us down to talk to Col Trowbridge, the Executive Officer along with Major Ludwigsen from Baughman's office, and two company COs. Ludwigsen is a long, narrow-faced, dark girl I wanted to use for her leaves as detachment CO. We seemed to get it all fixed except possibly the weather. I brought Anderson back by noon with the arrangement that we would try it out on the ramp tomorrow morning. The afternoon went mostly into telephone calls and fixing up a 'schedule' for the General. . . .

Thursday 30 March 1944

Over to Bolling at about 9.30 with Lt Anderson. . . . We had some standing around down at Operations with Col Trowbridge and the WAC company lts and Capt Brooks who improved in my estimation, being suddenly full of sense, and Major Ludwigsen, who, I really thought, was fine before I finished—that is, I began to realize as a Captain Hasse there, more or less in charge of protocol, worked out the ceremony that for her it was a pretty large order to step out of Hq and take over the thing as ostensible CO—she even had to go home and get an overcoat as it was planned to parade them in coats. Dempsey had represented to me that it should be given to them in the talk as more to their advantage and less as their duty, so I had to write that over, dictating some new remarks to a WAC Pfc, very handy at shorthand, in Major Gray's office, with the telephone ringing all the while about who was coming and who wasn't. Dempsey telephoned me at 11 and said I'd better make myself part of the Gen's luncheon, which threw us all off as we were going to spend the luncheon interval on the ramp. I managed to get to the Officers Club only a little late with copies of the new remarks and the approved schedule. Mr A was ten minutes late himself, but in fine spirits, and we sat down—he, Col Hastey, Col Trowbridge, Lt Col Baughman, a Wac major named Gates, Major Gray, Dempsey, Capt Brooks and I, to a lot of chicken patty (made of superior parts of chicken, I soon realized). The Gen rode Col Baughman very hard on how the Wacs did not know how to recruit; and first appalled, she rallied, and began to answer back, so he barked across the table to me; What do you think of her talking back to me, Captain? I said I thought she had some good points, sir—all very jovial. However, from where I was sitting I could see down to the gates where the Wac detachments were formed up halted, showing that Major Gray or someone hadn't had the gates opened. After twenty five minutes I could stand it no longer and had Dempsey excuse Capt Brooks and me. We went rushing down and to the guard, and got the gates open, and they went in—all good and cold, I think, since they weren't using overcoats after all. The newsreels had turned up in great force, to my relief, and though it seemed out of the question to expect it, everything went off nicely—Mr A was easy and composed, and spoke to the right Wacs on inspection, and they marched well, and Major Ludwigsen in spite of her engaging jitters, did everything right. I could see Col Hastey was much pleased and he even thanked me by name; and Mr A himself said to me, Well, are you satisfied? so I began to feel that I had had quite a triumph, though very relieved also to have it over. . . .

Friday 31 March 1944

. . . The office was in a state of unbroken repose except for Newhouse trying to compose a letter to the president of the Dominican Republic expressing the Gen's pleasure at his naming a new national airfield for some Marine corps General I had never heard of. . . .

Saturday 1 April 1944

We had nothing to do beyond measure the floor of our rooms while George worked out a distribution of desks to include the next big room beyond us. The general impression I get is that though Smith may be technically CO, he is a benefit rather than a trouble to George since he has delegated his authority on all important points, so George can now do what he wants and if any one doesn't like it, Smith, not he, will be to blame. We had a new AAF T/O [table of organization] and sure enough we were out from under AC/AS Intelligence and off on the edge on a par with the Air Judge Advocate and the Air Chaplain. I am still a long way from knowing what is actually going on.

Sunday 2 April 1944

On as duty officer. At 10 Lt Col Barber called up and said he thought George wasn't coming in but if he did, would I ask him to call. He did not, and there were no other signs of life. I thought again that Smith being technically CO considerably eased George's burden, and I don't mean that he takes the relief in any spirit of pique or all-right-now-you-do-it, but simply quite justly and equably, that he will do the work faithfully and carefully as directed; but, not having the command, he will not on his own take the responsibility for anything he is not directed to do. I was pleased to see in the *Herald Trib* a photo of Mr A with Major Ludwigsen at Bolling Thursday, everything as I thought looking good & trim. . . .

Monday 3 April 1944

We had little to do. George sent me up to see Col Baughman about some interview she was just giving to a *NY Herald Trib* wench who seemed to be somebody named Hamilton, but she had touched on nothing but background and I thought had not likely jeopardized policy. She said, propping up her neat small feet and offering me a Camel, that she wondered if I could help her get an historical pic done on the Air

Wac anniversary and I said to put in an R&R and I would do what I could. . . .

Tuesday 4 April 1944

. . .The AAF camera crew pictures at Bolling turned up and I went to see them with Baughman and Varn and Capt Smoak, where we were magically joined by Lt Col Prewitt, I guess with the hope of establishing some relation with Varn. As one always is, I was taken back to see myself—and might well have been, since the shot that featured me was of the Gen reading his speech, and there I was good and plain behind him, to the right, wincing at various phrases he had changed and rolling my eyes around—enough, I should imagine to get me court martialled if he ever saw it. For some reason I wasn't aware that I was in the picture then. Later Baughman sent down her Lt Floyd with a few messages to be coordinated and a protest about some scene in a GI 8th Air Force show called *Skirts* in which, it seemed, some enlisted men dressed up as Wacs reflected on their morals and manners. George, I thought, felt that this Wac business might be being over-done. . . .

Wednesday 5 April 1944

. . . the latest policy 'pitch' was that Mr A would stop boasting—who is going to enforce the ban remains to be seen. . . .

Thursday 6 April 1944

. . . With some precautions, George passed me a piece of Reeves' in which the Gen was appealing in the *War Times*, a Pentagon pub of no importance, for blood donors.* It was indeed an awkward piece as written but I could not see that it mattered much, but somebody up the line was fussing. We have in now the 2nd Lt called Doulens and a Major Cecil Holland who used to work with the Col on the *Star*. I have not been able to make much of either, but they can plainly handle the detail, which leaves us with little to do—again a circumstance that everyone seems to relish but me.

Friday 7 April 1944

. . . At the office there was nothing to do. George was busy with the Pentagon people, sergeants and civilians, about telephones and more desks for the new room, in which it developed that Chamberlin and Newhouse and Bradshaw and Reeves and I would be put with Miss Johnson, a situation Newhouse described as roughly analogous to that of the Black Hole of Calcutta; but, in fact, the room is much bigger than 3C128. He then asked who would buy the cotton for Miss Johnson's ears—which seemed in

*See Appendix.

any event likely to come too late, as he had yesterday assured her privately that I was one-eighth Negro, and had been deeply wounded by some remarks of hers about feeling that she could never, for instance, date a Negro. He takes a peculiar pleasure—which in theory I would take myself, but in practise find irksome and boring—in drawing out people of simple ideas and encouraging them to express themselves. Miss Johnson apparently had been wounded because his solemn manner made her first believe him, and then she did not like the fact that she had believed him. She is a very thin Kansas girl with a mop of remarkable dark red, though not either pretty or beautiful, hair; and a thin white widemouthed face, always in paroxysms of grimaces and gesticulations—she laughs, distorting her face a good deal, if anyone looks at her; and if no one does, soon stamps her foot or exclaims under her breath over mishaps in her typing. When not self-conscious, she whistles loudly and cheerfully and far off the key, being at bottom I think simple, amiable, and good-natured. . . . I am sure she never saw anything like Newhouse before—but then, neither did I. . . .

Saturday 8 April 1944

. . . At the office there was nothing to do—that is; George showed me an appalling cable continuity for a Major James Stewart, a motion picture actor with the AAF in England, to do with a Wac; and asked if I knew about it. I did not (though S told me, in the eve, that Robert Carson, another Hollywood major, had been summoned down to some rush job, and I felt sure that was it). He asked me if I thought it was all right and on reflection I could not help believing that the hideous corny-ness was probably just about right. I then had a call from Capt Smoak, representing Col Baughman who was concerned when the Bolling Field business did not turn up in yesterday's newsreel. I made a few calls about that and the rest of the day sat with my feet on the desk reading and listening to Reeves tease Miss Johnson, which she seemed greatly to enjoy.

Monday 10 April 1944

. . . We did our moving into the new room, which I must say gives us a spacious or leisurely effect. . . . George came in and grumbled rather sharply—together in a room, Smith had apparently started to tell him something of his cockeyed plans for public relations, and, no doubt, for self-aggrandizement. Capt Smoak from Baughman's office came down in the morning with the R&R for the Wac picture, an earnest square-faced, open-eyed blonde woman with some notion that she wanted something along the lines of an air force picture she had seen somewhere. Jo Chamberlin pricked up his ears, and the picture proved to be a musical treatment of a 'poem' that he had written called, Do you know what the air force is? not yet released. However, on the word, he had it set up in 5E229, to which Smoak summoned Baughman and we looked at it. It seemed to be a version of the I-am-an-American technique run on the radios around the last election, in this case implying that the AAF was much more than planes and flyers, being in fact the whole American people. It was moderately wince-making, but Smoak said she thought it was wonderful and Baughman said she thought it was fine, and I said I thought that was a good job, Jo; and Chamberlin, who had a credit line on it, received our reports with modest pleasure.

Tuesday 11 April 1944

. . . In the office matters still seemed disorganized with nothing to do. . . .

Thursday 13 April 1944

. . . We still had nothing to do but there were some signs of renewed activity. . . .

Friday 14 April 1944

. . . There were no signs of life in the office. . . . George wandered in once, not in good spirits, so I supposed more complications were afoot, and felt, for one, somewhat fed up with it—it seems so stupid to sit around here doing (though, of course, through my own incapacity or lack of discipline) nothing, when certainly no one would be the loser if I were home and about my business; yet, on the other hand I would not like being a civilian right now. The plain solution would be, like Newhouse or Chamberlin, to get about my own work; and, if I don't feel like it, why, do it anyway. . . .

Saturday 15 April 1944

. . . There was nothing to do in the office but George was in better spirits and driving him home, he indicated to me yesterday's trouble as having to do with Smith's reluctance to take his word that a Capt Goldstein on *Air Force* ought to be a major and expressed his intention of 'going-into' *Air Force* as soon as he had time, probably to tear it all apart on the grounds that, as a former *Newsweek* man, he understood magazines. George with his inimitable manner of being candid, and yet, without disingenuousness or deceit, not telling you anything there was no need for you to know, seemed (I judged) to have resurveyed the situation and found that in the Smith matter he was still sitting pretty. That particular trait or manner deserves a better description, since the thing and the important thing, is that I think I am beyond doubt right in realizing that he tells no more than he wants to, but he does it so that you do not feel a trace of resentment at being what might after all be deemed unworthy of confidence. You really like and respect him for the ability to, soberly and with convincingly friendliness, keep his mouth shut. I can see that it is probably common in men used to negotiation, in politicians who are really competent and powerful, and probably in everyone who gets anywhere in large affairs involving dealings with people; but I have never seen it before—it is the real art & science of managing people, as opposed to, say, the small time political aptitudes of someone like John Fox—the promises, the exaggerated friendliness which, while maybe not rejected, outright, by anyone, are still seen through soon by almost everyone.

Monday 17 April 1944

We were undisturbed all day and so all got on with our reading. . . .

Tuesday 18 April 1944

. . . George turned up a request from Gen Hall to provide the Secty of War with stuff for his Thursday press interviews, the idea being to use them to make AAF propaganda and sent me to see Lt Col Dall, who seems to be the President's ex-son-in-law. . . . The idea was that Gen Kuter[31] might have some points to make; but he talked on every other subject, finally even causing a Col Whitney who shared the office with him to suggest that he was missing the point. I looked at the Col then and realized that he must be one of the horse people—it somehow surprised me to note that he looked quite sensible and earnest and anxious, or at least, neither idle nor rich. Later George came around (there was no connection) and said Gen Kuter was speaking sometime and I should see him tomorrow and find out what he would like ten minutes of.* Shortly afterwards Col Smith came in and addressed me as Jim, causing me to start, to say before I saw the Gen, would I see a Col Milton in his office. I said I would.

Wednesday 19 April 1944

I went in to see Col Milton, who had been on Kuter's trip with him, at 8.45 and he was drinking tomato juice and holding his head in a way which made me feel sympathetic, and taking handsful of his graying hair to pull while he went into what Kuter would probably want to say with energy and reasonable precision. He has a son, a fighter pilot, with the XIVth whom he had seen in China three weeks ago, and the morale there, he said, was very high. I could not help wondering whether that was good evidence—ie knowing his son, could he tell; or would he be the last person his son would actually tell anything to? At 9.30 I went in to Gen Kuter, who has got his second star. He has a scraggly though short black moustache and long flat cheeks. He talked for about three quarters of an hour, and I was interested to observe him, for he is supposed to be the coming man and a very smart guy. He seemed pleasant

*See Appendix.

and unaffected, but disconcerted me a little [by] what you would ordinarily think of as a kind of naivete—describing his trip and adventures, so much seemed to surprise him (I don't mean it wouldn't surprise me) like the ingenuity of the men at the advance posts in China making showers out of oildrums (every illustrated paper has had pictures of it), or flush toilets in the great new base in Markham valley in New Guinea. In the afternoon his girl called me up to ask if I could get an invitation for Mrs K to go to the dinner with him, so I called a Casey Jones who is editor or something of the *Post*, and got it all right, but it all seemed part of a simple, and by no means unpleasant, air of slight bewilderment. Jo Chamberlin had us up to projection room three at noon—he also had up Caroline Varn and Lt Col Baughman . . . to look at the film on the General's report, which was harmless, or a little better.

Thursday 20 April 1944

Busy with the remarks for Gen K, and, I could not help noticing, feeling quite lively and blithe as I fed sheets to Miss Johnson and was generally very occupied. I took a version in to Col Milton at 11 and he surprised me by suggesting sensibly that a pay-off might better be, for the Association of Editors, the need to maintain a determination to carry on the war rather than the need to see supplies were available. However, he also questioned in a moderate wise-acre way the build-up I had provided for the XIVth Air Force pushing out its line of battle until it was over Japan. He said knowingly, how did I know it would be that way? So I said he would know better than I (since presumably Kuter and he were doing the planning) and he said, Ah, Yes. However, George told me on the way home that Milton really knew nothing. Gen K had not got to the speech when the afternoon was over so I pulled out at six. In the morning Bill Harris telephoned me, and I went up to a foot army section in contracts where he was waiting. . . . Like so many others, he remarked that compared to the British we did not seem to know there was a war on. It seemed to me, as it had before, that far from being a reproach or sign of weakness, this might very well, if really true, be a sign of strength.

Friday 21 April 1944

. . . There was some delay in finding out about Kuter's piece, but it finally came around to me about noon, as rewritten by the Gen, which was really something. I ought to be used to it, but it still flabbergasts me—the changes are always so awful—that is, beyond any possibility of difference in taste or opinion, so bad; not just ungrammatical or ineptly worded, but fundamentally muddled in thought, with a maddening disregard for both sense and sound. I suppose it is a professional prejudice, but it always seems impossible that a man who hasn't the sense to express himself could have sense in any other direction; because that is so simple, at least relatively speaking. How in God's name, you ask yourself, can a man who rewrites a simple sentence stating a plain fact into three lines of incoherent gibberish because he plainly thinks it is better that way have the wit to make a sensible plan for the incredibly complicated operations of a whole air force? Of course, the answer is; he can, perfectly well. I know that is the case; but it is one of the hardest things for me really to believe. However, I know now better than to waste time trying to patch the patches so I just showed it to George who said; God, he screwed it up, didn't he? . . .

Saturday 22 April 1944

The Kuter matter, involving a great number of telephone calls, went on. I talked to Mr Jones and Mr Jones' secretary and a Mrs Pitts who was secretary of the association and a lot of people at the Navy, where a Commander McCarthy said their speakers were to be an Admiral Lowe and an Admiral Radford. Meanwhile Kuter was making more changes and Col Smith had some ideas, but his ideas came to nothing because when I finally called in and got to see Kuter at noon, he was about to go to Stimson's office, gave me a copy, said (with what gall, I felt) I had done a fine job, and left without adding any more jokes. Earlier George came in and said that Smith was burned up because I left yesterday; but when I started to say, if he liked, I would tell Smith I left because Kuter had rewritten it the way he wanted it and what could I do, he said; I told him you left because I said you could. Or, in short, we are about to have a show-down, a matter confirmed in the afternoon when Bradshaw was going to go on leave though Smith had not approved it. George came in and told him to go ahead anyway. It was plain that Monday he was simply going to tell Smith that he had given Bradshaw leave, more or less inviting Smith to make something of it. Either Smith would, and George would get out, or he wouldn't, and it would be established once and for all that Smith could tell George what to do or have done, but George would run the outfit that was doing it. I daresay the moment was well chosen, as Smith has looked extremely harassed and would probably be sunk altogether if he quarreled with George.

Monday 24 April 1944

. . . There was nothing to do except to cook up an R&R for Kuter through Dall about the stuff for Stimson's Thursday press conferences. I could not tell whether anything would come of it, except, I would bet, a lot of trouble with Dall. . . . Since everyone was idle I was entertained to see Newhouse teasing Miss Johnson with a sort of clinical interest on his part. No doubt it is the company she is obliged to keep; but she, I think insensibly to her, has begun to take a broader view and submitted with nothing but laughter to a sufficiently dry and sardonic but relentlessly pressed interrogation on whether or not she was really a virgin. She said she was; but even if she wasn't, would she say so? He said; Now Maggie, honesty is the best policy. I think it made her feel that she was quite a woman of the world.

Tuesday 25 April 1944

In the morning there was little to do as Kuter was out and Dall though so voluble was clearly unwilling to risk decisions on his own. . . . About 3 pm George came in with an R&R for two minutes by Mr A for the RAAF [Royal Australian Air Force] to be made on a record tomorrow; the occasion, the 4th Anniversary of their 'participation' in the Empire Training Scheme.* I went in to the Munitions Building to see a Group Captain Thomas, a stout short young fellow with a moustache and a fairly British accent (though I observed that he called it Austry-lyer) and some British habits, like answering the telephone by saying; Thomas, here. . . . It then developed through Dempsey that Mr A wanted his remarks right away. By six I had some, and gave them in, but Mr A had gone home. . . .

Wednesday 26 April 1944

. . . Though in early and so reporting myself to Mr A's office, he did not squawk and it finally came back to be typed in large type with only the words differentiate and unfailing taken out, they being too hard for him to pronounce. We had as a result an idle day with Ed coaxing Miss Johnson to define what was meant by the word orgasm.

Thursday 27 April 1944

. . . nothing to do, though George was in once or twice to say that some trouble had come up about the unified armed services department business which congress was fooling with, and Mr A had the notion that all AAF posts should send their COs or PROs around to the local papers to explain why what is presumably the Navy was wrong—a project George understandably regarded with horror since in the great majority of cases it was certain that those sent to do the delicate job would screw it up and accomplish nothing but, in one stroke, irritating hundreds of editors. Smith has been in NY all week at the Publishers' convention, so, I meant to say before, I was wrong about the show-down. The picture would be somewhat different if Smith came back and discovered that Bradshaw had gone a week ago, and the point established would be merely that when Smith was away George would run things, or else.

Friday 28 April 1944

. . . We had nothing to do, and it occurred to me that it was, of course, of the nature

*See Appendix.

of war, for whatever reason; and at least we shared fully with those in the field the futile waiting and the wearing idleness which, by every account I have ever heard, makes up most of most operations from the standpoint of the individual. I was reading in Freeman's first volume of *Lee's Lieutenants* the account of the first battle of Bull Run while I waited and it seemed very graphic on that point. You might presume that with experience the command would get somewhat more adept at disposing the troops, but probably not much more, really; and a battle would still remain, and must still remain, a sort of blundering together of forces, most of them in fact out of any actual rational control;—quite different from the after-the-battle maps showing position of troop bodies and their apparently planned movements. That is, obvious movements, like turning a flank or overrunning an enemy position, would plainly disconcert the enemy, and so the troops would be arranged and pointed in the general direction to accomplish one of these; but once started, whether or not they did it would be the result of just luck, several good breaks, and several guesses proving right. What I mean is that all the waiting and all the wasted time, both here and in the field, that seem so unreasonable, really aren't; they are simply consonant with the nature of war. If I and nine other officers do nothing for days on end, that is all right; for no matter how busy we were, nothing we did could affect the outcome since the movements are already initiated, and it remains only to be seen whether our guesses prove, as it seems they will, right; and whether we get the breaks, as it seems probable from the overwhelming scope of our preparations, we will. . . .

Saturday 29 April 1944

. . . We still had nothing to do, but it was plain that in the background a great struggle was going on to prevent General Kuter, to whom the business had apparently been delegated by Mr A, from carrying out the plan to start some active air force propaganda for the unified war department. The issue seemed to have engaged and exhausted everyone on the air staff, and on the general staff, for the last three days. As of the late afternoon, George's counsels had definitely prevailed—a good job, and even a necessary one. As soon as you put people in high places it is plainly necessary to provide a certain number of other people who will stubbornly and resolutely work full time at keeping them from making fools of themselves. . . . The later afternoon Newhouse devoted to questioning Miss Johnson on literature, history, and geography. Her ideas, avowed with a not unpleasant earnest perplexity, were amazing; she did not know where Spain was exactly, and seemed to think Joan of Arc had something to do with the Trojan horse, and that Tennyson and Shakespeare were contemporaries about a hundred years ago. The truth is, she never reads anything, not even a paper in the morning, and I suppose this is the surprising result.

Monday 1 May 1944

. . . Up to have some coffee about 10 with George and Major Holland where we started again on the stuff for Stimson's conferences. I went to talk to an amiable Capt Sweeney and a Major Theobald in Stat Control where they thought they could get some new and significant figures on the ETO [European Theatre of Operations]. Late in the afternoon to see Miss Cochran again. She had just flown in, very creased and worn looking. George came over presently, and Major Carr, who was not much needed. What was wanted was something the Secty could say about the WASP situation. George with great gentleness and delicacy worked her away from some ideas of hers and especially from the notion she was toying with—to give an interview to a man from the *NY News*. As George said, walking back with me, she was so wrought up about her girls that given a good reporter she would say anything and so cook matters properly with congress. I thought her again—I suppose because of the fanatic earnestness in her constantly widening light brown eyes—a good kind of girl, if not too long on brains or common sense.

Tuesday 2 May 1944

. . . It was finally decided that the Secty would not discuss the WASPs. In the afternoon a matter blew up suddenly about the 20th Air Force and the apparently imminent use of the B29s; so they had Major Simon of BPR writing a statement for the president, and Major Spence writing one for General Marshall and me writing one for General Arnold. Since it was all top secret the atmosphere was feverish at least, and I read with interest the background material on the production of the plane, the organization of the air force, and the preparation of the fields. You got the feeling that the operation had better be good. . . .

Wednesday 3 May 1944

. . . George came in early with a piece for Mr A for some Latin American nonsense of Nelson Rockefeller's next week in New York.* It was difficult to figure out why the Gen should be talking to them anyway—it seemed to have to do with postwar economic planning, or how best to sew up the South American trade. The material was agonizingly dull, and I did not seem to get any farther ahead than reading the hand-outs.

Thursday 4 May 1944

. . . I spent all day writing up the Gen's remarks for the Inter-American Development

*See Appendix.

Commissions which served the usual purpose of making me feel busy and energetic. . . .

Friday 5 May 1944

I did a few more things to the speech and handed it over to George, but he did not get to it until noon. . . .

Saturday 6 May 1944

. . . I spent most of the day—it was my own fault, and I do not mean that I would not rather be doing it than do nothing—on a memorandum to BPR about an article on the WASPs in this week's *Time* which had some misstatements. The one that really made the trouble was the representation, about half by *Time*, about half by alleged protestors to congress against giving them military status, that pilots from the WASPs were necessarily grounded several days each month. I went up to the Air Surgeon's office and a lanky young major, a southerner named Clark, got out a number of report sheets from Avenger Field and we soon concluded that we could say that less than 1/5 of them (it sounded better than 20%) were grounded even one day a month because of menstrual difficulties. I went down and shot the memo through to BPR and went in town with Newhouse to have lunch at the Lafayette. When I got back hell was popping because it seemed that Major Clark had been beat-on plenty for so pronouncing—not that it wasn't true, but that (a) WASPs were not part of the AAF yet, so the Air Surgeon had no business to have figures on them (b) from the scientific standpoint the figures were not adequate—only for a few months. Clark was really in a sweat to get me to telephone at once so that BPR wouldn't publish his figure instantly. I guessed that he must have been a young practising physician brought in directly and he had hardly realized that he was in the army now and not free to give his professional opinion. A prolonged hash-over, shifting the phrasing, went on then with a Col Ball and finally (no one denied the truth of the statement; they just didn't want no trouble, scientific or military) I was allowed to say: The degree to which a woman is incapacitated by menstruation naturally depends on the individual; but medical reports indicate that in the case of most WASPs their ability to fly is not seriously affected and they do not need to be grounded. Col Ball made the revealing remark to me that this was perhaps mostly because in their physical examinations the matter was gone into pretty thoroughly and those likely to be incapacitated were screened out to start with. He also said; I wish I could say the same about psychiatric difficulties. I said I thought we need not bring that up; and he said, My God, no; leading me to suppose that there were a few things Miss Cochran had not told me.

Monday 8 May 1944

. . . We had a few revisions to do on Mr A's speech—he had been working on it himself and with his usual accuracy hit the right passages to make horrible. . . .

Tuesday 9 May 1944

Still fussing with a last few details on Mr A's speech and we got it retyped just about in time for him to fly to NY with it. . . .

Thursday 11 May 1944

Did nothing all day. Something seemed, as so often, to be up somewhere but we did not hear about it. . . .

Friday 12 May 1944

What was up was apparently some agitation by Mr A about how BPR was not doing right. George asked me if I would run him in to the dentist's at noon and he cursed heartily all the way about the impossibility of doing anything for the old bastard, or indeed putting up with him at all; but I could by now guess that his reaction was only temporary and tomorrow he would go on doing what he could. I was delayed in getting off by some suggestion that something might be coming up but nothing did, except some expostulation by Smith that Newhouse seemed to work at home a lot and would he come in, which he did.

Saturday 13 May 1944

When I got in I discovered that Newhouse had won yesterday's bout and was working at home again. Smith came in about ten and sent me up to Gen Gates of Management Control over a plan to make a speech for some 400 rural editors at Chicago, all to be done at once; but Gates, a gray-headed, I thought sensible and agreeable, swearing fellow said no, he would make no such speech unless Smith planned it out and took it with him and submitted it to Mr A, because he said he knew Gen Marshall had asked the Air Force to stop talking out of turn and he didn't purpose to hold the bag and get sent to Panama or somewhere. I reported this to Smith, who said vaguely to write him a speech anyway, he would bring him around. Soon he came back and said he hadn't brought him around, but to do it anyway, someone else would make it. Sometime later it developed that no one would, and no speech was needed, making a confusing day, but on the whole all right with me since nobody seemed agreed on what would be said if anything by anyone.

Tuesday 16 May 1944

. . . In the morning we did nothing. At noon, very warm, took George out to his place to pick up a speech of Newhouse's that he had left home and I was set about doing 15 minutes for Mr A next Sunday for the painfully called I Am An American Day show-down at Chicago. George said we had better hedge on the invasion situation—that is, the Germans would have plenty of planes at first even if we did obliterate them and obliterate them again. I laid myself a private bet that Mr A would never allow it but went ahead.

Wednesday 17 May 1944

I got on with Mr A's remarks, enlivened by the memo from BPR which George brought in saying Par 2 it should be of patriotic sentiment and emotional appeal. I said as how there were not only privileges connected with being an American, but obligations and responsibilities and introduced the required data on how D Day would find plenty of GAF [German Air Force], but how long could they last. We also had a flurry on Mr A going over to the labor relations board and telling them (and I thought, good for him) that their foremen's strike had cost us 250 P51s, and what a hell of a time to do it. We were fairly sure of the figures and, showing that he can when it suits him, he did all right too, saying that he was too busy to answer questions instead of making a speech, as was to be feared. In to see Jo Chamberlin about his *Nat Geo Mag* piece on the Burma commandos was Col Allison.[32] I observed him with interest. He is a short slight young man, rather like what you would expect in a junior professor of math or physics with a head shaped like an egg, much of his thin brownish-blonde hair gone in front, and a flexible, humorous, lively face—smiling a great deal and speaking good-naturedly about the captions for the pictures. He seemed to want to get as many men as possible mentioned by name because their wives would like it. He had on a green shirt with eagles much askew, no wings, and pink pants. It seemed to go to show that there was no way of telling what you could make a fighter out of.

Thursday 18 May 1944

I got the lines for Chicago finished, but around noon Col Barber was in and felt that we had too much emphasis on the air force end. He suggested with lazy smiles and in a mild way that a few stories might be better. I did not think George liked it very well; but he said yes; so I went up to see a Major Van der Wolf in Awards and Decorations, who gave me some new stories of heroism, including one Barber liked about a mechanic, a corporal who had his foot smashed in trying to put out a fire on a B17 newly delivered to a local field. He was alleged to have said when they told him in the hospital his foot would have to come off; To hell with the foot; I lost my plane. The truth is, I suppose, people do say things like that. We finally got a new version done by six, but George said then to let it ride, word having just come through that review was not allowing the use of the term 'invasion.' They also said they were not allowing the use of the word 'malaria' which was reassuring, as seeming to indicate that someone was crazy down there. We will try it in the morning, though that will be hot work as Mr A is supposed to be off by noon. . . .

Friday 19 May 1944

. . . I was around to get the speech down to review at 8.30 but no one got there until nine so I mildly did what I could to spread consternation, saying Mr A was waiting. The executive, a little bald lt col called Curtin read it rapidly and made no objection to the invasion business. Upstairs it developed that Mr A was not leaving at all, so we had that on our hands. . . .

Saturday 20 May 1944

. . . It was reported that Mr A got off with his speeches about 10 and we did nothing all day—that is, Newhouse wrote letters and Reeves read the papers until noon when he went off for exercise, and Chamberlin was obscurely busy with his many 'articles' (which will turn up in anything from the *Reader's Digest* to the *Farm Journal*) and Bradshaw kept his feet on the desk with a really impressive sustained vacancy, actually doing nothing by the hour, and I read Wiley's *Life of Johnny Reb* which is a good job on the Confederate soldier, often sensible or shrewd, and well documented, and Miss Johnson read Ilka Chase asking me every little while what such words as metaphysics and altercation and bibelot and imponderable meant, or how they were pronounced. I could not help thinking that the reading must be hard for her, but she was resolved and constant in a way that made me guess she was going to improve her mind if it killed her. . . .

Tuesday 23 May 1944

. . . We had nothing to do all day; but, as George Haddock confirmed me by remarking while we were driving in town in a light rainfall; What do you think you'd be doing most days if you were out risking your life and limb in some honest to God theatre? . . .

Wednesday 24 May 1944

. . . We turned up a speech for a Gen Pratt who was to make it Friday when they open for Cities Service a 100-octane plant at Lake Charles, La and I went into the Munitions building to see what some petroleum officers wanted.* A Major Benedum, who had both ends of his blonde moustache waxed, but was not bad, took

*See Appendix.

me in to a mild blue eyed Col Lingle whose face, though it was not hot, was running with sweat, and he told me a few vague things while I laid on the Hq business and questioned him closely, I'm afraid for the hell of it, so that he would know it wasn't everyone who had Mr A's men helping him out. This, he seemed to like very much; as I have discovered before. . . .

Thursday 25 May 1944

. . . Major Benedum called me about 2 minutes after eight (when very few people would be in their offices, but I had just got down from breakfast, and I thought it was commendable of me to be there) to say that Col Lingle was leaving at 10. I told him I would call the Col in half an hour, and what he wanted was for me to read the remarks to a machine, which I did. It then developed that he was not going until 11, and would I get copies over, which I did by ten. By twelve a Lt Col French was fussing because Gen Pratt was about to leave San Antonio and could not seem to wait for the copies Lingle was flying down with him, so they solved that by sending me around there, and I read it again to a recording machine in San Antonio on a private line—it seemed to me an extraordinary waste of time and money; but no doubt it is right that you should get something out of being a major general. After that everything was quiet. . . .

Friday 26 May 1944

. . . At the office there was nothing to do and nothing going on but an order from Gen Giles to say that people would stop using WD stationery for their private correspondence, a spot check having shown that fifty some percent of the Pentagon mail consisted of that. Bradshaw and Reeves went downstairs and bought themselves some envelopes at Walgreen's. . . .

Saturday 27 May 1944

. . . All was idle in the office except for my activities with Newhouse in stapling up the sheets of a beautiful 1-500,000 map of southern England and the European coast, in case we were going to have an invasion. Getting the sheets from the map section and cutting and folding and joining them, not to mention finding a staple gun, took all morning. . . . George sent me in to Col Bentley, Gen White's executive, who was trying to write a manual for air attaches, with very little success from the standpoint of English prose. His idea seemed to be that we could fix it today & tomorrow (he was going on leave Monday) but I managed to get over the suggestion that this was an important matter and should be done right, and need not, after all, be ready until he got back in the middle of June. This he took down quite readily, saying, yes, that's true; this will probably be standard for the next five years. He is a large pale man, plainly once very handsome, who used to be air attache in Italy. His stuff, when you could figure out what he meant from what he wrote, seemed to show that he did know all about it and had sensible if incoherent ideas.

Monday 29 May 1944

. . . Col Bentley was making some changes in his work before pulling out at noon and his girl was then typing it. Late in the afternoon George came in with some stuff for a dinner Mr A was giving for some Russians tomorrow—Newhouse was already working on some toasts which were then to be translated into Russian (quite a waste of time, you could not help thinking) and I was to do some remarks for McNarney or someone to make when Mr A introduced them. Then it was decided they could wait until tomorrow. . . .

Tuesday 30 May 1944

. . . The remarks for the dinner did not come up but Smith put in to me at ten to see Col Pool about some remarks Gen Harper was to make before the alumni of the Harvard Business School on Saturday.* Neither Pool nor Harper seemed to have any idea of what they would say, though Pool, looking much fatter and older than the last time I saw him (and so, indeed, I am sure I do myself if he were to tell me) thought the Gen might describe the training program. I went around to Stat Control where the invaluable Capt Sweeney took me in to see some people on training figures and I then loitered around Harper's place seeing others. In this process I suddenly encountered Miss Cochran in the hall and she wheeled, backing me against the wall, and asked if I had seen what the Ramspeck committee[33] was trying to do—nothing good, I gathered, trying to imply that I knew already and expressing indignation. She looked quite worn and ill, and in spite of the absurdity of it all I found myself feeling a pang and would willingly have fixed it for her if by turning a hand I could. After lunch which I had with Ed Newhouse, who now I think of it, has what must have been the Ancient Mariner's glittering eye and way of fixing you while he discusses the bad work of Theodore Dreiser or James T. Farrell (who could doubt it was bad; but he seems to wish to establish it once and for all) working on phrases for Harper. I spoke to Smith about it and he thought we might tie it in somehow with the subject of the conference but mostly left it to me to do it, looking all the while worn and red-eyed and holding his face or head, but still speaking to the point. Since he has never been anything but pleasant and even considerate to me I find myself resisting a little Ed's dislike of him—which is to say, I suppose, I would settle with anyone for a smile.

*See Appendix.

56

Wednesday 31 May 1944

I got Harper's piece done by noon, but he was engaged in a conference much of the afternoon and Pool reported that he took it home with him at 4, so I suppose we will have trouble tomorrow. At the office we all stayed in until six because Smith had indicated that someone from OWI [Office of War Information] was coming in and he wanted us to meet him. He came in, but apparently had more sense than you would expect from someone in that outfit, and went right out without giving us the pleasure. . . .

Thursday 1 June 1944

. . . Pool told me in the morning that Gen Harper was making do with the speech, quite unheard of in our experience. . . .

Friday 2 June 1944

. . . I managed in the morning to get a version of a statement from Mr A for the West Point magazine shaped up, including in it (I will probably be cashiered) all the more dreadful phrases from a telegram which, originally written by Ed, had been revised by Dempsey and Mr A and sent back to him as an example of how to write. It irked Ed more than you would expect—or rather, now I think about it, just as much as it would have irked me; which I guess means that criticism is criticism, even if obviously imbecile or idiotic. . . .

Saturday 3 June 1944

. . . I worked more or less at Bentley's stuff, having much trouble with the first paragraphs because I had little to go on about AAF policy except what he had written and I found that by consulting that constantly I suffered a sort of corruption of style in which it seemed almost impossible to write the stated facts without putting them in something like the same fantastically stilted phrases. . . . Late in the afternoon we were busy contradicting a UP rumor that the invasion had started but the contradiction was so curiously phrased that it seemed possible it might have— except that Mr A's son is getting married next week and Mr A is going, and he seemed hardly likely to let the two coincide.

Monday 5 June 1944

. . . Late in the afternoon Bill Chambers called me from NY (he had been made a Lt Col) and wanted to know if there was any chance that they could get the use of me briefly to do a chapter in the FM [field manual] about landing operations. However, it did not mean getting back to NY for a month as at first I thought so I spoke to

George Haddock and he said he would call tomorrow and say no I could not be spared. . . .

Tuesday 6 June 1944

Picking up a 1st Lt of engineers on the way in, he said to me well I suppose this is it; which seemed to indicate that the invasion must be on. I said yes, though I had not listened to the radio. In the office we had installed (very conveniently, perhaps) yesterday a teletype machine grinding out the FCC bulletins, of which there were a hundred feet on the floor at seven thirty, it having apparently turned itself on. We did not get much work done, what with that, and everyone standing in groups around it while it poured out what was in fact very little and mostly German at that. Reactions seemed about half and half—my own, which was a good deal of anxiety and vague distress, and Johnny's which began by being, Hooray! with which she came in but she soon seemed to catch the infection and began to pace up and down and look at the teletype every three minutes, too. . . . I suppose the general unspoken feeling was that if we got on with this, it might be over sometime; and if we didn't, God knew when. . . .

Wednesday 7 June 1944

. . . In spite of the teletype it began to get fairly apparent today that nobody knew anything, and nobody would for a week or so, and everyone might just as well relax. The most efficient form of it, I thought came up in Dempsey's office where I brought along a new text for Mr A's piece to the cadets in the *Pointer* next fall.[34] This did not suit him and he settled down to what amounted finally to an hour of comment and effort to formulate what Mr A might like to say—very warm and friendly so I was some time in realizing that what he was after was Col Smith. He found fault with what was written because it followed the suggestions sent from West Point, and I thought his objection was sensible (though I had not thought of it myself). Their idea was that flying training was wonderful because aviation after the war would be something, because of what we had learned. What the hell, said Dempsey, are we training them at great expense to get a job in civil aviation? I would suppose that the answer is probably yes; but I could see that the CGAAF [Commanding General, Army Air Forces] didn't have to suggest it to them. However, this seemed pretty much aside from the point, which plainly was that Col Smith did not give us 'guidance' in the way Dempsey thought (and would no doubt tell Mr A) he should. I did not encourage the idea, since, though without any intimate bond of affection to tie me to Smith, I still like him better than Dempsey, who was plainly out to make him all the trouble he could. Sitting there amid the walnut and red morocco with the main business on hand a subtle interdepartmental knifing, you could obviously contrast to your heart's content the war here and the war around Caen; but I am quite prepared to believe that one really isn't possible without the other.

Thursday 8 June 1944

. . . I did not get far with Dempsey's project as Col Pool could suggest no one but Col Ward (away) for dope he thought I might get there, and Gen Kuter's somewhat mincing little round Major Berg could think of no one but a Col Moffat who was making a plan for the Joint Chiefs of Staff. I did grudgingly and very gradually what I could by myself. . . . In the afternoon the news seemed fairly good both on the teletype and by word of mouth. Dempsey had not yet been to see Smith, who seemed fairly belligerent on the subject. Driving George Haddock home, he said to me that he was reasonably satisfied with the situation, meaning him & Smith, and so was apparently ready to oppose Dempsey if he started to mix in. . . .

Friday 9 June 1944

. . . I finished up the new *Pointer* version but there seemed little hurry about it since Mr A had flown to England yesterday (perhaps sharing the local fidgets or unease, and being better able to do something to relieve himself) so I mostly watched Bradshaw, who with fine nonchalance was doing nothing about a speech for Gen Giles due this afternoon—that is, when I left at noon to exercise, he had written five pencil lines and I almost wanted to stay to see whether he was going suddenly to get it done by three oclock, or what he was going to say if he hadn't got it done. What news we had about the state of affairs in Normandy added up to little, but it was plain that already it had dropped out of the foreground and things were proceeding as usual—and, indeed, when you think of it, why shouldn't they?

Saturday 10 June 1944

. . . I went down to get Mr A's *Pointer* piece cleared with Review which took some time as they had a few fancy new regulations about the 'processing' of pieces by general officers ending with a somewhat gross coast artillery col . . . who re-initiated in blue pencil the stamp already initialled in red pencil by Major Parker. We seemed to get mostly good or at least not bad news from France and Chamberlin suggested we go in and have luncheon at the Lafayette which we did—he had his concerns equally divided between whether we were getting somewhere and so might hope to get out sometime, and a project Col Clemson was operosely fumbling over; viz.; could a film be made which would encourage the AAF personnel when they discovered that licking Germany did them no good, they would all be engaged with Japan while 3 million foot army people were released and went home and got the good jobs. . . .

Monday 12 June 1944

. . . Things were calm in the office and I went on with Bentley's stuff, though slowly. . . . Miss Johnson was somewhat miffed because she had been assured Saturday (an idle afternoon) that it was true about Chinese women; and it seemed that there were some Chinese girls at Arlington Farms and she had found in the shower room that it wasn't.

Tuesday 13 June 1944

. . . We spent most of the morning putting up the sheets of the 1-1 million European map to cover the eastern front on the wall behind the table—no doubt as profitable a way to spend time as any other. Before we finished Jo Chamberlin's promotion came through so he insisted on having Ed and Reeves and me in to have lunch at the Lafayette. It was plain that he was much relieved to be a Lt Col after a year and a half as major in the Pentagon where it is certainly established that if you are less than a Lt Col you can't amount to much. This is what might be called the active side of it and presumably if you are a major—which is the passive side; you are all right, you cannot be pushed around; but, at the same time, you can't hope to push anyone else around or to have anything you say seriously considered—you get to want it. I can see that in the nature of things I ought to be a major myself in a couple of months; and while I would not mind that, considering the majors there are, that seems to me all I could ever conceive of wanting to be—but I suppose you learn. . . .

Wednesday 14 June 1944

. . . There was some unease in the backroom as it seemed that Smith was going ahead with his idea of farming out Reeves and Bradshaw, and it was also indicated that he said he would not stand in Haddock's way if he could get a job in India, which was offered him. The Air Surgeon took care of that but it all suggested a certain amount of general insecurity. However, after all these months I realize that the proper treatment for these stirs is to pay no attention to them. We had little to do since I could not get Bentley's piece, at last finished, typed and I spent much of the afternoon putting up north Italy in the 1:200,000 sheets behind me to replace south Italy. . . .

Thursday 15 June 1944

. . . When I got in at 7.30 Smith and Spence and Doulens were there already, apparently waiting on some stuff to do with the Navy going ashore on Saipan and the 20th Air Force being in the process of sending the B29s over Japan. The official releases did not come until afternoon and there were no details about the 29 mission then—still everyone felt quite lively. . . .

Friday 16 June 1944

. . . Little that was definite on the 20th Air Force operation had come in and outside the back room—showing I suppose how little we have to do with Smith's business or activities—everything was bustle with much animated coming and going though plainly all of it was pointless or fruitless, since visiting a dozen offices, as Major Spence seemed to be doing, would not be likely to uncover details not yet put on the wire from China. Col Bentley came in about quarter of twelve and gave me a turn as I was about to go out, by suggesting that he would like to work on his piece after lunch. I decided I might as well speak out, so he amiably agreed tomorrow would do as well—indeed, he was very polite and full of expressions of thanks, not seeming to take it entirely for granted that we should be working for him. . . .

Saturday 17 June 1944

. . . I was busy with Col Bentley who was a pleasure to work with since he had what I considered sense enough to see that when I rephrased a thing it was better and clearer than when he wrote it and gladly agreed to a rearrangement of material into some kind of order. One doesn't generally expect so much cooperation. Col Smith was looking doleful in the morning for it seemed that on one of the four 29s lost had been the *Time* and the *Newsweek* writers, both he claimed old friends of his. In the afternoon he had a birthday cake which he jovially compelled us all to accept pieces of. In fact, he is agreeable and amiable, except perhaps for a certain real or imaginary taint of conniving or paltering which seems to hang around him.

Monday 19 June 1944

. . . Col Smith had gone away on a junket and everything was calm and idle. . . . with George to the Mayflower where I came in to have a drink with him. . . . We sat in the Men's bar where presently a young fellow in civilian clothes joined up with us—he proved to be a former Eagle Squadron pilot . . . and was now trying to get back on flying status. The remarkable thing about him was a most extensive plastic surgery job—a curious, regular, but disconcertingly unlined face, which he said was mostly skin off his legs, and considerably repaired hands. Because the face job lacked a few nerves the Air Surgeon was jibbing for no apparent reason. Perhaps more peculiar, after all, was the obvious anxiety he felt about whether they would let him go back and really buy it. No doubt fortunately for us, you can conclude that the fighter pilot can be relied on to have little adult intelligence and less imagination.

Tuesday 20 June 1944

. . . We were still idle, but I had discovered that they had some Link Trainers[35] on the fifth floor E ring and that by seeing a Major Zacherle, the Bolling Field liaison man,

I could, for no more than an R & R filled out by myself, get onto them, so I did that. In with Chamberlin to have lunch at the Lafayette. When we got out the R & R was back approved so I went up with Reeves and found my hand somewhat out but it was pleasant. They have four trainers and the complement of sergeants and apparently very little to do, so they seemed to welcome me.

Wednesday 21 June 1944

. . . We had nothing to do but worry about the Navy's pronouncements, Nimitz[36] very bumptious and cocky but shy about figures on what the 5th & 3rd fleets were doing plainly in fending the Japs off from Saipan. I went up and had a little Link Trainer where I had some difficulty with the artificial horizon which they now make you use, but which I had always been told to ignore. . . .

Thursday 22 June 1944

. . . I read Gilbert & Sullivan all morning. About 2 oclock George Haddock came in and wanted 1 minute for Gen Wooten for the Bond business at the Shot From the Sky Show by the monument, so I spent the rest of the time cooking that up. . . . We began early to get the secret reports on the Navy's business, which seemed all right but I think everyone was hoping that we would destroy the Jap fleet and thus make it possible to get out of this that much earlier. . . .

Friday 23 June 1944

. . . There was nothing to do in the morning, though I was relieved to hear that Gen Wooten liked his speech very much, thus making it certain that I would not have something to do in the afternoon. . . .

Saturday 24 June 1944

. . . It developed or perhaps transpired from our Lt Doulens that Col Smith got himself married last night. . . . Mr A, back since Thursday, was off on a talking jag, we supposed, since I got one for the Business Advisory Council for Tuesday* and Bradshaw got one for something else for Wednesday.

Monday 26 June 1944

. . . I went on with Business Advisory business. Haddock went in with Bradshaw and me to have dinner at Hall's and afterwards to have a drink at the Mayflower bar and I drove Haddock home. He said that he had met Mr A in the hall late in the afternoon and the old man had stopped and been quite civil to him, the first time he

*See Appendix.

had seen any civility in him since he had known him, so he supposed he must have been mistaken for somebody else.

Tuesday 27 June 1944

. . . I got in early and finished up Mr A's piece which I took up to Dempsey who seemed to be in a pettish mood and took issue with Smith's failure to endorse the R & R saying he saw no reason why Smith couldn't follow standard military prac- tise. . . . Later Haddock presented us with a true-or-false test which we were required to 'accomplish' on security measures—it is fantastic when you imagine, or try to, someone actually getting up the idea and having it mimeographed and given to all personnel in AAF Hq. The idea was to see whether you understood procedures for safeguarding security in five minutes, and I believe that only Bradshaw and Johnny proved, when the papers were marked, to understand it less than I did. We got a reaction from Dempsey, or rather Mr A's Miss Adkins, on the speech, which she described as the worst she had ever seen and so she did not show it to the Gen. George was enraged—since, in fact, it was not bad at all, and even a little better than usual; and I began to wonder myself if I wouldn't do better to try again to get back to TAD—I mean, what the hell can you do with them?

Wednesday 28 June 1944

. . . I heard no more about the speech, though we expected to all morning. Later in the afternoon it became known that Mr A had taken it home to make a few changes in it, so it seemed likely that Dempsey's report of Miss Adkins' reaction may have been merely part of his campaign to needle or otherwise annoy Smith. . . .

Thursday 29 June 1944

. . . Nothing to do all day but we seemed to pass it well enough reading (I was reading Harry Brown's piece on a platoon in Italy[37] with many good parts and much phoney dialogue)—the difficulty a writer has in doing things all of a piece is one of our great literary problems—at what point in realism do you add imagination to fact, and why?—I was glad to go up to the Link Trainer where I got on better for an hour. . . .

Saturday 1 July 1944

. . . Did nothing all day. In with George Haddock to have lunch at the Lafayette. Discussing what we were going to do and what would become of us he said that Smith had laid aside his promotions, but he was purposing Monday to put it to him for me and if he said no, to say that then he could not consider me necessary or valuable there, and how about letting me go back to TAD where they were short and would clearly have more use for me. I though that was fine, being pretty well fed up (and perhaps being very little pleased, which was George's own reaction, since it implied that Smith was not taking his word for anything, by the notion that Smith did not think there was any reason to make me a major. This, of course, is exactly the case, but certainly anyone must feel an affront if he found himself held in less regard than the numerous odd characters who were being made majors.) Up on the Link Trainer in the afternoon, where I was clearly getting better. . . .

Monday 3 July 1944

. . . We found ourselves in an incredible minor fuss brought on by Kelly whose RC or lace-curtain Irish got the best of her . . . and she moved Miss Johnson out of our room, alleging that her morals were being impaired by our conversation. This upset Miss Johnson very much, she answering that maybe we did talk about some things but we did not talk about them in a nasty way, and being there was the only interesting thing she had had in her work in Washington, and she would quit. . . . [Kelly] ended by bawling with George, poor fellow, saying she guessed she shouldn't have done it, but just the same she thought it pretty fast company for a 20 year old Kansas girl. This somewhat overlaid the matter of Smith & his ways—something to be continued tomorrow, but in the few minutes he had George gathered that he was ready to promote us rather than let us (or specifically me) go.

Tuesday 4 July 1944

. . . when I came back there was no one in the office but [Kelly] and me so nerving myself not to mind my own business, I went in and said: Look Becky, why don't you drop all this nonsense? You're making things very tough for George who is trying to get away and everybody is unhappy so let's forget it all and you send her back where she belongs and we'll all skip the whole business. She was somewhat flushed and blowsy looking (due I think to weeping) and she said that was all right with her. . . . George came in soon with Newhouse so I said to him that I had spoken out of turn to Becky and it was all fixed, if it was right with him. He seemed much relieved, and said sure. I was struck by a highly ungenerous [thought]—since no one could be more gentle, agreeable, and attractive in character, or more sensible and better balanced in judgment on most matters, by the fact that so simple and obvious a solution startled him. It could be guessed that some of the difficulties he has, and some of his failure to win out higher up is probably associated with some similar trouble with what might be called human relationships—something I am no good at myself, and in this case, simply blundered into; but if I, why not he? At any rate, Miss J came back, pleased in a nice way—that is, not cocky or gloating, and all seemed well. Driving home with George who is leaving on leave tomorrow, he said that Smith seemed prepared to go ahead and if I wanted more work I could have it in keeping track of the Training Command.

Wednesday 5 July 1944

I went in early and needled Col Smith about Training, so he called Col Pool and said he was sending up 'a very able officer, Captain Jim Cozzens'—the phrasing seemed worth preserving—to find out what troubles they had now or impending. Up there, Pool was very cordial and cooperative and took me to see a Col Garrett, a lanky pouch-eyed man with wings, plainly an old airlines flyer, who got in a Major Zell from Management Control and taking me to a vacant room discussed the new Operations Division they were getting up to take over Flight Control from Flying Safety. There seemed some likelihood of a squawk from the air lines because the new system would affect their control of their own flights. He then told me to see a Col Estes in Flying Safety to find out just what the changes were going to be, but he did not tell me that Flying Safety didn't yet know that about a third of their organization was being taken over. Estes was no longer working there, so I put it to a Major Swayne and the sensation was something—it was the first they had heard, and I saw at once (too late) that I had put my foot in it. There followed (I learned) much telephoning especially to Winston-Salem & Zell and Garrett were fit to be tied because they had meant to keep still about it until the project was definitely finished. It did not seem the best possible introduction to my new duties, but Col Pool (I was relieved to find) regarded it as a joke on Garrett and we managed to fix it up amiably—in fact, the fault was at least half his. At any rate, I was busy all day what with that and some stuff with a Lt Col Gardener, in Gunnery and, as I expected, it did much to shorten the time.

Thursday 6 July 1944

. . . I went up in the morning to see Pool again and he passed me on to a number of other people, including the amiable thin faced Col Ryan, and so I got together stuff for a second memorandum. This suited me very well. A Lt Col Deichler of Management Control came down later and Smith turned me over to him, as to say there was another I could keep track of. He twitted me somewhat on yesterday's matter, but seemed amiably disposed. . . .

Friday 7 July 1944

. . . Back by two for a very long staff conference of Organizational Planning in Management Control—there was little to our purpose but I made the 16 officers an address explaining what we wanted. What I heard seemed to me very good evidence

WAR DEPARTMENT
HEADQUARTERS OF THE ARMY AIR FORCES
WASHINGTON

5 July 1944

MEMORANDUM FOR THE CHIEF, OFFICE OF TECHNICAL INFORMATION

Subject: Information from Office of AC/AS, Training.

1. <u>Flight Operations Division</u>:

This is a new division in the process of being established (Hq.
Office Instruction No. 20-17 26 June 1944) under Lt. Col. Garrett.
The new plan will involve several changes in Flight Control processes,
especially let-down procedure. Col. Garrett thinks that it is likely
that the Airlines will object because they are used to controlling
their own traffic to suit themselves.
(Confidential) When the new division is fully functioning it is
planned to take Flight Control away from Flying Safety. This will
greatly cut down the size of the Winston-Salem office. Flying Safety
personnel does not know this yet and in the interests of avoiding
friction while Management Control works with the plans, Col. Garrett
does not want them to know. However, he thinks that Winston-Salem
papers who have been very zealous about keeping as much AAF stuff in
town as possible, will join the squawk when they know.

2. <u>Gunnery Training</u>:

During March and April a large number of gunners were held for vary-
ingly long periods waiting to go overseas without being allowed to
take leave which they said General Arnold had 'promised' them. Most
of them wrote complaining letters home, and AC/AS Training is now
hearing a good deal about unjust and inhuman treatment. They think
it won't be long before Drew Pearson or his equivalent cites it as
an example of AAF bad management and stupidity.

Lt. Col. Gardner in charge of Gunnery Training feels that a serious
sore point has to do with proper assignment of returned combat personnel. They have been getting men as gunnery instructors who weren't
gunners and didn't want to be.

Another serious problem is expected to arise when they start ordering
gunners on a second tour of duty. It is not planned to do this until
an arrangement has been made to return pilots, bombardiers, navigators
(i.e. officers). To date only those gunners who volunteered have been
sent on a second tour. There were extremely few of them.

J. G. COZZENS
Captain, Air Corps

FOR VICTORY BUY UNITED STATES WAR BONDS AND STAMPS

of the fact that if you want to do nothing in a long and roundabout way, you should always call a conference. Still, I liked fussing and being busy. . . .

Saturday 8 July 1944

. . . In the afternoon I was happy and busy pursuing a hint from AC/AS Training's daily activity report that all was not well with the helicopter program, and duly, having seen a Major Greenleaf in OC&R and finally a Col Bradbury in MM&D [Materiel, Maintenance, and Distribution], discovered it was not. This I put into a tasteful memorandum, trusting Col Smith would appreciate my acumen and industry (which seems unlikely), told him I was off tomorrow, to which he said: have a nice time, and drove Newhouse home, more relieved than I would have expected at the idea that I would not be back for two weeks.

Monday 24 July 1944

. . . Though it seemed hardly possible, I found myself pleased at least mildly to get back to the office. . . .

Wednesday 26 July 1944

. . . I spent my time running around AC/AS Training and had some fairly grisly conversations with a Major Towey in charge of 'directed missiles' who told me something about the GB-4, the so-called television bomb, which they expect to get in quantity early in the fall and some others which he remarked with regret might not be ready for this war but we would have for the next. I don't know whether they are more frightening to the uninstructed mind than the first appearance of gunpowder was—perhaps not, and perhaps all they mean is that the possibility of a quick and decisive settlement of a war has again been restored but you feel as if this was surely the end of everything—not this time, but in twenty years or so when we try it again. .

Thursday 27 July 1944

. . . I went to see Miss Cochran about a WASP point and found her somewhat flustered with three large packing cases in her office. One had been opened, and from it taken a bronze intensely nude female figure which was said to represent the average WASP—that is, constructed according to the average measurements. She said the Qm [quartermaster] had brought them while she was away, she did not know where from or why. I suggested that surely the breasts were a little large for average, being at loss for something to say, and she said they certainly were, with energy, and she didn't think anything was right, except maybe the height—which was about 5 feet 5 inches.

WAR DEPARTMENT

HEADQUARTERS OF THE ARMY AIR FORCES

WASHINGTON

8 July 1944

MEMORANDUM FOR CHIEF, OFFICE OF TECHNICAL INFORMATION

Subject: Information from Office of AC/AS, Training.

1. <u>Helicopter Pilot Training</u> (Major Ryan, ext. 71595)

In Daily Activity Report 5 July Major Ryan noted that all training classes for helicopter pilots would be set back thirty days due to unavailability of equipment and maintenance difficulties. He did this on the advice of Major W. H. Greenleaf, Airborne & Liaison Branch, OC&R. Major Greenleaf said that at present no R5 helicopters would be ready until 1945, and only 17 R6's would be delivered by December, 1944. 13R5's and 111 R6's were supposed to be delivered in 1944. Present plans call for the employment of 235 R5's and 369 R6's.

In an R&R signed by General Gros on June 20th, OC&R asked the Materiel Division Production Branch MM&D for an explanation of the delays and a report on the present status. Lt. Col. L. T. Bradbury, Assistant Chief is completing a statement for Col. Phillips, Chief, Materiel Division, <u>Availability of Helicopters</u>, answering General Gros in detail. A copy of this will be sent to the Chief, OTI, probably on July 10th.

The difficulty seems to lie in the decision to proceed simultaneously with development and production. Most of the problems are development problems. Col. Bradbury explains this by pointing out that in 1942 there was not a flyable helicopter in the United States, and no plants, tools, or equipment were available for large scale production. In spite of this, the submarine menace was held to make large scale production vital and it was undertaken with the recognition that there would be plenty of trouble - which there has been.

Speaking off the record, Col. Bradbury said there was reason to believe that a certain amount of difficulty and delay has resulted directly from the designer's determination to keep helicopters as much as monopoly as possible in view of real or imaginary tremendous post-war markets. The AAF has done all it can in many conferences to adjust this aspect of helicopter production.

J. G. COZZENS
Captain, Air Corps

Friday 28 July 1944

. . . Up to see a Major Van Cleave in Training who had little on the item I was interested in but gave me some good tips—one of them about training devices—just how much money had been spent on how many that did not pan out. I went to see John Fox who was glowing, affectionate and expansive and it will interest me to see how far he may be from the facts for I thought I'd better put an R&R through Col Pool asking TAD to stand and deliver. To my astonishment Col Smith said he wanted to speak to me when I came back, and what he had to say was that my memoranda were just what he wanted and had always been trying to get—I thought this probably true, but I could not help wondering if he had heard somehow that I had been thinking of trying to get out and considered that a reasonably good and cheap way to forestall me—not for me, but just to keep what he had. However, I was pleased. . . .

Saturday 29 July 1944

. . . I began to exert myself by indicating that *Air Force* ought not to publish a piece on helicopters, which George agreed to, and Ben Grant, now a major, consented to—it made me feel useful, though Straubel in NY might not think so. . . . Up to see Col Belshe in Personnel in the afternoon—a stocky, white headed swearing man who had a plan of his own to handle air gunners so that they did not get second tours of duty too quick. I thought it a good one, and said I would see Smith heard about it. In the morning Chambers called me from NY to see if I could get loose, and I said not— the truth being that my present job, if I can keep it, interests and stimulates me. . . .

Monday 31 July 1944

. . . Up to MM&D (I learn, now rechristened, Materiel & Service) where Col Sessums, Gen Echols' executive officer, wondered if it was necessary for me to have the daily activity report. I said well maybe Col Smith could take it up with Gen Echols & he said; Are you threatening me, Captain? I said hastily, no; but it occurred to me that maybe I was getting a little high-falutin. In the end I got it. To talk to a Lt Col Newhall in the afternoon about the disposal of excess aircraft and I could see there were some stories in there if I could manage to get them.

Tuesday 1 August 1944

. . . I went on with Newhall and got up a memo for George Haddock on the disposal of excess aircraft. In the morning he took me into the hall and said that Smith had said to him Cozzens is a damn good reporter, did you know? To which he said he said yes, I told you that before; you're just finding it out, so how about promoting him? So Smith said yes. I felt a certain sense of ignobility, but readiness to accede. . . .

69

Wednesday 2 August 1944

. . . We had a light blow-up with Jackie Cochran in the pm, I having been directed to ask her if it were still honest-to-god true that she was not cooking anything about the WASPs so that Rex would be ready for a conference with Mr A. To Mr A the (I-had-to-feel, two-faced bitch, since she had been easy enough with me) said Col Smith (PRO, that is) had done nothing to get her anything and simply sent his Capt Cozzens to ask her 'peculiar' questions and would Mr A tell him to do so and so. Mr A, plainly in his role of doddering old ape, said; Col, this is an order, get them some publicity. Smith was much annoyed by the direction but seemed to think more favorably of me than not. He said he said that I was a competent officer and if I asked questions it was because I felt it my duty to get him the information he asked me to get. My feelings were as usual mixed.

Thursday 3 August 1944

. . . Smith seemed to reverse Jackie's field in the morning by persuading Mr A that he had better not, after all, mix up with Jackie's schemes since her husband[38] had mixed in politics to the extent of $150,000 in the last campaign; and was it to be said that was how she got to be an army colonel? Up to see a Major Anthony who was exercised about a morale problem with the 4 thousand odd officers the AAF needed to assign to contract termination work and could we write them a pep talk from the old man to put in a leaflet to be given to them when they were assigned.* The utility of it seemed doubtful, but yes we could. I then went down to see a Mr McVeagh who was supposed to be able to give examples of how important the work was. He proved to be Charlton McVeagh, whom I had not seen for twenty years. He said, not too encouragingly; My God, are you Cozzens? and we shook hands with more warmth than we ever had in the *Advocate*[39] days; and apparently on the basis of the connection, he dropped everything and made himself very helpful. . . .

Friday 4 August 1944

. . . In, at McVeagh's suggestion, to see a man named Boyle at Douglas Aircraft in the Shoreham Building. He is a relative big shot, lean and not unintelligent, with a fancy tie; but he nonetheless seemed to entertain the idea that I, if I would, and if I were made to understand the real issues (they boiled down to this; that the aircraft companies shouldn't lose anything, no matter what happens) could set the War Department right, and start them on really renegotiating contracts and terminations, instead of applying what he described as formula terminations (very unjust, he said). I thought if he could believe I had such powers, he might as well; so

*See Appendix.

simply assured him that I knew General Arnold's (my old pal) line of thought was very much the same. I added significant looks or wags of the head to imply that I would use my influence. . . .

Saturday 5 August 1944

. . . I went on with my morale piece after some early coffee with Haddock. . . . [His] seems in some ways the most fortunate disposition in the world, since no one can see it or meet it without liking it. Since he has with it a sort of natural acuteness and common sense he would seem to have everything.

Sunday 6 August 1944

. . . In as duty officer and I was able to finish up Major Anthony's piece. . . .

Monday 7 August 1944

. . . I brought my effort up to Major Anthony. He had the nerve to find unsatisfactory—a matter that took me aback, until I realized that in fact he is a little obtuse, and did not understand how well I had made Mr A appear to promise without doing it. The major thought he ought to come right out and promise, so I had to read him a lecture on what became the CG/AAF. Haddock said, when I reported, that we would bypass him and take it to Mr Lovett, who shook hands with me in shy confusion. I mentioned the circumstance, and Haddock said (what I had never thought of before) that he sometimes wondered if Mr L were not professionally modest. He also told me, driving him home, that Smith has signed the recommendation for my promotion and I should get my just deserts sooner or later.

Tuesday 8 August 1944

. . . We heard no more from Mr Lovett's Col Brownell, so I was free to waste the morning trying to find out what Col Edgerton told Col Smith about a so-called 19th Tactical Air Force. In all AAF Hq nobody knew anything, but finally a prim little gum-chewing buck general named Barker in OPD [Operations Division, War Dept. General Staff] instructed me that it was the 19th T.A. Command, in the 9th Air Force, assigned to support the Third Army. This seemed to simplify everything. . . . In the late pm Newhouse conducted one of his remarkable examinations of Miss Johnson; Who was Robert E. Lee? (She figured it out in about ten minutes); What is the difference between Christopher Marlowe and Christopher Morley (she never figured it out); Who was fighting against whom in the last world war (she thought maybe the US and England were fighting France, Germany and Russia). In one way it staggers you, but in another I expect it shows Henry Ford really had something when he said history was bunk.

Wednesday 9 August 1944

. . . I told Col Smith that I did not see why I couldn't add OC&R to my collection, which he seemed gratified to hear and telephoned General Craig so that I actually got their daily activity report by afternoon and what with it, and M&S [Materiel & Service], and Management Control, and Training, was able to cook up a nice gossipy memo for Rex. I spent several hours in the pm, while Haddock was exercising, sitting in there and Rex spent much of them telling me about his early life in southwest Va and indicating by his use of their first names his familiarity with many prominent people in the government. . . .

Thursday 10 August 1944

. . . I was busy again investigating my various staff sources, which seems a pleasant way to pass the day. . . .

Friday 11 August 1944

. . . to my surprise, for I could hardly believe there would not be some hitch, I got my majority as of yesterday, which was all right with me since it gets more & more apparent that it is the minimum level of subsistence or minimum standard of decency in the Pentagon. I would not be surprised if it got in just about under the wire since the mass of majors and lt cols is becoming a kind of joke. Ed assisted me to pin on one of the envelopes of leaves Jo had left me, and Johnny got very busy calling up the telephone directory and typing out new pay vouchers and, I daresay, there was a general sense of encouragement, as it seemed to show the local dam was broken. . . . About four Gerald Carter having called the office, got on to me at home in great agitation, saying his Fitzgerald had written that he had lost his corporal's stripes and this circumstance in Gerald's words cut him to the heart. I don't know whether he imagined wildly that I could get them back for the boy, but he was audibly upset to a high degree. It seemed Fitzgerald's organization had changed, which was a break for me, so I explained that it didn't mean he had got into trouble, but only that probably in the new outfit there was no room for another corporal at the moment, but undoubtedly when there was he would get it back. This seemed to comfort him a little, but certainly not much.

Saturday 12 August 1944

. . . Col Brownell had some new ideas about the contract termination business and I worked fitfully at that while Newhouse discoursed with Johnny. . . .

Monday 14 August 1944

. . . We got Col Pardy's report in from TAD showing that they had junked some one million seven hundred thousand dollars worth of training devices, which did not include the Waller Trainer from the Navy at $120,000 apiece (50 of them) which, it seems, are about to be adjudged of little or no value. This seemed well worth digging into and I had a nice day putting people's backs up.

Tuesday 15 August 1944

Both George Haddock and Smith went to New York, so the usual result was that there seemed little hurry about doing anything. I poked idly at the Navy to see what they knew about the Waller Trainer which seemed to be nothing. . . .

Wednesday 16 August 1944

Continued very hot and idle in the office, everyone everywhere disclaiming all knowledge of the Waller Trainer, and there seemed no point in writing memoranda since Smith wasn't there to read them.

Thursday 17 August 1944

. . . In to the Navy Department to see an assortment of people on the track of the Waller Trainer matter. I finally located, though I did not see, a Lt Commander Weiler who was supposed to know something. In the process I could appreciate the Pentagon more, as very few parts of the Navy Building are air-conditioned and most people just sit in rooms with the shades down sweating. I was interested to note that being a major was useful, for they don't seem to be so lavish with promotions. You rank almost everybody you find in the run of the offices, a circumstance that seems to make them very civil. . . .

Friday 18 August 1944

. . . It developed that Lt Com Weiler was out of town so I put the morning into doing a report to date, which amused me, but I could not help reflecting, had little, certainly, to do with the War End of it. Major Hirsch was in with what was presumably the General Staff's word that the Germans had largely extricated themselves from their Normandy situation. Apparently hopes had been higher than I knew, for they seemed glum now over the likelihood that the war in Europe might last quite a bit longer. . . .

Saturday 19 August 1944

. . . Rex had me busy in the morning on some odd jobs such as seeing about getting Charlie Murphy cleared by the JAG [Judge Advocate General] to receive some special A2 information and inquiring into the misadventure of some Major Haydon who dropped 40,000 feet with a parachute at the Air Surgeon's suggestion and so

ADDRESS REPLY TO
COMMANDING GENERAL, ARMY AIR FORCES
WASHINGTON 25, D. C.

ATTENTION:

HEADQUARTERS, ARMY AIR FORCES
WASHINGTON

18 August 1944

MEMORANDUM FOR CHIEF, OFFICE OF TECHNICAL INFORMATION

Subject: Information from Office of AC/AS, Training.

1. **Waller Gunnery Trainer.** Lt. Curtis, Navy Bu Aer Gunnery Training, states that of the fifty odd Waller Trainers made by the Vitarama Corporation, Long Island City, NY, the Navy has only one. Following an evaluation by Navy gunnery experts early in 1943 it was decided that the very much greater expense($120,000 installed, as opposed to the Jam Handy gunnery trainer, about $3000) was not justified by demonstrably greater training value, and that the Navy would therefore install no more of them. The circumstances under which the AAF decided, in spite of this finding of the Navy's, that the expense was justified and that it would be a good idea to take the fifty odd machines for which the Navy contracted off the Navy's hands are not yet clear. I learn in the Navy Department that Lt. Commander Weiler, Bu Ord, who is returning to Washington tomorrow, handled the original contracts. The opinion in AC/AS, Training, Gunnery, is that Lt. Col. ▆▆▆▆▆▆, CC&R, now on leave until 28 August, had much to do with getting the trainers for the AAF, mostly by telephone or other verbal arrangements. There seems to be no correspondence on the subject in the files. Lt. Curtis, and Lt. Clark of Lt. Commander Weiler's office, agreed that Mr. Waller and some others who joined to form the so-called Vitarama Corporation did so at the representation of the Navy (and perhaps the War Department) that it was their patriotic duty to make the devide available. The contracts were cost plus and netted no money for anyone, and apparently many headaches for Weiler's office. Waller and his associates had, however, some idea that they could develop something of commercial value when they first began to fool with it, more or less as a hobby. Essentially, the trainer consists of six simultaneously projected films on a concave surface with added devices to indicate points of aim and to register "hits" on the photographs of attacking planes. I have shot in a Waller Trainer at Buckingham Field, Florida and the effect is great fun. You seem to be sitting in space in the tail turret of a bomber and the attacking planes appear three dimentional and scare the hell out of you. Probably this realistic effect had much to do with persuading the AAF officers involved that it must be good. Major Hart, AC/AS, Training, is still trying to get results from the current evaluation tests being conducted at Loredo.

J. G. COZZENS
Major, Air Corps

died. This I could see was a slight danger attending my otherwise good job. In to see Capt Wright, the Aide to the Assistant Secretary of the Navy for Air in the afternoon. He was complete with chicken guts[40] and though small headed and bald, extremely smooth and soft spoken. I learned a little from him about the first steps in the Waller Trainer matter, which from 1940 on he had been interested in. So also, I was surprised to find, had been my former Col Carr (1940), a matter which did not appear later. He at least gave me enough names and file numbers to go on with and Haddock commended my industry so I took occasion to say that I thought I could take care of the rest of the AC/AS sections in my daily gossip sheet and let him know that I hoped I would be too busy for any more speeches. He said fine, if I wanted it that way and that Smith was much pleased with me, leading me to hope that at long last I had built up the customary comfortable little job for myself.

Monday 21 August 1944

. . . Haddock got me the rest of the staff sections in the morning, except for Plans where Major Berg pointed out that their activity report was all top secret. I then went to talk to him and he seemed to feel that something might be done to see that Rex heard about anything concerning him. I told him I personally did not want to know anything I did not need to know, which was partly true, though perhaps edged a little with the thought that anything judged to be safe with so clear a little moron would not be unsafe with anyone. Up to talk to Fox and Sessums in TAD liaison and then to Col Pool who said that the plain way to handle the Waller business was to go to TAD, and at once dictated a letter telling them to show me their files. I had not thought of such a trip, but the idea seemed good, and I put it up to Haddock, who seemed willing, perhaps because Smith was going on leave tonight.

Tuesday 22 August 1944

. . . Busy with deployment all day, a top secret affair from Lt Col Faith of Plans.

Wednesday 23 August 1944

. . . I got in an analysis of AFF LTR 55-3 for George which seemed a refinement as it was already an analysis of an analysis. Lt Col Skeele of TAD came in to see me, talking long and loud and to little point, but I could see that Col Pardy had fluttered the cote about my impending visit. In the afternoon (I had a solemn bowl of soup with Chamberlin in the Officers Cafeteria where we saw Col Cochran[41] and some of his officers in high spirits—forcing on you the reflection; dumb as a flyer. Though in fact they also are generally agreeable in a simple way) to see Col Ward in Training about the 25,000 program afterwards and it was well borne out. He is a young-oldish man with small even features on a round face and I had some trouble with

ADDRESS REPLY TO
COMMANDING GENERAL, ARMY AIR FORCES
WASHINGTON 25, D. C.

ATTENTION:

HEADQUARTERS, ARMY AIR FORCES
WASHINGTON

21 August 1944

MEMORANDUM FOR CHIEF, OFFICE OF TECHNICAL INFORMATION

Subject: Information from AC/AS Offices.

1. <u>Operations from French Bases</u> (MC) As of 8 August 58 AAF
and 42 RAF squadrons were operating from fields in France. Squadrons included 1097 AAF fighter planes, 76 AAF Reconnaissance, 803
RAF fighters.

2. <u>Bombs on Berlin</u>. (MC) From the beginning of operations to
August 15th, 1944, 54,960 tons of bombs have been dropped on Berlin.
About 1/5 of this total was dropped by the AAF.

3. <u>Turret Motors & German JP Planes</u>. (OC&R, Capt. Michehl) A
1-A priority project is being set up immediately to supply drive
motors which will give gun turrets slewing speeds of 85 degrees
per second, and to convert all existing gun-sights for computation
at a differential speed of 300 mph. This is intended to give the
gunners some chance of hitting JP planes. It seems to indicate
that at present gunners on an attacked bomber are just out of luck.
They hope to have the new equipment "en route to the European Air
Forces" in about 90 days.

4. <u>Report on Redeployment AAF/MTO</u>. (OC&R Lt. Col. Machinist 73274)
The Col. has just returned from AAF/MTO with a "detailed study" of
how to work out redeployment. This includes (1) rules for screening
personnel (2) actual unit requirements for redeployment to Far
Eastern theaters (3) requirements and plan for POM inspection of
units moved. A summary of the complete report is being prepared by
Col. Machinist and his Capt. Freeman will send one to Chief, OTI
some time this week.

5. <u>Bomb Safety Lines</u>. (OC&R Col. Macklin) The foot army will
probably be relieved to hear that a first priority project has been
established with the AAF Board to "develop adequate reliable procedures"
for fixing the position of front lines when visibility is poor. The
way they put it is "for the benefit of aircraft engaged in support
of ground operations". Several types of electronic devices will be
tested.

6. <u>JP Engines</u> (M&S) Production of JP engines by the Allison Division
of General Motors is to be increased from 500 to 1,100 a month.

SECRET

7. <u>Strikes</u> (R&S) In plants producing wholly for the AAF approximately 350,000 man-days were lost due to strikes during the first 32 weeks of 1944. Being already $2\frac{1}{2}$ times the man-days lost during the whole of 1943, this is a real achievement.

J. G. COZZENS
Major, Air Corps

him. He could not seem to understand fairly simple statements and the effect was soon to make you feel that they were indeed incomprehensible. . . . The staff was full of rumors about things falling apart in Europe, which was a nice idea.

Thursday 24 August 1944

. . . I got in my memorandum dealing with training, pigeons, the C46 & the C47, bombs dropped on south France and so on, went up to see a Lt Col Richardson about the chances of a robot bomb for the Ordnance exhibit in New York, waited on Col Faith to show him my 55-3 analysis and so heard a dismaying conference between five or six officers and Col Whitney in his office—I was quite wrong about Col Whitney having any sense. The conference, which seemed to be an inane discussion about uncertain subjects by subnormal people, went beyond burlesque and I could see that Col Belshe in Personnel who had spoken disrespectfully of the outfit was understating it.

Saturday 26 August 1944

. . . To TAD in the morning which seems to be more and more a shambles—the whole place has a crammed, confused and vaguely futile air. Col Pardy talked to me some and I found out what I could from a disgruntled blondish Capt Travis. . . .

Monday 28 August 1944

. . . To TAD in the morning to check on a few points and then to *Fortune* where I talked to Bill Furth and a Kenneth Galbraith on Smith's prospective material. . . . Back to TAD and much of the afternoon with Ray Zimmer trying to find out what the cost of the Waller Trainer film had been—in the end it appeared about $600,000. . . .

Tuesday 29 August 1944

. . . To Washington on the 8.30 train. There I seemed to have been little missed, as though Smith were indeed content for me to amuse myself as I chose. I thought my brief report of what I had been doing made him a little restive, so I said I would presently have it in in writing. He said Fine, Fine. . . .

Wednesday 30 August 1944

. . . I was busy getting my memoranda in and they did not seem very clear because I suppose they weren't very clear to me—do what you will, you cannot seem to get at the point; that is, who in early 1942 decided to buy the Waller Trainer. . . .

HEADQUARTERS, ARMY AIR FORCES
WASHINGTON

30 August 1944

MEMORANDUM FOR THE CHIEF, OFFICE OF TECHNICAL INFORMATION

Subject: Waller Flexible Gunnery Trainer (Preliminary Report)

1. <u>Discussion with Training Aids Division</u>. At the suggestion of Col. Pool, Training (my memorandum 22 August) General Harper directed Col. Pardy, Chief, TAD, to make available all material in their files on the Waller Trainer. On August 26 and 28 I visited the TAD offices in New York and discussed the matter with these TAD officers:

Col. George W. Pardy, Chief, TAD
Col. James S. Waters, Deputy
Lt. Col. C. W. Skeele, Executive
Lt. Col. Earl V. Compton, Chief, Operations Section
Lt. Col. R. S. Zimmer, Chief, Training Films Section
Capt. A. C. Travis, Jr., Ass't. for Gunnery

2. <u>General Situation</u>. There are at present 56 Waller Trainers owned by the AAF. All except 2 (at Honolulu) are in the Training Command. Since January 1944 relatively little use has been made of them, pending the completion of films for Course III. This is due to an order 8 January 44 from Training Command Hq directing that Course II-A would not be used. The order was at the suggestion of the Central Instructors School, Flexible Gunnery, Laredo, Texas. In the opinion of Col. R. K. Waugh, Director; Major Nicholas Hobbs, Coordinator of Research, and Major Robert Bragarnick, Director of Proof Section, Course II-A had "negative training value" because the attacking planes were not flying standard curves of pursuit. Work on films showing such curves was started in November 1943. The process was very complicated because special camera equipment had to be built into a B-17 and further difficulty was found in getting fighter pilots who could fly such curves accurately. In fact, no matter how good the pilots were, they seemed to get on the curves mostly by luck or accident. This seemed to throw doubt on the CIS contention that Course III should contain nothing but these curves, since it was obvious that gunners would rarely or never have to fire at attackers flying them. (The CIS point, for what it is worth, was, of course, that the attacker flying those curves was mathematically certain to score hits on the bomber he was attacking; while, if he was not flying the curve, he would not score hits.) The result has been an enormous consumption of film and months of delay, because the CIS officers refused to accept anything short of perfection on this point of debatable importance. I was assured by the officers of TAD who had been dealing with the matter that ███████████████,

who seems to have an unfortunate personality, was personally responsible for many senseless delays and difficulties.

3. Costs of the Waller Trainer.

    a. Trainers. Fifty-eight Waller trainers have been taken over
from the Navy, who accepted them on a cost plus contract with
the Vitarama Corporation. As a result the first few trainers
cost over $100,000 apiece, but this figure was soon reduced and
Air Service estimates the average cost as $55,000 apiece (es-
timated total, $3,190,000)

    b. Housing. The Waller trainer requires special housing of a
fairly elaborate sort, including air conditioning. This
housing was requested through AAS and largely accomplished by
the Corps of Engineers. It is therefore difficult to obtain
costs. An estimate is being prepared.

    c. Film. If and when Course III is finished and distributed
the cost of film will be more than $650,000.

4. Evaluation of the Waller Trainer.
There appears to be no difference of opinion in the Air Force (and
for that matter, in the Navy) that the Trainer is a realistic,
interesting and useful device. There are great and even violent
differences of opinion on: (a) whether in actual training results it
is superior to the 3A2 (Jam Handy) trainer whose present cost is about
$800 (however, it should be noted that the Waller can train four
gunners at once); (b) whether in view of the difficulties of maintenance (it requires a crew of 9 for every two trainers) and the
mechanical complications both in showing and preparing the films, the
trainer, even if definitely superior, should have been taken over when
the Navy judged it too expensive for their use. The fact that
relatively little use has been made of those installed in the Training
Command since January (a pieced-together 15 minute film was prepared
from Course I and Course II which the CIS approved, and used until
it wore out at some schools) certainly appears to bear out the view
that the whole thing was too complicated. However, a great part of
this trouble may be, and probably was, due to the difficult and ill-
advised attitude of ███████████ and others at CIS. (Par 2)

5. History of the Waller Trainer.
Capt. A. C. Travis, Jr., TAD, prepared at Col. Pardy's direction a
history of the Waller Trainer based on what material could be found
in TAD's files. This proved very sketchy on all important points
dealing with the original procurement arrangements. Action was taken
by TAD to supplement this. Mr. Jack P. Probst, Air Service Command
Hq., was requested by telephone to supply material from their files.

He has made it available to Mr. Joseph J. Brandenstein, AC/AS
M&S, who is adding material from the Hq files here. This should
be ready tomorrow and may clear up most of the points which
Capt. Travis was not able to get at.

                        JAMES G. COZZENS
                        Major, Air Corps

Thursday 31 August 1944

. . . I proceeded placidly along with my fussing and reporting until the late afternoon when I hit an item in the Personnel activity report which brought me up to see Col Ward in Training—what was training going to do with the ACER [Air Cadet Enlisted Reserve] kids, for whom the training command said it was not ready until December, but they were going to take a little less than 1,500 a month even so? I had the same baffling experience I remembered having before—he looked at me in his dumb sloe-eyed way and said it was up to Personnel, I didn't understand how Hq worked if I asked him. But, sir, I said, it can't be up to Personnel after the TC accepts them and puts them at Sheppard Field. But it was, he said, if Personnel sent them, Personnel had better say what to do with them. But meanwhile, sir, I said, what is the policy? He said there was none. I said, shall I tell Col Smith Gen Harper has no policy? He said, I tell you it's up to Personnel. . . .

Friday 1 September 1944

. . . I managed to get in to the Pentagon still intent on tying a can to Col Ward but I found as usual I had little actual firmness of purpose and finding Pool out—I had thought of saying; By the way, sir, between you and me, is Col Ward hard to get on with? If he said yes, as I expected, I would know that the wind lay about where I expected too and it would be easy to say; Well, sir, frankly, I don't think he's quite bright. I've had to go to him a few times and he never seems to know what anything is all about. Any stick being good to beat a dog, I could imagine Pool saying to Gen Harper sooner or later; There are a lot of squawks about Ward, General. I can't help wondering etc. At any rate, he was out, so I saw Col Ryan instead and he explained simply and lucidly enough the situation as they saw it (showing that in simple truth Ward is less than bright) so I said nothing and went down and put in my memorandum. My scheme to do no more speech etc writing was damaged because George Haddock came in and said I would have to do a piece for Lovett for the *Army & Navy Journal* anniversary issue,* because he had requested me by name—ill fruits of the readjustment piece for Arnold, which he had heartily approved and so got his Col Brownell to find out who wrote it. I could see a grave danger if I did this piece and he liked it, too. On the other hand, the course of wisdom—to so write it that he couldn't possibly like it, was not easy either. . . .

Saturday 2 September 1944

. . . I went to see Lovett. He received me with shy grimaces, turning his patulous, somewhat sunken intelligent eyes on me for fractions of a second and then at his

*See Appendix.

82

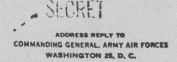

HEADQUARTERS, ARMY AIR FORCES
WASHINGTON

31 August 1944

MEMORANDUM FOR CHIEF, OFFICE OF TECHNICAL INFORMATION

Subject: Information from AC/AS Offices

1. Redeployment (Personnel, Col. Belshe). In connection with a note in the Personnel DAR 30 August, Col. Belshe says that a general discussion of redeployment and rotation policies will take place Monday or Tuesday with General Harmon. He expects that a directive to the Training Command will come out of this, and thus oblige the gunnery schools, for instance, to follow the the principles of his plan (my memoranda; 29 July, 7 Aug). The 30 August note concerned 2,649 e.m. returned from the ETO and given to the 2nd Air Force to work as mechanics on the B-29's. Col. Belshe suggests that in addition to General Ent's desire to get experienced mechanics, there was some concern about the 2nd Air Force M/R which was not showing enough personnel returned from the theatres in proportion to personnel that had never been overseas.

2. B-29's in Europe. (OC&R, Requirements) The summary of deliveries as of August 23 shows 105 B-29's delivered to the 8th Air Force, and 13 on the way. The 15th Air Force has received 91, and one more is on the way. Presumably they are not being sent just for the trip.

3. K-14 Gun Sights. (OC&R, Requirements) Extensive tests with the 412 Fighter Group (JP) net the following conclusion: "The K-14 is a satisfactory sight for jet propelled aircraft. Additional tests are being run to better determine the efficiency of the sight and to see how soon a pilot can become proficient in its use". (An interesting point in regard to "proficiency" was the testing pilot's report that "he was kept half-blacked out at all times because of excessive G pull and had difficulty in seeing the gyro".)

4. Excess P-39's. (OC&R, Commitments) M&S has concurred in the declaration of all P-39's, except the P-39Q's (which we seem to hope to get off on Russia; my memorandum, 17 August), excess to the AAF as soon as they are declared excess to any individual air force.

5. Mexican Air Force. (OC&R, Troop Basis) AC/AS, Plans, has requested AC/AS, Training to make a study of personnel requirements for setting up pilot, bombardier, navigator, radio, gunner and mechanics schools to train and support a Mexican Air Force "with

an assumed number of training transport, tactical and liaison aircraft". Troop Basis has been asked to compute the number and types of units. This has been prepared and transmitted to AC/AS, Plans. "The size and composition of the Air Force. ...is entirely hypothetical and is being computed for planning purposes only". However it seems possible that the enlightened public might sometime wonder why we find it necessary to go to the trouble and expense of building those greasers up as an air power just south of the border down Mexico way.

6. AAF casualties. (Management Control)

Battle Casualties.

Dead	16,272
Missing	24,477
POW or Internee	21,945
Wounded	10,955
	73,649

Non-Battle Casualties

Dead	6,911
Missing	914
Sick-Injured	1,971
	9,796

TOTAL   83,445

7. Pearl Harbor Material. (Intelligence) On 30 August "archival material on AAF activities centering about 7 December 1941" was completed.

8. Activity Report for AC/AS Plans. There has been a delay in supplying me with this material due to its top secret classification. However, Major ███ has arranged a meeting for Saturday morning. He hopes to work out a system by which items of interest to Chief, OTI, will be made available to me.

JAMES G. COZZENS
Major, Air Corps

shoes or the end of a cigarette which he changed from hand to hand. We seemed in agreement about what I suggested we'd better write on; but he had a number of positive suggestions about what Gen Arnold had better write on—news not very welcome in the office where Reeves had long ago written it up and put it in. . . .

Monday 4 September 1944

. . . I spent my time writing around something for Mr Lovett and investigating a few items for Rex, uncovering another though pleasanter sort of Col Ward in OC&R Troop Basis—a Col Ford, whose note in the activity report was incomprehensible and his explanations no better. Since it concerned training & surplus pilots I took it up to Col Ryan, who was again invaluable, understanding exactly what they were trying to say and then saying it himself in a clear homely way.

Tuesday 5 September 1944

. . . I worked a little on Lovett's piece and got out a long memorandum for Smith, who told Haddock who told me that he was toying with a scheme to get me as his personal spy into Plans where he seemed to think I might do great execution. I said to Haddock all right, if I could keep my desk here, but I did not purpose to be shut up in an office with Major Berg—did Col Smith want to get rid of me? He said, oh no, I was the fair haired boy par excellence at the moment. The idea was simply that if I got into higher and more secret counsels my memoranda would make even better reading. . . .

Wednesday 6 September 1944

. . . Smith's scheme if any did not materialize, because, presumably, he did not himself. . . . I had a quiet busy day putting in memoranda (with no one to read them) and finishing up Mr Lovett's piece. In the morning I went up to talk to Lt Col Baughman about the WAC situation which upset her—her scrubbed and serious small face showed some inner exercise as she tried to figure out what they were going to do—more recruiting, or no more. She did not think that some slogan such as Join the WAC and release a man to come home to his wife would have any great appeal. . . .

Thursday 7 September 1944

. . . Smith still did not show. I amused myself by talking to a Major Miller in Personnel on rotation policies and getting in Mr Lovett's piece—he phoned late in the afternoon to say that he had not had time to read it but he would on a plane to NY this afternoon and would see me Saturday—and in getting the Air Inspector's activity report out of them. Haddock was a little restive over what Smith might or might not be up to. . . .

WAR DEPARTMENT
HEADQUARTERS OF THE ARMY AIR FORCES
WASHINGTON

6 September 1944

MEMORANDUM FOR THE CHIEF, OFFICE OF TECHNICAL INFORMATION

Subject: Waller Flexible Gunnery Trainer.

1. <u>Summary of the Situation</u>. The AAF is in possession of
56 (2 others were destroyed by fire at Las Vegas) Waller Flexible
Gunnery Trainers. The average cost, including housing was about
$90,000 a unit. The cost of film, including Course III now in
preparation, is more than $650,000. Total cost for the whole
program – trainers, special housing, and film – is about $5,870,000.

A difference of opinion exists about the value of these
trainers. Three evaluations by the Navy held it in no way superior
to the Jam Handy trainer (average present cost about $800) An
AC/AS Training evaluation made in July, 1943 concurred in this
finding. At the time we had about 40, and General Harper directed
that no more be procured. A few months later this directive was
cancelled on the grounds that the Gunnery School Tables of Equipment proved for a certain number, and therefore that number would
be made up.

Since January, 1944, very limited use has been made of the
trainers because the film for Course II, with which they were
supplied, did not meet the specifications of the Central Instructors School. This was in line with the switch-over in gunnery
training theory which accompanied the introduction of position
sighting. The Training Aids Division has been working on a new
Course III since last November. More than a thousand fighter
attacks were photographed, none of which completely suited the
CIS experts. The objections seem in many instances to have been
absurd and captious. The situation was remedied in a conference,
29 August called by Col. Pardy, Chief, TAD, in New York. (Incidentally, the principal factor in Col. Pardy's decision to call it
was undoubtedly this office's interest in the subject) Here a compromise was reached and work is now going ahead on Course III.
However, it will still be several months before the trainers are
working full time and any newspaper man so disposed, using facts
and unfavorable comment which he could get with little difficulty
and no violation of technical security from a large number of AAF
officers in the Training Command, might present an interesting story
of how the Navy sold the AAF six million dollars worth of pup and
what's more they can't even decide how to use the damn thing.

CONFIDENTIAL

2. <u>AAF Explanation</u>. The Waller Trainer was secured on the recommendation of a board of 10 AAF officers meeting in conference April 15-28, 1941 at Wright Field. This board recommended (Par 13, Memo to Chief of the Air Corps, 28 April 1941) that the trainer be procured "since it appears to have qualities which no other training device known to be in existence incorporates." In fact, the Jam Handy trainer did not exist at that time.

The Navy placed the original order and signed the contract; but by the time the first trainer had been delivered (early in 1942) the development of the much simpler and cheaper Jam Handy had begun. The Navy's argument was not that the Waller was less effective, but that the small size of the Navy gunnery training program, and the desirability of smaller portable units for its special training needs made the expensive, permanently installed and complicated Waller too much of an investment for them. The AAF, setting up a number of more or less permanent schools in a vastly larger gunnery training program felt that the best equipment would always be worth the price. The Waller Trainer was regarded as the best trainer - at that time it was considerably more effective than the Jam Handy, whose first models were soon changed and improved. The most expeditious way of getting trainers was to take over by Procurement Orders those which the Navy had contracted for, and which were already in the process of production. Time was a most important element.

Thousands of our air gunners have been trained on the Waller and there is no reason to doubt that the use of it greatly improved their marksmanship. The AAF had months of full use of all installations. The use was suspended only when an increased knowledge of the theory and practise of air to air firing suggested important improvements in gunnery training. The truth is that nobody, our enemies or ourselves, really understood the principles of air to air firing. This can hardly be charged to the Waller Trainer, which, with the new course III based on these new principles, will again come into full use.

NOTE: No really convincing or satisfactory system for exactly evaluating a device of this kind has ever been worked out. Critics could not possibly <u>prove</u> that the Waller Trainer did not train. Those who doubt its value have mostly the probably-correct feeling or hunch that there is no way to get good at aerial gunnery except by practise (if you live that long) in firing in the air at planes making actual firing attacks on you. None the less it seems fair to assume that the Waller's extremely realistic effect of being at a gun position moving in space, complete with combat noise and vibration, does prepare the trainee to a certain degree by showing him something very close to what he will see when he is actually attacked.

J. G. COZZENS
Major, Air Corps

Friday 8 September 1944

. . . Rex turned up in the morning not visibly the worse for wear and I presume relieved Haddock's mind. I had a quiet morning mulling over my memorandum. . . .

Saturday 9 September 1944

. . . George Bradshaw got back looking well-sunned and in good spirits, with many tales of the P-80 and the general jp [jet propelled] furor on the coast, so Chamberlin and Reeves and I took him in to luncheon at the Lafayette. I spent the rest of my time getting up such subjects as Personnel's policy on the discharge of officers over 38 following the defeat of Germany (in which I felt some interest)—and the Air Provost Marshal's plans for handling AAF personnel who might feel the urge to cut up on the same occasion.

Monday 11 September 1944

I started fussing with an R&R from Col Clemson about various policy angles on various V Day developments (but, you can't help thinking, the Germans still have to accommodate us on the date). Haddock thought that I could help Maj Holland but it soon appeared that my extensive knowledge of the Air Staff fitted me to do it myself. . . .

Wednesday 13 September 1944

. . . Col Smith had himself some idea about material on losses & accomplishments since D Day in ETO and I threw Maj Osborne of Stat Control into a tizzy over it, the dope being in theory required for Gen Giles[42] by 3 pm. It did not get in then, and in fact by 5 or 6, though I had a sort of summary of some of it written up, the Gen's need seemed less than acute. George Haddock explained it by saying that the Col Commanding was in his executive mood. At any rate for lunch I had a sandwich and some milk at my desk which is a rite which seems to mean that you are really winning the war single-handed and which I had no occasion to perform before. . . .

Thursday 14 September 1944

. . . The Giles matter went on and involved a session with him and Gen Eubank lasting from half past eleven to half past one. He was sitting at Gen Arnold's desk in Gen Arnold's office and I soon suspected that part of this business was his non-aversion to taking advantage of the Gen's absence at Quebec to have a talk as deputy commander with the newspaper people. No one could be worse fitted. He is a gray squat little fellow with a slow open wrinkled face—when he advanced to the wall to point out some things familiar to everyone on a map I observed that he was shorter than Smith who is shorter than I am. Gen Eubank, fiddling with plane models on

WAR DEPARTMENT
HEADQUARTERS OF THE ARMY AIR FORCES
WASHINGTON

9 September 1944

MEMORANDUM FOR CHIEF, OFFICE OF TECHNICAL INFORMATION

Subject: Information from AC/AS Offices

1. Discharge of AAF Officers.

    a. (Management Control) Officer separations from the AAF other than death and battle losses totaled 2,242 during the first seven months of 1944. 751 were men physically disqualified; 473 were due to misconduct, inefficiency, etc; 95 resulted from the action of general court martial 86 "miscellaneous honorable separations"; and 837 were officers over 38 years old with no suitable assignment (see b.)

    b. (Personnel) General Bevans reports 8 September that a memorandum was forwarded to G-1, WDGS "pointing out reasons why officers over 38 years of age for whom no suitable duty assignment exists should be relieved from active duty". Lt. Col. Hewitt, Classification & Separations Branch, was about to send me a copy of this when Col. ████████████████████████████████ called up in what seemed to be agitation and said the memorandum was a "private" memorandum to Gen. Henry and should not have been mentioned in the activity report and it was not available to anybody. This led me to suppose that somebody was trying to pull something in the way of arranging to let out a few of his airline executive friends or the equivalent. In view of the 837 mentioned above this point of who gets out and who doesn't among AAF officers may not be long in becoming a sore one.

2. Preparations for V-Day. (M&S) On the head "Possible V-Day Disturbances" M&S reports that the Air Provost Marshal's Office has worked out plans "for adequate control of AAF military personnel upon publication of news indicating cessation of German resistance". Further consideration is being given to "measures necessary for the protection of industrial facilities against vandalism likely to occur." Col. Trimble, Air Provost Marshal's Office, is forwarding a copy of the directives involved.

3. B-29 (M&S) In summarizing aircraft production for August (total acceptances, 7,937, or 96% of W-11 Working Schedule) M&S reports that all plants manufacturing the B-29 made or exceeded their quota except Bell, Atlanta, which fell short of W-11 by 29 "due to incorporation of modifications in the production line and also

to a shortage of skilled labor."

4. <u>P-39's & P-63's for USSR.</u> (M&S) The plan to dispose of surplus P-39's and P-63's to the Russians (my memorandum, 17 August) has hit a snag. "Representatives of the Soviet Purchasing Commission advise that the Soviet High Command do not see why they should recommend that the Soviet Government request any of the used P-39's and P-63's which the AAF advised would be available for their consideration". It seems that their engineers checked 481 of these airplanes and found 416 no good at all.

5. <u>Unsatisfactory Messing Conditions in CBI</u> (Air Inspector) The WASC (Agency of the Chinese government charged with quartering and messing Air Force personnel in China) has been doing so badly that General Jones, personnally inspecting the works, informed the Air Inspector that "the hostels operated by this agency are notable for their lack of supervision and disgraceful messes. The personnel operating the messes are ignorant, untrained and unspeakably filthy in their personal habits in and about the mess halls and kitchens...There is a great scarcity of edible food, even though in some localities there is an abundance of fresh vegetables and fruits. The diet is monotonous and unbalanced. Pure drinking water is almost unknown." General Herwig plans to send an inspection team of mess experts to this theater, but meanwhile there will probably be plenty of squawks coming home.

J. G. COZZENS
Major, Air Corps

WAR DEPARTMENT
HEADQUARTERS OF THE ARMY AIR FORCES
WASHINGTON

13 September 1944

MEMORANDUM FOR CHIEF, OFFICE OF TECHNICAL INFORMATION

Subject: Information from AC/AS Offices.

1. <u>ACER Procurement</u>. (Personnel) Total ACER enlistments for
August were 5060, about 400 less than in July, but still far
in excess of anything that the new training program (my memoranda
24 Aug, 1 Sept, 5 Sept) contemplates handling. It is hard to
understand the policy, if any, which accepts enlistments in numbers beyond what we will be prepared to train when the ACER course
is finished and the young men reach the age of induction into
the AAF. In this connection (continued recruiting and continued
advertising campaigns) Col. Pool of General Harper's office expressed to me the informal opinion that somebody must be nuts.
He feels that there is a PRO and morale angle here that might
interest the Chief, OTI and that Personnel, or whatever agency
is running the advertising campaign, should be asked as a matter
of information, what they think they're doing.

2. <u>Structural Failures on B-29</u>. (Air Inspector) General
Jones reported 11 September that a new B-29 structural failure
(skin cracks and spot weld failures in the trailing edge skin
adjacent to rear spar) was being checked "in view of numerous
field and theater reports of such failures". Though these seem
to be mostly in Bell B-29's, Col. B. M. Jacobs of the Air Inspector's Office showed me a wire from the Director, ATSC, stating
that there were similar, "though not so extensive" troubles in
B-29's manufactured elsewhere. The Director, ATSC, added that
"Unsatisfactory workmanship and inspection at Marietta is being
corrected. Douglas rivet expert is assisting." However, Col.
Jacobs, who has made several trips to Marietta, tells me, off the
record, that he expects no improvement in that situation as
long as (a) the work is done by dim-witted Georgia crackers (b)
the officer who accepts planes for the AAF is "under such tremendous pressure" (presumably from the top). Col. Jacobs (I
gather he is an engineer of some experience) believes the plane
is all right except for these minor annoyances, and considers the
accident rate due not to structural failure, but to "pilot error".
I gather that as soon as all the pilots who can't manage to
learn how to fly the brute are killed attrition by crack-up will
go to normal.

3. **A-26.** (Management Control) On 6 September A-26's of the Ninth Air Force flew their initial combat mission in the ETO. Brest harbor was attacked by 13 A-26's, each dropping 4 one thousand pound bombs.

4. **Specialized Theater Training.** (Training) General Harper requested 11 September, the CGs of the continental Air Forces to take steps to see that fighter pilots were classified for training by the specific theater to which they were to be assigned. This is intended to make possible specific-theater-training at specific stations in the TC. An effort is being made to see that each such station is as fully staffed as possible with instructors who are returned combat pilots from the theater in question. This is a long overdue and very desirable measure.

5. **WACS to Australia.** (Personnel) 241 Enlisted Women originally scheduled to be sent to North Africa have been diverted to Australia. An additional 247 will be given two weeks extended field service training at Fort Oglethorpe and also sent to Australia. The ordinary ratio of Wacs to other personnel suggests greatly enlarged AAF Australian bases.

6. **Agitation in Brazil Against U.S.** (Plans) Much fuss seems to be going on in Brazil as the political opposition to Vargas makes charges about the "Secret Military Aviation Agreement with the U.S." which is alleged to have ceded Brazil's sovereign authority. Col. Brownell suggests that the actual agreement should be published. However, the Brazilian Government is opposed to publication and the U.S. will not release it without the consent of the Brazilian government. This seems to be a little outside the purview of the Chief, OTI, but Capt. Danforth, Plans, said that Major ███████, Plans, felt that Chief, OTI, should know about it. In view of the fact that we have just got a system for obtaining information from Plans working, I did not wish to discourage Capt. Danforth and promised to report the item.

J. G. COZZENS
Major, Air Corps

Arnold's desk and getting up and sitting down and unbuttoning his sleeves to scratch above his elbows engaged him in a sort of Who-dat-say-who-dat exchange on a lot of questions submitted by newsmen which Smith was feeding to him and he was answering to a stenographer, with infinite complications, delays and ramblings. The effect of the two of them was disconcerting—they looked and sounded like a pair of comic rustics, knowing nothing about anything, and I could see that Smith's role was really vital. He could check and direct the Lt Gen. . . . I presume and can believe both of them have special great abilities but you would not know it to listen to them for two hours. The afternoon went into fixing the overall remarks for Giles and getting it through the system so that copies would be ready tomorrow. . . .

Friday 15 September 1944

. . . We began again on the Giles matter and Mr Lovett called about his article to add to the confusion, but the initial effect at least was amusing. I had gone up to see Col Belshe in Personnel, giving his phone number to Johnny in case Giles did call and Smith wanted me. When I got up there the Col was standing somewhat perplexed and his girl said to me that Col Smith had called, Gen Giles wanted me right away. I started to excuse myself to Belshe and the telephone rang again. The girl listened a moment and then said to me; That was Mr Lovett's office, Major. Mr Lovett wants to see you as soon as possible. By this time Belshe had dropped his jaw a little and I thought I would not spoil it, so I said perhaps not without pleasure: I'm sorry sir, I don't know when I'll get through, may I call you tomorrow? Lovett had rewritten his piece, which he complimented me on, though it bore no resemblance to mine; and had me read it while he watched me anxiously. I said I thought it was fine and bore it off. We finally got through with Giles about 1. . . .

Saturday 16 September 1944

. . . The Waller Trainer business broke out again this morning in the moderately satisfactory form of a new conference next week to decide whether they should junk the whole business or take over (it now develops; incredibly enough, no one seemed to know before) the $1,200,000 a year payments being made to the Vitarama Corporation by the Navy, which it purposes to stop. No money, no Vitarama Corp; no VC, no course III; no course III, no further use of the more than 6 million dollar investment. Haddock told me to write an endorsement on the basic communication requesting my presence saying yes I would be there Monday the 25th. . . . In the pm to see a BG named Lauris Norstad,[43] a personably thin-faced blonde boy, though I found later he was not such a boy being only four years younger than I am. He was of Norwegian extraction and Rex had had some notion that mention of him ought to be made on something OWI was beaming to Norway tonight (I suppose we must be

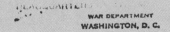

WAR DEPARTMENT
HEADQUARTERS OF THE ARMY AIR FORCES
WASHINGTON

14 September 1944

MEMORANDUM FOR CHIEF, OFFICE OF TECHNICAL INFORMATION

Subject: Information from AC/AS Offices.

1. <u>Talks on Fighter Aircraft with Navy</u>. (CC&R) Col. Holloway reports 12 Sept. that he "made visit and informal talk on latest fighter aircraft trends to a group of about 30 Navy and Marine Corps officers "of the Materiel and Fighter Requirements Sections of the Bureau of Aeronautics. One problem discussed was how to adapt jet aircraft to carrier operations. "Landing rather than take-off presents the most difficulty...However, they are very jet conscious and display a progressive attitude of 'how can we change our methods' rather than 'we can't use jets'." Col. Holloway concludes: "An excellent relationship has existed between Army and Navy fighter sections in this manner for some time and it has been found to pay excellent dividends in exchange of ideas and in constructive analysis of mutual problems".

2. <u>Complaint of Facial Discrimination</u>. (Air Inspector) One Pvt. Archie Gittens of Dale Mabry Field, Florida seems to have been incited by a Mr. D. A. Wilkerson, executive editor of something called The People's Voice to supply this periodical with a front page story on discrimination against and abuse of negro personnel. What got Pvt. Gittens was, apparently, the provision of two prophylaxis stations at Dale Mabry with "white" and "colored" signs on them. The Air Inspector observes somewhat obscurely: "These have since been changed."

3. <u>Complaint of Religious Discrimination</u>. (Air Inspector) Chaplain ███████████, RC, has written to President Roosevelt saying that he and all RC priests are discriminated against. The Air Inspector says that no discrimination appeared and he has furnished the Chief of Chaplains with a report recommending "That the desire of Chaplain ██████ to resign be considered favorably." Showing a lively and prudent sense of the powers of the RC lobby, the Air Inspector adds: "Although an industrious and conscientious priest, he (Father ██████) has not been able to orient himself successfully in the Army."

4. <u>Complaint Alleging Excess AAF Stationery Purchases</u>. (Air Inspector) Mr. Charles P. Garvin, General Manager of the National Stationers Association, told a Senate sub-committee that the AAF has purchased "large excesses of filing folders". The Air Inspector

SECRET

reports that investigation reveals no such excesses. (Half the time I can't even find one around here).

5. Overseas Awards. (Personnel) The Secretary, WDGS, has informed Gen. Bevans that the policy of withholding presentations of overseas awards to senior officers stationed in Washington has been "rescinded". However, it is directed that presentations be made without"publicity".

6. Status of the Waller Trainer. (Training Aids Division) In connection with the Waller Trainer difficulties (my memoranda, 6 September) Col. Pardy, Chief, TAD, has sent me a moranda which states that a temporary course III will be distributed by 1 November and the Permanent Course III by 1 February 1945. This should mean that all trainers will be in full use in about six weeks.

J. G. COZZENS
Major, Air Corps

planning to put some people ashore there). He did not mind saying to me that he, on graduating from West Point in 1930, had transferred from the cavalry to the air corps because he thought that was the logical trend, the air corps being the knights of the day. The Norwegian business was pretty thin, depending on a grandfather who came here in 1873, but I passed it on to a Mr Mann in OWI who I daresay made something of it.

Monday 18 September 1944

. . . Johnny came in in the morning with some symptoms of being distraught and it soon developed that a brother of hers who was at Westover, Mass. on the B29 business had been killed in a crash yesterday. . . . Becky came to the rescue by letting her know that of course she should go home, so that was arranged and she left to fly out on TWA for sixteen days. She is a nice kid. . . .

Tuesday 19 September 1944

. . . Gen Giles had us—Smith & his 'staff' in to the air conference room to listen to a recording of Mr A's American Legion speech . . . because he thought it was an example of Mr A's definitive statement on present policy. With us were a few generals—Norstad, Wilson, Kuter, Hodges and an unidentified buck general and we all sat silent around the long table while the deplorable effusion went on for two dictaphone rolls. When it finished Gen Giles remarked that it was good, a statement so staggering that no one said anything. He then went on to make a few remarks on post-war policy and how we would have to keep at least 27 thousand officers in the Air Force. . . . Coming out, we all went in and had luncheon at the Lafayette. Later in the afternoon I went up to see a narrow-faced gray-headed and explosive Col Scott in the Air Inspector's office about a mess coming rapidly to a head. . . . I was cheerfully assured that if Col Smith wanted to explain things away, the folly and ignorance of the Air Service Command would keep him busy now that they were catching up with it. George Bradshaw got promoted in the afternoon, which seemed to me at least to make everything easier around the office—I could not help reflecting that as a captain he had had several months on me.

Wednesday 20 September 1944

. . . Joe Furnas came over in the morning and I took him up to Gen Jones, the Air Inspector. I had seen the General beforehand and represented to him that Col Smith thought we might do ourselves some good if in the *Sat Eve Post* Furnas were to more or less anticipate such matters as [   ] by showing how these things could happen, but how the Air Inspector could swoop on them so quickly & well. . . . In the afternoon it developed that Furnas thought he might do something with the Air Inspector's stuff, so we talked that over. . . .

CONFIDENTIAL

WAR DEPARTMENT
HEADQUARTERS OF THE ARMY AIR FORCES
WASHINGTON

19 September 1944

SPECIAL MEMORANDUM FOR CHIEF, OFFICE OF TECHNICAL INFORMATION

Subject: Situation at ▮▮▮▮ Air Depot

1. Colonel Scott and Colonel Outcalt of the Air Inspector's Office have outlined for me the status of a complicated and unpleasant situation at the ▮▮▮▮ Air Depot. Colonel Outcalt went with General Owens and Colonel Brossman to consult with the US District Attorney at ▮▮▮▮ who was about to take action against various officers and officials of the Air Depot, apparently as a result of the public outcry. This was on three counts:

   a. An alleged illegal contract (cost plus fixed fee) with a local contractor named ▮▮▮▮ ▮▮▮▮ s cut was $10,000 a month.

   b. The fancy fixing up of the officer's club, and especially bar, which furnishing was estimated to be worth $20,000 though it did not cost that much because they used lots of GI labor and plenty of government material. The US Attorney is planning to bring a civil suit about this, come what may; though Colonel Scott has a $3,800 cheque from the Club which he is trying to get him to accept as a compromise.

   c. Destruction and discarding of government property alleged to amount to $250,000, due to the dumbness or laziness of the civilian inspectors. They dumped out dozens or hundreds of brand new parts and whatnot because they could not find the right bin to put them in.

2. Colonel Outcalt feels that it is a distinct possibility that the Grand Jury at the US Attorney's instigation will indict everybody from the CO ▮▮▮▮ up or down. ▮▮▮▮

▮▮▮▮ Colonel Scott and Colonel Outcalt feel that this is only the first of many such unpleasantness,and that the inefficiency and stupidity of the Air Service Command is to blame. As I suspected, the Memphis Air Depot matter (my memorandum, 18 September) is more of the same thing. The Air Inspector has a man down there now trying to anticipate another investigation.

J. G. COZZENS
Major, Air Corps

Thursday 21 September 1944

. . . Smith had gone to Nashville for undisclosed reasons so we had a quiet day. I went up to see a Col Kern in the morning about the frangible bullet project—he proved to be a handsome senior pilot with a lot of CBI [China-Burma-India] ribbons—there can hardly be anyone in the AAF who has ever been in combat anywhere who hasn't the Silver Star, the Distinguished Flying Cross, the Air Medal, some of them with clusters—it's just like everyone in the Pentagon being a major. He sounded off with some heat on the rottenness of the gunnery training program and how he personally thought the Waller Trainer was all right. I was not long in realizing that he didn't know anything about it, but the fact that he had somehow shot down some Japs made him think he must know something. He walked over with me to talk to Col James in Training and they got nowhere together fast. It is plainly a definite phenomenon, this dumb-as-a-pilot, and yet, the great majority of cases, a nice pleasant sort, too.

Friday 22 September 1944

. . . I was busy with my memoranda which ran very long and was certainly regretting Johnny. . . .

Saturday 23 September 1944

. . . I was busying myself to get off without fuss . . . when Gen Jones' Major Simpson came in and fetched me up to see the Gen. It pleased me to think that Jones was ready to see I heard about things, but this was fairly ticklish. He wanted to talk about the Rolls-Royce Corp which seems to have been pulling a fairly fast one in Detroit for a couple of years, but from the record, which was long and which I had to read while he sat over me twitching his long nose and blinking his rather ill-looking eyes, I could not help thinking privately that the Air Judge Advocate, who was preventing him by way of Gen Timberlake from getting administrative reprimands for a Bg & 3 Cols involved, might have something. Indeed, I suspected that Jones had been stung a little by some unnamed needlings from the Inspector General, who, in turn, being told to keep out of Air Force matters, was restless. I just made the 1 pm train, having finally told him where I was going, so he immediately said he would like to hear about that, too.

Monday 25 September 1944

. . . To TAD early, which has the same somewhat tawdry air. The conference finally got started in the projection room about half past ten with Col Waters mildly in charge. We talked around the subject for some time, but it was soon apparent that we were going on with the Waller and that a Mr Probst of ATSC [Air Technical

SECRET

WAR DEPARTMENT
HEADQUARTERS OF THE ARMY AIR FORCES
WASHINGTON

22 September 1944

MEMORANDUM FOR CHIEF OFFICE OF TECHNICAL INFORMATION

Subject: Information from AC/AS Offices

1. **AAF Proposals on Negotiations with Sweden.** (Plans) General Kuter has proposed to the State Department (at a meeting with Messrs. Morgan, Trimble, Roper, Jarvis) that the U.S. Minister in Stockholm be instructed; (1) that additional B-17s on a loan basis, and 5 C-47s could be made available (2) that the Swedes be asked to authorize ATC to operate into Stockholm from Iceland or UK openly instead of disguising personnel as civilians (3) that the Swedish government be informed that no aircraft of any type can be made available until an agreement is reached about the release of our internees.

The State Department does not concur, representing (1) that no answer has been received to our previous proposal to sell up to 150 P-47s and to loan 4 interned B-17s if all our internees were released, (2) that the matter of landing rights at Stockholm should not be discussed at this time (3) that the loan of additional B-17s would enable Swedish airlines to start service into Russia "to detriment of our own hopes for undertaking operation of a service into Russia."

2. **Reply to Mead Committee on Post War Plans.** (Plans) PWD coordinated memorandum prepared by the Office of Legislative Services (Lt Colonel Reuschlin) for Mr. Amberg containing information on which to base a reply to the Mead Committee's request for dope on the status of plans for a post-war air force. The Committee is to be told that "plans are tentative and cannot be released at this time."

3. **Retaliatory Chemical Warfare against Japan.** (Plans) In examining a number of AC/AS Plans activity reports I noticed that during the past week, almost daily conferences and discussions are reported on this subject. The only entry is the bare statement; but it may be significant that the extensive tests conducted by the Sixth Air Force on the use of gas in connection with jungle and amphibious operations were reported by OC&R as highly successful a few weeks ago.

4. **Night Bombing Operations.** (OC&R) Requirements Division has prepared a directive to the AAF Board requiring the Board to "investigate implications and make recommendations concerning the development of night and bad weather operating capabilities in selected combat units after the defeat of Germany." The letter to the Board points out that the RAF "has been almost wholly responsible for night attacks" and that the RAF "may not always be available for this purpose in fighting the Japs."

5. **P-80A Combat Evaluation with B-29.** (M&S) Operational trials conducted at Alamagordo indicate that the P-47 cannot match the B-29 (whatever that may mean) at 40,000 feet. OC&R is therefore putting on trials "to see whether the P-80A will do better." The immediate reason for it is that General Spaatz "has requested information which can be answered only by bomber vs. P-80A combat evaluation." It seems probable that what General Spaatz wants to find out is whether the B-29 could operate against German jet jobs (my memorandum, 7 September) at less of a disadvantage. This might shed some light on the possible use of the 200 odd B-29s now in ETO (my memorandum, 29 August). Three day tests will be held at Muroc, with ATSC pilots provided for the P-80As, beginning 25 September.

6. **Camp Springs AAF, Maryland.** (M&S) The Camp Springs project (my memorandum, 11 August) has advanced to the point of a recommendation to the CG, AAF that authority be granted to proceed with construction and improvements (a dual runway @ $4\frac{1}{2}$ million dollars; additional parking apron @ $1\frac{1}{4}$ million dollars; permanent post construction @ $2\frac{1}{2}$ million dollars). The purpose of the project, you will remember, was to provide a sort of air force permanent show to keep Congress and others air-minded. There seems to be one slight hitch; viz. "Cognizance must be given (sic) to the fact that there are no suitable nearby range facilities."

7. **State Department & the Bahrein Refinery.** (M&S) Arrangements have been made to keep the State Department informed on various problems that have arisen in connection with the construction of the high octane aviation gasoline refinery on Bahrein Island in the Persian Gulf "in which the State Department is interested."

8. **Controlled Missiles Program.** (M&S) An agreement has been reached with the ASF on division of responsibility in the development of controlled missiles. AAF is to be responsible for air launched missiles and for all types of aerodynamic missiles. ASF is responsible for ground launched "momentum" missiles. Even if they are exclusively for the use of the AGF, the AAF will develop and produce all controlled missiles of the types for which it is responsible.

9. **JB-1 Flying Bomb** (M&S) The Northrop JB-1 has been given its first flight test. It was towed to 14,000 feet and turned loose carrying a pilot in the space normally occupied by one of the 2,000 lb. bombs. He had quite a time, because the JB-1 showed "decided longitudinal instability at 150-190 mph" but he stayed with the thing, which, on landing, bounced 75 feet. "The pilot was not seriously injured."

10. Pin point Bombing. (Management Control) 45% of the 47,696 tons of bombs dropped by the Eighth Air Force in August "fell within 1,000 feet of the aiming point." 75% fell within 2,000 feet. "This is the best accuracy yet shown by this Air Force."

J. G. COZZENS
Major, Air Corps

WAR DEPARTMENT
HEADQUARTERS OF THE ARMY AIR FORCES
WASHINGTON

23 September 1944

MEMORANDUM FOR CHIEF, OFFICE OF TECHNICAL INFORMATION

Subject: Information from AC/AS Offices.

1. <u>Production Requirements for Bombardiers & Navigators.</u> (Training) AC/AS Training has received a directive on the rate of training of bombardiers and navigators for the coming year. They will turn our 12,400 bombardiers and 16,900 navigators. Almost all of these will be in excess of estimated requirements (my memorandum, 21 September).

2. <u>Staff Officers for Post War Europe.</u> (OC&R, Requirements) General Giles has proposed in a memorandum for G-3, WDGS that some 200 selected AAF staff officers be given special training to equip them to deal with "the varied military-political problems which will arise in our European occupational forces." General Anderson recently recommended some such step, feeling that we might find ourselves with a lot of dumb air-plane drivers and hicks from the Texas sticks up against suave and I-daresay-morning-coated old world diplomats, who would soon take them for all they had. He feels this could be remedied by a six months course "at an institution like Columbia University" under "the best obtainable academically, economically, and diplomatically qualified instructors."
While perhaps unlikely to do much good, it is not clear how such a course could do any harm; but both the AGF and the ASF non-concur. General Lear says there is an acute shortage of officers "eligible to attend such a course" while ample officers should be available in Europe after the defeat of Germany. (This does not appear to answer General Giles point; they may be ample and they may be available, but without six months at Columbia, how can they be suave, polished men-of-the-world?) General Somervell non-concurs because he thinks such training of staff officers would "encroach upon State Department prerogatives." However, the memorandum is now being coordinated with Mr. McCloy and will then be coordinated with Mr. Lovett.

3. <u>Personnel Scheduling Procedures.</u> (OC&R) The Advisor for Program Control has transmitted to AC/AS Training, AC/AS, Personnel, and Management Control a draft of proposed Hq Office Instruction 150-1 outlining procedures for revision of personnel and training scheduling. This seems to represent the abandonment of German defeat on 1 October as a planning date. The new monthly cycle schedule will start on 25 September and end in November, with the new assumption of Germany defeat on 1 November.

J. G. COZZENS
Major, Air Corps

Service Command], who plainly knew his business, was prepared to take over the Vitarama job when they finished course three. Major Bahr, of CIS [Central Instruction School], proved less objectionable than I had been led to believe, so I contented myself with rising from time to time to ask them to put into the record various informal understandings that everyone else was content with. I could see that I was being quite a nuisance, but on the other hand (and to my surprise and I daresay not displeasure) I could see, too, that the Navy and Bahr and others began to regard me with a sort of respectful apprehension. A whole day full of it is quite wearing.

Tuesday 26 September 1944

. . . We did not get far with the conference business in the morning, it being already all done anyway. . . . We did some more checking of the conference record in the afternoon and I talked to Col Pardy late. He seemed willing to say that the opinion of TAD was that the thing was good. . . .

Wednesday 27 September 1944

To Washington on 8.30 train . . . I got into the office at one and found a thousand daily activity reports carefully saved for me. . . .

Thursday 28 September 1944

. . . I had my hands full putting in no less than three memoranda and listening to a plan of Rex's to get me a little deeper into Gen Kuter's outfit. Late in the afternoon, around with Haddock to see the Gen, who seems, as I had thought before, well-intentioned if vacuous. His problem is fixing up topics to tell an off-the-record press conference, which I was supposed to help him with by examining all his top secret stuff, incidentally perhaps finding a few things his WAC Capt Danforth had not been giving me for Smith. The Gen has a curious, self-conscious way of pursing his long mouth up and talking over the edges of it, which made me think he was very little at ease in this PRO world, and perhaps not always comfortable in his reputed role as brains of the staff—a grim thought, too. . . .

Friday 29 September 1944

. . . I went around to Kuter's office in the morning and Major Berg, the Gen being out, in a finicky and perhaps obfuscated sort of way, allowed that he thought maybe I'd better be cleared with A-2 for Top Secret first. This was done without offense. I had noticed before a hardly credible, yet not-to-be-doubted, change in attitude when I became a major, too—as though, in preserving the status of his caste, he must and did change his attitude toward me. (We had not got on too well up till then.) This brought everything to a stand-still, which was really all right with me. George asked

WAR DEPARTMENT

HEADQUARTERS OF THE ARMY AIR FORCES

WASHINGTON

28 September 1944

MEMORANDUM FOR CHIEF, OFFICE OF TECHNICAL INFORMATION

Subject: Information from the Office of the Air Inspector.

1. <u>Situation Involving Rolls Royce Inc.</u> General Jones suggested to me that the Chief, OTI, should be aware of a mess at Rolls Royce Inc. at Detroit which has been cooking for two years and which he feels may soon come to a head because the corporation is taking court action to resist renegotiation of its contracts. These involve $14,000,000 in a prime contract and about $6,000,000 in subsidiary contracts. The corporation was to make propellor assemblies. The Inspector General discovered two years ago that the Rolls Royce Corp was a dummy, and made representations to the Air Inspector, who in turn made representations to everyone in sight in the Air Service Command but action was persistently, and General Jones feels, deliberately postponed, pigeon-holed, and otherwise given no attention. The Inspector General persisted, and I think General Jones has found and finds himself considerably embarrassed by his inability to make the now-ATSC act. He prepared last week a memorandum recommending renegotiation of the contracts, which have, apparently, produced little if anything, and administrative reprimands for a Brigadier General ████████ ████████████████████ and three Colonels. The reprimands were disapproved by General ████████ on the advice of the Air Judge Advocate. General Jones is not satisfied. He feels that "in order to adequately protect General Arnold the case cannot be dismissed without some action against individuals responsible for this unusual and indefensible situation." The General says he will keep the Chief, OTI, informed. He thinks that if the Corporation's suit brings the matter into the newspapers or to the attention of Congress it will be most unfortunate.

2. <u>Memphis Air Depot Investigation.</u> The officer sent to Memphis (my memorandum, 19 Sept) reports that the allegations given the Mead Committee were unfounded in all respects, except that General ████████ had indeed been using an Army car for his "personal business." ███████████████████████████ ██ ██ General Jones appeared much relieved.

3. <u>Pipe Line to Drew Pearson.</u> General Jones' executive, Major Simpson, tells me that their office is satisfied that Mr. Pearson has received information (specifically, the leak-proof tank matter), and continues to receive it, from either or both Lt Colonel ████ formerly in the Troop Carrier Command office, and a girl named ████████, supposed to be intimate with Mr. Pearson.

J. G. COZZENS
Major, Air Corps

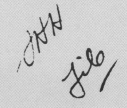

WAR DEPARTMENT
HEADQUARTERS OF THE ARMY AIR FORCES
WASHINGTON

28 September 1944

MEMORANDUM FOR CHIEF, OFFICE OF TECHNICAL INFORMATION

Subject: Information from AC/AS Offices.

1. <u>Negotiations with Sweden</u>. (Plans). In spite of, or perhaps because of, the non-concurrence of the State Department (my memorandum, 22 September) General Giles has directed AC/AS Plans to prepare a letter to Mr. Stettinius "requesting that he give his personal attention to instructing the US Minister in Stockholm." The instructions are to carry out General Kuter's proposals to make available a certain number of aircraft wanted by the Swedes in exchange for the release of AAF internees and for permission to establish "an independent ATC station in Sweden."

2. <u>Post-War AAF Commissions</u>. (Plans) General Kuter has forwarded a memorandum to the Chief of the Air Staff "pointing out the strong need for prompt Congressional authorization for 5,000 additional regular Air Force commissions to permit granting regular commissions to the best qualified of the present non-regulars before they slip through our fingers and make other post war commitments." (Slip through our fingers is right).

3. <u>P-80 Project</u>. (M&S) The AAF Committee for Release of Technical Information has "down-graded" the P-80 project to "restricted" for production, maintenance and training purposes. The principal object, I gather, is to enable the P-80 to be flown away from the factory, instead of being taken down and shipped in pieces as a security measure.

4. <u>Jacket, Field, Wool, O.D.</u> (Personnel) The Chief of Staff approved (27 Sept) the optional wearing of the jacket, field, wool, O.D. (battle jacket) by military personnel in the United States, including the Military District of Washington. Appropriate instructions from A/C of Staff, G-1, will issue within the next few days.

5. <u>AFTRC Directive on Frozen Trainees</u>. (Personnel) Steps are now being taken by the Training Command to do something about the situation resulting from the training program freeze (my memorandum, 15 September). General Bevans reports that "because of longer delays than anticipated in the assignment of trainees to pre-flight classes the importance of appropriate training during this interim period is greater than ever." The directive divides this training into phases A (Basic Training and firing of small arms); B (Administration, supply, and aircraft engineering); C (specific assignments on post, such as, weather section, message center clerks, airplane mechanics, etc.). Trainees will not be required to take A if they have already had it. In C phase, furloughs will be rather freely authorized, not to exceed 15 days including travel time. 25% of

total strength may be authorized at one time "thereby assuring furloughs for 100% of the personnel over a period of two months." These measures are so unlike the Training Command that it is a good bet that the morale situation was enough to scare even General ▓▓▓.

6. Latin American Air Forces. (OC&R) AC/AS Plans has requested the Troop Basis Division for plans similar to those prepared for The Republic of Mexico (my memorandum, 31 August) for setting up suitable air forces for: Bolivia, Brazil, Chile, Columbia, Costa Rica, Cuba, Dominican Republic, Ecuador, El Salvador, Guatemale, Haiti, Honduras, Nicaragua, Panama, Paraguay, Peru, Uruguay, Venezuela (what, not the Argentine?). "These studies are being made as a result of an OPD directive to prepare initial estimates of the post war size of air forces in Latin American countries as a basis of plans for earmarking equipment."

7. Report of AAF Evaluation Board SWPA. (OC&R) The Board's evaluation of attack aviation in this area concluded that "we have no aircraft suitable for low altitude strafing and bombing missions and that we should develop for this purpose a two-engine attack airplane which has maximum forward firing power, good visibility for pilot and formation work, long range, and bomb-bay area for the maximum pay-load of small bombs carried internally."

8. Post-war Disposal of AAF Materiel. (OC&R) In connection with a stated non-concurrence on a G-4 WDGS Memorandum "Post-war Requirements for Enemy Materiel" General Gross made recommendations going somewhat beyond the subject memorandum: specifically; "b. That a public relations policy be established and carried out to explain to the general public the overall reasons for avoiding the accumulation of 1944 enemy equipment. c. That the War Department, as a corollary policy, avoid taking back lend-lease equipment which can indirectly further stifle development for the post-war period. d. That the War Department, as a corollary policy, avoid placing in strategic reserve beyond the needs of our initial peace-time establishment, large quantities of 1940-44...equipment which may indirectly, by providing Congress with a false sense of security, prove a burden on post war development." General Gross adds: "Because of the highly controversial nature of the original proposal, preliminary appearance of excessive waste, and presumed additional cost to the tax payers in the post war period, concurrences were secured from AFACO, AFDCH, AFACT, AFAAA, AFAEP, AFRER, AFAMS, AFDAO, AFTAS." (But not, apparently, AFOTI).

9. Plan to Burn Kobe. (OC&R, AAF Board Control Office). The AAF Board has made a study of requirements for destroying "the inner-most inflammable section of Kobe, Japan". The Board concludes that 84 B-29s over the target in clear weather would probably be able to destroy most of the area with bomb loads of 80% M69 incendiaries and 20% M41 fragmentation bombs. 168 B-29s would be required with 3/10-6/10 cloud cover. More than 6/10 cover would require BTO methods.

10. B-29 Accidents. (Management Control) From figures presented by Mr. Wood of Boeing (at a Second Air Force conference on accident prevention) it appears that "63% of B-29 accidents are due to power plant failures (including fires, failures in maintenance, and failures of electrical equipment)". In a comparable number of accidents involving B-17s, only 8% were due to these causes.

11. Revised ZI Bulk Allotments. (OC&R) Effective 1 September the authorized allotment of personnel for Hq AAF will include 5,380 officers, 107 nurses, 83 WOs and 6,893 EM. Or, each officer has 1 and a fraction man to kick around.

12. Overstrength of AAF in ZI. (OC&R) The squawk of the General Council (my memorandum, 6 September) on excessive ZI AAF personnel has been prolonged and continued. General Giles required the Troop Basis Division to "brief" him on the subject, 25 September. General Giles interest seems to have been aroused by a chart produced by General Nelson showing that the strength of the Army as a whole had increased approximately 20,000 between 31 July and 31 August. Since General Marshall stated to the President that the Army will reduce to 7.7 millions, this seems to be making somebody a liar. General Nelson stated that "the AAF are particularly bad." It is overstrength in the ZI by approximately 100,000 and has decreased only 2,000 in actual strength during August. OC&R suggested that the Chief of the Air Staff might represent that this overstrength was "particularly offset" by shortages in overseas Air Forces, and that the total overstrength of the AAF as of 31 August was approximately 50,000, while (if General Nelson wanted to know) the overstrength of the whole Army was over 300,000.

13. Status of XB-36 & XB-35 Airplanes. (M&S) The XB-36 (Consolidated 10,000 mile-10,000 pound superduper) is 100% complete in point of flight engineering, and 40% complete in construction. 100 have been ordered (this is the one with 6 pusher engines). The XB-35 (Northrop's 19 million dollar flying wing) is 65% complete in engineering, and construction on the first article is 25% complete. 2 XB-35s and 13 YB-35s are on procurement.

J. G. COZZENS
Major, Air Corps

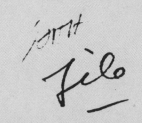

WAR DEPARTMENT
HEADQUARTERS OF THE ARMY AIR FORCES
WASHINGTON

28 September 1944

SPECIAL MEMORANDUM FOR CHIEF OFFICE OF TECHNICAL INFORMATION

Subject: Waller Gunnery Trainer Conference at the Training
Aids Division

1. On Monday and Tuesday, 25 and 26 September, a conference sug-
gested by Colonel George W. Pardy, Chief, TAD (my memorandum, 16 Sep-
tember) was held at the offices of the Training Aids Division in New
York to consider the status of the Waller Flexible Gunnery Trainer.
Representatives of AC/AS, Training, Gunnery; AC/AS Intelligence, Motion
Picture Services; Air Technical Service Command, OTI; and the US Navy
Bureau of Ordnance, Devices, were present. Colonel James Waters, Deputy
Chief, TAD, presided.

2. The finding of the conference was that the Waller Gunnery Trainer was a valuable training aid and its use would be continued. To this
end it was decided:

a. The Vitarama Corp would continue to work on permanent Course
III until it was completed.

b. On completion of Course III, the services of the Vitarama
Corp would be dispensed with and ATSC would take over the maintenance of
the trainers and the production of future films.

3. At my request, the following points were made part of the record, (which is expected to be available shortly):

a. The US Navy is prepared to continue the $100,000 monthly
payments to Vitarama until Course III is finished.

b. The Central Instructors' School is now definitely agreed
that the Trainer is an effective and valuable training device.

c. No changes or improvements will be allowed to postpone the
use of Temporary Course III, which is now about to be sent out, and which
will bring the AAF trainers, largely idle since last spring, into full
daily use within the next few weeks.

4. Copies of the transcript of the proceedings will be sent to the Air Inspector, who expressed an interest in the matter in a conversation with me Saturday. In view of the decision of the conference there seems to be no reason to suppose that the Air Inspector will wish to take any action at this point.

J. G. COZZENS
Major, Air Corps

us to go up and see the showing of the film which is meant to explain, on the defeat of Germany, the army's policy of demobilization, or more particularly why there will not be much until the Japanese matter is fixed. It is in technicolor and quite fancy and perhaps more effective than it seemed to me—the truth was that even in so comfortable a funk hole as the Pentagon I am pretty sick of this war, or at least, want to get home. It seemed to me that what this served to do principally was remind the troops that it might be a long time before they got home—something it seemed to me, too, that they would like as well or as little if they were just allowed to find it out for themselves. There might be a certain unnecessary psychological burden in trying to get a man to agree that he ought to do what he is going to have to do anyway. . . .

Saturday 30 September 1944

. . . They had me cleared for Top Secret and I spent some time looking at stuff in Kuter's office, most of it naturally of little immediate interest; the disposition of this or that air force, and what it had, being of importance only to those who might be unexpectedly attacked by it. . . . Matter for a conference did not seem to be shaping up particularly, but I now realize that the whole thing may be forgotten before it is needed anyway.

Sunday 1 October 1944

. . . On as duty officer, but I had hardly got a few bills paid and letters written when George Haddock turned up and we sat waiting for Smith who did not show while we fooled with Stat Control on figures for an article by Charlie Murphy for *Life*. It developed then that Smith had had an automobile accident and would not be in until later. . . .

Monday 2 October 1944

. . . Rex was out with his contusions and George was fretting, though more calmly than I would have, about whether he really was going to Paris or not. Meanwhile he had both arms loaded with shots—typhus, cholera and yellow fever in one, typhoid, tetanus and a new smallpox in the other. He said to me, from my standpoint, rather grimly, This is a hell of a load for one day; the rest of you ought to try spacing them out. With Smith in his present mood, you might any of you get sent anywhere on one day's notice, anytime. . . .

Tuesday 3 October 1944

. . . Haddock, with his arms good and sore, got around at last to Kuter's conference tomorrow and we fooled some with Stat Control and some with Flying Safety—

2 October 1944

MEMORANDUM FOR CHIEF, OFFICE OF TECHNICAL INFORMATION

Subject: Information from AC/AS Offices.

1. Latin American Air Forces (OC&R) The Troop Basis Division
has drawn up the following table of strengths in answer to the OPD
directive (my memorandum, 28 September). It will be noted that crack
about the Argentine was unwarranted.

COUNTRY	NUMBER OF SQUANDRONS	TOTAL PERSONNEL	COUNTRY	NUMBER OF SQUANDRONS	TOTAL PERSONNEL
Argentine	13	11,956	Guatemala	2	412
Bolivia	8	5,916	Haiti	2	412
Brazil	35	26,874	Honduras	2	412
Chile	16	13,582	Mexico	15	13,698
Colombia	7	5,549	Nicaragua	2	412
Costa Rica	1	178	Panama	0	0
Cuba	4	2,525	Paraguay	2	412
Dominican Rep.	2	412	Peru	12	11,869
Ecuador	5	2,752	Uruguay	7	5,708
El Sal Vador	2	412	Venezuela	7	5,551
			Total –	144	109,042

Incidentally, AC/AS Plans notes in 30 September Activity Report
that AC/AS Intelligence has commended our Mil Air Attache in Mexico City
for his diligence "in forwarding information concerning movements of
Royal Canadian Air Force representatives" in Mexico and requests additional reports.

2. Retaliatory Chemical Warfare Against Japan (M&S) Gen Echols
reports that the Subcommittee of the Joint Logistics Committee, Joint
Chiefs of Staff, has completed its work in computing requirements and
availability of ammunition, equipment and personnel necessary for waging
retaliatory gas warfare against Japan. This seems to be the matter that
was agitating AC/AS Plans a couple of weeks ago (my memorandum, 22 Sept)
General Echols expects that the Joint Chiefs of Staff will accept this
study and approve the indicated theater stock levels. "These requirements take into consideration the Twentieth, Twenty-first, Twenty-second
Bomber Commands as well as augmentations due to redeployment".

3. Reduction in Training Program (OC&R) General Arnold has approved
reduction in the training program following X Day along the lines suggested by Dr. Learned's tabulations (my memorandum, 21 September). Dr.
Learned says that Major Holland will be given all the details.

- 2 -

4. <u>Notes from In and Out Log 30 September, 1 October.</u>

a. (From G-2 AMMISCA) Present Jap force moving on Kweilin must be credited with intention of continuing to Liuchow, our last large base in east China for Fourteenth Air Force Operations.

b. (Stockholm) Signed Rayens. 330 internees have been released by Swedish government. Rayens believes "internee problem now solved" (my memoranda, 22 September, 28 September)

c. (Paris) signed Eisenhower. SHAEF Main (hq) moved to Trianon Palace Hotel, Versailles. (29 September)

d. Signed LeMay. Reconnaissance photos of steel works at Anshan show approximately 168 craters, largely in open ground to north, east and south of targets at distance of 5000 to 13,000 feet.

e. (London) signed Spaatz. Suggestion that in view of recent loss of 2 major gens and 6 bgs that some of the "extremely competent general officers who will remain in the Air Force after the war" but are now stationed in ZI be sent over to get some "combat theater experience."

f. Signed Spaatz. Slight increase in enemy fighter "reaction" is credited to:

1. Relative stabilization of front line which has allowed regrouping of GAF on new bases in Germany.

2. Area being defended is much smaller and the 350 single-engine German fighters committed to Reich defense are all based well within interception range of vital targets.

g. Arnold to Spaatz. Asks what's this about Seventh Army report (in message from General Walter Smith to General Handy, 23 Sept.) that we sank small German lighter in bay of Marsailles by direct hit with "4 tons of psychological warfare material signed by General Wilson". CGAAF says it sounds like a lot of bull.

J. G. COZZENS
Major, Air Corps

part of the trouble was the release of AAF plane loss figures yesterday along with something about dropping our millionth bomb. I did not know at the time who dreamed that up, but I suppose, if a hard school, fools will indeed learn in no other. Naturally, the papers had seized on the 42,000 planes, not on the million tons of bombs and it seemed wise to explain what we meant by the 17,500 planes lost over here. This took so much fussing that Haddock and I and Cecil Brown stayed to have a revolting supper in the cafeteria and on until after eight, so Kuter could see what he was expected to say. It could all have been done earlier, except the squawk on the release, and maybe next week we can do it earlier.

Wednesday 4 October 1944

. . . Haddock got a directive of sorts from Spaatz early and Murphy turned up to go with him, but still they did not go and had not gone when the day was over. Meanwhile the Kuter business complicated itself with suggestions from the incredible ass Col Clarke in Stat Control and talk from Col Delaney in BPR, and finally . . . two hours with Kuter who (I suppose because he was so civil to me and paid heed to what I said when he suggested one or two obviously outrageous statements he thought he might make) struck me as having better sense than I had seen in him before. We met up in the AAF conference room at 4.15—some forty newspaper people (and a seedy lot—shop-worn men and homely energetic females) where he did quite well, reading his text with ease and some expression, and deviating from it with relative naturalness. He had donned (who knows why?) battle dress for the occasion—that is, the new mess-jacket field jacket with stars and some miniature ribbons and miniature wings. While we were in his office he spoke to Gen Bevans on the interphone and asked if it was all right yet to wear the outfit. Ans. Yes. I wondered what he had been thinking about in the morning when he put it on.

Thursday 5 October 1944

. . . I went in to read the Log in Kuter's office early, and presently he turned up himself, coming behind me where I sat at a table between Major Berg's desk and Capt Danforth's. Spying the two stars, I started to spring to my feet but he put a hand on my shoulder and holding me down, said; Don't get up, my boy. I thought of saying, Well, sir, when you get to be my age you'll appreciate being able to sit down; however, I said only, yes, sir. He had some ideas about what we would talk on next week and they made pretty good sense and I continued to take a bright view of him. We had a little trouble in the afternoon trying to shake down A2 for some of it—a squirt of a Major Marks making most of the trouble—I suppose he would describe me as bossy and arrogant and too stupid to understand the difficulties in making up certain information—but it is nice to be a major in that line of work because they

ADDRESS REPLY TO
COMMANDING GENERAL, ARMY AIR FORCES
WASHINGTON 25, D. C.

ATTENTION:

HEADQUARTERS, ARMY AIR FORCES
WASHINGTON

5 October 1944

MEMORANDUM FOR CHIEF, OFFICE OF TECHNICAL INFORMATION

Subject: Information from AC/AS Offices

1. <u>Service Rating Card.</u> (Personnel) At a meeting of the Special Planning Division the matter of the point score to be used on the service rating card was taken up. (It was recommended at the General Council Meeting 25 September -- General Henry particularly urging it -- that this system on which demobilization after X day will be based, should be given a trial run as a means of reducing the current excess of personnel over troop bases -- <u>Minutes of the General Council 25 September pp 3,4).</u> The point score to be used will be 1 point for each month of service, 1 point for each month of overseas service, 5 points for each combat award, and 8 points for each child (not to include more than three).

2. <u>Heavy (including VHB) Bomber Figures.</u> (Management Control) The 25,000th heavy bomber produced in the US since 1 July 1940 was delivered on 27 September. 22,601 have gone to the AAF. 9,521 have been lost from all causes. This is the breakdown by types:

Model	Total Delivered	Delivered to AAF	Lost, Redesignated or Reallocated	Still on Hand With AAF First Line	Restricted	Total
B-29	754	754	110	639	5 a/	644
B-32	3	3	1	-	2	2
B-17	10,113	9,951	4,679	4,561	711 b/	5,272
B-19	1	1	-	-	1	1
B-24	14,151	11,892	4,681	5,991	1,220	7,211
Losses on Models Not Yet Known			50	-50	-	-50
Total	25,022	22,601	9,521	11,141	1,939	13,080

a/ Includes XB-39
b/ Includes B-40's

3. <u>Physical Profiles for EM.</u> (Personnel) A project is underway to -er - accomplish physical profiles for all enlisted men in the ZI not previously profiled. General Bevans points out that G-1 points out "that profiling would materially reduce present overstrength of armed forces in the US by weeding out many physically unfit enlisted men who were drafted during the 'blitz' period of induction some months ago." I'll have more information coming on this situation.

4. <u>Discharge of AAF Officers</u>. (Personnel) General McCormick reports that G-1, WDGS has sent a paper to the War Department Separations Board establishing " a policy eliminating any special consideration for officers of any component, and eliminating manner-of-performance ratings (other than unsatisfactory) as a factor in determining whether an officer should be relieved or not." As nearly as I can find out, this is trying to say that neither the officer's particular job nor his performance rating in it will be considered in finding him excess. If his job is unnecessary, or his performance lousy, or both, it still won't necessarily make him excess. In the same piece of paper the WDSB is informed that future cases will not be submitted to them for review (my memorandum, 21 September). The Adjutant General will from now on issue orders at the request of Ho AAF, AGF, or ASF.

5. <u>Powered Aircraft Training for Glider Pilots</u>. (OC&R) General Gross has concurred in an AC/AS Training plan to "increase the professional usefulness of glider pilots" by qualifying them to be airplane drivers. It is held that the ultimate aim of the Troop Carrier portion of the post-war Air Force is for all pilot personnel to be able to fly all equipment assigned to these units, whether gliders or airplanes. The post-war recommendations are to authorize returned combat officer glider pilots meeting present qualifications to go to primary flying schools. (In this connection, somebody seems to have forgotten that fact that, at South Plains, glider pilots in training get a good deal of time on Piper cubs and ought to be, dumb as a pilot or not, a little past the primary stage); to continue glider schools at a production rate of 150 a month and limit eligibility to Troop Carrier pilots who have had no glider training.

6. <u>Selected Service Personnel for AAF</u>. (OC&R, Troop Basis) In a conference in General McNarney's office on 30 September the personnel situation in the AAF was discussed. Very little seems to have come of it. The AAF's request "to receive absolutely no personnel from selective service was received but not formally approved"; apparently because WDGS, G-3 "stated that the Army as a whole required the selective service replacement system and could not stop new intake" (and so though God knows why, the AAF will have to continue to take its share, exacerbating the feelings of the General Council (above), and making of little avail such measures as stopping ACER recruiting and folding up Miss Cochran's birdwomen.)

7. <u>Notes from In and Out Log, 3, 4 October</u>.

a. <u>SHAEF, signed Eisenhower 2 October</u>. Directs every effort to be made "to preserve from destruction by Allied Force" passenger liners observed in enemy ports unless the enemy is actually using them.

b. <u>Ankara, USMA, 2 October.</u> "Popularity of Russians and communism has suffered noticeably in Turkey as a result of wide-spread siezure of property in Bulgaria and ruthless conduct."

c. <u>France, signed Eisenhower, 2 October.</u> Imperative need is still felt in Ninth Air Force for minimum of 12 "working press type" public relations officers in grades of Lt and Capt. "Time for telling true accomplishment and capabilities of tactical air power is rapidly running out. Feel very strongly that if story is not related during western European campaign opportunities will be materially lessened and there will be a host of disbelievers after war". They feel they have nobody there who knows how to write. (Judged correct feeling).

d. <u>New Delhi, Sultan to Marshall, 3 October.</u> "Night strikes at east China and XX Bomber Command bases by Japs are becoming serious." Four night fighters are being sent into China next week but aren't expected to be much good because of shortage of GCI radar personnel.

e. <u>London, signed Spaatz, 2 October.</u> Fighter strength: 32 groups

Eighth Air Force	12 P-51 groups
	3 P-47 groups
Ninth Air Force	3 P-38 groups
	1 P-51 group
	13 P-47 groups

f. <u>Eglin Field, signed Gardner, 2 October.</u> Tests of No 1 P-75 showed maximum true air speed, 375 mph at 16,000 feet. Take off and landing characteristics excellent; general flying characteristics, good.

g. <u>London, signed Winant, 29 September.</u> Poles claim reliable reports that Germans are increasing "extermination activities" in Polish concentration camps. Can we bomb extermination chambers and barracks (what's the idea, help the Germans?), or can we warn Hitler some more? (ARNOLD answers it is up to Spaatz).

h. <u>Brisbane, signed McArthur, 4 October.</u> Communique describes Balikpapan (oil storage, etc) as "the most lucrative strategic target in the Pacific." MacArthur says it was "destroyed".

i. <u>SHAEF, signed Eisenhower, 4 October.</u> Continued inquiries about who (Swiss or German governments) controls flow of water into Rhine from Lake Konstanz. "Suggest inquiries be kept discreet." (Object is plainly to find out if the Germans can suddenly flood the upper Rhine valley).

j. <u>Lisbon, signed Solborg, 4 October.</u> In regard to "Global Proposal" (major AAF airfield near Lisbon), "Feel critical situation existing here cannot be over-emphasized."

k. London, signed Spaatz, 3 October. Goes on with joke about four tons of literature sinking the German lighter in bay of Marseilles. Getting a little long.

JAMES G. COZZENS
Major, Air Corps

cannot brush you off as they would a Capt. George seemingly got to Paris with Murphy, and Smith got his chicken this morning, so everyone else was happy, we presume. . . .

Friday 6 October 1944

. . . I spent the morning struggling somewhat with a Col Rothrock on the H2X bombing. He was bald, short, jolly and explosive, and seemed to feel unlike Bright in A2 that there was something in it, showing issues of a magazine called *Radar*, a confidential job got out by the Air Communications Officer on the size and scale of *Impact* which I had never seen or heard of before. Things like that always astonish me by the revelation of how big or even enormous the AAF is—I mean that relatively speaking I am in a position to be very well-informed about it—and am—but there are all kinds of activities, all engaging a lot of people and all going on all the time, of which I'm completely ignorant. However, Bright in one sense had the last word since he was still dragging his feet and saying it couldn't be done, so I was driven to say; Well, will you tell Kuter that? I could see there were all kinds of things he hadn't heard of, too; for he seemed taken aback and slightly incredulous (I don't know what he thought was going on) when I telephoned Berg and said I wanted to bring Col Bright around to see Gen Kuter, and Berg said yes. Kuter was very affable to me and agreed that maybe we'd better drop the subject, and this too, affected Berg, a somewhat truculent freckle-faced crop-headed youth. When we got into the hall he and his Major Marks became immediately very cordial and friendly as opposed to the impatient and captious airs of yesterday, as to say: He really did know the Gen after all.

Saturday 7 October 1944

. . . Miss Johnson turned up, assuredly to everyone's relief, and just as much, it was soon plain, to hers. You could see without too much trouble that she had in fact been living to get back—her parents and Dodge City were all right and no doubt she loved them but it was never like this. George Bradshaw with a characteristic natural grace of feeling suddenly said, as we were planning to go in for lunch to the Lafayette; We'll take Johnny. She demurred mildly, but soon called some girl friend and came with us. Plainly very happy, for she was actually skipping along with Jo Chamberlin ahead of us to the parking spaces, at least until she recollected herself. Meanwhile, coming out into the sunshine I think she astonished us all—she had no hat on—by the astounding effect of the sun on her dark red hair which lit up to knock your eye out—the whole effect being gay, youthful, and in an impersonal sense affecting. Back again, she went with vigor into the long & tedious job of catching up with my memoranda index. I thought it was quite a load and said so, but she said again, I love

118

it; which I believe is no joke. Casting back in my own mind to figure what, fantastically (when compared with the literal reality) it must have to be like to her, I could only think of coming down from school (about her age) and encountering Dickey Doubs[44] and his (now I know) more or less dubious and phoney art people in Greenwich Village in 1921.

Monday 9 October 1944

. . . I made some gestures with Cecil Holland about Kuter's material but there were various delays here and there and it was plain that the customary rat race was in the making, and indeed inevitable. . . .

Tuesday 10 October 1944

. . . We worked off and on with Gen Kuter all day and in the end finally did get it finished about 4. The Gen received me very affably at that time and seemed satisfied and also, in that amusing simple way, conscious of his affability, so that you could see him thinking—sign of a good heart, after all, that graciousness really meant something to someone in my position and what did it cost him? . . .

Wednesday 11 October 1944

We had a few touches to put on Kuter's matter in the morning and putting up his maps and plans in the Air Conference Room. . . . The Gen gaining ease, did very well and everyone seemed, though exhausted, satisfied. Bill Harris was in town and to his place at the Raleigh where he and his wife had a crowded cocktail party whose principal feature proved to be the Secty of Labor[45], which amused me because I did not catch the name of this voluble, fancy-talking elderly female at first; but I had already noted a peculiar technique in her manner when the rest of the roomful were presented to her—what struck me was that she acted as if she were somebody to so high a degree that I thought she must be mad—all this in a very easy and affable way, insisting on shaking hands with every single person who was introduced. So I was entertained when I found she was indeed Mme. Scty. She seemed on good terms with Jane Grant[46] and had a mole on her upper lip—really on the lip, which seemed awkward. Out after half an hour and home. I seem to find myself more and more unsuited for social life—that is, I keep wondering why in hell we are all there.

Thursday 12 October 1944

. . . A little difficulty turned up in regard to the conference yesterday—Gen K had noted in the Log and asked me to put into his text a reference to the recent capture of a German weather outfit in Greenland. It developed today that this was the item of most interest to most of the press and that—the Log didn't say and it seems neither I

WAR DEPARTMENT
HEADQUARTERS OF THE ARMY AIR FORCES
WASHINGTON

9 October 1944

MEMORANDUM FOR THE CHIEF, OFFICE OF TECHNICAL INFORMATION

Subject: Information from AC/AS Offices.

1. <u>A-26 in SWPA</u>. (OC&R) General Gross states that General Kenney has again (Log b., my memo 7 Oct) "indicated preference for B-25 and A-20 in lieu of A-26." Action is being taken to keep Gen. Kenney supplied with them as long as possible. However Gen. Gross observes: "It is believed that as this airplane (A-26) proves itself more and more in other theatres, it will be demanded in SWPA. Recent reports from ETO are enthusiastic over the A-26."

2. <u>Night Air Operations</u> (OC&R) "Numerous staff agencies are beginning to indicate interest in the question of adapting, for the war against Japan, a definite proportion of the AAF to night operations." (my memo 22 Sept) "The suggestion has been made that the B-32 might be developed specifically as a night bomber. Both Gen. Norstad and Gen. Gross have suggested this possibility to Gen. Craig." Gen. Kuter told me, in discussing the answer to the question on the B-32 in his 4 Oct press conference, that he believed that the B-32 was unlikely to go into production; and that probably the three built to date will be the only ones ever built. I gather that it is felt more and more that future development should center around the XB-35 and the XB-36 (my memo 28 Sept). The AAF Board has not yet reached the point of final report and recommendations.

3. <u>Aircraft Delivery Losses</u>. (OC&R) During September, 1124 AAF aircraft were flown to overseas theatres for delivery. Only 6 were lost enroute.

4. <u>German Aircraft Performance</u>. (OC&R) "On August 31, a German aircraft was plotted over the Messina Straits. Two Spitfires were scrambled to intercept and they climbed to 43,000 feet without intercepting. From calculations, the enemy plane was estimated to be flying at an altitude of 51,000 (sic) feet. It is not yet known whether this plane was a jet job or not. It is not believed a jet plane due to the distance from any possible base."

5. Chaplain's Conference. (Personnel) "A representative of this command attended the Chaplain's Conference of the ETTC on 3 October. The general problem discussed was the contributions of chaplains to guardhouse problems." (!)

6. Chemical Bombs for VHB Airplanes. (OC&R) Every indication continues that "retaliatory gas warfare against Japan" is not far off (my memoranda, 22 Sept, 2 Oct). Gen. Gross reports that "Air Chemical Officer was advised that the present lack of suitable chemical bombs loaded with persistent chemical agents for use by VHB airplanes is becoming more serious in view of the proposed retaliatory planning now being considered. Requirements for suitable munitions have been outstanding for over two years."

7. Fighter Aircraft Losses. (OC&R) An increase in the fighter aircraft loss planning factors has been recommended. This will be from 12% to 16% in Pacific Theatres. The present 20% rate in European Theatres will be continued. Losses for the first 8 months of 1944 averaged 23.5% in Europe and 16.6% in the Pacific.

8. Show at National Airport. (OC&R) "A demonstration of aircraft employed in the movement of airborne and standard ground force elements and their equipment" will be held on 1&2 November over at the Airport. All "interest officer personnel" are invited and apparently admission is free. The display will include the C-46, C-47, C-54, and XC-82 (the twin boom, 2 engine Fairchild job, considered very hot stuff)

9. Rate of Missions Flown by AAF Personnel. (Management Control) From October 1943 through August 1944 officers were found to have flown a greater number of missions than air crew enlisted men. (This is easily explained, if MC wants to know, by the fact that fighter missions are included). A tabulation of the median number of missions flown and the number of months spent overseas:

| | Rated Officers | | | Air Crew EM | | |
	Cumulative	July	Aug	Cumulative	July	Aug
Median no. of missions	41	39	37	36	35	37
Median no. of months	10	11	10	11	10	11

10. AAF & RAF Bomber Strength. (Management Control) As of 25 September, AAF squadrons in combat theatres had 4,027 HB, 1,483 Medium Bombers, 518 light bombers. Of these, 84% (3,382) of the heavy bombers are in operation against Germany. On the same date the RAF had 1,961 HB, 597 Medium Bombers, 719 Light Bombers. Of RAF heavy bombers 95% (1,862) are operating against Germany.

11. **Notes from In and Out Log, 7, 8 October.**

    a. <u>COM Task Force 32, 6 Oct.</u> Peleliu bomber runway usable 6 October.

    b. <u>SHAEF for Joint Intelligence Committee</u>, 6 Oct. In view of possible surplus bomber capacity "after all targets required to ensure enemy's defeat have been covered" it is again urgently suggested (Log e. my memo 7 Oct) that we attack "other targets...destruction of which would be in long term interests of the United Nations. For strategic or economic reasons, further attacks against particular industries might be desirable." (Industries suggested: shipbuilding, chemical, synthetic rubber).

    c. <u>Cairo, signed Giles, 6 Oct.</u> Saudi Arabian Foreign Minister is reported "reluctant to press our request for permission to construct airport at Dhahran" with his boss the King. Gen. Giles hears a couple of Britishers in civilian clothes have been fooling around there and H. M. Gov't is not going to let us in if they can help it.

    d. <u>Hollandia, signed MacArthur 7 Oct.</u> From this communique it is plain that we took an unexpected pasting on the last trip to Balikpapan. (MacArthur described Balikpapan as "destroyed" 4 Oct). Of 21 B-24's attacking, 7 were shot down and 13 damaged. 30-40 Jap fighters were up, and though reported as familiar types, it is felt that identification was at fault, and they may have been the new Rob and the new Frank. Request is for A-2 here to forward all (if anything) that we know about them.

    e. <u>London, from Doolittle signed Spaatz 8 Oct.</u> Recommends holding Cols. Zemke, Blakeslea, and Cummings, considered the best of the 8th AF group commanders, in ZI jobs "in the interest of conserving these valuable officers and assuring availability of their leadership and experience in post-war Air Force."

J. G. COZZENS
Major, Air Corps

nor the Gen knew—it was done by the Coast Guard, and the Navy did not at all approve of its being released. There was quite a flurry, but the Gen seemed to be holding the bag firmly. S came down on the 6.30 train, and in with George Bradshaw to meet her and have dinner at the Chinese place. I had on a green shirt and pinks and was somewhat taken aback when, waiting at the gate, a 2nd Lt MP came up and informed me civilly that I was out of uniform and took my name and serial number. In fact, of course, I knew it; but it is much worn in the Pentagon and I had not seriously imagined anyone would bother me in the Military District of Washington. As George remarked, it makes you suddenly realize you are in the army, or something.

Friday 13 October 1944

. . . In to Plans in the morning where I found a nice item on the CAP [Civil Air Patrol] which I then took up to Col Risen in Training for a little enlightenment, not realizing until I got through getting what he knew that I was, whatever my good opinion of my wit or adroitness, little fitted for delicate negotiation, for, though he did not let on, I suddenly realized at the end that I was the one who had enlightened him; and, for whatever reason, he had not before been told that the Board had taken such and such resolutions, all likely to affect his job. I went off at noon not sure whether I had spilled the beans or not. . . .

Saturday 14 October 1944

. . . We had a fairly quiet day, though I had a very long memorandum to get in. . . . I was up in Gen Jones' office where they had prepared me a summary of their pending cases, all duller than I would have expected; and a session with Kuter in the afternoon in which he seemed to give the lie to the rumor that he was to be replaced by Gen Smith by his active planning of what he was going to say Wednesday. We had a fairly good subject for him on what should be said about the newspaper misapprehensions in regard to Gen Eaker's 12 Oct Italian operations. I thought he might simply take the news stories, read them to the gang, and tactfully explain in an informal way why it seemed to him that the point had been missed. Afterwards I wondered if he could handle it without putting their backs up, as to say (like Mr A) he was telling them how to run their papers; but I still felt it might go on the basis of a frank man-to-man discussion on how the sometimes obscure communiques ought to be interpreted. It seemed a day's work by the time it was over.

Monday 16 October 1944

. . . The teletype through the morning was full of the Jap claims about what they did to the Navy, and though palpably lies, I found myself disturbed, remembering a

WAR DEPARTMENT
HEADQUARTERS OF THE ARMY AIR FORCES
WASHINGTON

12 October 1944

MEMORANDUM TO THE CHIEF, OFFICE OF TECHNICAL INFORMATION

Subject: Information from AC/AS Offices.

1. <u>Russian Participation Against Japan</u>. (Plans) <u>This item
is Top Secret</u>. Note from OPD, Plans. "Worked on final draft
of paper "Russian Participation in the War Against Japan" with
representatives of WD,OPD Strategy Section. This paper outlines
our concepts of the part which we desire to assign to the Soviets
upon their entry into the war against Japan." (Col. Bonnevalle)
In this connection, a list of Siberian bases which we will wish
to use for our air operations is being prepared.

2. <u>Monkey Business in Saudi Arabia</u>. (Plans) The U.S. Minister
has been instructed to offer King Ibn Saud "a small flight training mission" -- 4 officer pilots, 10 EM, 6 training planes and a
cash outlay of about a quarter million dollars. This seems to
be a U.S. countermove to alleged British-inspired obstructions
(my memo 9Oct, Log c.) or more simply, a U.S. bribe.

3. <u>Conference on Heavy Transport Type Aircraft</u>. (OC&R)
Representatives of OC&R, M&S, and ATC met 4-5 Oct to determine
characteristics desired in a new transport type aircraft capable
of being operated profitably carrying passengers paying not more
than 3¢ a mile. "AAF participation in its development is more
than justified because the construction of such an airplane would
result in much more general air travel, a greater public air-
mindedness, and the creation of a large corps of trained operation
and maintenance personnel which would constitute a potentially
powerful asset in the event of national emergency." Specifications
agreed on will be forwarded to AC/AS, M&S.

4. <u>P-59A Airplane Production</u>. (OC&R) Deliveries from Bell
will be terminated with the fiftieth article. Decision was made
in view of the higher priority requirements for I-16 engines in
the Navy FR-1, a first line carrier plane, and "the limited requirement for the P-59". Col. Holloway adds that it is not
contemplated training and equipping any specialized jet fighter
groups other than the 412th. (my memo, 7 Oct) and that P-80's
will be "put directly into combat as replacement aircraft." It
is believed that the fifty P-59's "will be sufficient to equip
the 412th group, supply the needs of the ATSC, and fulfill training
requirements for jet mechanics."

TOP SECRET

5. **M-Series Bomb Sights**. (OC&R) "Except for the visibility problem created by interposing clouds and haze", it is felt that the four major modifications, tested and approved by the AAF Board and now being incorporated in the M-Series bombsight "make it suitable for all operations up to 40,000 feet at speeds up to 400 mph."

6. **JB-1 and JB-2 Robot Bombs**. (OC&R) "Since the JB-1 project (Northrop tail-less aircraft) may be dropped or in any event will not become operationally suitable for many months" it was recommended that the answer to a cable from Spaatz asking how they were coming should be restricted to JB-2 (Chinese Copy of Robot bomb) "which is at present in a satisfactory state of development." (my memo, 5 Sept)

7. **Air Judge Advocate & War Crimes**. (OC&R) AC/AS, Intelligence, Personnel, & Management Control & the Air Judge Advocate are redommending to the Chief of the Air Staff that the Air Judge Advocate be made "office of primary responsibility as respects atrocities and war crimes perpetuated (sic) against AAF personnel in hands of enemy, particularly the Bulgarians." Investigation had disclosed that no AAF agency was directly responsible for establishing policy or processing information on cases in which AAF personnel were involved. However, the JAG was directed by the Secretary of War on 15 Sept. to assume "full War Department war crimes responsibility."

8. **Report No. 1 AAF Evaluation Board, CBI**. (OC&R) Report No. 1., dated 15 Sept. has been received from the AAF Evaluation Board in CBI. It presents a general evaluation of the air actions by various components of the Allied Air Forces in the theater. "No outstanding conclusions or evaluations were made", but the following points were submitted:

    a. Air power, almost alone, has to date saved East China and the air bases there.

    b. An increase in air striking power in China can be secured only by an increase in the movement of supplies.

    c. Air Commando operations are practical but all phases thereof must be carefully coordinated.

    d. Determined troops cannot be isolated; they can be supplied, reinforced and evacuated by air.

    e. Operations of the XX Bomber Command are extremely costly and have detracted from the air effort of other Air Forces in the Theater, but are considered worthwhile due to their tremendous effect on Japanese morale.

f. Air bases should be nearer enemy lines to reduce wasteful flying over friendly territory.

g. Completion of the Lido Road and pipe line may not be practical and this project should be carefully restudied at this time. Changed conditions indicate that a port on the Burma Coast or the South or East Coast of China can be secured far quicker and more economically.

h. Close air-ground cooperation is very important in jungle warfare.

i. The "fire bomb" has not proven efficient as an incendiary during the monsoons.

j. The "spike bomb" is an efficient device of limited application.

k. Fighter-bombing is considered the most efficient type of operation for third phase operations.

l. More photographic responsibilities should be given the AAF by Army Regulations.

m. More attention should be given to bomb fuzing.

This report was submitted through Headquarters U. S. Army Forces in the CBI and OPD, WDGS. U. S. Army Forces in the CBI commented on a. and g. of the above conclusions. Their comments were concurred in by OPD. They were "air power alone cannot stop a determined ground enemy" and "The completion of the Lido Road and the pipe line to China is considered a must by this Theater." They stated that "it is estimated that a one-track, dry-weather road will be opened to China by 1 Feb 1945 and the pipe line will be in operation to Kunming by 1 Apr 1945."

9. C-109 Tankers. (Management Control) A study of the VHB program has been prepared by Stat. Control. It is pointed out in this study that the allocation of C-109 tankers to the CBI will so augment present supply as to permit performance of 350-400 sorties a month.

10. Allied Air Strength Figures. (Management Control) As a result of G-2's revision of its estimate of Russian Air Forces personnel strength, total Allied Air Forces strength as of 1 Sept 44 now exceeds 6,000,000 (6,063,661) in comparison with the 1 Mar 1944 figure of 5,625,731. The breakdown of Allied Air Force strength is listed below:

ALLIED AIR FORCES - SUMMARY OF PERSONNEL
(1 Sep 44)

USAAF	2,403,056	39.63%
US Navy Air Arm	702,610	11.59
RAF	1,275,252 a/	21.03

Royal Fleet Air Arm	57,545	.95
RCAF	149,133	2.46
RAAF	161,912	2.67
RNZAF	35,140	.58
Red Air Forces	1,207,500 a/	19.91
French Air Forces	47,483	.78
Netherlands East Indies AF	1,328	.02
Chinese Air Force	4,559 b/	.08
Latin American Allied AF's	13,943	.23
Other Allied Air Forces	4,200	.07
	6,063,661	100.00%

a/ Best estimate available
b/ Includes Chinese personnel of CACW

11. Decorations Situation. (Management Control) Stat. Control
has prepared a summary the percentages of officers and enlisted
men returning on flying status from the various air forces who
have been decorated. (Conclusion: an invidious distinction is
being made against an extremely small minority. This could be
corrected by automatically giving everyone the Silver Star, the
DFC, and the Air Medal)

	Percent Decorated -Air Forces-		No. Decorations for Each man receiving at least one decoration.	
	vs Germany	vs Japan	vs Germany	vs Japan
Officers	90.1	80.9	1.7	1.7
Enlisted Men	79.3	67.1	1.6	1.6

12. Notes from In & Out Log. 9., 10, 11 Oct.

a. Stockholm, signed Johnson 6 Oct. Reports that plan
for arranging an exchange of POW mail via Stockholm carried by
ATC is approved. In connection with a series of German conditions
and provisions it was noted that "the German government would be
grateful if there might be included...mail to and from German
civilian internees and POW in Canada."

b. Kunming, signed Chennault, 7 Oct. "14th Air Forces
losses due enemy aerial combat continue to be minor. Continued
loss of gasoline stores due to night attacks can create critical
shortage."

c. Kunming, from CAKRM, 9 Oct. Estimates Jap air strength
at Chinese bases: North China, no data on bombers, 145 fighters;
Central China 150 bombers, 280 fighters; South China, 55 bombers,
125 fighters. "Jap airdrome development indicates practically

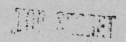

     d. <u>Madrid, signed Hayes, 6 Oct</u>. "A difficult situation would be created should the U.S. sell or furnish commercial aircraft to Portugal without similar concessions to Spain, in my opinion." This would perhaps indicate that the Spanish are onto the Global deal.

     e. <u>London, signed Spaatz, 10 Oct</u>. "Encounters with enemy jet planes on 7 Oct resulted in claims of 4 destroyed by fighter escort. These were 3 ME-262's and 1 ME-163. Fighters reported scattered encounters with 20 to 25 jet and rocket propelled aircraft over a wide area from the Zuider Zee to Bruz... several instances of attacks by jet planes on straggling bombers were reported, although all of these attacks were ineffective." Pilots of the jet jobs were judged to be inexperienced and somewhat nervous.

     f. <u>Caserta, signed Eaker, 10 Oct</u>. Answers at length the charge by the president of the Rumanian Red Cross that AAF planes had been shooting up civilians. The Gen. says there is nothing to support it and that it may be definitely stated on unimpeachable authority (including his own, because he was there himself) that the people bore no ill-will toward Americans and "said they could always tell we were bombing military objectives and with remarkable accuracy considering the great height at which we flew."

     g. <u>San Salvador, signed Massey, 11 Oct</u>. Reports that 2 forces of Honduran refugees are secretly leaving San Salvador to invade Honduras. "Equipment considered inadequate but support promised from Mexico if invasion progresses successfully". However, the attempt is judged unlikely to succeed due to political divisions.

JAMES G. COZZENS
Major, Air Corps

remark of Gen Giles some weeks ago that they were going to get the worst licking they ever had when they tried their new plan. Fooling with Kuter's stuff all day and around to see him late. He was again amiable and I found it not hard to have him get in his secty and we 'together' dictated most of the conference material—certainly a wonderful labor-saving device unless he suddenly realizes that what I had him do was all our work for us. Still, it makes little sense to guess at what he means and then make him correct it.

Tuesday 17 October 1944

. . . It began to develop that there was something in the rumor that Kuter was to do no more conferences—the Navy was mad enough to have the Secretary, Mr Forrestal, write a note to Stimson. Cecil Holland later drafted a cringing reply, but Col Smith's blood was somewhat up and he was promising late to take it to Gen Giles—that this was no time to change from Kuter, for whatever reason because whoever was wrong on the Greenland matter (it was we), who was running this air force? I think he may make it stick; but meanwhile we went up to see Gen Smith,[47] a pleasant little round faced fellow with a snub nose and agreeable grin—I should think about five years my junior. I could see he would do, but I was getting on all right with Kuter and did not wish it to happen. . . .

Wednesday 18 October 1944

. . . It soon developed that Col Smith had won and I went in with the text to sit with Kuter while he made some changes. On the box he rang up Gen Smith and said; Look, I want you to be there and I'll introduce you. I don't want to give them the impression that I am being fired. This seemed to show that the case was indeed that; but Kuter is going on a trip tomorrow, so I phrased up some concluding remarks to make it reasonably graceful. Much scurrying and finally we got off all right at 13.30, with Smith and poor Col Archer, now the Air Engineer. He was earnest and long and dull, but Kuter who had a pencilled note put in front of him—I was sitting at the table to keep the pages straight in case he had to check back—saying *Gen Arnold wants you, the meeting has begun*, pulled out short of the end and I would have to admit that Smith, to whom he turned it over, was much his superior—shrewd, smiling, easy, making them all laugh, while he gave straight short answers and knocked off lightly (and with much judgment) what he did not feel ready to answer. Kuter, though he had improved and I had come to like him, lacked this natural gift. By the end of the afternoon it was plain that the Japs had been fantastically lying about the fleet action off Formosa (we weren't sure until then, and it did seem that they must really have done something when they loaded the teletype with their national holidays and so on) so everyone felt better.

WAR DEPARTMENT
HEADQUARTERS OF THE ARMY AIR FORCES
WASHINGTON

18 October 1944

MEMORANDUM FOR THE CHIEF, OFFICE OF TECHNICAL INFORMATION

Subject: Information from AC/AS Offices.

1. <u>AAF Violation of Uniform Regulations</u>. (Personnel) The Air Provost Marshal conferred with PM of MDW "with regard to violations of uniforms regulations by AAF commissioned personnel in and around Annex #1. The Military District stated that they would be pleased to have the AAF take any steps necessary to correct this condition. An occasional officers' patrol will be assigned to duty at this building." (Assume this was all brought on by apprehension on 12 Oct. of undersigned officer at Union Station in a green shirt).

2. <u>AAF Officer Candidate School Classes</u>. (Personnel) The continental air forces and commands were notified 17 October that in selecting candidates for future AAF, OCS classes preference will be given to applicants who have served overseas. However, "this does not mean that poorly qualified returnees will be selected over outstanding applicants who have not had overseas service." Preference will be given only when qualifications are approximately equal.

3. <u>Tests of JB-2 Flying Bomb</u>. (M&S) Tests of the JB-2 are under way at Eglin Field (my memo, 12 Oct.) The first launching, 12 October, was considered successful and the bomb flew approximately one mile. Development and procurement are being carried on by the ATSC at Wright Field. At Eglin Field the tests are under the AAF Board. AC/AS, OC&R will report the Board's conclusions.

4. <u>Excess Aircraft</u>. (M&S) On 14 October M&S incorporated in its activity report a summary covering four pages of all types of aircraft declared excess and the number so declared up to 11 October. This is the first time this information has been available. Totals are: Excess to AAF (my memo, 2 Aug.) 14,803; Declared Excess by MAC (Air), 13,040; Balance of Inventory of Models under AAF Letter 65-16 Not yet Declared Excess by AAF, 16,843.

5. <u>Status of XB-39</u>. (M&S) (The XB-39 is the B-39 with 4 Allison V-3420-A16 engines instead of R-3350s) Estimated completed date for shopwork remains late October. Engine installations are 95% complete.

SECRET

Empennage has been reinstalled with safety changes incorporated.
First flight date is supposed to be 31 October.

6. _Weary Willie Project._ (M&S) Additional fuss about termin-
ology (my memo, 14 Oct.) nets the following. "It has been decided
to use the term 'Willie' for all projects covering war weary airplanes as robot aircraft. The Willie project control airplanes are
called 'Mothers', the missile airplanes controlled by 'Mothers' are
called 'Babies' and the missile airplanes controlled from the
ground will be called 'Orphans'." (Suggest you now chase me)

7. _Status of GB-7B Bomb._ (M&S) The GB-7B bomb (2000 lb-radar
target-seeker) will be subject to reduced procurement as "no theater
requirement exists at present time" and they are also trying a few
further tests at Wright Field.

8. _Lapel Buttons for WASPS._ (Personnel) Gen. Bevans reports
that "investigation is being made of the possibility of creating
special insignia to be used by WASPS to represent honorable service
with the AAF. Since they are not eligible for the usual discharge
lapel button, it is thought that a special insignia might be devised."

9. _Gas Tests._ (M&S) Tests, no doubt associated with retaliation
plans (my memo, 22 Sept, 2 Oct., 9 Oct.) tests have been conducted
at the Dugway Proving Grounds "to determine suitable concentrations
of H (mustard) by low altitude spray." One phase of the tests developed the fact that two-layer protective clothing now available
provides adequate protection against any field concentration of H
spray likely to be produced with unthickened mustard gas. "Further
work is being done to determine the casualty producing qualities of
thickened mustard when used as a spray."

10. _Status of XP-77._ (This is the all-wood fighter-interceptor)
(M&S) Plane is now at Wright Field, where it will be used to study
the control system "inasmuch as this airplane has the best balance for
stick forces in stick and rudder combination of any of our current
fighters".

11. _Production of Jet Engines._ (M&S) Upon signing of a contract
at present being processed at Wright Field there will be on order a
total of 124 TG-180 engines and 32 TG-100 engines. AAF applications
for these units thus far are:

XB-81	- one each TG-100
XB-43	- two each TG-180
XB-45	- four each TG-180

(The XP-81 is a fighter with combination jet and propeller propulsion. The XB-43 is a medium bomber with 2 jet engines. The XB-45 is a heavy bomber with 4 jet engines)

12. Atlantic City Hotels for AAF. (M&S) The Undersecretary of War has been requested to grant authority for the acquisition of the Madison, Marlboro, Blenheim, Lafayette, Crillon, and Knights of Columbus Hotels, Atlantic City, New Jersey, to provide housing for the personnel being processed by the AAF Personnel Distribution Command.

13. Returned Combat Crew Personnel. (M&S) Representatives of AC/AS, Personnel conferred with representatives of the Air Surgeon "relative to problems posed by enlisted combat crew personnel returned from overseas who are not amiable (sic) to military duties and discipline". It was decided that they should not be discharged on C.D.D. but retained on duty status "until it is finally determined that they are adjusted to normal living or that such adjustment cannot be attained." Further study is being given this matter.

14. Notes from In and Out Log.

a. London, signed Spaatz, 14 Oct. On German jet planes: "There is no evidence to indicate that large numbers of any type are yet in training. It is doubtful if there are more than 40/50 ME 262's and possible 20 ME 163's at present operational..it is not felt GAF is withholding these fighters..but are putting them up piecemeal as they become operational....Because of their great speed both of these fighters present threat to all types of Allied aircraft. However, it appears that Allied fighters can outturn either type. ME 262 is considered most dangerous German jet type and there is evidence that greater emphasis is placed on its production."

JAMES G. COZZENS
Major, Air Corps

Thursday 19 October 1944

. . . I had a great pile of stuff to catch up with on my memoranda—not that it is a full time job, but when I began to count I was astonished or even aghast to realize that every day this week I had sent Johnny or some one up to get me a ham sandwich and some malted milk for lunch. . . .

Friday 20 October 1944

. . . I stirred around in the morning, bothering a Col Durant and Gen Bevans about an R&R from Gen Smith which, fantastically, wanted something written up on AAF policy and so on for the use of people when they were out of it after the war—that is, so they could correct any popular misconceptions. Gen Bevans (also in battle jacket) said somewhat shortly that he thought the idea was foolish (as I did myself) but they would cooperate. I went down then and decided to take steps to let the whole thing drop, as it was unlikely Gen Smith or anyone else would remember it a week from now. . . .

Saturday 21 October 1944

. . . Mostly busy with a long memorandum and putting off the AAF policy matter. We had a quiet day, though it appeared that Gen Smith would indeed expect his conference to be got up for him, but beginning Monday as usual, so we would go crazy for two days.

Monday 23 October 1944

. . . We got started on the conference and I talked to a meek and really nice little BG named Reuben Hood who had been in charge of the Air Service Command stuff in China and who was to say a few words. He was sitting lost and forlorn in Gen Wilson's office and agreed with alacrity. I spent the rest of the time getting together stuff from A2 where the Far Eastern division under a very energetic Lt Col Martin and a nervous and somewhat jerk-like Capt Chandler did much of the work so we had things fairly well under control. . . .

Tuesday 24 October 1944

. . . We got down to the rat race and I managed to get a text out by 3. It was then supposed that Gen Giles would do the thing, which was painful as I saw I would have to rewrite almost everything into words of one syllable, but we took a chance anyway; and for once were rewarded. I went down with Col Smith to see Gen Smith and while we were there word came through that he, not Giles would have to take it. He was amenable and even gave up his idea of picking a fight with the Navy over land-based vs carrier planes when Rex led him a little. He had said, reading an

WAR DEPARTMENT
HEADQUARTERS OF THE ARMY AIR FORCES
WASHINGTON

19 October 1944

SPECIAL MEMORANDUM FOR THE CHIEF, OFFICE OF TECHNICAL INFORMATION

Subject: Current Cases in Special Investigations Division,
Office of the Air Inspector.

At General Jones' direction, Colonel Scott, Chief of the Special
Investigations Division, has supplied me with information on his
pending cases. There are about 150, but most of them concern individuals and would be unlikely to make a large-scale stink or get
into the papers. Those that Colonel Scott feels might have an angle
of interest to the Chief, OTI, are briefly summarized below. Those
that the Air Inspector views with special concern are marked with
an asterisk.

*1. Conditions at Richmond Army Air Base Guardhouse, Richmond,
Virginia. Several complaints were received regarding mistreatment of
prisoners in this guardhouse. Most of these were substantiated by an
investigation, including insufficient and poor quality food, placing
prisoners on bread and water diets without proper authorization or
cause, dirty bedding and no blankets, extreme cold (at times there was
no fuel) and restriction to a bare cell for minor infraction of rules.
Corrective action taken.

2. Indiscriminate Firing Near Mandeville, Louisiana. Several
complaints have been received, some through Congressional channels of
danger to civilians in this area from stray bullets. One 50-calibre
bullet from a machine gun firing at a tow target went through the roof
of a civilian's house (Percy Jenkins) and landed about two feet from
where Mrs. Jenkins was sitting. Action is under way to eliminate the
danger to civilians in this area.

*3. Pollock Army Air Field, Alexandria, Louisiana, Sanitary Conditions.
Two complaints from constituents living near this base were forwarded
by Representative Allen regarding the sewage from the Air Base being
turned loose into the creek near their homes; that the odor is very bad;
mosquitoes are breeding and that the water is unfit for farm animals.
It is surprising that more complaints have not been received inasmuch
as investigation disclosed complaints were entirely justifiable. Septic
tanks at the field are not adequate to take care of the sewage. Inasmuch
as this is a small base, with very poor housing facilities, it has been
recommended that this field be abandoned without delay. This recommendation is under consideration by The Air Inspector's office before
submission to higher authority.

CONFIDENTIAL

4. Racial Trouble.

a. Mutiny at Herbert Smart Airport, Macon, Georgia, 457th Aviation Squadron. On 11 May 1944 the 457th Aviation Squadron collectively went on a "sit-down" strike", refusing to obey a direct order of the Squadron Commander to meet formation or go on duty call, in resentment of the Commander's reducing in rank a First Sergeant and transferring into the organization a new First Sergeant. The matter was brought to the attention of the Air Forces as a result of letter written by the "Members of the 457th Aviation Squadron" addressed to Secretary of War; Commanding General, Army Air Forces; Commanding officer, Patterson Field, and Commanding Officer, Herbert Smart Airport.

b. Racial Discrimination at Nashville Army Air Center (Hospital). Allegation sustained as to discrimination existing in posting of sigh that colored people would ride only in rear of bus (furnished by Army). This, of course, was in violation of War Department regulations. There was said to be "voluntary segregation" in the post theater. Commanding Officer of the base, and higher echelons, are aware of racial unrest at this base and apparently are taking adequate measures to correct the situation.

c. Racial Discrimination at the following Bases: Tyndall Field, Florida; Davis-Monthan Field; Bryan Field, Texas; Clovis, N. Mex.; Bolling Field, D. C.; MacDill Field, Fla; Hammer Field, Calif; Tuskegee, Alabama.

If C.O. at Nashville has found any "adequate measures" perhaps he'd better tell the CGAAF what they are.

5. Mistreatment of Prisoners (Colored and White) at McChord Field, Tacoma, Washington. Three prisoners were beaten and there was general abuse of prisoners by profanity, threats, use of leg irons and unusual punishments for minor offenses. Responsible officer is being reclassified and other corrective action taken.

6. Crash of A-26 Airplane 1/2 Mile South of Portland, Maine, Municipal Airport. 15 civilians were killed, property in trailer camp damaged by fire and otherwise, 22 civilians injured and 2 AAF personnel killed. Crash occurred on 11 July. Matter now under investigation.

7. Alleged Restrictions at Kelly Field. This concerns enlisted men not being permitted to live off the post with their wives (many of the wives are employed by Air Service Command installations there) and only 50% of the men being allowed off the post in the evenings. Several complaints have been received by General Arnold's office. Matter is currently under investigation. Restrictions are reputed to be causing low morale at the base.

8. **Accidental Drowning of Pfc** ███████████████, Truax Field, Wisconsin. The peculiar circumstances surrounding the death of Pfc ████████ caused the father of this enlisted man to go to his Congressman (Rooney) and request an investigation. Investigation was made and the following conclusions were reached: ███████ was believed to be a homo-sexual, had approached two enlisted men and some scuffling ensued. They were near the edge of the water. ███████ fell in, apparently after the scuffling had stopped and while he was a few feet away from the two enlisted men. Death was considered accidental. Two enlisted men have not been identified. The Madison Police do not consider the case closed and have assigned detectives to it.

9. **Hunting on Laredo Aerial Gunnery Range, Texas.** (360,000 acres leased for exclusive use as a gunnery range). This subject has caused considerable correspondence between the War Department and Senator Connally, and the Governor of Texas. Citizens feared excessive amounts of wild game, particularly deer, would be killed if hunting were permitted. Hunting was prohibited for a time but order was later rescinded. Evidence indicates State Game Laws are not being violated. Some question also arose regarding grazing of cattle on this range. Information has recently come to the Air Inspector's office that a Mr. ████████ of Laredo, who is presumed to be the ███████████████████████████ for Texas, has secured a copy of a confidential report of investigation of this matter. Recent inquiry from one of Senator Connally's constituents asks if this is true. If it is, he wants a copy for the Game Commission of Texas. This aspect of the matter is currently under investigation.

*10. **Contracts with Rolls-Royce.** (my memo, 28 Sept.) Pursuant to a directive of Chief of the Air Staff, an investigation was conducted into AAF contracts with Rolls-Royce, Inc., which disclosed that $17,000,000 in Air Corps contracts placed with Rolls-Royce were not negotiated in best interests of the U. S. Government. Recommendations were made for thorough discussion of the matter with the British followed by appropriate steps for renegotiation and revision of contracts. This being accomplished by Ass't Chief of Air Staff, Materiel and Services. Recommendations for disciplinary action were not approved by the Air Staff. (Gen. Jones is not satisfied and has sent the whole matter to the Inspector General)

11. **Alleged Burning and Dumping of Gasoline at Gowen Field, Boise, Idaho.** This subject was publicized during the period 9-12 September 1944 through newspaper articles published locally (Boise, Spokane, Denver) and nationwide releases through Associated Press, quoting a resident of Boise, Idaho, as having stated that Army authorities at Gowen Field were burning sub-standard grade gasoline. Representative Compton White proposed a Congressional investigation. Colonel Kane refuted these charges in an article in the Statesman, 10 September 1944. An investigation was made by the Second Air Force and it was determined that

the only gasoline burned is a low-test gasoline used for cleaning purposes and this is burned only after it has become so adulterated as to have no further value for cleaning. (Note: Investigation did reveal that some salvageable oil was being burned and other salvageable items of brass, lumber, etc. destroyed. Thus far, these items have not been given any publicity and action has been taken to prevent the continuance of this practice).

12. Aircraft Accident near Glenwood Springs, Colorado. Accident occurred on 18 November 1943 but wreck was not found until July 1944. Later a sheep-herder complained that he had been in the area and there were parts of human bodies lying around, skulls with hair still on them, etc. Another party was sent out to recover and properly dispose of these remains and to burn the area. (there have been several cases like this.)

*13. Misuse of Government Material, Marana Army Air Base, Arizona. Investigation substantiated allegations that government property was being misused. 22 civilians complained to Secretary of War. ███████ ████████████████ has been relieved and further inquiry is being made as to additional action to be taken.

*14. ████████ Air Depot, ███████████████████ (my memo, 19 Sept) Three complaints through U. S. Attorney at ███████ - concerning (1) disposition of surplus property; illegal labor contract and construction of Officer's Club and Bar. The U. S. Attorney has not yet let Gen. Jones know what he proposes to do, but it probably won't be pleasant.

                          J. G. COZZENS
                          Major, Air Corps

ADDRESS REPLY TO
HEADQUARTERS OF THE ARMY AIR FORCES
WAR DEPARTMENT
WASHINGTON, D. C.

WAR DEPARTMENT
HEADQUARTERS OF THE ARMY AIR FORCES
WASHINGTON

19 October 1944

MEMORANDUM FOR THE CHIEF, OFFICE OF TECHNICAL INFORMATION

Subject: Information from AC/AS Offices.

1. C.A.P. Affair. (Plans) Capt. Green of AC/AS Plans told me this morning that the recommendations of the Board of Officers (my memo, 14 October) had been adopted by the Air Staff. Gen. Giles attended the New York meeting, 16 October, and is supposed to have confined his remarks to suitable applesauce on the great achievements of CAP pilots in our hour of need. Among statements presented to the Board of Officers, according to Capt. Green who was present, were indignant charges of favoritism against Col. ████. It was claimed that CAP activities in ████ (the Col's home state) got 'everything', while those in Alabama and other inconsequential (and incidentally, Democratic) command areas got 'nothing'. It was reported, and seems unquestionably true, that there was a certain amount of regular funny business about providing new planes. Cut-backs and insurance rebates were involved. All CAP bookkeeping was much neglected and there is no record which will account for the disappearance of several million dollars. The Board was shown a letter from Mr. Beck to General Welsh making other unspecified charges against Col. ████, but this letter was held to be off the record. Capt. Green thinks the fundamental trouble lay in an enthusiastically uncritical acceptance by the high command of any plan that seemed to show civilian interest in aviation. The WASP program would be another example of the same thing. The Air Inspector is starting the investigation recommended by the Board. It would probably be well to keep in touch with this because the factional row is very bitter and plenty of people could, and no doubt will, tell their interesting troubles to the papers.

2. German Composite Aircraft. (OC&R) "Investigation disclosed that suitable weather and 'close following' (1 mile) by directing aircraft were prerequisites for successful German operations. Willie projects (my memoranda, 14, 18 October) appear to have greater tactical advantages and Willie weapons can be used in this war, some this winter. Recommended no further consideration be given composite aircraft projects at this time."

3. Excess Aircraft. (OC&R) An R&R to AC/AS, M&S points out that delays have been encountered in the disposal of excess and surplus aircraft. The indication is that this matter, which had assumed

serious proportions last summer (my memo, 2 August) is assuming proportions again. "The domestic air forces and commands have been required to store and maintain aircraft as long as three months after they were declared excess. This situation has required the organizations to expend excessive man hours on surplus airplanes." (More to the point, it undoubtedly means that once again hundreds of aircraft are standing in rows around the country with resulting reports about AAF waste and inefficiency) Recommended by OC&R Commitments Division:

"a. A more aggressive policy be followed in surveying aircraft of doubtful value, especially combat types.

b. The Air Technical Service Command or the appropriate civilian agency store and maintain those aircraft which have been declared excess until final disposition is made."

(All this was supposed to have been arranged by the Aircraft Distribution Control Branch, M&S - my memo, 2 September) OC&R points out to M&S "that, after the defeat of Germany, this problem will undoubtedly become much more acute."

4. Soldier Voting. (Personnel) "The Coordinator for Soldier Voting, Office of the Secretary of War, who has just returned from a tour of the seven service commands informally reported excellent cooperation between service commands and the AAF installations on Soldier Voting matters, and that all Soldier Voting procedures at AAF installations had been executed in a highly satisfactory and efficient manner."

5. Notes from In and Out Log.

a. Moscow, signed Deane, 16 Oct. Reports a meeting with Marshal Astakhov, Chief of Soviet Civil Aviation. USSR agrees in principal to establishment of northern air line route but the Marshal didn't want to put anything on paper. For the southern route via Cairo the Marshal wanted the U.S. to hand over 5 C-54's. Deane said they were not available. There was also some bickering about C-47's for the Teheran run. Deane: "I think they are most anxious to get service started and recommend you (Arnold) give me favorable replies."

b. Kharagpur from LeMay 16 Oct. Mission 11 results. "First formation over Ucito took strike photos which show center of bombing pattern approximately 1,700 feet to left and 500 feet short of aiming point. Excellent results are shown by strike photos of later formations."

c. Stockholm, signed Johnson to State Dept. 12 Oct.
"The Department is urgently asked by Swedish Foreign Office to
inform press representatives confidentially...in order to put
an end to attacks on SKF, that all shipments of ball and roller
bearings...to Germany have been ended by SKF voluntarily." (!)
It is emphasized that "there must not be any publicity with
regard to decision of SKF."

d. COM 3rd Fleet, 17 Oct. "On 16th Cabot and Cowpens..
shot down 50 out of 60 planes attacking the cripples ... enemy
fleet reluctant and enemy air forces seem to be having trouble
scraping up attack crews. All 3rd Fleet ships reported by radio
Tokyo as sunk have now been salvaged and are retiring towards (sic)
the enemy."

e. Hollandia, signed Kenny, 17 Oct. Escorting P-47's
on Balikpapah strike; "Mission produced serious pilot fatigue
and must be considered special mission until more pilot comfort
can be incorporated in P-47 airplane. Capability of P-47 exceeds
capability of pilot to perform frequent missions to maximum
radius of action."

f. London, signed Knerr, 17 Oct. A long message on
"heavy bomber losses due to hydromatic propeller feathering
difficulties." Reports from crews of shot-down B-17's indicated that
it proved impossible to feather the prop in the case of 70 out
of 167 damaged engines (on 121 aircraft). Operation Research
Division opines: "Feathering probably is still the biggest single
item left for improvement in losses."

g. Rio de Janeiro sighed Donnelley to State Dept. 9 Oct.
Reports general aviation equipment and surplus aircraft are being
offered prospective buyers in Brazil by Canadian Government. Wants
to know if U.S. surplusses could not be made available "to protect
competitive position."

J. G. COZZENS
Major, Air Corps

ADDRESS REPLY TO
HEADQUARTERS OF THE ARMY AIR FORCES
WAR DEPARTMENT
WASHINGTON, D. C.

WAR DEPARTMENT
HEADQUARTERS OF THE ARMY AIR FORCES
WASHINGTON

21 October 1944

MEMORANDUM FOR THE CHIEF, OFFICE OF TECHNICAL INFORMATION

Subject: Information from AC/AS Offices.

1. <u>Post-War AAF Commissions.</u> (Personnel) Memorandum to Chief of Staff recommending the appointment of 7,000 officers in the Regular Army Air Corps was submitted 20 Oct. to Gen. Giles for signature. This seems to be the final action on Gen. Kuter's suggestion (my memo. 28 Sept.) that 5,000 such commissions should be made available so that the post-war AAF would not lose the services of a certain number of its talented amateurs of the moment.

2. <u>Education of Career Air Officers.</u> (OC&R) The draft proposal submitted by Post-war Plans Division for future training of air officers (my memo, 25 August) has resulted in an AAF Board report which reached OC&R 10 October. The AAF Board recommends:

    a. Undergraduate Training.
      (1) No compulsory military training requirement for appointment to 'Combined Service Academy'.
      (2) A 2 year course at a 'Combined Service Academy'
      (3) A short flying adaptability course to determine which cadets should be selected for the Air Academy.
      (4) A 2 year Air Academy course containing the flying training necessary for a rating if it is determined by further study that this is practical.
      (5) A commission in the Air Forces at the end of the above 4 years training.
      (6) A fifth year of flying training if it is determined that it is not practical to include flying training in the 2 year Air Academy course.
    b. Post-graduate Education. (The Board wants these recommendations "effected" as soon as possible so that they may be applied to present officers in the AAF.)
      (1) Squadron officers course - 4 months - to be attended between the first and third year of service.
      (2) Tactical officers course - 6 months - between the fifth and ninth year of service.
      (3) Advanced officers course - 9 months - between the ninth and fifteenth year of service.
      (4) Combined services staff course - 9/12 months - to be limited to selected graduates of Advanced course who have had 15 years service.

3. <u>Discharge of AAF Officers</u>. (Personnel)Gen. Bevans reports that AC/AS Personnel has been asked to review the draft of a War Department circular on the "relief from active duty of officers for personal hardships". General Bevans feels that the "basic policy to be adopted should be that relief from active duty for hardship should be authorized only when the hardship is of permanent nature." If the hardship isn't permanent, emergency leave or special leave ought to do. "Officers being relieved from active duty for hardship reasons of a permanent nature will normally be completely separated regardless of age." At the same time, Sec. 5, AR 615-360 (Discharge of Enlisted Personnel) is being revised "to recognize other types of hardship beyond purely financial destitution." The General adds, somewhat cryptically; "The prime underlying purpose behind this is recognition that hardship cases in which female military personnel are involved are sometimes authentically based on other than financial reasons." (Suggested meaning: Love, Love, Love).

4. <u>CDD Discharges</u>. (Personnel) AC/AS Personnel has been conferring with Psychological Branch, Research Division, Office of the Air Surgeon, about CDD discharges of returned enlisted combat crew members who have been given the diagnosis of "psychoneurosis severe" This seems to tie in with conferences M&S had with the Air Surgeon (my memo, 18 October) on air crew members who were "not amiable to military duties and discipline". The Air Surgeon is engaged on a study of 900 psychoneurosis severe cases and expects to have it ready in two weeks. Further consideration will follow.

5. <u>XCG-16 Glider Project</u>. (OC&R) A board under Brig. Gen. William D. Old will convene to evaluate the XCG-16 Glider Program "from beginning to end starting with the original proposal and ending with production possibilities and tactical suitability." The board is expected to reach a definite decision "as to whether or not the XCG-16 Glider project has sufficient merit to be continued and whether or not this glider can be effectively employed in this war."

6. <u>Camp SpringsAAF</u> (Air Inspector) Senator Wherry complained to the Air Inspector that "the site of Camp Springs was selected despite prevalent fogs because of the fact that a man by the name of ████ had an option on the land" (Camp Springs is to be the great Air Force base in this area after the war; my memos, 11 Aug, 22 Sept) Col. Scott says: "Inquiry reflects there is no reference to the name of ████ in any of the files pertaining to Camp Springs. From meteorological and smoke conditions reports, the Camp Springs site compares favorably with the othre three air fields in the vicinity of Washington. Foregoing information supplied I&I Division, stating it is not believed possible to determine whether or not 'a man named ████ exerted any undue influence upon the War Department, or was prompted by ulterior moves, if he did so. Suggestion made that if Senator Wherry cares to furnish the identity of his informants, a more thorough investigation can be conducted."

7. **AAF in Troop Basis, 1 October 1944 Revision.**

CATEGORY	AUTHORIZED STRENGTH AS OF 30 SEPT. 1944	TROOP BASIS STRENGTH AS OF 30 JUNE 1945
Combat Air Forces	524,154	534,352
Air Corps Services	217,135	231,399
Misc Operating Personnel	129,375	167,859
Arms and Services	319,535	323,644
Students and Replacements	370,615	354,025
Z. I. Allotment	748,412	704,463
TOTAL ARMY AIR FORCES	2,309,226	2,315,742

(Col. J.J. Ladd -4563)

8. **Notes from In and Out Log.**

a. **Versailles, signed Eisenhower, 19 Oct.** Reports that Gen. DeGaulle wants to withdraw black troops in 9th Colonial Infantry Division (about 2/3 total strength) and replace them with personnel drawn from French Forces of the Interior. The blacks will be sent to garrison duty along the Mediterranean coast "where they will ultimately be employed in the constitution of units likely to take part in 1945 operations in the Far East."

b. **Kharagpur, signed LaMay, 19 Oct.** "Observation of last three missions in forward area shows results of particular importance to you. Every airplane which aborted, and three lost operationally, due the engine or prop governor failing. Airplanes loaded around 132,000 lbs. operating off rough muddy slow runways and taking off using full emergency war power from 5 to 8 minutes...may be cause of short life on engines.....Command has experienced further difficulties in attempting to feather engines." (See note from Knerr, my memo19 Oct)

c. **Wright Field, signed Knudsen, 19 Oct.** "This command has requested Allison Division to accelerate production of type I-40 engines (jet) as rapidly as possible, reaching a production of 1100 engines per month."

d. **Southwest Pacific, signed MacArthur, 20 Oct.** "Strategically enemy seemed caught unawares, apparently in anticipation of attack southward. His Mindanao forces are already practically isolated and are no longer an immediate factor in the campaign."

e. **To Deane, from Arnold, 17 Oct.** "Not enthusiastic is our reaction" to Deane's report (my memo log a. 19 Oct) of discussion with Marshal Astakhov. Soviet objection to northern route regarded as "political rather than military". Deane was right to refuse C-54's. "However, we will play along...in hopes of improving services in the future."

f. <u>To Ravens, signed Bissell, 19 Oct.</u> The price of the 70 P-47's wanted by Sweden will be approximately $100,000. apiece, with standard armament and radio equipment, including modification and delivery charges. (These are P-47D's)

g. <u>Versailles, from Eisenhower, 20 Oct.</u> "The only French authority with whom we can deal is the present Council of Ministers and we <u>urge</u> that every support be given to it, including formal recognition as the Provisional Government of France." (A Zone of the Interior, to be administered by the frogs, will be set up during the next few days and Eisenhower would like such recognition to be "simultaneous with the announcement.")

J. G. COZZENS
Major, Air Corps

WAR DEPARTMENT
HEADQUARTERS OF THE ARMY AIR FORCES
WASHINGTON

23 October 1944

MEMORANDUM FOR THE CHIEF, OFFICE OF TECHNICAL INFORMATION

Subject: Information from AC/AS Offices.

1. <u>Transfer of AAF Personnel to Foot Army</u>. (Personnel) In selecting the AAF personnel being transferred at the direction of the War Department to AGF (5000 a month during October, November, December) the following principles will be observed:

    a. Only personnel with SSN's common to the AGF and the AAF, or surplus, will be selected.

    b. No enlisted man will be reduced as a result of transfer, "Nor will promotions be made to fill vacancies until personnel in exchange has been received from the AGF"

    c. Personnel in any of these categories will not be transferred:

        Former AC Enlisted Reserve Corps,
        Former Air Crew Trainees,
        Those who entered service for express purpose of air
            crew or combat crew training,
        Voluntary inductees,
        Volunteers for flying Regular Army Air Corps,
        Those eligible for discharge under current WD directives,
        Enlisted men under charges,
        Those attending factory or technical schools to become
          AAF specialists,
        Graduates of technical schools,
        Returnees from overseas,
        Personnel in committed units.

More or less in this connection were discussions with G-3, WDGS on the matter of the AAF furnishing 700 to 1,500 negro enlisted men to the AGF for Infantry replacements. The idea was to complete a regiment of negro infantry. G-3 was told that "we had planned to use quite a number of negro enlisted men and to activate a number of Aviation Engineer Battalions. There is actually no surplus negro personnel in the AAF. However, it would be agreeable to the AAF to furnish any number of negro personnel up to 1,500, or even more, as replacements for a part of the 15,000 white, physically disqualified personnel that are being sent to the AAF from the GAF."

2. <u>Recruiting for Post-war Air Force</u>. (Personnel) AC/AS Personnel has prepared for the signature of the Chief of the Air Staff a "program" to facilitate recruiting for the post-war Air Force. "Selective Service Act prohibits recruiting for the permanent establishment and this division proposes to the War Department that the advantages of the Army as a career for the enlisted man be brought to the attention of all AAF enlisted personnel through information material, posters, etc."

3. <u>Unsatisfactory Messing Conditions in CBI</u> (Personnel) General Bevans reports that he has approved grades for seven Mess Teams that are to be sent to CBI theater to instruct Chinese personnel in AAF messes. General Jones, the Air Inspector, personally examined CBI messing conditions last August and found them "disgraceful" and the Chinese in question "unspeakably filthy" (my memo, 9 Sept). It ought to be a real source of satisfaction to those who eat in these messes to know that barely two months later the Air Staff got around to approving grades, and in a few months more mess teams may actually turn up and start doing something.

4. <u>Use for Chaplains</u>. (Personnel) AC/AS Personnel notes with satisfaction that "On October 19 a War Department press release stated: 'Air Chaplains to Visit Families of AAF Personnel Killed in Action'. On October 20, after the press release had been read by officers of the ASF, this matter was called to the attention of the Chief of Chaplains by the CG, ASF, asking what was to be done by them in regard to the same situation. Apparently the Air Forces placed into effect a new idea ahead of the Ground and Service Forces." (i.e., we got there firstest with the mostest.)

5. <u>AAF Personnel in Switzerland</u>. (Intelligence) General Hodges reports that he conferred with the Under Secretary of War "relative to the disposition of aircraft to the Swiss. It was indicated that if a quid pro quo (Latin) such as release of interned airmen could be accomplished by agreeing to sell the interned aircraft and equipment, there would be no objection from the Under Secretary's office."

6. <u>Tests of Navy Anti-G Suits</u>. (OC&R) Tests were made in an F6F-5 (Grumman Hellcat) on pull-out readings of between 6 and 7 G. Pilot experienced no ill effects. In 20 minutes simulated combat with another F6F, pilot equipped with the anti-G suit was able to out-maneuver the other pilot at all times and remain in firing position. "Very noticeable in this suit is fact that automatically applied pressure creeps up on pilot through the thigh regions instead of suddenly slamming tight around the stomach. In sustained pull-outs a heavy 'gray-out' is experienced, but only if the pull-out is held for some time." The bladder equipment in the suit is made of nylon instead of rubber and can be washed or dry cleaned. All navy pilots reported much in favor of it. OC&R says that they are making an investigation of "the desirability of this suit in comparison with AAF equipment."

7. <u>Some Obliteration at Brest.</u> (OC&R) General Fickel, making
an initial survey for the ETO Evaluation Board on bomb damage to
Brest, reported 5 October that damage to the submarine pens was
"Practically nil." There were 9 hits by 12,000 pound bombs, of which
4 penetrated the roof. Other bombs had no effect at all. However, the
destruction of the town was "practically complete." In the town
itself Gen. Fickel estimates that "only about 31 buildings" can be
made habitable and that over 50% of the buildings in surrounding areas
were damaged beyond repair.

8. <u>Post-War Military Establishment.</u> (OC&R) AFRAL prepared estimates of aircraft requirements for the post-war air force on two
bases:

     a. <u>War Dept. Plan No. 1</u> which involves 75 tactical groups
and assumes universal military training.

     b. <u>War Dept. Plan No. 2</u> providing for 103 groups, without
universal military training.

Under Plan 1, the Air Force would consist of approximately 12,000
aircraft and require annual aircraft production of approximately 2,500
articles. Under Plan 2 there would be 14,600 aircraft with annual
production requirement of 3,200. (It will be interesting to see whether
aircraft manufacturers will or will not favor universal military training.)

9. <u>Eager Beaver in 13th Air Force.</u> (Air Inspector) A Lt. ████
████ felt called on to give out the news "that he was ordered to
take several officers on a fishing trip at his overseas station in an
emergency rescue boat." However, "Investigation revealed that use of
the boats for recreational purposes was standard procedure for morale
purposes, providing such uses did not interfere with primary purpose
of the boats" (and they could use something for morale purposes in
that AF – my memo, 22 Aug & OAR No. 6, Air Surgeon). Investigating
officer suggested dinging Lt. ████ under 104th AW, but the CG, 13th
Air Force, tempered justice with mercy and decided an admonition would
be sufficient "in view of the fact that Lt. ████ had been motivated
by a desire to correct what he thought was improper use of Govt.
property." (Sooner or later the Lt. will probably learn not to think
in this army)

10. <u>Notes from In and Out Log.</u>
     a. <u>Quarry Heights (CG) signed Brett 21 Oct</u>. On the situation
in Guatemala: Rebelling forces flanking Guatemalan Air Force Area.
Pan American ceased operations (one pilot seriously wounded, one
mechanic killed) and evacuated personnel to US Army Air base. Military
attache in Guatemala was instructed that it was most inadvisable to
consider giving up base "due to complete loss of prestige and valuable
property" and was promised, if needed to protect "US Govt. property
and vital communications center", one fully armed company of Continental
Infantry accompanied by bombardment aircraft". (Marshall replied to
Brett 21 Oct. that he would send no such thing as we wanted no trouble
with the Spics. 22 Oct., the Mil. Attache said things were quieting
down.)

b. <u>SHAEF Versailles, Book Message from Strong, 20 Oct.</u>
A long counter-intelligence summary, promised as a weekly feature
henceforth. <u>Espionage</u>: "There remain still to be captured in France
and Belgium a few agents with WT communications but fact that German
intelligence still asking for simple tactical information which
efficient net work could easily supply suggests value of this remainder
not considerable." <u>Sabotage</u>: "German sabotage plans on a larger
scale than we anticipated. Buried sabotage dumps widely distributed.
13 have been discovered. Presumed for future use when enemy agents
could return to them." <u>Political Factors</u>: "It is evident that the
enemy has not yet lost all hope of resurrecting elements of the
Fascist Fifth Column." <u>France</u>: Political tension high in southwest
where 25% of FFI are Communists and are joined up with an estimated
20,000 Spanish republican maquis. <u>Belgium</u>: "By withholding recognition
from some groups have been cooperative but not unified as in France
or Belgium. Dutch police have not played the important role of the
police in France and Belgium."

c. <u>London, signed Winant, 18 Oct.</u> A long message on "Increasing uneasiness evidenced in British aviation circles that fundamental difference of opinion exists between US and GB covering degree
of economic control over international air routes."

d. <u>Caserta, signed Kirk, 19 Oct.</u> Reports Sofia "terribly
damaged", and that Gen. Hall's people are being given quite a run-around
by Red Gen. Berezov who said he had no instructions from Moscow and
in general didn't know nothing. British mission under Oxley reported
similar "polite but not warm" relations with the Russians.

                              J. G. COZZENS
                              Major, Air Corps

evasive answer of mine, Christ Jesus, who is running us, the Navy Department? I could see he would roundly relish a nice row. Our Capt McClung came back at noon from the fighter plane business with the Navy where he had had a wonderful time. They gave him, with no check out, a F6F Grumman to fly and an anti-G suit to wear. He came in to tell us while I was eating a sandwich for lunch and I was again surprised (how often I have been) to find that like most pilots (perhaps part of the dumb as a pilot business) far from being cocky and despising the desk officers, he regarded us with a sort of temperate but genuine awe, and liked our company or conversation. I went over to Plans late in the afternoon to catch up with the Log when we had the good news from Gen Smith and saw an officer talking to a few others. We exchanged a stare and it proved to be Charlie Bond, now a chicken col, just back from the Russian operation. I was surprised again by the warmth with which he said; For God's sake, what are you doing here?—the very remark I was making. Deserting Gen Fairchild and some others he came over full of warmth, as though I were an old buddy of his, causing both the Gen and Major Berg to stare appreciatively too. It occurred to me that for psychological reasons of their own they like to keep hold of people who do not fly, getting some kind of reassurance out of it to balance against their own vaguely shocking and astonishing lives.

Wednesday 25 October 1944

. . . Spence was asleep on the cot in our room when I came in at 7.30 but the B-29 mission seemed somewhat overshadowed by the fleet action in the Sulu Sea or wherever it was. On the ticker the Tokyo radio was going good and no matter how many times they do it, it still gives you pause. There was no other news until ten. The conference business was so easily settled that I felt almost at loss—10.30 Wednesday morning and everything done. As expected, Gen Smith managed the conference well, his little pug-nosed face pleasant and his manner easy, humorous, but also soberly authoritative. We were somewhat harassed in the afternoon later. . . . There was nobody there but Holland and me and all kinds of nonsense coming up—including a message of congratulation from Arnold to Spaatz on winning the German war, if and when we did.

Thursday 26 October 1944

. . . I found I was a little wrong about the conference going well yesterday since the *Washington Post* had picked up its story from a vague answer of Gen Smith's to a question about atomic bombs and announced that it was 'revealed' that we were preparing them.[48] We had a desperate scramble all morning to get hold of Miss Southworth, who was over at the Navy taking something, to find out what he had said actually. We finally got her transcript notes and Johnny, seemingly proving that she was quite a bright girl and had profited by her course, succeeded in finding and mostly reading off the machine symbols—however, we had to have it exactly and Miss S didn't turn up until 1 pm. It was hard to figure out why the upset, since he had in fact said nothing and the article said little more, and God knows like everyone else we have certainly been working on it. This was hardly over when Holland in agitation due to a call from Rex in NY asked us all to turn to on some stuff Chamberlin (who was home sick) had been supposed to prepare for a presentation by Gen Arnold to the Joint Chiefs of Staff on how wonderful the air force—an essentially idiotic project that probably had some connection with Gen Eaker's presence and a persistent little shrimp of a chicken col. . . . At any rate, Col Bright's section in intelligence (he and his Major Marks, heading it are prime fat-heads) was not ready with the stuff but we all sat and struggled late. . . .

Friday 27 October 1944

. . . The conference business went a bit further in the form of a confidential release from Gen Surles to all editors pointing out that the AAF spokesman spoke from his own ignorance (all this quite sharply phrased) and it was requested that no more be made of the subject or incident. Holland brought in word with it that Giles himself would take the next meeting and all I had to do was figure out what it would be on. . . .

Saturday 28 October 1944

. . . I was busy all day getting together a memorandum which seemed to run to four pages. . . .

Monday 30 October 1944

. . . I was engaged with the stuff for the Wednesday conference which Giles is resolved to take himself and spent some time with Col Clarke in Stat Control. He has seemed to me, and he seems to me, of considerably less than average intelligence—an absurd, puzzle-headed, grimacing and gesticulating rather flabby and not-too-little, gnome who is always correcting his figures and laughing at his own lamentable jokes and grinning and writhing behind his gray moustache, so it astounded me to hear a young major of his named Blake, a serious pointed-faced youth with glasses, observe that the old man—Clarke—was really a genius. I thought it a joke in somewhat doubtful taste, and was about to snigger—Clarke had ducked out a moment—when I saw Blake meant it. I hardly knew what to say except, oh yes. . . .

Tuesday 31 October 1944

. . . Gen Giles' stuff finally got done about 1 pm and when Smith took it to him he made little or no objection, which was a relief, though no doubt we will have some

ADDRESS REPLY TO
HEADQUARTERS OF THE ARMY AIR FORCES
WAR DEPARTMENT
WASHINGTON, D. C.

WAR DEPARTMENT
HEADQUARTERS OF THE ARMY AIR FORCES
WASHINGTON

29 October 1944

MEMORANDUM FOR THE CHIEF, OFFICE OF TECHNICAL INFORMATION

Subject: Information from AC/AS Offices.

1. <u>Action Under AW 48</u>. (Air Judge Advocate) Reports that
the language of the WD circular that "attempts to set forth the
provisions" for disposition of officers returned to the U.S.
after court martial to await action under AW 48 (Provides that
there must be confirmation by the President of any court martial
sentence imposed on a general officer; or any that involves dismissal of any officer or cadet; or any sentence of death, except
in time of war for murder, rape, mutiny, desertion, or espionage)
"is so difficult, ambiguous and confusing, as a matter of law"
that nobody can make head or tail of it. The AJA requests that
he be allowed to draft something somebody can understand.

2. <u>Tactical Availability of B-32</u>. (OC&R) Gen. Echols has
concurred in the suggestion that the first forty B-32 airplanes
(to be delivered to the Training Command) be stripped, but he
stipulates that all aircraft thereafter be as fully combat modified as possible. (From material on the B-32 gathered by a Board
meeting two weeks ago, Gen. Arnold reached a decision to go ahead
with the production of the B-32, after all. OC&R, Commitments,
(Bombardments Section , Col. Bronson) was not informed of the
reasons for this decision. Gen. Kuter stated to me definitely
about three weeks ago that all idea of further production had been
given up.)

3. <u>Glider Training for Power Pilots</u>. (OC&R) Complementing
the scheme to train all glider pilots to be airplane drivers (my
memo, 5 October) it is now proposed that all pilot personnel assigned
to Troop Carrier Command be given glider training "within the I
Troop Carrier Command after V-E Day". Gen. Gross' recommendations:
> <u>a</u>. Continue glider schools at the present production
> rate of 150 per month. Limit eligibility for glider
> training to power pilots graduated from advanced flying
> schools.
> <u>b</u>. After V-E Day, transfer the responsibility for glider
> training to the I Troop Carrier Command. Continue pro-
> duction rate of 150 per month, but limit eligibility for
> such training to Troop Carrier pilots assigned to Troop
> Carrier units available for redeployment or strategic
> reserve. First priority should be given to personnel
> returned from overseas duty.

2

4. <u>Overseas Delivery of Aircraft</u>. (OC&R) Through September 1944, 14,844 aircraft have been delivered overseas this year (12,171 by combat crew; 2,673 by ATC). 156 aircraft have been lost en route. This is approximately 1% of the total. By months, the losses were highest in January, February, March and (1.9, highest of all) May. For the last three months the percentage of loss has been 0.5 (24 aircraft in the three months, to 4,806 delivered)

5. <u>Release of Aircraft to Air Lines</u>. (OC&R) As of 19 October the Air Staff approved recommendation of AC/AS OC&R that approximately 91 DC-3 type and 70 Lodestar Type aircraft be released from the AAF for ultimate disposal to commercial air lines. The I Troop Carrier Command is being requested to make the DC-3's available "as soon as possible". Since the AAF has just turned over (my memo, 26 October) DC-3's to bring the total airlines planes up to the limit permitted by the Presidential directive 29 April 1944 it is now necessary to get this limit lifted. Major Young, OC&R Committments, tells me that action is being taken along these lines and they think something may be done within a month. There is probably an interesting story in how pressure was put on the AAF and what it consisted of. Two weeks ago further releases were not being considered, according to Col. Mosley. (Committments)

6. <u>Unsatisfactory Messing Conditions in CBI</u>. (Con) (Personnel) Prognostications (my memo, 23 October) on this subject seem well borne out by this note (27 October) from Gen. Bevans: "Completed formation of five Mess Teams to be sent to CBI on TD as directed by the War Department to alleviate the extremely unsanitary conditions now existing in China area of that theatre." Each team consists of one mess officer, one sanitation engineer, and seven enlisted men. "<u>Officers were ordered to Camp Luna, Las Vegas, N. M. for a brief period of indoctrination before departing for overseas</u>." Presume all eating in China area, CBI, will be suspended until they arrive.

7. "Eagle" Radar BTO Equipment Program. (OC&R) AN/APW 7 Eagle (the new radar bombing through the overcast equipment) has reached the "initial stage of production whereby plans can now be made on a priority basis for a limited number of installations." If further tests prove successful, Eagle will replace all present BTO equipment in VHB aircraft.

8. <u>A-26 Combat Suitability</u>. (OC&R) Gen. Giles is writing Gen. Kenney and forwarding a "condensation of Ninth Air Force A-26 combat suitability report" recently received at this Hq. This is clearly

an effort to persuade Gen. Kenney to change his mind about not
wanting the damn things (my memo, 9 October). Production of A-20's,
which Gen. Kenney likes better, was stopped last month, but we
have approximately 400 new ones in storage which it was planned
to dole out to Kenney as replacements. However, this Hq. plainly
hopes he will see the light and take A-26's.

9. <u>Patuxent Fighter Conference Findings</u>. (OC&R) At the joint
Army-Navy party (16-23 October) Patuxent Navl Air Station "the
principal topic of conversation during the entire conference was
pilot comfort for fighter pilots on long range escort missions and
it is believed that the aircraft manufacturers have been made to
realize that this subject is of extreme importance. The manufacturers admitted that the following improvements should be made to our
fighters:

    <u>a</u>. Reduce engine noise and vibration.
    <u>b</u>. Improve cockpit heating and ventilating systems.
    <u>c</u>. Change seats and controls to allow freedom of
movement for pilot.
    <u>d</u>. Install automatic pilot. (see Par. 10, below)"

Fighter aircraft on display were:
    <u>a</u>. P-47M. This is a special model of the P-47, and 130
aircraft are being produced for the U.K. It is a combination of the
N fuselage and the D wing with the R-2800-C-CH-5 turbo combination.
This power plant installation gives a War Emergency Rating of 2800
H.P. at 32,000 feet and a Military Power critical of 39,000 feet.
Top speed is in excess of 470 mph at 32,000 feet.
    <u>b</u>. F7F. This is a twin engine medium range Navy fighter.
Power plants are 2-R-2800-C, single stage two speed engines. Armament,
4x20 MM and 4x50 caliber guns. High speed approximately 450 mph
at critical altitude. It is not expected that this fighter will be
operated from carriers, but will be used principally by the Marines
from land bases. The Marines also intend to use this aircraft modified as a two place night fighter.
    <u>c</u>. F8F. Experimental. This is a small Navy fighter.
Gross weight, 8,200, Power Plant R-2800-C, single stage two speed
engines. Armament consists of 4x50 caliber guns. Internal fuel is
162 gallons. Performance data was not available, but a rate of
climb in excess of 5000 feet a minute and a high speed in excess of
450 is expected.
    <u>d</u>. F2G. Experimental. This is the Corsair with the Pratt
and Whitney 4360. Performance data was not available as only a few
flights have been made in this aircraft.

10. Automatic Pilots for VLR Fighters. (CC&R) The importance of an automatic pilot in fighter planes that must fly many hours in escort for the B-29's was stressed at the Patuxent Conference (above). "At the present time the most likely prospects, taking into consideration all aspects of production, performance, and installation, are the General -lectric G-1 (96 lbs.) and the newly developed Grumman pilot (26 lbs.)." The G-1 is now being tested in the P-47. Stock and production are such that, if performance proves satisfactory, it can be made available almost at once. An improved lighter version is in production, but will not be ready for tests before January 1945. Republic and Grumman are working on production engineering for installing the Grumman pilot in P-47N's. One technical difficulty is that the gadget was designed to operate with a high pressure hydraulic system. It is expected that definite decisions on the whole matter can be made within two weeks.

11. Proposed Court Martial of POW's for Talking Too Much. (Air Judge Advocate) It is recommended by Gen. Hedrick that proposed AAF Letter "Conduct of AAF Personnel in Event of Capture" should require all flying personnel to be briefed "with respect to possible consequences of their furnishing information to the enemy, inadvertently or otherwise." It is urged that emphasis be put on the fact that they can and will be court martialed under (a) the 95 and 96 AW (Conduct unbecoming an officer and gent; and disorders and neglects to the prejudice of good order and military discipline) or (b) the 81 AW (Relieving, Corresponding With, or Aiding the Enemy)

12. Notes from In and Out Log.
    a. Messages on 3rd and 7th Fleet Action. A succession of messages from COM 3rd Fleet, COM Task Force 77, CINCSWPA (signed MacArthur), and Com Task Force 38 are rather confusing. Some points: COM 3rd Fleet reports 26 Oct "Upon recovery of second strike, Task Force 34 and Task Group 38.2 departed for Leyte in response to Task Force 77 reporting critical situation." COM Task Force 77 26 Oct. "Mid morning enemy force which apparently sortied through San Bernadino strait estimated as 4 BB 7 AC 2 CL 12 DD joined in attack on our aircraft carriers." This was reported turned back by "repeated strikes from aircraft carriers supported in afternoon by strikes from Task Group 38.2" which "arrived in time to prevent what might have been a serious situation" Damage "Our own reports fragementary but considerable damage suffered by 2 aircraft carrier groups." COM Task Force 38 25 Oct. (apparently delayed) "Force torpedo, bomb, and food expenditures have reached point of almost complete exhaustion."

The general effect is that our 'victory' is not quite that — what we succeeded in doing was just missing getting the hell licked out of MacArthur's naval support.

    b. <u>London from Spaatz 26 Oct.</u> Urges loading all
bombs with Minol (we are still using TNT or Amatol as in
1918) "Production prepared to accept risks connected with
loading Minol because of its increased efficiency...no
unusual number of accidents has occurred in England since
development period was completed."

    c. <u>Madrid, signed Sharp, 26 Oct.</u> "Franco regime seems
assured for present at least due to loyalty of army and to
lesser extent inability of opposition groups getting together."

    d. <u>Versailles, signed Eisenhower 27 Oct.</u> Recent reports
of "restive movements" by German troops in Biscay garrisons.
There is "quite good water communication" between them. At
Gironde fortresses, much coming and going, and periodic reports
that they are about to make a break for Spain. It is considered
more likely that they may be "plotting extensive foraging
expeditions on lines of those carried out by S. Nazaire garrison." Estimated strengths; Rochelle, 8000; Oleron, 4000;
Gironde north, 5000; Gironde south, 5000.

    e. <u>For MacArthur from Arnold 26 Oct.</u> "My congratulations
...the victories of your air ground and sea forces...will
hammer the forces of Hirohito to a pulp..."

<u>For Halsey through Nimitz from Arnold 26 Oct.</u> "Another resounding
well done...you can't get what's left too soon as far as I'm
concerned." (Judged to mean; no objection if you sink more
of Jap fleet).

                    J. G. COZZENS
                    Major, Air Corps

tomorrow. I walked the copies around and argued with a few people about some stuff in my memoranda, but it seemed still more incredible to have the thing apparently done, not just on Wednesday but actually on Tuesday.

Wednesday 1 November 1944

. . . We found this morning that Gen Smith was going to take it instead of Giles, something I congratulated Col Smith on, and he accepted it as though he had done it; so maybe he did. As for the Gen, he flabbergasted me by addressing me as Jim when I came in with the text—the awkward circumstance was that I half-turned my head, thinking somebody must be behind me; but it didn't discourage him for he so continued to address me. I don't know why it makes me uncomfortable—unless, of course, because I do not quite see my way to calling him Freddy. He is, however, a nice little guy, in the general category of those people that everyone likes on sight. At the conference he was good again—easy, pleasant without loss of dignity, with a quick natural warm smile when that was needed, and always without exertion a half a thought ahead of his questioners. When Rex asked me, I told him I was sure we couldn't do better on the Air Staff and we should by all means cling to him. . . .

Monday 6 November 1944

In to see Gen Smith about his conference which we had few questions for, as most of the people involved were out in Kansas to see the B-29s. I hoped he might have ideas, but, harried in aspect, he said he was leaving that to us. After some thought I decided we'd better not have a conference, what with the election and all. With difficulty I sold the idea to Holland. . . . Finally he did propose it to Gen Smith and that was all right so we calmed down come six oclock. . . .

Tuesday 7 November 1944

. . . I made up memoranda all day and in the evening . . . we listened to the election returns—rather boring—until 12—though I must admit I would have been disconcerted if Dewey had shown any likelihood of winning. You could imagine the shambles in this Hq if they had to wait around some months to find out who was going to be on top in a new and hungry Republican administration in the War Department.

Wednesday 8 November 1944

. . . We had a leisurely day while I picked up items for Gen Smith's conference next week and fussed with cases in the Air Inspector's office.

Thursday 9 November 1944

. . . I went in to see Gen Smith about his conference for next week which was to be on

HEADQUARTERS, ARMY AIR FORCES
WASHINGTON

2 November 1944

MEMORANDUM FOR THE CHIEF, OFFICE OF INFORMATION SERVICES

Subject: Information from AC/AS Offices.

1. <u>Summary of B-29 Accidents</u>. (Flying Safety) There were 18 B-29 accidents reported for the month of September, bringing the total since February 1943 to 131. The September accidents compare with a high of 28 in June, 25 in July, and 20 in August. However accident rates for B-29 flying in the continental U. S. were sharply above August (39 per 100,000 Hours; September, 62 per 100,000 Hours). These September accidents resulted in 8 wrecked aircraft and 22 fatalities. (Totals from February 1943: 61 wrecked aircraft, 208 fatalities).

2. <u>Weather Factors in AAF Accidents</u>. (OC&R) The Weather Division complying with a directive from CAS to suggest ways and means to reduce the air accident rate in the continental U. S., suggests:

    a. that the Combined Chiefs of Staff approve the removal of restrictions on weather information in North America.
    b. that additional stress be placed on instrument and weather flying.
    c. that weather forecasters be required to participate in flying missions in order to give them a concept of the weather forecasting problem from the flyer's standpoint.

3. <u>Lack of Leave for 60 Troop Carrier Crews</u>. (OC&R) The I Troop Carrier Command reported on 22 Oct. that 163 troop carrier crews scheduled for departure overseas in November had not received leave during the last six months. Delay in shipment dates was requested to permit granting of leave. This was concurred in, 60 crews excepted. Reason for exception: if these crews are not ready to leave on 4 November as specified, there would be no transportation for them until mid-December. Judged TS for them.

4. <u>Insecticide DDT Solution</u>. (OC&R) The AAF Board reports that it is practicable to emit the insecticide DDT in oily solution from M-10 and M-33 chemical tanks on fighters or medium bombers. A 90% to 99% "kill" of mosquitos in the area affected results. This persists from 5 to 7 days. "It is estimated that effective mosquito control can be accomplished over a normal beachhead area (.5 x 1.5 miles) in the SW Pacific by 9 to 12 A-20's, each carrying four M-10 chemical tanks". The report has been submitted to the Air Surgeon for evaluation.

5. <u>Refractory Wac</u>. (Air Judge Advocate) Opinion; "that Wac who was AWOL and who was apprehended in Philadelphia may legally be tried or otherwise punished at the point of apprehension rather than be returned to her home station in Texas, especially where her hysterical and violent conduct would necessitate the use of handcuffs and armed guard on such return."

6. <u>Personal Conference Hour</u>. (Air Inspector) Gen. Jones has forwarded to Management Control for publication an AAF letter "establishing a monthly personal conference hour at all AAF activities. Purpose of this hour is to enable all personnel to present to the CO complaints and suggestions. This is designed to keep the CO informed as to what the men are thinking and to enable him to be alert to dissatisfaction in its incipiency." (Judged likely also to enable him to go nuts)

7. <u>Notes from In and Out Log</u>.
    a. <u>London from Gallman 31 Oct</u>. "Conferred with officials of the Foreign Office since Russia indicated that she would not take part in Civil Air Conference, Chicago...a surprise to all and no one takes Russia's reasons (participation of Switzerland) seriously...all my conferees feel there is more behind Russia's move." (Suggest one thing behind it might be leak on Deane's 23 Oct message (my memo, 26 Oct.) about ██████ being our pal).

    b. <u>CINCPAC 1 Nov</u>. "It is directed that no public discussions take place on Japanese suicide plane attacks. The knowledge of possible effectiveness of such attacks would be of great value to the enemy."

                            J. G. COZZENS
                            Major, Air Corps

SECRET

HEADQUARTERS, ARMY AIR FORCES
WASHINGTON

10 November 1944

MEMORANDUM FOR THE CHIEF, OFFICE OF INFORMATION SERVICES

Subject: Information from AC/AS Offices.

1. **Hiring of AAF Pilots by Airlines.** (Air Inspector) At the request of the Adjutant General, Col. Scott of the Air Inspector's Office conferred with Col. A. G. Atkinson, ATC, "concerning the possibility of a working arrangement with commercial airlines to discourage employment of former AAF pilots discharged as psycho-neurotic cases by board procedure in overseas theatres." General Doolittle seems to have cabled the Adjutant General "that unconfirmed reports of such employment of former crew members is creating an undesirable morale problem." (Apparently the feeling would be that if a pilot wasn't too psychoneurotic to get a good safe job here, he wasn't too psychoneurotic to go on flying there. This way a certain premium would be put on pretending you were crazy.) Col. Atkinson thought that some agreement with the commercial airlines about employing former pilots separated for reasons other than honorable might be worked out, but he agreed with Col. Scott that "any effort to interfere with employment of personnel discharged for medical reasons is highly undesirable and would probably result in severe political repercussions." This was reported to the Adjutant General.

2. **332nd Fighter Group.** (Management Control) A special report been prepared on the operations of the 332nd Group (colored). "This study shows that the 332nd Group compares favorably with other groups flying the same model aircraft during the same period of time." (The 332nd has flown successively P-39's, P-47's, and P-51's.)

3. **RAF General Officers.** (Management Control) As of 1 Sept. the number of RAF General Officers was 273. In the AAF we had a mere 259, though RAF personnel, including dominion and allied air forces num-bered no more than 1,275,252. AAF personnel was 2,403,056 on 1 September.

4. **AAF Training Standard 30-1-1.** (Training) Information from CBI has represented the training received by L-5 replacement pilots in the Third Air Force as totally inadequate. This brings up again the long-standing training safety argument - will you kill them in training, or will you save them to kill later? In the case of the L-5 pilots, Gen. Welsh remarks: "Informally, information from the Third Air Force indicates that it has been a positive policy not to conduct the training in accordance with AAF Training Standard 30-1-1,

SECRET

because of the directive, this headquarters, emphasizing safety."
Col. Barber, Gen. Welsh's executive, says that in spite of the
phrasing, no specific directive was in mind, but only the CGAAF's
repeated letters to the CG, Third Air Force, telling him he must
have fewer training accidents or else. The general staff feeling
seems to be that somehow, and very soon, too, the CGAAF must be
told that he cannot have both - that is, a low accident rate in
training, and pilots really capable of flying under theatre-of-
operation conditions. The whole problem, incidentally, seems sure
to be complicated by the poorer and poorer maintenance situation,
brought about by shipping out the more experienced ground crewmen.
- and certain to get worse still if G-3's scheme to swipe 100,000
AAF personnel goes through. (my memo, 9 Nov.)

    5. _Doron Requirements_. (M&S) AAF Doron (plastic armor made
of laminated glass) requirements have been cancelled "pending
completion of further ballistic tests now in progress at the
Aberdeen Proving Ground to determine relative merits of various
protective materials." Doron was adopted a couple of months ago
as a suitable material for flak curtains. I learn from M&S that
it was fine except that flak went right through it.

    6. _AAF Gasoline Requirements_. (M&S) At the Chicago meeting
of the Aviation Gasoline Advisory Committee it became plain that a
number of oil executives had got the idea that the AAF attached
little importance to the production of Grade 115/145 gasoline and
were consequently much inclined to ease up. The AAF Petroleum
Branch says quite the contrary and thus states the AAF position;
"The AAF wants first, adequate supplies of 100/130 Grade of adequate
quality to meet the requirements of the air effort, and second that
the AAF will make the most advantageous use possible (with the Navy)
of that quantity of 115/145 which can be made from production
facilities after requirements of 100/130 Grade have been met."
(Judged to mean that the Advisory Committee was pretty close to
right.)

    7. _After the Ball is Over_. (Air Judge Advocate) In General
Hedrick's opinion, there is no regulation or established policy
that prohibits the detail and use of garrison prisoners for the
purpose of cleaning an officers' club following a Saturday night
dance. He says, however, "that the practice of using prisoners
for this purpose is regarded as undesirable."

                                J. G. COZZENS
                                Major, Air Corps

ADDRESS REPLY TO
COMMANDING GENERAL, ARMY AIR FORCES
WASHINGTON 25, D. C.

ATTENTION:

HEADQUARTERS, ARMY AIR FORCES
WASHINGTON

11 November 1944

MEMORANDUM FOR THE CHIEF, OFFICE OF INFORMATION SERVICES

Subject: Information for AC/AS Offices.

1. <u>Naval Air Units Training with Foot Army</u>. (Training) AC/AS Training has been discussing with the Air Section, Hq AGF, the proposed joint training of Naval Air Force units and Army Ground Force units. The Navy will furnish this Hq with a schedule of exercises when the details have been worked out. This does not go down very well with Gen. Welsh, who observes: "It appears that the Navy intends to gain the benefit of joint air ground training and at the same time demonstrate to the ground forces that the Navy system of control and liaison used in their employment of air power, coordinating with the ground forces, more nearly agrees with many ground force commanders' ideas on command and employment of air power." It seems that the Navy system "provides for an excessive employment of 'air alert' flights and control by numerous 'air liaison parties' stationed with small ground force units in forward positions." I gather that Gen. Welsh feels that the AAF is being undercut by such aerial fawning on the foot army, though he admits that "the ground forces participating in these exercises may later be employed in operations in the Pacific in which a large proportion of the air power will be furnished by the Navy." Still and all, if the foot army were to join the Navy en masse we'd certainly be left rattling around in the Pentagon.

2. <u>Preflight and Flight Training Delays</u>. (Air Inspector) The expected and inevitable result of the 11 September cut in the training program (my memo, 24 Aug) has begun to catch up with the Air Inspector. Congressman Lawrence H. Smith has been squawking on behalf of pilot trainees at Napier Field, Alabama who "were compelled to perform duties other than required" (whatever that may mean). Gen. Jones informed Mr. Smith "that the reduction of the AAF pilot training program has caused a backlog of trainees awaiting preflight and flight training, and that these men are being given 'on the line' training, and basic military training while awaiting assignment. Every effort is being made to assign these men with the least possible delay." Very much in this connection, AC/AS Personnel reports a conference with AC/AS Training at which it was agreed "that the Training Command should prepare a plan of action for advising all air crew trainees prior to pre-flight as to the wait involved for pilot, bombardier, or navigator assignment and their opportunities for immediate training as a gunner. This action is intended to reduce, on a voluntary basis, the pools awaiting pre-flight training."

3. <u>Civilian Employment in Washington</u>. (Personnel) "A meeting has been held with representatives of the Civil Service Commission to solicit help of the Commission in presenting to the Office of War Information the urgent need to undertake publicity to present Washington in a more favorable viewpoint with respect to civilian employment." (I am told in AC/AS Personnel that, among other factors, the rumor through the sticks that if you do it with a Marine down on Hains Point you get killed, is supposed to have given pause to a certain number of employees, who after all can do it at home with only the ordinary risks).

4. <u>Service Rating Card</u>. (Personnel) A representative of AC/AS Personnel attended the conference 10 Nov. at the Special Planning Division, WDSS "to consider the point scores of the adjusted service rating cards." (Defined in Demobilization Regulation RR1-1; my memo, 5 Oct). Reports Gen. McCormick; "The meeting was confused and in-conclusive, but the consensus appeared to be that while the current ratio of 1-1-5-8-" (one month's service - one month's overseas service - each combat award - each child) "- may be satisfactory, it needs to be tested against the 2% sample now being taken in all theatres and in the U. S. G-1 has already prepared some statistical material and will analyze the 2% sample as rapidly as the information is received. It is anticipated that another meeting will be held not later than 15 December."

5. <u>Tribute to the President</u>. (Personnel) "Because of the statement appearing in the Washington Post that government employees would be excused to greet the President on his return to Washington," AC/AS Personnel checked with the Office of the Secretary of War on 9 November, "and was advised that it was the feeling of the Secretary of War that the best tribute which could be paid the President by civilian employees would be to remain on the job and that War Department employees would not be excused to view the parade."

6. <u>Incidental Pickings for AAF Officers</u>. (Air Judge Advocate) There is no legal objection to an officer "accepting employment as consultant for a private company in connection with the construction of civilian air fields and receiving pay for services so rendered, provided the work does not interfere with the officer's performance of his official duties." However, it is recommended that any officer with such a job in mind "address a communication to the War Department reporting the facts in accordance with the provisions of par. 2e (2) (b), AR 600-10, 8 July 1944."

7. <u>Fourteenth Air Force Supply</u>. (Management Control) From study "Effect of Supply on Operations of the XIV Air Force," (SC-SS-299): "17,000 tons of supplies must be delivered over the Hump monthly to sustain a reasonably high level of combat activity." (Defined as

3

336 HB sorties, 576 MB sorties, 4,770 Fighter sorties). Included
in the 17,000 tons are 9,000 tons broken down thus:

Housekeeping (.36 tons per man)	4,000
Gas for Troop Carrier & Photo Activity	1,250
Chinese Air Force allocation	850
Composite Wing allocation	1,800
Fixed reserves and losses	1,100
	9,000

Total combat potentialities of heavy bombers in China appear
to be around 8 sorties per month per U.E. This requires 2,880
tons of gasoline and bombs per month. Activity has generally been
restricted to around 6 sorties per U.E. because, on an average,
only 2,200 tons of supply have been available.

8. <u>Missing C-47</u>. (Air Inspector) They are still looking for
the C-47 missing out of Syracuse N. Y. since 19 Sept. (my memo,
31 Oct). Col. Martenstein, Rome Air Service Command, has advised
Gen. Jones that "search will be completed in two or three days.
He believes that it will be unproductive, but has continued it to
date in view of the fact that Mrs. Ambrose, sister of Sgt. Poska,
has been continuing a search on her own initiative with civilian
airplanes." (my guess: it fell in one of the Finger Lakes).

9. <u>Electronic Interference with Aircraft Engines</u>. (OC&R) The
Air Communications Officer has been asked to comment on the advisability of instituting a project to develop some method of shielding
aircraft engine electrical systems from possible electronic interference, and at the same time to investigate the status of any
current efforts of our own along this line. "The logic which dictates this advance counter-measure thinking on our part," says Col.
Giffin, "stems from our continuing air superiority, the enemy's
necessity for finding adequate means of combating our air power,
demonstrated German ingenuity in developing new methods and techniques,
and the enormous interference with air operations which would
immediately result from enemy use of a device capable of stopping
aircraft engines."

10. <u>Notes from In and Out Log</u>.
    a. <u>Ankara no sig 9 Nov</u>. Turkish gov't desires weather and
communications equipment we are about to install in Turkey be
sold to them...we consider it very important to immediately
agree in principle...so that installation and operation may
proceed without further delay and other nations will be faced
with a fait accompli...

b. London signed Gallman 7 Nov. The Royal Aeronautical Society...publicly dissociates themselves from recent comments on U.S. airline plans made by Brigadier A. C. Critchley..("the U.S. has 200 civil air attaches who are nothing more than high powered business men...etc.")

c. USMA Bern signed Legge 8 Nov. Monthly German plane production 900 plus 200 Italy...

d. Caserta from Eaker 10 Nov. Preliminary reports indicate that P-38 fighters of the Strategic Air Force on strafing mission in Yugoslavia 7 Nov. became engaged Soviet fighters and possibly attacked Soviet columns...possibility of navigational error,...believe 2 YAK fighters destroyed and 2 MASAF fighters also missing...recognition signals then exchanged...would like to point out that Russians have not appreciated necessity for bomb line...tardy in giving approval for liaison mission...in view of fluid situation..incidents such as that reported are apt occasionally to occur.

e. CINCPOA Nimitz to Arnold 10 Nov. We appreciate your message of good will and in conjunction with your forces we will continue to harass the Nips at every opportunity.

f. To Spaatz signed Arnold 10 Nov. Negotiations with Sweden how nearing completion make allocation of 25 new P-47D's to them from your stocks a matter of urgency..tacit understanding with Swedes on release of our interned airmen...

g. To Solberg (Lisbon) from George 10 Nov. ...we find it difficult to understand why a nation whose territory (Timor) has been overrun by foreign troops feels that it must have additional justification for taking steps (furnishing air base facilities at Santa Maria) to recover its territories...

J. G. COZZENS
Major, Air Corps

the air support at Leyte and found him agreeably clear and vigorous about what he thought, though I could see it might take some tempering, unless we wanted a row with the Navy. His general contention, and I think he probably contended correctly, was that anyone who thought as a result of the action that carrier-based planes could take the place of land-based planes was wrong. He also lost little time in telling off the Air Inspector's notion for a complaint hour and assured me it would not get by the staff so there would be no need to have Gen Jones there to explain it. . . .

Saturday 11 November 1944

. . . I was busy with Smith's remarks on Leyte all morning and my memoranda all afternoon. Everybody else was idle and after lunch began to drift off. . . .

Monday 13 November 1944

. . . While busy writing up Gen Smith's remarks on Leyte, Maj Simpson suddenly called me and announced with modest triumph that Mr A had approved the cry-baby-hour; so what? I said we wanted it, and took myself off to Gen Smith. He bristled somewhat, but when I said I thought it would be gracious of him, since he disapproved it (as of Thursday), to introduce Gen Jones while it was propounded, he gave me that engaging wry or rueful grin that the newspaper people like, humorously swallowed twice, and held up the ok O with his thumb and first finger. At the same time he reached for his box phone and I left. Simpson came down later and I discovered that he had that minute used it to call Gen Jones and ask him himself to be part of the party. All in all I thought, as I had before, that he was a very nice little buck general. Finally I got the text finished and saw that Maj Dahlstrom in charts was making us a beautiful map, so I felt I had done all right for the day. . . .

Tuesday 14 November 1944

. . . I had Gen Smith's stuff together by 10, but did not get to see him until 2, when I carted in a large map Maj Dahlstrom had made for me and saw him through his text. He took it well, only wanting to point out that if we had land-based planes the Japs never could have succeeded in reinforcing Leyte at all. I ventured to ask him if he was sure of that; and he said yes, or at least they'd fire any group commander who let it happen, because they had prevented it on all other Pacific islands. Later it seemed to develop that though everyone had passed the text, Gen Marshall was sensitive to any implication that (as the case was) we had not decided to go into Leyte until the middle of September on the basis of Navy carrier reports. It looked likely that much of it might have to be done over tomorrow. The sense of the objection was not clear. . . . Maj Simpson, by his telephone communications, spent the day feebly fighting over Gen Jones' remarks and he at least was pleased whenat the last minute we had to postpone the conference to 4 tomorrow to make way for another WD demonstration for newspaper people on the 'portable harbor' they had used on D Day.

Wednesday 15 November 1944

. . . We were stuck awhile on the conference matter, Joint Security still insisting it was all right (or at least a brooding, bespectacled Col Butler so insisted. I do not think he has much sense). Haddock and I went from there to Gen Marshall's Col McCarthy, a very dapper fellow in a British-made blouse. It would have seemed simple to me to take it to Gen Marshall, since he was the squawker; but that could not be done because the Gen was busy with a round-fronted, aged, civilian on something so special that McCarthy had been asked to leave for a few minutes. This confirmed me in the notion I had grasped before this, that though relatively I am deep in secret information, in fact the real dirt is in a category at which the top secret and secret stuff I had merely hints. The end was that Gen Bissell and Gen Handy decided we had to take out a large section that made Gen Smith's remarks make sense. We excised it. Smith did well as usual; but Gen Jones did deplorably, dumbly and harshly reading with his earnest big-nosed face bent down. His Major Simpson had been fluttering around for an hour beforehand and afterwards Jones delayed until everyone was gone, and then walked me through many corridors, anxious over a mis-placed comma in his mimeographed release. He is a nice old man and I tried to comfort myself with the reflection that it did me no harm in the E ring to be seen in intense and intimate colloquy with a major general. . . .

Thursday 16 November 1944

. . . Though not in the Washington papers, in the New York papers Gen Jones got some space and Simpson was soon on the phone to express his appreciation (I begin to think that he wildly imagines I do it, and am a good person to keep in with) and to ask if I had heard any unfavorable comment in the staff. It seems he had heard something from Giles' Col Coe, a poor limitary and frustrated tough soldier up there, who has, however, only nuisance value. I was busy getting up some special information for Rex on what the pay-off on the Russian planes we shot down in Yugoslavia was, and what Maj Gen Walsh was going to do on the Air Staff. The higher echelon was somewhat preoccupied as the big offensive in Europe was supposed to open today and we were supposed to hit Tokyo with the 29s tonight— all the top secret people (I suppose, including myself) looking demure.

Friday 17 November 1944

. . . However, the Tokyo business was put off until tonight, when it seemed it would go—a perhaps too-obviously curious or odd circumstance to reflect that I knew now

ADDRESS REPLY TO
COMMANDING GENERAL, ARMY AIR FORCES
WASHINGTON 25, D. C.

HEADQUARTERS, ARMY AIR FORCES
WASHINGTON

16 November 1944

SPECIAL MEMORANDUM FOR THE CHIEF, OFFICE OF INFORMATION SERVICES

Subject: Attack on Reds in Yugoslavia by MAAF Fighters'
November 1944.

1. General Antonov's Account. (10 Nov.)

From General Deane in Moscow. Gen. Antonov, Deputy Chief of the Red Army Staff, reported that at 1250, 7 Nov., between Nis and Aleksinao in Yugoslavia, a motor column of Red Army troops was attacked by a group of American fighters composed of 27 P-38's. A protecting group of 9 Soviet fighters took off from Nis airdrome. The Soviet planes were attacked while gaining altitude in spite of the fact that they were clearly marked, to defend themselves. The attack was stopped only after the Soviet group leader, Captain Koldunov, "at risk of being shot down, took a position under the leader of the group of American fighters and showed him the markings of his plane." . As a result of the attack, Lieut. Gen. Kotov, Commander of the TZE Corps, was killed along with two other officers and three men. 20 motor vehicles with equipment were set on fire. 3 of the Soviet fighters were shot down, two of the pilots being killed. In the region of the airdrome, 4 more people were killed by American fire. "This unwarranted instance of an attack by American planes on a column of troops and the group of Red Army planes completely perplexes us, since the attack was 50 kilometers behind the front line...on 14 and 16 October information given in Soviet communiques that these towns (Nis and Aleksinao) had been captured..There is no justification for these operation by the AAF not having been coordinated with the General Staff of the Red Army. Please inform combined Chiefs of Staff of the altogether deplorable facts...ask immediate investigation..punish those responsible...henceforth not allow flights of allied aviation into Zone of Activity of the Soviet troops without preliminary agreement..."

2. General Deane's Action.

Deane immediately expressed the regrets of our Chiefs of Staff and of the AAF, and assured Gen. Antonov that we would take the measures suggested. However, when Deane proposed "liaison between the hq's. concerned in the field", Antonov insisted it was unnecessary, and that liaison should be effected with the General Staff in Moscow. Deane disagreed, but suggested as an alternative that a boundary line should be established beyond which we would not operate. Antonov said he favored this, but could not speak without consulting the staff. His view was, also, that "when our ground forces come closer together" it would be time enough for liaison in the field.

3. <u>Regrets from General Arnold.</u> (10 Nov.) "...In the meantime I wish to express to you (Marshal Novikov, Red AF) my personal regret ...my admiration of the described conduct of the Red flyers..sincere hope successful method of cooperation..in area of your magnificent and successful operations...will be effected...."

4. <u>Account from AF Hq at Caserta.</u> (13 Nov.) "The 82nd Fighter Group was dispatched on adequate information to attack a legitimate target after proper briefing." Group Commander was Col. ███████████, a pilot with more than 4,000 hours and veteran of 27 combat mission. He had been assigned to attack enemy columns and rail movements between Sjenica, Novipasar, Baska, and Nitrovica. About 60 miles SW of Sjenica, Col. ██████████ threw up a squadron for top cover and brought his other two squadrons down on the deck. ████████████ own squadron arrived at what he thought was Novipasar, found the road "heavily trafficked", and proceeded to straf. "Actually, as verified by his cameras, he began his strafing at Krusevac and continued through Cicevan." As his squadron pulled off, it was attacked by Red Yak fighters. ----(this is the one point that contradicts Antonov's account; Antonov says the Red planes were attacked while trying to gain altitude from the Nis field, and the detail about 4 persons killed by American fire around the field seems to bear him out) ---- Col. ██████████ says that he recognized the Yaks at once, but 1 P-38 had been shot down in the first pass; and another was shot down, and so were two or three Yaks, before he could round up his planes. "The Yak flight leader then slid up to him and confirmed mutual identification." Hq. Caserta observes: "There is a startling similarity between the map appearance of the briefed target and the actual target." (They were roughly 45 miles apart) "All pilots will readily understand how even one as experienced as Col. ██████████, flying on the deck in such rugged country, under frequent flak attack, could make a mistake of ten minutes in navigation." Hq. also points out that this was the first such mistake in 37 missions flown between 18 Aug. and 11 Nov. in aid of the Soviets.

5. <u>Action of the Joint Chiefs of Staff.</u> (15 Nov.)
Gen. Deane was instructed to hand to the Red Army General Staff a paper expressing more regrets and remarking that the best way, in our experience, to avoid such incidents was to maintain close liaison between air and ground forces. Gen. Lindsay recommended that Col. ██████████ be immediately ordered to return to the U. S. for reassignment "without prejudice". Gen. Loutzenheiser is implementing this recommendation, and Gen. Lindsay assumes (15 Nov.) that the Joint Chiefs of Staff have approved.

J. G. COZZENS
Major, Air Corps

ADDRESS REPLY TO
COMMANDING GENERAL. ARMY AIR FORCES
WASHINGTON 25, D. C.

"TENTION:

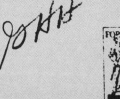

HEADQUARTERS, ARMY AIR FORCES
WASHINGTON

16 November 1944

MEMORANDUM FOR THE CHIEF, OFFICE OF INFORMATION SERVICES

Subject: Information from AC/AS Offices

1. <u>Utilization of P-80</u>. (OC&R) The CG Fourth Air Force has been informed by the Requirements Division of the general plan for utilization of jet fighters. Jet equipment and units will not be treated as "special". Existing practices will be followed as far as possible. Jet fighters will not be committed to action until adequate field tests with 20 or more P-80's had been performed by the 412th Group. A training cadre has been authorized, to consist of 21 officers and 45 mechanics, "for transitioning conventional fighter groups to jet equipment" (This seems to represent a slight change of opinion. AC/AS Training previously concluded that no transition was necessary. My memo, 7 Oct.). Thirteen YP-80A's and the first 30 P-80A-1 aircraft are allocated (my memo, 14 Nov). Assignment of 2 YP-80A's to UK and 2 YP-80A's to MTO are included. Wright Field, AAF Board (Orlando), Training Command, and 412th Group receive proportionate shares.

2. <u>P-61E as Day Fighter</u>. (OC&R) The P-61E, designated as a long range day fighter, has been modified from the standard P-61B fuselage. Two pilots ride in tandem. The combat radius is 1,400 miles (1,172 gallons carried ingernally, 1,200 gallons externally). A top speed of 430 mph is expected. Test aircraft will fly about 15 December.

3. <u>Air Force ZI Strength</u>. (OC&R) The presentation to Gen. Arnold reported by Management Control (my memo, 14 Nov) is summarized by the Troop Baisis Division. The several charts "emphasized the following facts."
(1) AAF is overstrength about 50,000, the Army about 250,000. The AAF, with 29% of the Army strength, has 13% of the overstrength.
(2) AAF losses are about 15,000 persons per month, and gains are about 5,000, mostly prospective air cadets. Net loss, 10,000 per month. (Col. Chamberlain, G-3, seems to regard this calculation as disingenuous, apparently regarding the in-take of AAF personnel as the right figure for gains, rather than the output of trained individuals. The great glut of prospective trainees (my memos, 11, 14 Nov), now sitting around, G-3 perhaps not unreasonably considers part of the Air Force)
(3) "The AAF has a decreasing number of students planned, but cannot cut permanent party proportionally because, while we reduce low-cost projects such as BTCs, Primary and Basic Flying, and technical training, we add high cost projects such as BTO schools, Four Engine, and VHB Transition, fighter transition, etc." (High and low "cost" here means number of permanent party personnel required)
(4) "Because the AAF has reduced intake and pilot production below that necessary to fight a continuing two-front war, some savings in students and ZI authorizations now appear possible by April 1945."

This authorization, however, is needed on redeployment or for the flexibility to provide either for new units or resumption of basic and flying training when intake is again necessary." (This is a very good sample of the conflicting and confusing sort of argument that is being fed to the Old Man. Probably it is due to what Gen. Gates (my memo, 14 Nov) called "a combined effort" on the part of 5 staff divisions. Either we have decided that we are not going to produce pilots for a continuing two-front war, and so are not going to need personnel to provide for new units or the resumption of basic and flying training, or else we are behaving like damn fools and somebody ought to be court-martialed)
(5) Delivery of personnel qualified for overseas service and now directed by WDGS includes 15,000 men who are to be "exchanged" for 15,000 ASF limited service personnel "plus 25,000 more" (For whom no exchange" seems yet to have been arranged. Col. ▊▊▊ feels that "further deliveries from the AAF should be limited to an even exchange by SSN grade and color.")

(The general impression to be got from the various AC/AS reports is that the AAF has been put, and is being kept, strictly on the defensive by the attitude and findings of the General Council; and that there is some internal conflict of interest and confusion of thought so great that nobody can formulate any clear or coherent plans, policies, or even desires for the CG to express in defense of the Air Force position.)

4. <u>Discharge of AAF Officers</u>. (Personnel) Gen. Bevans' people and G-1, WDGS are again discussing changes in the policy on the relief from active duty of AAF officers who are surplus. "It was recommended that relief from active duty be again placed on such a basis so that it can be voluntarily requested by officers over 38 years of age." G-1 has concurred, and circular 341, 1944 will be amended accordingly. "A recommendation was also made that officers who are recommended for relief from active duty and for whom no suitable assignment can be found by the three major commands will automatically be separated by the WD Separations Board." I learn, not from AC/AS Personnel's limpid style, but from a direct inquiry, that this refers to other, perhaps younger-type, officers. At any rate, G-1 has concurred here, too; "and will present it to the Chief of Staff for approval early part of this week. This policy has already been discussed informally by G-1 and the Separations Board. As soon as this recommendation receives final approval, several cases which are in this category and pending at this Hq. will be disposed of."

5. <u>Major Gen. R. L. Walsh</u>. (Plans) Confirming my reported rumor of yesterday, AC/AS Plans' activity report 16 Nov. stated; "R&R to CGAAF through Deputy Chief of the Air Staff inclosing a memorandum to the Chief of the Air Staff prepared for Gen. Arnold's signature designating Major General R. L. Walsh as his Special Assistant to represent him in all matters of interest to this Hq. in relation to other American republics." (Col. J. D. Gillett seems to have the matter in charge.)

6. <u>Proposed B-29 Deal with Reds</u>. (Plans) AC/AS Plans has prepared a message at Gen. Arnold's direction to go to Gen. Deane in Moscow "offering to give the two B-29's which forcelanded in Siberia to the Soviets in return for Russian authorization for ATC to operate routes in USSR. Requested Deane's recommendations in this matter." (In fact, my memo 31 Oct., and some letter Log items, the Reds have taken the planes anyway and were yesterday supposed to have flown one to Moscow.) Perhaps not incidentally, Col. Hickman reports that "agreement has been reached that is is inimical to our future national interest to provide the Russians with a Strategic Air Force."

7. <u>Allied Air Strength</u>. (Management Control)

As of 30 October 1944, there were 1561 Allied <u>Front Line</u> Squadrons (excluding all Russian and all Troop Carrier and Combat Cargo Type units). These were comprised of the following:

	Number	Percent
Army Air Forces	712	46
Naval Air Arm -Land Based	154	10
Carrier Based	85	5
TOTAL U. S.	951	61%
Royal Air Force	448	29
Royal Fleet Air Arm	62	4
Royal Canadian Air Force	11	1
Royal Australian Air Force	29	2
Royal New Zealand Air Force	12	1
TOTAL BRITISH EMPIRE	562	37%
Chinese Air Force (including Chinese American Composite Wing)	20	1
French Air Force	20	1
Other	8	-
TOTAL OTHER	48	2%
GRAND TOTAL	1561	100%

8. <u>Notes from In and Out Log</u>.
   a. <u>USMA Stockholm 14 Nov</u>. Reliable contact reports with reservation that Hitler is showing symptoms of brain concussion resulting from July incident with necessity of operation indicated.

J. G. COZZENS
Major, Air Corps

what a number of people on the other side of the world did not know—that a certain number of them would assuredly be dead by tomorrow. We occupied ourselves with some new announcements by Drew Pearson on quick-release parachutes, so I talked to Col Griffis in the Air Surgeon's office (Gen Glenn, Gen Grant's deputy, having ducked it after arranging on the telephone to see me—I gathered from his girl and Griffis, because he feared I would get him mixed up in something) and Col Hanson in Mr Lovett's office. I was gradually getting mixed up myself, but at least I have the experience and presence of mind to fend things off until tomorrow when necessary, so I was able to get out at noon after all. . . .

Monday 20 November 1944

. . . It developed that Rex had flown to Paris on Mr A's declaration that he was not pleased with his publicity. Smith said it had to be cooked at overseas Hqs, so Mr A said: for God's sake go and cook it. Whipping around then, he found Lt Doulens, who happened to be in Sunday, asked him if he had ever been overseas, and hearing, no, said, go on, right away. This took him (Doulens) aback some, but he had his shots today. I could not help thinking that I was glad it had not been my Sunday in, since I haven't any desire to sit around present day Paris in December at all. We experimented with a few topics for Gen Smith's party and got nowhere—Gen Craig, moved from OC&R to OPD, and now wearing two stars, brushed me off well—for really the first time since I had had to do with General officers . . . I felt what Newhouse seems to feel all the time—like saying; Look, stupid, I'm trying to help out your dumb army. If you won't help me help you out, to hell with you! However, I said only; yes, sir, and withdrew. In the morning I had already talked to Col Sessums in M&S about the parachute business and decided to drop that, so by the end of the day we had nothing for Gen Smith and could expect to go crazy tomorrow.

Tuesday 21 November 1944

. . . The conference matter was solved in the easiest and probably best way by deciding not to hold it "because of the holiday." . . .

Wednesday 22 November 1944

. . . There was some talk that Ziff-Davis, an oddity connected with *Flying* magazine, had sold Mr A a bill and was about to move in on Rex's province; but George Haddock told me going home that he thought it had been stopped. He also told me, however, that he was not sure that Rex was ever coming back, hoping or meaning to move elsewhere when he finished in ETO—in part, maybe, because of the implied lack of confidence in whatever the Ziff thing was; in part because he perhaps felt that as it worked out, there was less and less chance of anything for him in the present set-up. In to see Gen Smith in the pm, and I began to suspect that he was not pleased with the calling-off of the conference today. He showed me a log item of little use or interest and said, somewhat reproachfully, that he thought our office ought to spot and develop without suggestion from him such conference material. I ventured to point out some of the obvious reasons why it was no special use for the purpose, and he took it in good part; but, I think, remained still discontented. . . .

Friday 24 November 1944

. . . I had the usual trouble with the moronic Maj Marks in A-2 over whether or not he would give on the stuff Gen Smith wanted. There is a certain baffled sullen quality about him that defeats me, though I've seen one or two more, now I think of it—Col Ward in Training; and Col Ford in OC&R Troop Basis—you say something entirely simple to them and they say what does that mean, I don't know what you want. At any rate we got apart without striking blows and I went back and told George, nettled, that I thought he'd better speak to Gen Hodges, I would have no more to do with Marks. He accepted it patiently and I went upstairs to talk to Col Harris in Gen Jones' office. He is a graying lawyer with a loud clear court room voice and an admirably lucid manner which he used, pacing up and down his office, to explain some trouble with the Mead Committee[49] over some goings-on at Eglin Field. . . .

Saturday 25 November 1944

. . . When I got in, there was the material from Major Marks, so I was inclined to forgive him, though his motivation had probably been an exchange with Col Bright, when he came in, along the lines of; Col B: Yeah, I know the son of a bitch; but they have the inside track somehow, and we don't want any trouble with them; so get it over to them. . . .

Monday 27 November 1944

. . . Promptly at 9 turned up M/S Hadlow from Bolling Field to be looked over as a possible speaker for Gen Smith Wednesday when he was to talk about the MAAF [Mediterannean Allied Air Forces] ground crews. The Sgt had been there two years—a blond smooth-faced old air force man—he had enlisted in 1930 and was now only 32. I thought he would do—reasonably personable and strictly army—he pulled up and saluted me when he came in, surely the first time such a thing had ever happened in this office. I could see George Haddock was a little more doubtful—about his being fluent enough, but after some talk with him and the inspection of some stuff he wrote out on his work over there (he said that he wasn't a very good

ADDRESS REPLY TO
COMMANDING GENERAL, ARMY AIR FORCES
WASHINGTON 25, D. C.

ATTENTION:

HEADQUARTERS, ARMY AIR FORCES
WASHINGTON

24 November 1944

SPECIAL MEMORANDUM FOR THE CHIEF, OFFICE OF INFORMATION SERVICES

Subject: Mead Committee Investigation of Case of Lt. Phillips.
(Air Inspector)

1. <u>Death of 2nd Lt. Mark Phillips</u>. At Eglin Field, Florida, on 5 October AT6A airplane 41-530, piloted by Lt. Phillips, dived suddenly, crashed and burned killing the pilot. The only witness was 1st Lt. ████████████, who was in the air in another plane at the time.

2. <u>Representations of Lt. ████</u> Lt. ██████████████ ████████████████████, a utility pilot who washed out of fighter training, and who had been stationed at Eglin Field for about 3 months, wrote his father, alleging in great detail that Lt. Phillips' AT-6 was in no condition to fly and that this was well-known to supervisory personnel at Eglin Field; and that, moreover, utility pilots, (of which Lt. Phillips was also one) were treated like dirt and generally discriminated against. Mr. ████ immediately wrote letters to the President and to Senators Byrd, Kilgore, and Bailey.

3. <u>Action of the Air Inspector</u>. General Jones directed Lt. Col. ████████████████████████████ to make an investigation. This investigation did not substantiate the allegations; but Col. F. E. Harris, of Gen. Jones' office, who outlined the case to me at Major Simpson's suggestion, said that the report by Lt. Col. ████ was in fact insufficiently thorough. This was also the opinion of Lt. ████, who wrote his father again, to say that the investigation had been a white-washing job. His father immediately made fresh representations to Washington, which resulted in the Mead Committee sending down a Mr. Sparks to investigate at Eglin Field. The War Department was told that they were sending a man to Eglin Field, but not told what for.

4. <u>Mr. Sparks' Investigation</u>. Mr. Sparks interviewed a number of officers at Eglin Field but gave most of his attention to Lt. ████ and three friends of his, also utility pilots, Lts. ████, ████, and ████, who agreed on charges of negligence against supervisory personnel, and extended their remarks about discrimination against themselves as utility pilots.

5. <u>Alleged Disciplinary Action against Lt. ███ and Friends.</u>
As soon as Mr. Sparks left, Lt. ███ and the three others were
rated by Major ███████ of the Eastern Flying Training Command;
██████ and ████████, unsatisfactory; ████ and ██████, satisfactory.
Major ████ also reported to Col. Rodeick, the Wing Commander, that
the four were highly undesirable because of their general attitude.
He accused them of disloyalty in making charges and complaints out
of channels (i.e., to ███████ father and to Mr. Sparks). Col. Harris
tells me that there is little doubt that they all were and had been
chronic sore-heads and trouble-makers ever since they had been at
Eglin, and that everyone was sick and tired of them. As a result,
they were all four transferred out. ██████ was sent to Napier Field,
where the CO, Col. Daley, informed him of his unsatisfactory rating,
and told him he would be on "informal probation" for a month. ███████
immediately wrote his father again, alleging that he was being
disciplined for testifying to the Mead Committee's Mr. Sparks.

6. <u>Reaction of the Mead Committee.</u> Prompted particularly by
Senator Kilgore, who, according to informal advices from Col. Harris,
is always very ready or even eager to do the AAF in the eye, the
Mead Committee reacted sharply to Col. Knowles (in Mr. Amberg's
office. He acts as WD contact man to or for the Mead Committee)
who requested Gen. Jones to provide a full report at once. This was
done, but Col. Knowles said that the Committee was far from mollified
and seemed anxious to make an issue or even stink out of the allegation that the AAF cracked down on officers who gave the Mead
Committee information.

7. <u>Present Status.</u> Col. Scott yesterday outlined the situation
to Gen. Owens. At the same time, Gen. Jones sent Col. Outcalt and
Col. Watson of his office to Eglin Field to make a new investigation
both into the charges of negligence about Lt. Phillips death and
the matter of 'disciplinary action' against Lt. ██████ and the
others. Today, Senator Mead has taken off for the south, first to
Memphis, but Col. Harris believes he will turn up at Eglin within a
few days and has alerted those concerned. Gen. Jones is much
concerned over the apparent high probability that the Mead Committee
will in fact use the incident for an attack of some kind on the
Air Force. Col. Harris will keep this office informed.

J. G. COZZENS
Major, Air Corps

writer, but if that was what he understood me to say we wanted, he could say it all right) I persisted in saying he would do, and George visibly took my say-so and sold it to Gen Smith, so he'd better do. With this to help I got the text of the conference mostly set up and typed by Johnny, except for interruptions due to her having a nose bleed.

Tuesday 28 November 1944

. . . I was busy with Gen Smith's stuff all day and we got to see him late in the afternoon, when he broke the disturbing news that maybe Gen Giles would take the conference—it shook me because the questions, at least, were full of three syllable words. . . .

Wednesday 29 November 1944

. . . The conference went off very well and the Sgt did his part, plain, earnest, blunt and not unduly grammatical, very effectively. Smith himself was superior—he gets better and better—simple, easy, quick-witted and humorous so they both like and respect him—I was amused to hear him referring to the sergeant in direct address as 'son'—I suppose there is perhaps six years difference in their ages.

Thursday 30 November 1944

. . . I was busy with my memoranda, including some conversation with a Major Hanscom in A2 on what they might give me—nothing, it seemed, because they were already passing on everything they had to other agencies, and with Miss Thompson, Gen Smith's girl, while I waited for him, but he did not come, being busy talking to this Ziff fellow making me wonder again if Col Smith's flight to Paris meant or did not mean anything. Miss T is a very plain, very well-washed-looking intelligent girl, and so I got little out of her. . . .

Friday 1 December 1944

. . . Gen Smith sent for me at 10 oclock and proved to be in an animated mood, requesting me to shut the door when I came in, and falling at once on his subject which was Admiral Mitscher's[50] remarks yesterday on the advantages of carrier-based over land-based aircraft. I had read them myself and they were sufficiently full of absurdities, only to be accounted for by some feeling in the Admiral that anything the Navy had was good & the best in the world. Gen Smith justly remarked that the Admiral had stuck his neck out—we had refrained from invidious comparisons, but since he wanted to make them, that's what we'd do next Wednesday. This was a brisk and enlivening idea, but I am getting old or responsible or something and when I had the chance I ventured to insert the suggestion that this seemed to be a matter

176

ADDRESS REPLY TO
COMMANDING GENERAL, ARMY AIR FORCES
WASHINGTON 25, D. C.

ATTENTION:

SECRET

HEADQUARTERS, ARMY AIR FORCES
WASHINGTON

30 November 1944

MEMORANDUM FOR THE CHIEF, OFFICE OF INFORMATION SERVICES

Subject: Information from AC/AS Offices

1. **Discharge of AAF Officers**. (Personnel) Col. Hewett and
Lt. Col. Laking are continuing coordination with G-1, WDGS, on
revisions of WD Circular 341, Subject: Relief from Active Duty
of Officers for Whom no Suitable Assignments Exist (my memo,
16 Nov.). It is expected that AC/AS Personnel's recommendations
(mostly already agreed on) will be in final form early next
week, and Col. Laking will inform this office. Meanwhile two
additional categories of officers who may request relief from
active duty have been agreed on:

    a. **Recovered prisoners of war**, or those who landed
in enemy territory and evaded imprisonment. All who are not
regular army officers may request relief from active duty, regardless of age, if they were "in excess of 60 days prisoner in
enemy hands or evading capture in enemy controlled territory."

    b. **Combat wounded officers**, who, as a result of their
wounds are permanently below the physical standards for general
service. "In other words, combat disabled officers will normally
not be encouraged to remain on active duty, as rehabilitation and
adjustment to their disability is finally facilitated by return to
civilian environment and employment, and can be accomplished better
during the war than during the general demobilization period after
the war is terminated." (Judged to mean that it would be easier
to get them jobs now when they are war heroes than later when
everyone is sick and tired of veterans, and will see little percentage in taking a fellow with one arm when they can get plenty
with two arms for the same money).

2. **Douglas Jet Bomber**. (M&S) The Douglas Aircraft Corporation
is preparing a proposal for a medium bomber of the B-42 type (engines
mounted to rear of pilot, driving counter-rotating propellors in
the tail - my memo, 2 Nov.), but "designed around" two TG-180A jet
propulsion engines. (The TG-180A differs from the TG-180 in having
a different turbine wheel and incorporating a reduction gear and
a propellor). M&S informed the Douglas representative that development on TG-180A had been stopped for the time being, but he
said Douglas would submit the proposal anyway because it was felt
the advantages of the projected plane would be sufficiently obvious
to bring about resumed development of TG-180A.

SECRET

3. **XP-61E.** (MGS) The first XP-61E is scheduled for flight on or before 15 December (my memo, 16 Nov.) This is the P-61 adapted as a long range escort fighter. It will allow a pilot and a relief pilot to change places in flight. The normal radar equipment is replaced by a 4 gun .50 caliber nose installation. It will have in addition four 20 mm. guns in the wings.

4. **B-29 Production to Date.** (Management Control) The 1,000th Very Long Range bomber was delivered to the AAF on 22 November 1944, the total through that date being 1,004.

Disposition has been as follows:

Received		1,004
Less: Domestic Losses	52	
Overseas Losses	100	
Balance on Hand		152
		852

The balance on hand (852) is distributed as follows:

B-29 Domestic	502	
Overseas	296	798
F-13 Domestic	14	
Overseas	13	
		27
XB-29 Domestic		2
YB-29 Domestic		2
TB-29 Domestic		20
XB-39 Domestic		1
YB-32 Domestic		2
Balance on Hand		852

5. **Fighter Production to Date.** (Management Control) The 75,000th fighter produced since 1 July 1940 was delivered on 25 November 1944. Of this number 52,741 were Army-type fighters and 22,261 were Navy types.

Planes had been distributed, as of 25 November, as follows:

AAF	35,281
Navy	18,171
British Empire	10,787
U.S.S.R.	9,034
China	757
All Others	972
	75,002

b. <u>Notes from In and Out Log.</u>

    a. <u>USMA Lisbon signed Solberg 28 Nov.</u> Aggreements on
Santa Maria and Fimor were signed today by Salazar and Norweb...

    b. <u>USMA Ottawa from Graling 29 Nov.</u> Collective insub-
ordination is the term used by the Director of Military Operations
and Plans, Canadian Army General Staff, in discussing personallly
and confidentially...the west coast disturbances in Canadian army...
situation at Terrace, British Columbia..very serious...grave doubt
that men selected for overseas service will return from embarkation
leave....

    c. <u>Caserta from Schuyler (Rumania) 29 Nov.</u> Leaders of
major parties have agreed to withdraw support from present government (Sanatescu)...which is very weak and offering continued
appeasement to the Communists out of all proportion to what they
deserve on basis of their actual strength...new government will be
headed by General Radescu...much concerned over possible attitude
of Russia...some expecting her to intervene...all feel however that
situation will worsen rapidly unless strong stand against Communists
is taken at once.

                                    J. G. COZZENS
                                    Major, Air Corps

that concerned all air policy and ought to interest Gen Arnold. Smith had no trouble in getting the point; but seemed undisturbed by the impertinence, being, I suppose, and indeed could see, snapping with zest for battle, and simply said; Oh, I spoke to him this morning; he says go and get them. Less held back than perhaps I should have been by the childishness or even unwisdom of picking a fight with the Navy over remarks by an Admiral who is plainly a 'character' and probably an eccentric, I spent some twenty minutes giving and taking suggestions about what we could say, and accomplished little more (and maybe not that) for the cause of reason than to get him to agree that the right tone was a good-natured questioning of the Admiral's conclusions in light of certain inescapable facts. However, now that he is so much at ease and so well in command of his conferences, I doubt if he will let himself be held by any too temperate sayings in his prepared text. . . .

Saturday 2 December 1944

. . . I was busy with various researches on the Mitscher business, including eventually from a Major Thomas in BPR, the transcript of the conference showing what he really said—part of it seemed undoubtedly the out-blurtings of a confused old sea dog and professional tough man, pleased by the audience and aware that he was indeed a character, yet I still thought we could do all right with a little good-natured Now, Now, Admiral, stuff; a tone which Smith, if he will, should be able to manage. I was relatively at peace, since Smith, and Kuter, too, had gone to the football game at Baltimore, which it seemed the Army won—useful to me, as in the spirit of hearty ham, I figured we might point out that the Admiral was loyally Navy and so naturally thought it was the best outfit in the world, and everything about it (meaning also carrier aviation) was the best in the world, and probably he even bet his money that the team that went up to Baltimore today was the best in the world.

Sunday 3 December 1944

. . . In to the Pentagon at 10 to see Gen Kuter, but I did not get to see him until half past one, when I gave him seven or eight pages of the treatment for Gen Smith. He disconcerted me a good deal by reading it all dead pan, though there were some cracks I felt well-calculated to get a smile from anyone informed on the subject. I thought afterwards that no doubt some of his staff reputation is due to a cultivated impassivity. At the end, he said: This is for Freddy; I don't think anyone else could do it. The point, I soon realized, was to make sure that Giles didn't feel he had to lumber in himself—I thought it of the first importance, too, and concluded that Kuter would give me a hand in seeing that Giles didn't. I suggested that it might be represented to Giles that it dignified the whole business too much if we ceremoniously put a 3 star general to answering, and that seemed to go down all right. . . .

Monday 4 December 1944

I revised, not without pleasure, the remarks for Gen Smith, and eventually got it around to him after 4. . . . Smith read it with pleasure which was visible and certainly made me like him all the more—you feel with him, as so sharply opposed to 'with Gen Arnold or Gen Giles' you really could do something—that is, you don't write to no purpose; you can give him what it is right and natural for him to use, and he recognizes it and will make the very best, in his manner and delivery, of the stuff. He took it to clear with Giles and Mr A. Part of the day went into getting through a copy of the old FM 1-15[51] text which a Capt Ogilsby from the AAF Board in Orlando requested by telephone last week. S brought it down from my file and I was gratified to find that whatever the current value of its or Reade Tilley's doctrine, it seemed to read as I had tried to make it read—clear, easy, and simple. . . .

Tuesday 5 December 1944

. . . We were jolted back on the conference stuff, somewhat past noon, when it developed that while every one else concurred, Mr Lovett told Gen Smith that he advised against the piece, and Smith not unnaturally gave way. The introduction of what was clearly the adult view—why start a row?—stopped me too; but I thought Mr Lovett (who indeed said so to Smith himself) was a little overcautious. Smith gallantly said he did not expect us to replace it so late in the day, and that he would speak extemporaneously on the Tactical Air Forces, and I was to keep my text, which both he and Mr A thought good, for possible later use. This of course mollified me; and George Haddock, back late from Wright Field (to what infinite relief; you get a head again; calm, shrewd, able, and ready to decide as the dictates of good sense direct) concurred, though reluctantly. . . .

Wednesday 6 December 1944

. . . We got the conference matter set after some differences with Col Butler of JSC [Joint Section Chiefs] who was plainly reaching beyond security into policy and needed pushing back; and some complicated arrangements to make available, if anyone wanted to look into it, the stereogram pictures of bombing damage. Gen Smith did, as usual, very well; and his extemporaneous talk on the function of Tactical Air Forces amazed me—if it was not very interesting in itself, it was wonderfully lucid and orderly (with no notes, and plainly thought up as he went on) and I was pleased afterwards (and so I think was he) when Ransom applied from *Air Force* for the transcript to make an article out of, and one reporter at least phoned in to make sure that extensive quotes from it were or would be on the record, all right. I could not help regretting the lost battle with the Navy which would have been a sensation; but it was all the more credit to him, clearly, to make do with what he had so well. I admire his abilities and his personal qualities that make them, if not possible, natural, more and more.

Thursday 7 December 1944

. . . Up to talk to Gen Coupland, the Air Ordnance Officer, on something Smith might use next week on the munitions situation—all hampered a little by being, at least, in the AAF far from serious. Coupland was one of the worn, red-eyed, unmilitary, BGs who probably do nine-tenths of the business and production work, without which the West Pointers could do nothing. He was also civil and obliging; but to my surprise I prefer the military—I suppose because if you have to go around wearing a soldier suit and doing this kind of thing, it is easier if nothing reminds you of civilian matters and methods, and you are not disturbed by the implication that the army end of it has nothing to do with the real job—so true; but if you cannot feel that you are here because you are in the army, it is hard, at least in the unnecessary capacity in which I am here, to support being here at all. I had a long talk with Col Belshe in Personnel later about the transfer of 16,000 air crew trainees, and I was obliged to realize that his fundamental assumption that the army is the army was reassuring or sustaining. . . .

Friday 8 December 1944

. . . I was all morning writing up the transfer matter and a letter to a jerk who wanted to know why we did not bomb the Imperial Palace at Tokyo. . . .

Saturday 9 December 1944

. . . Up to see Col Sessums and Col Batchelder about Gen Echols' views in the morning, but there was little learned except that the Gen would not be averse to meeting the newspaper people himself if Gen Smith should happen to want him to. This took time and the rest of it went into a couple of memoranda and I felt as though I had done a full day's work by 5. . . .

Sunday 10 December 1944

. . . In at 10 to see Gen Smith with Haddock on what we were to do, and it seemed better finally to do nothing on the supply situation, since any good explanation could only imply (a) a criticism of Mr A (b) a criticism of the JCS [Joint Chiefs of Staff]. George later thought suddenly, and it seemed me well, that we could say something about the 11th and 13th Air Forces, mostly forgotten. . . .

Monday 11 December 1944

. . . I was about the matter of getting Gen Smith's stuff together and so encountered

ADDRESS REPLY TO
COMMANDING GENERAL, ARMY AIR FORCES
WASHINGTON 25, D. C.

ATTENTION:

HEADQUARTERS, ARMY AIR FORCES
WASHINGTON

12 December 1944

MEMORANDUM FOR THE CHIEF, OFFICE OF INFORMATION SERVICES

Subject: Information from AC/AS Offices.

1. <u>Case of Lt. Phillips</u>. (Air Inspector) Col. Scott reports that a final (he hopes) reply has been made to Mr. ████████████ (my memo, 24 Nov) "Mr. ██████ was advised that a reinvestigation was made by representatives of this headquarters; that the evidence obtained concerning the crash of an AT-6, cited in the complaint, refuted the charge that the crash was due to structural defects or negligence by supervisory personnel." Similarly, the charge that the remains of two pilots lost near Eglin Field "were mutilated by animals" was refuted. Copies of the letter to Mr. ██████ were sent to Senators Bailey, Kilgore, and Byrd. However, it is still not definitely known what action Kilgore may inspire the Mead Committee to make on the alleged "disciplining" of Mr. ██████' son for his testimony to the Mead Committee man. As this was the more serious aspect of the case, it may be considered still open.

2. <u>U.S. Pacific Air Strength</u>.(Management Control) Stat Control has prepared a special report on U.S. Army and Navy airplanes in the Pacific. As of 30 November, the AAF had 3,175. The Navy had 6,577 shore-based and carrier type airplanes ashore, and 2,424 planes on carriers. (A total of slightly less than 3 times as many as the AAF).

3. <u>Tallboy Bombs</u>. (M&S) The Very Large Bombs, under this new and felicitous title, which OC&R and Plans met to discuss last week (my memo, 4 Dec) have got to the stage of a direction that "engineering be accomplished" on a B-29 and a B-32 to accomodate them. "Engineering emphasis is to be placed on the B-29 in preference to the B-32, and 1-A priority is assigned to the project." (Incidentally, OC&R reports the cancellation of requirement for a 10,000 lb. bomb to fit the present B-29 bay, both because the limitations in dimension would necessarily have "very poor ballistics", and because of the decision on the 22,000 lb Tallboy).

4. <u>Attrition of Tactical Aircraft</u>. (OC&R) Actual losses of tactical aircraft in combat theaters for the month of November were, except in the case of B-17's approximately as estimated.

The B-17's lost 194 fewer than planned, due principally to curtailed activities of heavy bombers in ETO. If this "attrition saving" continues through the winter, the once prospective shortage of 600 B-17's by June 1945 will be eliminated.

5. TS on Swiss Consul. (Air Judge Advocate) Gen. Hedrick's office has "expressed concurrence" in the opinion that the Swiss government should be advised, with reference to the attack (alleged) by U.S. planes on the automobile of the Swiss Consul in Paris (18 August 1944) "that the U.S. government was not inclined to assume any responsibility whatsoever for such attacks and that a neutral government or its consul must realize that if he drives an automobile on a public highway in a battle zone during battle operations he exposes himself and his car to many serious and imminent dangers for which, unfortunately, no compensation can legally be expected; and that the U.S. Government sincerely regrets that the Consul and his wife were the innocent victims of the attack."

6. P-80 Production. (M&S) It has been directed that a study be made immediately of proposed P-80 production by North American, Kansas City. The study will include production schedules for rates of 100 a month and 200 a month.

J. G. COZZENS
Major, Air Corps

Col Fogle in Intelligence, a pursy, sandy-haired fellow from the 11th Air Force who soon displayed that invariable itch—he too would like to talk to the news men and in the end it was so arranged, it being decided that the inter-relation with the Navy we would meekly point to as proof of how well we got on with them. At noon Gen Loutzenheiser called me—he is the DC/AS [Deputy Chief/Air Staff] I had never had anything to do with, nor even seen. He proved to be a little fellow with a moustache and glasses and the manner and I should think mind of a small-town dentist. Gen Kuter had written my name on a buck slip about material for a press conference which, wildly enough, was to be telephoned to Mr A on the Pacific coast by three, so he could meet the boys there. We got it straightened out finally, George Haddock swearing some, and supplied a few items. . . .

Tuesday 12 December 1944

. . . I got Smith's stuff together, and arranged for his maps with Maj Dahlstrom, and got figures on the 11th & 13th Air Forces as a press release from Col Clarke, and picked up the odds and ends from Col Cannon in Plans to Major Hansen in A2, meanwhile 'briefing' Col Fogle about what he should say as a sample of the 11th Air Force. Still, there is nothing like it, if you have to do this business. The only fatal thing is to be any less busy. . . .

Wednesday 13 December 1944

. . . We were given a little pause when waiting with Miss Thompson in Gen Smith's office for him to come in at 8, he called to say he had been ill all night. However, his sense of duty was enough to bring him in by 11 and though plainly in some distress he carried off his conference with his usual success. Col Fogle, as one might have anticipated, was a little on the long side, but they seemed to like him and to take copious notes, so we considered it a success. Col Laking of Personnel brought over the draft of WD Circular 341 on Relief of Officers which I summarized in a memo— the most interesting piece of business in the office, really; though few could be affected but me. Those of us over 38 should apparently be able to get out as soon as it is published—or, I amend it in my own mind, as soon as the European business is finished. In perhaps too optimistic anticipating I keep reflecting that, strange as it feels to be in, it would certainly feel strange to be out, even with no more than the Pacific war still on—or, in short, what a wonderful relief if they would just stop fighting everywhere.

Thursday 14 December 1944

. . . I saw Gen Smith early on his notion of dealing with Harmon's Strategic Air Force and he sent me down to Loutzenheiser who still with that small-town dentist's

ADDRESS REPLY TO
COMMANDING GENERAL, ARMY AIR FORCES
WASHINGTON 25, D. C.

ATTENTION:

HEADQUARTERS, ARMY AIR FORCES
WASHINGTON

13 December 1944

MEMORANDUM FOR THE CHIEF, OFFICE OF INFORMATION SERVICES

Subject: Information from AC/AS Offices

1. ███████ Air Depot. (Air Inspector) This affair, which has been dragging on since last summer (my memo, 19 Sept), involved complaints to the U.S. Attorney at ████████: (1) illegal labor contracts; (2) use of government labor and material in building a fancy bar for the Army Air Base Officers Club; (3) improper destruction of new and repairable items at the Air Depot. Col. Scott conferred with Mr. Foley of the Claims Division, Department of Justice, this week. He was trying to get Mr. Foley to accept a proposed offer of settlement and to have the Department of Justice indicate in writing its willingness to accept the offer in full satisfaction.

Mr. Foley hedged, referring Col. Scott to a Mr. Friedman also of the Department of Justice. Mr. Friedman said that he had difficulty in persuading the U.S. Attorney at ████████ (Mr. ████████) to "submit definite recommendations in the premises". This is judged by both Col. Scott and Mr. Friedman to be due to Mr. ████████'s continuing resolve to prosecute criminally as well as to bring civil suit. Col. Scott's effort has been to get someone to order Mr. ████████ to settle the club bar matter separately - the club has posted $3,800 - and thus take out of it a number of officers who will be made defendants in a criminal action (the CO, the club board, etc). Mr. ████████ refuses to consider it separately. Since multiplying the defendants means increasing the difficulty of the case and the amount of work he will have to do, it seems clear that Mr. ██ is resolved, for whatever reasons of rancor or conscience, to smear the whole outfit if he can. Gen. Jones regards the matter with concern. Such action by Mr. ██ may set a sort of precedent for handling such cases, of which there are or will be plenty. "Mr. Friedman has renewed his efforts to obtain a final answer from Mr. ████████, but does not anticipate that such an answer will be given before 1 January 1945. This will be followed up after 1 January."

2. JB-1. (M&S) The first JB-1 (Northrop tail-less) flying bomb was launched from the horizontal track at Eglin 8 December. "The ground run was successful but due to causes unknown at this time the flight path was very steep and the missile fell off on one wing and crashed." (However, it was very instable on its flight tests; my memo, 22 Sept)

3. <u>Bahrein Refinery</u>. (M&S) The problems that interested the State Department in connection with this Persian Gulf development (my memo, 22 Sept) seem to have been settled. The Bahrein Petroleum Company reports that "the construction situation is much better. It is estimated that the completion date of 15 April 1945 will be met."

4. <u>Automatic Pilots for Fighter Planes</u>. (M&S) The action on automatic pilots for VLR fighters initiated by the Patuxent conference (my memo, 28 Oct) was determined as of 10 December with a direction to procure 2,000 Grumman automatic pilots. "Tests of the experimental General Electric pilot and of the Pioneer lightweight automatic pilot are to be continued on highest priority." Samples are supposed to be available about 1 January 1945. (The GE pilot weighed 96 pounds against the Grumman's 26, and nobody knew whether it would work. There is probably a story here about who was pulling what strings)

5. <u>B-29 Procurement</u>. (M&S) Procurement has been directed, to be carried on 1945 fiscal funds, of 350 B-29's from Bell, Atlanta; 400, from Boeing, Wichita; 300, from Martin Omaha. This procurement covers B-29's scheduled through June 1946.

6. <u>Negro Wacs.</u> (Personnel) Continuing this somewhat gingerly subject(my memo, 29 Nov), Gen. McCormick reports that colored AAF Wac Detachments are now located at 8 stations and include 733 enlisted women. (considerably under Col. Bandel's estimate). "Approximately 180 colored enlisted women allotted to the AAF are being held, unassigned, at First WAC Training Center, Fort Des Moines, Iowa, since housing facilities are not available. Tentative plans include approximately 200 AAF colored enlisted women in an overseas shipment. This will create vacancies to absorb the 180 now unassigned at Fort Des Moines." (If this overseas shipment does not go through, it is a fair bet that you will be hearing about the 180 before long).

7. <u>Notes from In and Out Log</u>.
   a. <u>Bern 9 Dec</u>. ...last bombardment Salzburg and especially Innsbruck other large number bombs failed to explode. Boche experts found all there contained small lead slab or ball placed near fuse. They of opinion this sabotage....

   b. <u>Greece ALUSNA 11 Dec</u>. British position Athens Piraeus grave. Large scale attacks by ELAS expected tonight or tommorow...

J. G. COZZENS
Major, Air Corps

ADDRESS REPLY TO
COMMANDING GENERAL, ARMY AIR FORCES
WASHINGTON 25, D. C.

ATTENTION:

HEADQUARTERS, ARMY AIR FORCES
WASHINGTON

14 December 1944

SPECIAL MEMORANDUM FOR THE CHIEF, OFFICE OF INFORMATION SERVICES

Subject: November Cases Pending in Special
           Investigations Division, Office of
           the Air Inspector.

1. <u>Resistance to Theatrical Entertainment</u>. Gen. Jones is
investigating a complaint about the conduct of AAF personnel
at an overseas base. Both commissioned and enlisted personnel
are alleged to have behaved improperly during theatrical enter-
tainments, "particularly those in which Pat O'Brien and Jinx
Falkenberg participated."

2. <u>Low Flying over Fox Farm</u>. Mrs. Sarah A. Davies of Great
Barrington, Massachusetts, has complained that low flying by AAF
aircraft has "seriously interfered with the successful raising
of silver foxes on her fox farm." This is being investigated.

3. <u>Alleged Beastly Goings-on at Big Springs</u>. An AWOL Wac
questioned at Bolling Field "made serious allegations" about
conditions at Big Springs Army Air Field (Texas) which led her
to absent herself. "These included conditions affecting both
physical and moral welfare."

4. <u>Treatment of Returnee Enlisted Personnel</u>. Many complaints
about the run-around, and general indifference and neglect, shown
AAF enlisted personnel returned from overseas and left idle here
and there have been received, investigated, and found largely
borne out. New procedures are to be recommended.

5. <u>Abusive Language of WAC CO</u>. "Conditions at ███████ Army
Air Field as regards Wacs are being investigated. Complaint
includes allegations that WAC Commanding Officer refuses to
listen to problems of enlisted women; refers to them as 'God damn
fools'; that Wacs are not wanted on the Base, etc."

                                J. G. COZZENS
                                Major, Air Corps

SECRET

HEADQUARTERS, ARMY AIR FORCES
WASHINGTON

14 December 1944

MEMORANDUM FOR THE CHIEF, OFFICE OF INFORMATION SERVICES

Subject: Information from AC/AS Offices.

1. <u>Dearth of Dog Handlers</u>. (Air Provost Marshal) The Quartermaster General has informed the Air Provost Marshal that the requisition for 40 sentry dogs by the Air Transport Command for shipment to an overseas station could be filled; but that trained Dog Handlers (SSN 458) are no longer available for assignment with the dogs. It will, therefore, be necessary for ATC to furnish 10 or 12 Dog Handlers in order to meet personnel requirements incident to this requisition.

2. <u>Bomb Tonnages on ETO Cities</u>. (Management Control) With the 5 December mission, Berlin became the city most heavily bombed by the AAF. Tonnages dropped by the AAF through 7 December on the most heavily bombed ETO points:

City	Tons
Berlin	13,517
Ploesti	13,098
Munich	12,937
Vienna	11,671
Merseberg	11,391
Cologne	11,326
Hamm	10,105
Brunswick	9,431
Kassel	9,270
Hamburg	8,481
Ludwigshaven	8,264
Budapest	7,007
Frankfort	6,642
Saarbrucken	6,476
Muenster	4,741
Hanover	4,697
Bucharest	4,403
Osnabruck	4,357
Wilhelmshaven	4,130

3. <u>New Aircraft Machine Guns</u>. (M&S) The Chief of Ordnance has reported on the current status and availability of the following four developmental machine guns:

a. <u>Caliber .50 machine gun, T36.</u> An improved
   caliber .50, interchangeable with the M2 gun.
   Greater belt pull and reliability are provided;
   rate of fire is 900 rounds per minute (present
   rate of fire, about 800 rounds per minute). Two
   guns have been tested successfully at Wright Field.
   Additional guns will be available 15 April 1945,
   and a production rate of 9,000 per month is expected
   in June, 1945. Existing AAF requirements are for
   31,336 guns.

b. <u>Caliber .50 machine gun, T25E3.</u> A new, high cyclic
   rate gun, similar to the standard M2, but not completely interchangeable. High belt pull and a rate
   of 1,200 rounds per minute are provided. Two guns
   have been shipped to Wright Field for test. Twenty
   additional guns will be ready 1 March 1945. By the
   end of May 1945, 2,000 guns will be available.

c. <u>Caliber .60 machine gun, T17E3.</u> This new gun has
   a muzzle velocity of 3,600 feet per second, fires
   650 rounds per minute. Two have been tested in an
   experimental Emerson turret. Additional guns are
   immediately available for installation in fighters for
   aerial test, but no promise has been made by Ordnance
   Department as to the date by which guns of proven performance will be delivered. Present AAF requirements
   are for 2525 guns.

d. <u>20mm. automatic gun, T31E2</u> (with T4 bolt). This gun
   was primarily designed for turret use; is equally applicable to fighters. Muzzle velocity is 2740 feet
   per second, rate of fire, 800 rounds per minute.
   Twenty guns will be available for official test 1 January 1945. Additional guns can be provided 90 days
   after notification by the Army Air Forces. Present
   AAF requirements are for 2,388 guns.

                              J. G. COZZENS
                              Major, Air Corps

or store-keeper's manner made himself useful without fuss, speaking in a firm way over the box to Col Stone, telling him to get together what I had just said I wanted. This was a great help since Stone and Col Cannon had then no choice but to do my work for me. . . . Ed Newhouse was made a major, to his own plain vast relief, making him a little coy about it—he simply appeared with leaves on and took refuge in reverting to a gag of last week in which Bradshaw suggested that he and I put on chaplain's insignia and see how soon anyone noticed. (It was about ten minutes, and we had already got some stares in the hall, since chaplains who are majors are rare and two together remarkable.)

Saturday 16 December 1944

. . . An AP story from New Delhi about smuggling into China by ATC and other personnel came over the ticker in the morning and I had an active day with Gen Jones' Deputy, Col Schneider, that office having heard nothing about it (and neither had the Air Provost Marshal or the Inspector General) but it seemed that OPD, WDGS [Operations Division, War Dept. General Staff] had known. I got through late in the afternoon with an R&R to Gen Smith asking him to ask Gen Giles to request WDGS to tell what they knew. At the same time I showed him the piece Gen Loutzenheiser's Col Cannon had written on the Pacific command, but it seemed to be all wrong so he sent me to Gen Kuter who agreed and arranged a conference for me tomorrow at noon with Gen Lindsay who was supposed to know about it. I could not see my way clear to observing that I was not on duty tomorrow; and that, I could easily see, was the difference between us—being a General was Kuter's whole life including Sundays, of course; while being a major was just a temporary work in which I found myself more or less engaged.

Sunday 17 December 1944

. . . Though I got down, Gen Lindsay didn't; and Col Johnson, his executive officer, thought 10 tomorrow would be a nice time, so Gen Kuter and I concurred. At least it enabled me to get home for lunch by two. . . .

Monday 18 December 1944

. . . Much seemed to be going on in the E ring in the morning and I was late in getting to see Gen Lindsay—from bits overheard here and there I gathered that it was being put to Mr A to use Brereton's 1st Air Borne Army to help out the hard-pressed 1st foot army, but the tension seemed to have relaxed later, making it seem possible that the force or the success of the German counter-offensive was over-estimated. Lindsay whom I had not seen or noticed before proved to be of the explosive opinion that nobody could really explain the Pacific set-up so why try—he is a tough alert, ruddy-

ADDRESS REPLY TO
COMMANDING GENERAL. ARMY AIR FORCES
WASHINGTON 25, D. C.

TENTION:

HEADQUARTERS, ARMY AIR FORCES
WASHINGTON

16 December 1944

SPECIAL MEMORANDUM FOR THE CHIEF, OFFICE OF INFORMATION SERVICES

Subject: 23 November Memorandum from AC/AS Personnel on
Air Crew Training Situation for the Use of Col.
McIntyre, Legislative and Liaison Division.

In conversations with Col. Belshe, Chief, Enlisted Branch,
AC/AS Personnel, about Gen. Bevans' 7 December directive to the
Training Command (my memo, 8 Dec.) it developed that "someone"
had, Col. Belshe thought, got together a statement on AAF personnel policy. The statement was apparently intended to guide
Colonel McIntyre in answers he might be required to make to
inquisitive congressmen. Lt. Col. ████ professed himself ignorant of the existence of any such paper; but a certain amount
of research, performed with the assiduity for which the undersigned
officer is noted, tracked it through Lt. Col. Fitch, Cadet Branch,
to Lt. Col. Clarke, Chief, Requirements & Resources, to Col. Maylon
who made it available with the cautionary comment of Gen. Bevans
that he did not want the damn thing aired all over the place.

1. Nature of the Memorandum. The memorandum is 8 pages, un-
dated, but stamped Secret 23 Nov. It is addressed to the Chief
of Staff, Attention Legislative and Liaison Division, and entitled:
Personnel of the Army Air Forces. Attached to it is the text of
Gen. Bevans' directive to the CG, AAF Training Command; and a form
letter addressed to "My dear Mr. Reservist", over the signature of
General Arnold. This appears to be the letter suggested by Gen.
Bevans last month (my memo, 29 Nov.); then abandoned; and then taken
up again. Col. Fitch tells me it has now gone out to all reser-
vists. In a perhaps-too-wheedling tone, it recognizes their disappointment, appreciates their volunteering, and says the transfer
'offer' is "intended only to accommodate those of you who prefer
immediate call to active duty".

2. Purpose of the Memorandum. "It would appear that there
is some misunderstanding of the operations of the Army Air Forces
by the War Department General Staff and perhaps by the Congress
and the country at large. It is anticipated that the facts contained herein will assist in clarifying the personnel policies
of the Army Air Forces." Col. McIntyre's "attention is invited
to the Minutes of the General Council, 20 November, which should
serve to answer questions relative to the progress of the AAF in
(a) reducing overstrength; (b) transferring overseas physically
qualified personne; (c) limiting size of ZI establishment." Part
of the purpose of the present paper is to indicate to Col. McIntyre

material that could be made available in the event of specific
questioning. "A detailed review of the AAF personnel scheduling
system can be arranged for representatives of the Legislative
and Liaison Division, and other War Department agencies at any
date desired." (Appointments will be made through AC/AS, OC&R,
Program Control Division).

3. <u>Air Crew Trainee Procurement Program</u>. The memorandum
rehearses the history of trainee procurement, with emphasis on
the necessity of very large procurement to start with. No more
than 24% of the candidates could meet the high mental and physical
requirements. We had no data on replacements, and so used
British figures, which have since proved too high even allowing
for our "chance of survival" plan. "The survival factor was to
be implemented by sending two replacement crews to the theatre for
each crew lost in combat." The cut-back in the Training Program
was initiated because "as early as December 1943 it could be
seen that the Training pipeline was too large." This August,
"due to the satisfactory progress of the European war", the
reduction to the 20,000 rate was made and it was further decided
that the November entrance into primary training would be at a
10,000 rate (that is; 800odd a month; the intake from ACER alone
is expected to average 4,000 a month, and, for January, will be
5,091)

4. <u>Present Plans for Utilizing Backlog of Air Crew Trainees.</u>
As of 22 October, there were 47,132 air crew trainees on duty.
To meet input requirements based on a 10,000 rate, approximately
21,000 are required in processing or pre-flight training. Therefore
the present trainee surplus amounts to about 26,000. "Freezing
pilot training in October, and a further training reduction in
November to meet the 10,000 rate, caused the trainee backlog to
become surplus to requirements." However, "An increase in the
training rate will be necessary to meet a continuing European
war. When the training rate is increased, current trainee reserve
will be largely wiped out."

Meanwhile, emphasis is to be put on the value of on-the-
line training. ("This experience and training has proved to be
valuable in making them better officers upon graduation."); and the
opportunity (offered by Gen. Arnold's letter) to transfer out with-out
prejudice if they get tired of on-the-line training (or 'temporary'
assignment to, say the Training Command permanent party, as in
the case of the 16,000 transferred by Gen. Bevans' 7 Dec directive.)

5. <u>Conclusion</u>. The most important point seems to be that made above, about the continuing European War. Though Col. McIntyre is not so advised, it seems to me obvious that he ought to be directed to make any inquiring congressmen realize that the whole apparently unfortunate screw-up was in fact a signal example of the AAF's prudence, resource in planning, and cool-headed refusal to get over-optimistic. We foresaw the possibility of the war in Europe continuing, and we are ready - we have this so-called surplus, and will not need to go into a frantic scramble to reverse an ill-advised policy of cutting input too soon. In short, given a few months more war in Europe, we ought to be out of the woods and functioning without embarrassment. Of course, the utility and advisability of Gen. Arnold's Dear-Mr.-Reservist letter thus becomes questionable; but that ought to be considerably easier to gloss over than a monthly intake of 3,200 more kids than we can train or begin to use.

                                        J. G. COZZENS
                                        Major, Air Corps

ADDRESS REPLY TO
COMMANDING GENERAL, ARMY AIR FORCES
WASHINGTON 25, D. C.

TENTION:

HEADQUARTERS, ARMY AIR FORCES
WASHINGTON

18 December 1944

MEMORANDUM FOR THE CHIEF, OFFICE OF INFORMATION SERVICES

Subject: Information from AC/AS Offices

1. Status of the B-32. (M&S) Acceptance and delivery status of the B-32 as of 16 December:

    Article No. 1 - Delivered to Consolidated-Vultee, San Diego, 9 December, for use as resident airplane. (a resident plane is one returned to the contractor for his experimental or other use)

    No. 3 - Accepted 9 December. Now in delivery pool.

    No. 4 - Delivered to Tarrant Field 9 Dec. for accelerated service test.

    No. 6 - In Army 262 inspection. (Final inspection prior to acceptance)

    No. 8 - Being flight tested by manufacturers.

    No. 9 - Static test article. Accepted 9 Dec. to be flown to Wright Field for static test (airplane is stripped and the frame subjected to breaking strains)

    No.15 - In engine run-up. Has had one flight by company pilots.

2. B-24 Accident Rate. (Training) At the request of Gen. Smith, reasons for the high accident rate of the B-24 (my memo, 15 Dec.) were summarized by AC/AS Training as follows: "Pilots require approximately 25% more training in the B-24 than in the B-17 to attain equal proficiency; the B-24 requires a greater degree of skill to avert an accident when trouble is encountered; the B-24 is more difficult to maintain, and therefore more failures are likely to occur because of poor maintenance." Recommended; Copilots be given 50 hours transition training in gunnery and technical schools, with emphasis on correct emergency procedure; that aerial engineers receive both aerial and ground training prior to shipment to CCTS's; that authorization be given to excuse maintenance personnel from physical training (my memo, 15 Dec.); that a four months' training period be established for B-24 CCTS; that a continued effort be made to return experienced personnel from combat theatres for assignment here; that every effort be made to expedite delivery of B-24N aircraft. (This is the B-24 with the single tail etc; my memo, 9 Dec.)

✓ 3. <u>German Jet Planes</u>. (Management Control) In a special

report on AAF heavy bomber losses (SC-SS-501), Stat Control notes
that in the month of October no bombers were lost to jet propelled German aircraft, although they were sighted on 13 missions.
"Reports received through 7 December continue to reflect no heavy
bomber losses as a result of jet fighters."

4. <u>National Aviation Trades Association Meeting</u>. (Training)
At a meeting of 2,000 members, at which Mr. Roscoe Turner was
re-elected president, representatives of AC/AS, Training heard
about their life and hard times. The Members say they are con-
fronted with a "very critical financial period of the next
several months prior to resumption of manufacture of light
civilian aircraft." Recommended: That the AAF "assist this
trades industry with their problem where possible in post war
thinking so as to preserve the unity of the industry." (probably
means something). "Specifically, they are desirous of the AAF
supporting a renewal of CAA's Civilian Pilot Training Program or
any comparable activity financed by government funds." They feel
this would be justified because, by keeping them in business, the
AAF would have available better facilities "for research, development, and manufacture in the future."

5. <u>XR-10 Helicopter</u>. (OC&R) A "subject mock-up" was viewed
at the Kellett Autogiro Company's plant last week. "This aircraft
is under development to fulfill military characteristics 'Helicopter, Utility-Cargo'." Specifications: Twin 525 hp engines;
twin three-bladed interlocking rotors; weight empty, 7,556; max.
gross weight, 13,500 (approximately 4,300 lbs. of cargo); high
speed sea-level, 126 mph; operating speed, 90 mph.; endurance
(hours) 3.1 at designed gross weight with full fuel load; 7.7
at alternate gross weight with fuel overload. Current estimates
indicate that prototype will not be ready for flight tests before
November 1945.

6. <u>XC-97</u>. (M&S) The Boeing XC-97 (cargo version of the B-29)
will be on view at the National Airport, 8 January.

7. <u>P-80</u>. (M&S) The contract with Lockheed Burbank covering
the purchase of 1,000 P-80A-1 airplanes was approved 15 December.

8. <u>Notes from In and Out Log</u>.
    a. <u>Com 3rd Fleet CINCSWPAC 13 Dec</u>. Our air plan con-
templates maintaining continuous day and night cap over Luzon
fields. Similar unrelenting pressure on Visayan fields should
mousetrap many Nips...

b. <u>Versailles from Schlatter 14 Dec</u>. ...Powered gliders can be landed in any area in which towed gliders can be landed, more accurately due to having power...believe up to 60 powered gliders should be made available at earliest possible date...

c. <u>Com 3rd Fleet 14 Dec</u>. Complete tactical surprise achieved as Task Force 38 ranged over Luzon fields...Navy blanket seems to have kept them smothered...

d. <u>Com 7th Fleet 12 Dec</u>. (Delayed) Estimated enemy strength 12 December. Luzon, 398 (146 fighters, 192 bombers); Visayas 186 (118 fighters, 44 bombers); Mindanao 100 (34 fighters, 48 bombers)... Japs have large plane reservation Formosa to replace losses...

e. <u>USMA Ankara 13 Dec</u>. Conditions in Greece causing much harm Allied cause in Turkey...immense loss of prestige for England...growing conviction U.S. turning back to isolationism...

J. G. COZZENS
Major, Air Corps

faced hell-for-leather (probably) drinking man with a cropped moustache—the type, if the truth were told, that I like in the Army for reasons not completely clear, except that he by God is a brigadier general and you're a major and everything is cut and dried. . . .

Tuesday 19 December 1944

. . . I saw Lindsay again in the morning and then Smith who was not of Lindsay's opinion so I got the text written up and Smith in the afternoon seemed happy about it. Up with Haddock to talk to Gen Norstad in the afternoon to see if he would release some figures on the 30th Air Force strength, and he wouldn't—a sort of stubborn Scandinavian streak in him in which reason consists in sticking to what he originally thought. . . .

Wednesday 20 December 1944

. . . Gen Beebe, the Acting CG of the Continental Air Force, gave me a slight turn by being late to the party to which I invited him yesterday on Gen Smith's behalf. He is a large & regular-featured, somewhat gray-complexioned and flat-spoken soldier's soldier who said to me disarmingly as he came up at last (I was hovering in the hall outside Smith's office); Guess I need somebody to tell me where I'm supposed to be. He did all right—I realize that the laborious 'speaking course' which they tucked into our tight enough OTS [Officers Training School] schedule must be derived from West Point, where they very properly figured that any officer must be able to make a speech, and so they learn the rudiments and can usually recover them. Gen Smith did his usual good job with nothing untoward but some asinine interruptions by Lt Col Gilder who grinning and bobbing offered a little advice on the problem of defining the relationship of the Deputy Chiefs of the Air Staff to the various organizations—Smith was flabbergasted yet composed and finally shut him off. He (Gilder) hung around and though Haddock had said to me behind his hand something must be done about him, when he (Haddock) with firmness but exemplary mildness started to do the something as we walked back, Gilder agreed so rapidly that it was not the thing to do that there was no catching him. We parted at the head of the tenth corridor and at least George and I could concur on Smith—he is really fine, or God's single solitary gift to George in his harassed job.

Thursday 21 December 1944

. . . The *Washington Post*[52] in the morning had extended Smith's remarks considerably to bring in the autonomy of the air forces and that took some fussing. . . .

ADDRESS REPLY TO
COMMANDING GENERAL, ARMY AIR FORCES
WASHINGTON 25, D. C.

TENTION:

HEADQUARTERS, ARMY AIR FORCES
WASHINGTON

21 December 1944

MEMORANDUM FOR THE CHIEF, OFFICE OF INFORMATION SERVICES

Subject: Information from AC/AS Offices.

1. <u>Adjusted Service Rating for Officers</u>. (Personnel) Though the text of WD Circular 341 <u>Relief of Officers from Active Duty</u> seems pretty well agreed on (my memo, 13 Dec), AC/AS, Personnel is having some differences of opinion with the War Department on "readjustment" (i.e., discharge) of officers following the defeat of Germany: and does not concur in a proposed regulation "which specifies an adjusted service rating for officers as a secondary consideration for demobilization is not considered to be in the best interests of the Army Air Forces." Long acquaintance with AC/AS, Personnel's prose style enables me to extract the actual meaning: we do not want it as any kind of a consideration, primary <u>or</u> secondary. "The AAF proposes an orderly reduction in officer strength, based on military necessity and the policies of the Commanding General. The use of an adjusted service rating would seriously hamper the Commanding General, AAF, in the full prosecution of his mission." (Judged to mean that the AAF does not want to be bound to get rid of anyone, or prevented from getting rid of anyone, just because a scale of points based on length of service, overseas service, decorations, and kiddies at home, has been worked out on a machine. This attitude would seem to be to the advantage of various desk officers who are getting sick and tired of it all.)

2. <u>Sound or Noise Warfare Against Japan</u>. (OC&R) A memorandum has been prepared for the Chief of the Air Staff "on the use of sonic devices in the persecution (sic) of psychological warfare against the Japanese. The study included a review of developments in bomb whistles, sirens, airborne loud speakers, deceptive charges (this is a device dropped at any desired point which by a successive explosion of separate charges simulates rifle shots, machine gun fire, mortar fire, and so on, leading the enemy to suppose that action is taking place at that point) and parachute dropped radio broadcasting speakers." (this is the so-called Bunsen Burner which will reproduce the sounds, for instance of an armored column in motion). Major Prout, who has had the subject in hand in the Requirements Division, says he thinks it unlikely that noise alone will lick the Japs, but the use of the last two types of noise-makers in conjunction with ground troops might someti es be effective. "Recommended that sound warfare not be adopted by the AAF in other than joint operations with surface (sic) forces, and that sound warfare be monitored by AAF Liaison with NDRC and by the ACO."

3. <u>Camp Springs Personnel</u>. (OC&R) At a conference held to estimate the necessary supply and maintenance personnel for the new Hq., Continental Air Force, at Camp Springs it was decided, on the basis of present Bolling Field personnel, that approximately 1,000 would be needed.

4. <u>Racial Difficulties at Midland Field</u>.(Air Inspector) In connection with a complaint signed by 22 colored officers (which was judged not substantiated, and the case closed) Col. Schneider remarks: "On 21 September 1944 the Commanding Officer of the base placed a temporary restriction on the use of the Officers Club by student officers (colored) to avoid race riot and bloodshed. The restriction was lifted on 16 October 1944. CFTC determined that action was necessary in the emergency."(The 'emergency' seems to have been the declared resolution of a number of white student officers, sufficient to intimidate the CO, to throw out any negro who tried to come in. The matter seems to have been very effectively hushed up.)

5. <u>Notes from In and Out Log</u>.
   a. <u>Chungking signed Hurley 17 Dec</u>. The threat to Chungking, Kunming and Kweiyang is still very real...operations of Japs in southwestern China are too large to warrant present optimism of the Chinese...

   b. <u>To Fort Worth signed Arnold 19 Dec</u>. You will receive TWX from CG 3rd AF stating his receipt from you of returnees who did not volunteer for second tour. We infer that this flow was prior to policy that all second tour flow must be volunteers. If epidemic of refusals in CCTS by returnees is allowed to develope it will cause serious ramifications. Problem cannot be minimized... (this is the first indication of what must be the next thing to a small mutiny on the part of returned combat crew members who have been assigned to CCTS units in preparation for going overseas again.)

   c. <u>To Caserta for McNarney 18 Dec</u>. Increase in frequency of attacks on German sanitary installations in Italy by British and American low level fighter bombers is subject of protest by German Government...

J. G. COZZENS
Major, Air Corps

Saturday 23 December 1944

. . . Gen Smith was stirring with interest over the improved weather in Europe and what the air force might now do, so I thought I would not go to Mr A's egg nog party, where I feared I would meet him and find myself perhaps involved a long time afterward figuring out a use for the news. . . .

Sunday 24 December 1944

. . . In as duty officer and little was up beyond a call from Gen Giles suggesting he would like someone in tomorrow. . . .

Monday 25 December 1944

. . . Down to the Pentagon about 11 to relieve Haddock, but I was not obliged to stay long, because he had obviously spoken to Gen Owens who shortly after 12 suggested that there was no reason for anyone to stay. . . . At the Pentagon the military news was mainly better. The fact that everyone is ready and willing to accept bad news at somewhat more than face value (I mean, everyone except the professional military men) must show something, though I do not know what—perhaps only that some subconscious assurance makes it possible to take dim and pessimistic views whenever anything goes wrong without impairing the fundamental sanguine acceptance of the certainty that we must win in the end, anyway—that is, you can criticize the delay without ever questioning the outcome.

Tuesday 26 December 1944

. . . We decided not to have a conference for Gen Smith since, though it began indeed in the Log (except for that part of it—the larger part—filled with an awkward sometimes fawning, sometimes embarrassed, exchange of Christmas messages and acknowledgement of those from Mr A, etc) to look as though we were getting the situation in hand and for the third straight day the air forces were pouring it in, we were not quite ready to say so. . . .

Wednesday 27 December 1944

. . . Drew Pearson had started the morning off with some sour comment on the Russian refusal to allow shuttle bombing, so we talked (Haddock and I) to Gen Lindsay about that—he has perhaps a narrow and limited mind; but it surprised me to hear him say, the doors closed and giving us what he thought was the low-down quite temperately that of course they did not want us in there supplying our bases, because it would do the government no good if the simple Reds were to see what the capitalistic world meant by 'supply'—the outpouring of goods and services and the effort to see that the men were amused and taken care of.[53] . . . After that we went

201

and talked to Smith about what to say to Gen Deane, and what to give Mr Stimson for his conference tomorrow on the subject, if it came up. I then went back and wrote the cable to Deane and the memo to Stimson.

Thursday 28 December 1944

. . . To Mr Stimson's press conference with Haddock at 10.30 on the chance he was going to talk about the Moscow stuff (he didn't). We had, punctually enough, two messages back from Deane, the second elaborately stating that the use of 'bases' in the first was for security reasons. I could not help reflecting that Smith's conferences were somewhat superior in conduct, animation, and interest; but the old man, halting through his text, had better news from the 1st Army front which was all anyone wanted. He also paid the AAF several forthright compliments so we felt more secure, and I went at once to get up stuff from Col Clarke and Col Fogle for Smith next week. . . .

Friday 29 December 1944

. . . I spent the morning marking up on a German communications-system map the air strikes of the last six days; and certainly the communiques begin to look as though that was it, and Smith was right. . . .

Saturday 30 December 1944

. . . I was busy with the Log cables, and roughing out what Gen Smith might say if things continued all right. In the Log, the reports were fragmentary, indicating that the real dispatches were coming through Top Secret; but, for once, at least, I deduced or just guessed, because they were very good rather than very bad. As far as Smith's piece went, it began to get vaguely clear that he must have been right—who (meaning Marshal von Rundstedt) in his right senses would undertake an offensive when he not merely lacked air superiority, but was outnumbered five or six to one if he sought as little as air equality? The only two conclusions seemed to be that (a) he did not understand the meaning of air power; or (b), he was so desperate that anything was better than nothing. If borne out over the next few days, the point would be good for the conference.

Sunday 31 December 1944

. . . To the Pentagon for a few minutes in the morning to see Smith, who seemed sanguine, but thought we had better take the German breakthrough as an accomplished fact, and never mind how it happened; since that involved SHAEF [Supreme Headquarters Allied Expeditionary Force] and why they had misjudged the German intention.

ADDRESS REPLY TO
COMMANDING GENERAL, ARMY AIR FORCES
WASHINGTON 25, D. C.

.TENTION:

HEADQUARTERS, ARMY AIR FORCES
WASHINGTON

26 December 1944

MEMORANDUM FOR THE CHIEF, OFFICE OF INFORMATION SERVICES

Subject: Information from AC/AS Offices

1. <u>Fixed-Fee Contract Altercation</u>. (Air Inspector) Since
last August the Air Inspector has undergone an odd and persistent needling at the hands of the Inspector General. The
IG has attacked practically every AAF contract, whether for
frames, engines, or completed aircraft, on the grounds that
fees for fixed-fee contracts are or were excessive. Lt. Col.
Logan, Chief, Contract Division, Office of the Air Inspector,
has repeatedly requested the IG to indicate more exactly his
objection - that is, why he considered the fees too big, or what
arrangement, in placed of cost-plus-fixed fee, he would recommend.
With this idea, and the assistance of Gen. Echols, a conference
was arranged a week ago Saturday in the office of the Under
Secretary of War. Here it was represented to the IG that (a)
the AAF was following the procurement policy established by the
War Department; and (b) that in the event of excessive fees or
profits, they were always subject to recovery through the renegotiation Statute. To this Gen. Peterson, (and Gen. Ahren, his Chief
of Procurement) seemed to answer little or nothing beyond
agreeing that "his office would review their past policies of
criticizing the amount of fees in cost-plus-fixed fee contracts."

This was highly unsatisfactory to the Air Inspector and
General Echols. General Jones believes (surely correctly) "that
the continuance of this type of criticism is detrimental to the
AAF." Gen. Echols, Col. Schneider, and Lt. Col. Logan therefore
had a second conference of their own, 21 December, and resolved
to draw up a 'definitive memorandum' to be signed jointly by
Gen. Jones and Gen. Echols protesting the IG's action or lack of
action. Major Simpson will send me a copy of this memorandum as
soon as it is ready (next week, probably). In a confidential
discussion with Lt. Col. Logan, who appears to be a sensible and
well-informed officer, I learned (for the information of the Chief
OIS, only) that he believed that the IG or some of his officers
were (a) definitely intent on building up a 'case' against the
Air Forces as inefficient in procurement; and in the case of some
of the officers (b) not averse to discrediting the whole so-called
profit system with an eye to having the army or the government
own its production facilities.

2. Misconduct at USO Performance. (Air Inspector) The nature
of the disorder complained about at a USO performance by Pat
O'Brien and Jinx Falkenberg at ███████ China, 25 October (my
memo, 14 Dec) now proves to have had nothing to do with the
performers or the performance. The "misconduct" consisted in
the CO appearing on the stage in a cockeyed condition requiring
two people to hold him up, and in his executive rushing out of
his quarters in a state of nature - scandalizing, if not the
assembled GI's, at least (presumably) Miss Falkenberg.

3. Very Large Bombs. (M&S) Priority for engineering and
modification of the bomb-bay of one B-29 to carry the Tall Boy
(my memo) 12 Dec) 12,000 lb. bomb has been raised from 1-B to
1-A. This project is in addition to that of "engineering an
installation" to carry the 22,000 lb. bomb (now differentiated
from Tall Boy by the title; 'Grand Slam'.)

4. Jet Propulsion Engine Procurement. (M&S) Procurement of
5,000 TG-180 JP engines and 1,000 TG-100 jet turbines (with pro-
pellers) has been directed. These engines (GE developed) will be
produced by Chevrolet at the former Jacobs Plant No. 2, Pottstown,
Pa. However, while the development of the TG series engines carries
a 1-A priority, production will be 2-B "in order to avoid interference with current R-3350BA engine and other programs."

5. Aircraft Carriers. (Management Control) Stat Control has
completed a special report "which presents a complete listing as of
29 November of US Naval Aircraft Carriers in the Atlantic and
Pacific Fleets and those carriers scheduled to be ready for service in the next three months." 85 carriers are in action at
present; 12 in the Atlantic, 73 in the Pacific.

6. Notes from the In and Out Log.
    a. Greenland att, AC/S Op. 23 Dec. ...Sledge patrol
reports Germans in northeast Greenland...request dispatch of three
B-17 aircraft...

    b. St. Germain signed Spaatz 25 Dec. Proposal to re-
turn technically trained maintenance personnel to ZI is subject...
latest strength figures available here indicate shortage of over
1,200 airplane engine mechanics...further drain would seriously
interfere with accomplishment of air force mission...we are not in
a position to accede to your request...

                                          J. G. COZZENS
                                          Major, Air Corps

ADDRESS REPLY TO
COMMANDING GENERAL, ARMY AIR FORCES
WASHINGTON 25, D. C.

ттENTION:

HEADQUARTERS, ARMY AIR FORCES
WASHINGTON

27 December 1944

MEMORANDUM FOR THE CHIEF, OFFICE OF INFORMATION SERVICES

Subject: Information from AC/AS Offices.

1. B-32. (OC&R) Lt. Col. Bailey, Requirements, has submitted a recommendation to C/AS that B-32's be used to replace B-24's in five MTO groups. "Study shows that tactical availability of aircraft will be sufficient, that necessary training can be accomplished, and that conversion of all five groups can be completed by March 1946." Questioned on the several interesting implications of this statement, Lt. Col. Bailey said that it was necessary to figure out something to do with them, since the CG had decided they were to be made and used. The first convenient hole to put them in was found in the plans prepared on an assumption (for planning purposes only, I hope) that the war would continue in Europe during 1946. The CG has also decided to include a Flight Engineer in B-32 crews. Col. Wallace has suggested several ways in which one of the present crew members can double as Flight Engineer, "obviating the necessity for including one more crew member." In view of these items, it seems safe now to consider the B-32 as definitely intended for operational use after all.

2. Helicopter School. (OC&R) "To provide training facilities soon to be needed, announcement is made that an AAF pilot School (Helicopter) is being established at Chanute Field, Ill., as of 1 December 1944." (Training) "Pending establishment of a definite helicopter training program by this Hq, approved request from the Training Command to: graduate present class of liaison pilots on 27 January 1945; enter 25 trainees next class beginning 22 January, classes to be of six weeks duration and overlap one week, resulting in a production of approximately 22 helicopter pilots each five weeks. Training Command also authorized to secure rated pilot volunteers under rank of Captain to fill vacancies in classes that are not filled by this Hq."

3. Burial of the Dead. (Training) In answer to an R&R from AC/AS, M&S, "calling attention to the fact that officers and enlisted men arriving in the ETO are not fully aware of the extreme importance of prompt burial of the dead, safeguarding and prompt evacuation of personal effects, prompt and accurate reporting of isolated burials," promulgation of an AAF Letter is recommended. This will require all units in training to listen to "a lecture of approximately one hour's duration covering the subjects enumerated above."

4. Colored Pilots. (Personnel) "A further step toward meeting a threatened shortage of qualified candidates for the colored pilot training program was taken when a directive was issued 22 December to all Continental Commands and Air Forces to screen all colored personnel for volunteers for pilot training who are between the ages of 18 and 26, physically qualified for overseas duty, having an AGCT score of one hundred or better, and who have not been previously eliminated from air crew training." (This directive might come in handy if and when the Afro-Americans squawk on the 322nd Group cut-down -- my memo, 18 Nov.)

5. Pilot Training Program Aircraft Requirements. (OC&R) In connection with the storage of training aircraft (my memo, 23 Dec) the Commitments Division observes; "if the two-front war continues beyond May 1945 it may be necessary to increase pilot production from the present 10,000 to 20,000 a year." This will require storage of 1,100 PT-17's; 1400 BT-13's; 1,200 AT-6's. "Most of the above aircraft are to be placed in storage over the next six months. Arrangements are being made to store the planes in fields released by reason of reduction in civil contract training schools. Personnel required to maintain the aircraft will be civilians already employed at these stations." The note concludes philosophically, "if either Germany or Japan is not defeated prior to December 1946, it would be necessary to eventually increase pilot production to 40,000 per year. However, in view of the remoteness of this requirement, no provision is being made at present for such an increase."

6. Racial Difficulties at Midland Field (Con.) (Air Inspector) The difficulty last fall at Midland Field (my memo, 21 Dec) was somewhat clarified by Major Henderson, of the Air Inspector's office, who looked up the file at Col. Scott's request. Major Henderson, whose accent makes it clear that he is qualified to understand the situation, said that he felt the action of the CO at Midland was essentially a declaration of temporary martial law. He informed me, apparently with first hand knowledge, that an acute person had little difficulty in telling when the southern boys were getting ready for "riot and blood-shed"; that there were no overt acts or representations to the CO, but an old southern hand would simply know that in a minute they were going to beat the hell out of those niggers. Question: do we wait until they do and then explain a lot of broken heads and maybe a few shootings, or do we step in and 'separate' the hostile elements, give them time to cool off, and then let the negroes back into the club? This was what was done, and it seemed to work. On this basis the Air Inspector closed the case.

3

7. <u>B-29 Inventory</u>. (Management Control)

The AAF inventory of B-29 type airplanes passed the 1000 mark in 23 December 1944. As of that date a total of 1002 B-29 type planes (including 41 F-13's and 1 XB-39) were on hand. Of this total 610 were in continental United States and 392 outside the U.S.

Derivation of the total is as follows:

Total Deliveries		1,207
Less: Overseas Losses	150	
Domestic Losses	<u>55</u>	
		205
On hand 23 December 1944		1,002

J. G. COZZENS
Major, Air Corps

ADDRESS REPLY TO
COMMANDING GENERAL. ARMY AIR FORCES
WASHINGTON 25, D. C.

TENTION:

HEADQUARTERS, ARMY AIR FORCES
WASHINGTON

30 December 1944

MEMORANDUM FOR THE CHIEF, OFFICE OF INFORMATION SERVICES

Subject: Information from AC/AS Offices.

(No doubt because of the celebrations traditionally associated with the winter solstice, all AC/AS Offices appear semi-sturned and little or nothing interesting or intelligible has come out of any of them since the Eve of the Nativity. On this occasion the Air Chaplain as usual reported "routine". The In and Out Log has similarly been much occupied with fawning acknowledgments of seasons' greetings from the Top Echelon. War expected to be resumed at Hq AAF next week.)

1. Bomber Sorites on 24 December. (Management Control) The Eighth Air Force operation of 24 December on which 2,034 heavy bombers were dispatched, represented the largest 'single' heavy bomber strike ever to be flown by the AAF. On D-Day 2,716 hb sorties were flown, but many aircraft and crews were used twice. On 24 December, 634 of the heavies attacked 14 enemy communications targets, and the remaining 1,400 struck at air fields in Western Germany.

2. On-the-deck Fighter Training. (Flying Safety) A "stricter policy" is to govern on-the-deck fighter training in this country. "It was agreed -" (with AC/AS, Training) "- that in all probability this will result in some increase in fighter accidents, though it is not believed that the 300-foot missions previously flown have resulted in any significant change in fighter accident statistics." (Suggest that valuable training would result from removing the present penalties on buzzing air-fields, control towers, cows, and goddam civilians driving cars down lonely roads.)

3. Twenty-First Bomber Command Reconnaissance. (OC&R) A recapitulation of the 3rd Reconnaissance Squadron (B-29) operations from Saipan "reveals the first mission was over Tokyo on 1 November. Many of the aircraft of the squadron did not arrive until 20 and 23 November. Yet from 1 November to 10 December 42 individual aircraft missions were flown." Of 26 photographic missions, 16 were unsuccessful because of the weather, 5 failed because of aircraft malfunction, 5 were successful. Of 10 weather missions, 8 were successful. Of 5 RCM flights, 4 were successful. "The 3rd Squadron is suffering from the fact that no service organization is responsible for its maintenance and care. This situation may be corrected when the organization has completed its move to the air depot field on Guam."

4. Notes from In and Out Log.

a. USMA Havana signed Tausch 27 Dec. Reliable sources rated B-3...a conspiracy among personnel of armed forces favorable to President Grau, object; ousting of present Army-Navy hierarchy...definitely known something is brewing in Armed Forces...

b. Caserta signed Alexander 28 Dec. ...if, as evidence of build-up implies, enemy intends major undertaking, consider likely that action in Serchio Valley likely to be preliminary and diversionary...

c. St. Germain signed Spaatz 28 Dec. There are twelve fields in UK which could be developed to standards indicated...(answers query on basing VHB squadrons in UK by July 1945)

d. Versailles signed Eisenhower 29 Dec. (This is an excerpt from Strong. Fuller reports must be coming in Top Secret) ...general battle for Bastogne spreading...enemy armor not yet employed...enemy perhaps hopes to stage one more attack with all his armor in north first. Signs of subsidiary or diversionary attack mounting in west Holland continue...

J. G. COZZENS
Major, Air Corps

A Time of War

Monday 1 January 1945

. . . Gen Smith's argument seemed to be shaping up all right for the conference, and I was able to get most of the questions off to sections of Plans and Intelligence on a new formula; Gen Smith would not wish to answer this without coordinating with you on policy. They then eagerly write the answers. . . .

Tuesday 2 January 1945

. . . Very busy all day finishing up Gen Smith's text and getting his maps done. Haddock and I saw him after 5 and it seemed to be all right. . . .

Wednesday 3 January 1945

. . . We had the usual Wednesday morning fuss—though, in fact, I find it enlivening if wearing—it makes me think sometimes that a man, or one of my temperament, is in fact easiest when there are ten things to do at once, and the phone never stops ringing, and you bustle around now; and now sit, and people keep coming in to say How about this; and; Is this what you want and, when, by degrees, it all straightens out, you know you have done something, it doesn't matter what. The conference was good and especially decorated by the presence of Major Bong, the kid they gave the Congressional medal to for his 40 Jap planes. He was the usual dumb-as-a-pilot infant with a cropped mop of fine slight wiry blond hair and the stolid good-natured face of a little, pleasant, composed and alert—well, pig; except that he had too all the steady good nature of the dumb-as-a-pilot type, which would outweigh the fresh, snoutish round face. He was very patient and amiable while the photographers shot him afterwards in Gen Smith's office, the General having turned him over to me and fled. . . . Incidentally, about Bong, I noticed again that certain look around the eyes which I am sure means extraordinarily quick and good sight, which every successful fighter pilot I have ever seen has.

Thursday 4 January 1945

. . . I had a quiet day with my memoranda, and in to lunch with Bradshaw at the Lafayette, and out to talk to Col Scott in the Air Inspector's office about a case involving the CO of a Lt Hoover, and whether he had or had not told the Lt not to testify to the Mead Committee. The point at issue was with the AJAG [Air Judge Advocate General] so I went down there, where I have had little business outside reading their activity reports and encountered some more well-poised lawyers in soldier suits, and accomplished little. . . .

Monday 8 January 1945

. . . Haddock seemed to support my absence with composure and I went at once to see

ADDRESS REPLY TO
COMMANDING GENERAL, ARMY AIR FORCES
WASHINGTON 25, D. C.

/ENTION:

HEADQUARTERS, ARMY AIR FORCES
WASHINGTON

3 January 1945

MEMORANDUM FOR THE CHIEF, OFFICE OF INFORMATION SERVICES

Subject: Information from AC/AS Offices.

1. CBI Evaluation Board Report No. 3. (OC&R) The report covers the period June, July, August 1944. Subject: Effectiveness of Air Attacks Against Burma and Siamese Railroads. Conclusions: (a) "Bombing effort in this period against railway targets was not completely satisfactory and there was surprising inaccuracy in these attacks." (b) Planning and target selections were unsatisfactory, (c) Adequate photographic coverage was not available. Recommended: (a) Careful preparation, selection and coordination of bombing effort against land lines of communication. (b) uniform methods in compilation of operational data (c) complete photo coverage of important targets. Hq AAF, India Burma Theatre in a 1st Ind. "comments on the statements in the report to the effect that ground force requirements dictated the amount of air effort against these targets in that period, and that certain classes of intelligence information which control priority and effort by air units cannot be made available to the Board." (Judged to mean: we are passing this buck).

2. B-29's Dispatched Overseas in 1944. (OC&R) Since 21 March 1944, 341 B-29's have been dispatched to the XX Bomber Command, of which 8 were lost through various accidents en route. 17 are still en route. 316 have been delivered as of 31 December. Since 7 October (initial departure) 271 B-29's have been dispatched to the XXI Bomber Command. 29 are still en route. There have been no losses en route. (Included are F-13's for both commands)

3. Allied Air Strength. (Management Control) As of 1 December the Allied Air Forces "inventory of combat and transport airplanes in all areas passed 150,000. The distribution:

	Aircraft Number	Percent of Total
U.S. Army Air Forces	51,979	35%
U.S. Navy Air Forces	27,230	18%
Total U.S.A.	79,209	53%
Royal Air Force	31,505	21%
Royal Fleet Air Arm	6,041	4%
Total British (Excluding Dominion Air Forces)	37,546	25%
Red Air Forces	26,700	18%
All Other Air Forces	6,896	4%
(Includes PCAF, RAAF, RNZAF, Chinese Air Force, NEIAF)		
TOTAL ALLIED AIR FORCES	150,351	100%

4. Case of Lt. Phillips, (Unexpected Aftermath) (Air Judge
Advocate) The Air Inspector's report on 2nd Lt. ████████████
(my memos, 24 Nov, 12 Dec) leads the AJA to the opinion that Col.
████████████'s instructions and directions "to the effect that
Lt. ████████ should not make any report other than through military
channels was not a suggestion that the Lt. refuse to testify before
a Congressional committee." However, the recommendation is that
Col. ████ "be given an administrative reprimand for the use of
ill-considered language in explaining War Department policy."
(Undersigned officer's opinion: better find out who his father is
before you ding a 2nd Lt.)

5. Camp Springs Snafu. (Air Provost Marshal) Asked by the
office of the Chief of Engineers if the employment of POW at
Camp Springs, Maryland had been approved ("The CG, ASF has issued
an order which prevents the use of any labor except POW on
demolition of buildings at posts, camps and stations. There are
some wooden buildings at Camp Springs which must be demolished
for their lumber which is a highly critical item at the present
time.") the Air Provost Marshal answered yes (1 Jan). However
(2 Jan) he was obliged to back-track. The Chief of Staff, First
Air Force, informed him that the request to use prisoners of war
at Camp Springs had been disapproved by the CG, Continental Air
Force.

6. Honorable Discharge Button & Mrs. Roosevelt. (Air Provost
Marshal) Mrs. R., after a luncheon with Gen. Hines, recently
observed in "My Day" that she hoped the WD would change the button
for wear by discharged military personnel. The APM observes;
"Some months ago this office initiated a paper (in itself quite a
trick) on a general service ribbon which was turned down by G-1...
it is felt this would be a good time to go back to G-1 with our
proposed General Service Ribbon. Considerable difficulty is
being encountered by discharged personnel because the button is very
similar to those of factory workers such as Pratt-Whitney and other
industries engaged in the manufacture of war materials. The War
Department has not authorized a General Service Ribbon for World
War I or II. There is a need for such a ribbon since so many have
been discharged from the service who did not see service outside the
continental limits of the US through no fault of their own."

7. White Shoe Dressing for MP's. (Air Provost Marshal) In
answer to an inquiry from the Air Quartermaster about requisitioning
white shoe dressing "for the purpose of whitening web equipment"
used by MP's at an AAF base, it was stated; "although the practice
of applying white coloring to web equipment was not prohibited by
the Inspector General, it was nevertheless not authorized by Army
Regulations, and that such coloring material was not available for
issue to any organization."

8. <u>Fun with Jeeps Etc</u>. (Air Inspector) "Investigation by the Western Flying Training Command revealed that at Pecos Field, Texas, a Negro prisoner had been double-timed in front of a jeep, a white soldier was kicked by an MP when he refused to keep quiet after arrest, and an MP lecturing guards used profane language. The practice of double timing was authorized in a guard regulation issued by the former CO, since killed in an airplane accident. The present CO had no knowledge of the regulation and rescinded it immediately upon learning of it. Reprimands were issued to two MP's. Guards were advised of proper methods in handling prisoners. The Training Command directed a survey of all subordinate commands to assure that double timing was not practiced elsewhere."

9. <u>Service Rating Credit Tests</u>. (Management Control) On the basis of the proposed point system for 'adjusted service rating cards' (who gets demobilized first) an analysis has been made by Stat Control. The system (my memo, 5 Oct 44) is: number of months service, 1 point; number of months overseas, 1 point; number of combat awards, 5 points; number of dependent children, 8 points. Analyzing on a sampling basis approximately 2% of all AAF enlisted personnel, they come up with the following estimates of those who would be released on the first cut:

13% -- of fathers in the AAF
9% -- of non-fathers
40% -- of father with overseas service
$\frac{1}{4}$ of 1% -- of all men without overseas service
3$\frac{1}{2}$% -- of all men in ZI
18% -- of all men in overseas theatres.

10. <u>Weather Factors in ETO Bombing</u>. (Management Control) The effect of bad weather in hampering ETO operations "is indicated by the fact that 75% of heavy bomber operations from September through November 1944 were done by non-visual methods. In contrast, during the same period, only 25% of XX Bomber Command operations were by non-visual means." In the past three months "only 1/3 of ETO heavy bombers air borne have succeeded in attacking their primary targets by either visual or non-visual means. "In September and October, 60% of ETO heavies bombing the primary target used visual means, but in November this figure dropped to 6%. Since only 1/3 of the heavy bombers airborne in the ETO attacked the primary target, only 2% (1/3 x 6%) of total heavies airborne in November attacked primary targets by visual means." (This quiet little analysis seems calculated to set Mr. A. back on his heels.)

J. G. COZZENS
Major, Air Corps

HEADQUARTERS, ARMY AIR FORCES
WASHINGTON

5 January 1945

MEMORANDUM FOR THE CHIEF, OFFICE OF INFORMATION SERVICES

Subject: Information from AC/AS Offices.

1. ▓▓▓▓▓▓▓▓▓▓▓▓▓ Case. (Going On & On). Col. Scott of the Special Investigations Division of Gen. Jones' office showed me with some swearing yesterday a 2 January memo from theAir Judge Advocate (signed by Col. ▓▓▓▓▓▓▓▓▓▓▓▓▓) which did not accord with the AJA Daily Activity report item (my memo, 3 Jan). Apparently taking a dim view of the ▓▓▓▓▓'s intellectual capacity, Col. Scott said it would give him pleasure if I would carry the two papers down and indicate the discrepancy. In the Activity Report, an administrative reprimand for Col. ▓▓ was recommended. The memo said:

"In further answer to your inquiry as to whether, in our opinion, an administrative reprimand to Col. ▓▓ would be sufficient to satisfy the Mead Committee, permit us to observe that we believe that it should be the consistent policy of the Commanding General, in the exercise of military discipline, to determine the character and extent of punishment to be meted out in any particular case upon the merits as we view them and in accordance with law, rather than attempt to satisfy the whims and caprices of a Congressional committee. We therefore suggest that the prospective views of the Mead Committee be not considered. Predicated upon the attacked record of investigation, it is the opinion of this office that no disciplinary or administrative action should be taken against Col. ▓▓ in the premises."

The lofty sentiments and high-falutin prose were perhaps in part responsible for Col. Scott's oaths. However, Col. Scott felt that the AJA, with such cracks as the one about whims and caprices, would help very little in the work of trying to keep the Mead Committee calmed down. He also felt that Col. ▓▓ had unquestionably behaved improperly and ought to get a reprimand for the record. In this view, Col. Kidner, of the AJA office, concurred. The discrepancy between the items was explained by the fact that Col. Kidner had written the activity report recommendation, supposing it was the recommendation of their office. Without telling Col. Kidner, Col. ▓▓▓▓▓▓▓▓ had changed his mind and written the memo to Gen. Jones. In neither office does Col. ▓▓ seem to inspire much confidence or affection.

2. **Allied & Enemy Plane Ratios.** (Management Control) Stat. Control has calculated the ratio between Allied and enemy first-line combat aircraft as of 25 December 1944:

Western Europe	4.9 to 1
Africa-Med-Italy	10.5 to 1
Eastern Europe	7.1 to 1
Asia	1.4 to 1
Far East	3.7 to 1
All Active Theatres	4.6 to 1

3. **Mine-Laying by CBI Aircraft.** (OC&R) Lt. Col. Younger, Requirements, reports at length of mine laying activities of the 10th and 14th Air Forces and the XX Bomber Command. Between 26 March 1943 and 23 November 1944, the 10th AF and the RAF laid 1,377 mines in 14 rivers and harbors and channels in Burma, Siam, Malay Peninsula, and the Andaman Islands. Between 16 October 1943 and 16 December 1944, the 14th laid 661 mines in 10 rivers, harbors and channels in China, Burma, Formosa and Haiman Island. On 10 August, the XX Bomber Command laid 16 mines in the channel approach to Palembang. Some results: "The harbor of Rangoon was completely neutralized. A ship, mined and sunk in the canal at Haiphong, blocked the entrance to an approaching convoy which was compelled to seek refuge in an emergency anchorage where 6 out of 10 ships were sunk by air attack. Haiphong was abandoned as a harbor in October 1943. Bangkok was closed from February through May 1944. Total tonnage of ships at Hong Kong fell to one quarter its initial value. General Chennault has stated that the mines laid in the Hong Kong-Canton area were more than any other factor responsible for the failure of the Japanese military forces to undertake a planned drive northward from this area in 1944. In addition to the foregoing strategic and tactical returns, it is known that a total of 19 enemy ships were sunk, 2 possibly sunk, and 8 damaged. The actual enemy shipping losses were undoubtedly considerably greater. These are the returns from a total of 555 aircraft sorties and the loss of 8 aircraft."

4. **AAF Day Fighter Strength in 1944.** (OC&R)

Type	1 Jan 1944	1 Jun 1944	1 Jan 1945	Gain or Loss During Year
A-36	227	131	87	-140
P-38	1796	2444	2709	+913
P-39	1994*	2027*	750	-1244
P-40	2220	2430	1722	-498
P-47	3734	5430	5056	+1322
P-51	1107	2331	3853	+2746
P-59	0	0	16	+ 16
P-63	*	*	320	+320
TOTAL	11,078	14,793	14,513	+3435

*P-39 totals include some P-63's.

This table indicates the rapid expansion of the AAF during the first half of 1944 with many of its day fighter units moving from operational training to combat duty. The second half of the year reflects a high level of activity in which the total fighter production has been insufficient to replace the total losses. However the replacement of obsolescent models has resulted in a distinct qualitative gain.

5. <u>Returnees at Scott Field & Elsewhere</u>. (Air Inspector) Some confusion and mismanagement in the handling of AAF personnel back from overseas for reassignment or further training has been repeatedly turning up in Gen. Jones' investigations (my memo, 14 Dec 44). The difficulties at Scott Field seem to have been corrected, but Gen. Jones regards the situation as still serious. His people have been working with the IG on "revised schedules". A detailed report from the IG to the Secretary of War on the subject is expected to be ready about 1 February.

J. G. COZZENS
Major, Air Corps

Gen Smith with him, where we decided to have no conference this week, planning a fine one on the Philippines next week—material for it he seemed to feel, with the same firm assurance he showed about the Ardennes matter, would be ready then. . . .

Tuesday 9 January 1945

. . . I got at my accumulated activity reports. To town for luncheon with Bradshaw and, my compilation done, we had an idle late afternoon which went mostly into Newhouse's expert questioning work on Johnny. . . . The pleasure she gets out of being questioned and resisting the questioning would, I suppose, be dull, except for a certain lively counterfeit of shame (yet half real), and the attractively energizing effects of the consciousness of holding the center of attention while the banter and kidding keeps it at just the right degree of intensity—what she says next, if she decides to say it, everyone will listen to.

Wednesday 10 January 1945

. . . Up to see Col Scott on some WAC difficulties (how they could be disciplined without loss of chivalry was the point involved. Col Scott, no doubt correctly, took the attitude of to hell with that; are they in the army or aren't they? and showed me a few records of lewd and insubordinate conduct). . . .

Thursday 11 January 1945

. . . I was busy getting stuff together on the Philippine business and making my memoranda. Driving home with George Haddock, he remarked that the efficiency reports were getting him down—it is a new form which does not stop with the general classifications of superior etc but asks scores on ten points and a short summary of what the officer is like. He said he was coming back this evening and would then do them all and get them out of the office before our practised snoopers could see what he said. This was only half a joke, because he could obviously see that though we might suspect we were not perfect, no one of us would really appreciate his stating in plain terms what we lacked; and would be more than likely to dispute to ourselves his judgment, and probably pick lacks more to our taste, or better suited to our prejudices. . . .

Friday 12 January 1945

. . . I was busy, out of the secret G-2 [Military Intelligence Section] chronological summary working up a schedule of air action on the Japs '41 invasion of the Philippines to compare with the present, and I was astonished to realize how grim the reading was (there were no really secret things in it; almost all of it was announced as fast as it happened and so I must have read it in the newspapers at the

ADDRESS REPLY TO
COMMANDING GENERAL, ARMY AIR FORCES
WASHINGTON 25, D. C.

ATTENTION:

HEADQUARTERS, ARMY AIR FORCES
WASHINGTON

9 January 1945

MEMORANDUM FOR THE CHIEF, OFFICE OF INFORMATION SERVICES

Subject: Information from AC/AS Offices

1. <u>Post War Troop Basis</u>. (OC&R) The Troop Basis Division, recovering somewhat from its low spirits brought on by the 'vest pocket air force' business (my memo, 6 Dec 44). "It has been tentatively decided to seek an AAF Post War Troop Basis limited to 700,000 military, including 200,000 universal military trainees. This personnel will be formed into an AAF organization which will support 75 groups and 30 separate squadrons in peace time, and provide for fighting as many groups as possible at the expiration of one year of war." (Translated from Col. ████'s everyday gibberish, this means that the organization will be so contrived that a maximum number of groups for combat will be available within one year from the word Go.) The division purposes to prepare another tentative troop basis "predicated on the above assumption, and also upon the assumption that this country will be warned and will take expansive action one year prior to the outbreak of hostilities." The Col. somewhat vacuously adds; "The latter assumption has been forced upon planning in view of the fact that because of the length and expense of combat crew training, this country cannot put an adequate air force into the field within one year of notice without excessive cost."

2. <u>Bush to Ding Major ████</u>. (Air Judge Advocate) Col. Patterson (my memo, 5 Jan) is of the opinion that subject officer (Major ████ ████) "should be punished under AW 104 for writing letters to the President, the Secretary of War, and the Under Secretary of War which criticized without foundation in fact his superior officers and his command. It is recommended that mentioned punishment be administered by Hq AAF to expedite same as Major ████ reverts to inactive status on 20 January 1945."

3. <u>Essential Aircraft Industry Workers</u>. (M&S) The Western Procurement District reports to Gen. Echols that any further release of 22-26 year old workers will result in definite loss of aircraft production. "Originally, approximately 12,000 men in this age group were deferred. At present, between 600 and 700 remain in a deferred status. It is claimed that these men are essential...Efforts are being made to establish a procedure which will result in review of each case at the national level prior to the induction of any of these 22-26 year old men. In view of the imminent induction of 26-29 year old men, the Western District and the West Coast aircraft industry consider it essential to develop some means for the retention of this small group of 22-26 year olds."

4. <u>Aircraft Production in 1944</u>. (M&S) Total US aircraft production for 1944 was 96,356 articles, of which 70,843 were produced in factories under AAF cognizance. March, with 9.117 acceptances, was the high month. There were 73,974 combat airplanes produced (76.4% of total production). New combat models produced in substantial numbers were B-29's and A-26's. B-32's and P-80's were just getting into production at the end of the year. Discontinued: A-20, A-30, RA-24, RA-25, A-35, P-39, P-40. All types of combat aircraft showed an increase over 1943. The largest decrease was in trainers (from 19,942 in 1943 to 7,578). The totals for previous years; 1941, 19,455; 1942, 47,805; 1943, 85,931.

5. <u>ZEC Types Vessels</u>. (M&S) Definite delivery dates have been received for the first 3 of the 16 new ZEC boats now under construction. (They are designed to ship assembled aircraft and relieve us from dependence on the Navy for CVE's - which the Navy is reluctant to make available: my memo, 6 Dec 44) Vessels will be delivered in time to permit loading at Pacific Coast ports; 11 February, 15 February, 17 February.

6. <u>Training Command Policy on Returnees</u>. (Training) Presumably aroused by the Air Inspector's findings (my memo, 5 Jan), AFTRC was directed by Gen. Welsh to take action to "(1) Train returnees in refresher courses, or for new MOS on a proficiency basis; (2) Extend to them all privileges consistent with a maintenance of proper military discipline; (3) Hold returnees in permanent party for a reasonable time before assignment to re-training." (In connection with (2) above, the Air Provost Marshal reports (8 Jan) that he "concurred in a paper prepared in the Foreign Assignments Branch, AC/AS, Personnel, which is aimed at correcting deficiencies in the appearance and conduct of personnel returning to the US through aerial ports of embarkation.")

7. <u>Frog Heroine Etc</u>. (Air Surgeon) "Madam (sic) Drue Tartiere, who directed the underground activities in Fontainbleau and was said to have aided many wounded airmen to get into the hands of the French underground and provided medical treatment for them, was brought to this office by Major Simon, BPR. The great desire of the doctors who aided these wounded airmen is to obtain some of the new and current medical books. Arrangements have been made for the Josiah Macy Foundation to furnish a portion of these books and the rest are to be gathered and will be sent to the doctors who have aided these men as a gift from the Josiah Macy Foundation and the AAF."

8. <u>B-36 & VLB's</u>. (OC&R) "Requirements were stated for a bomb of the present 'Tall boy'" - (they mean 'Grand Slam', not 'Tall Boy'; my memo, 26 Dec 44) "—design to fit the maximum space allowable by each bomb bay of the B-36. It is estimated that the bomb would weight approximately 45,000 pounds and the B-36 will have space available to carry two such bombs." (A check with Lt. Col. Fix, OC&R, indicates that '45,000' and 'two' are not misprints.)

9. <u>Fraternization with Wacs.</u> (Air Wac Officer) At the request
of ATC, Lt. Col. ███████ has issued a policy statement "on social
fraternization between male officers and WAC enlisted personnel and
women officers and enlisted men." She points out that WDGS, G-1,
holds that relationships between officer and enlisted personnel are
not governed by statutes or regulations, but by established and
accepted customs of the service. "It has been a generally accepted
rule of thumb at installations where Wacs are serving that enlisted
personnel should not fraternize with their immediate superiors. This
has been interpreted at the majority of AAF installations to mean that
officer and enlisted personnel stationed at the same installation should
not fraternize socially." (Col. ███████ informs me that the interpretation
would also be that a WAC enlisted woman, home, for instance, on furlough,
or off the post at which she was stationed, is free to go dining,
dancing, or (who knows?) shacking-up, with any male officer she might
meet. Similarly, WAC officers, if they are that hard up, need not
repulse the advances of GI's met off the post.)

10. <u>Post War AAF Commissions.</u> (Personnel)

- A study of the Officer Evaluation Reports, form 123, completed
recently at the AAF Tactical Center, Orlando, Florida, develops the
following factual data:

Total number of officers evaluated:
Rated	309	(26+%)
Non-rated	825	(73+%)
Total	1,134	

Recommended as qualified for Regular Army commissions:
Rated	179	(58% of rated group
Non-rated	447	(54% of non-rated group)
Total	626	(55% of 1134)

Of the total number recommended for RA commissions, 408 (or 65%)
stated that they were interested.

52% of all officers evaluated desire RA commissions.
80% of all officers evaluated desire either RA or ORC commissions.
20% of all officers evaluated did not desire any postwar
commissions (neither RA nor ORC)
91% of all officers evaluated were recommended for either RA or
ORC commissions.

11. <u>Notes from In & Out Log</u>
a. <u>Rumania from Schuyler 5 Jan.</u> Gen. Vinogradov...has spoken
in glowing terms of the growing friendship between US and Russia...
striking similarity in the line followed in all conversations...may be
part of a general Moscow policy to promote friendly relations...however,
it may also be a local effort to promote confidence and to camouflage
certain present or contemplated Russian actions which we might other-

wise consider detrimental to US interests...

SECRET

b. <u>Caserta from Faker 7 Jan.</u> (Answers request for more
information on recent hb losses) ...Narrative reports do not suggest
employment of proximity fuses or new projectiles (by Krauts)

c. <u>To Guam from Arnold 4 Jan.</u> ...your operations reports
show normal combat losses of about 1 airplane per mission but
operational losses...about 4. We cannot continue to have the large
number of operational losses for this type aircraft...

                         J. G. COZZENS
                         Major, Air Corps

ADDRESS REPLY TO
COMMANDING GENERAL. ARMY AIR FORCES
WASHINGTON 25, D. C.

ATTENTION:

HEADQUARTERS, ARMY AIR FORCES
WASHINGTON

LL January 1945

SPECIAL MEMORANDUM FOR THE CHIEF, OFFICE OF INFORMATION SERVICES

Subject: ██████ Air Depot Case. (Air Inspector)

1. Col. Scott, Special Investigations Division, sent for me this morning to say that the Department of Justice had informed him that the U.S. Attorney, Mr. ████████, will ask the Grand Jury meeting on 17 January for indictments against the officers and civilians involved in the Air depot mess at ████████ (my memo, 19 Sept 44). Originally there were three points: (1) the illegal labor contract (negotiated by a Col. ████████, Chief of Supply Section, with a local contractor named ██████; (2) a super-duper bar in the officers' club built with gov't material and army labor; (3) alleged destruction of a quarter of a million dollars worth of new supplies to save the depot the trouble of sorting and storing them.

2. The Air Inspector, through Col. Scott and others, has been trying ever since to reach some agreement with the Dep't. of Justice. Col. Scott had some talks with Mr. Foley of that Department last month, but the position of U.S. District Attorneys is such that the Dep't cannot effectively direct or control them. Mr. ████████, who is believed to have political ambitions, appears to see himself in a Tom-Dewey-type crusading role, and to like the sight fine. Probably at this point, he could not, even if he wanted to (or could be induced to want to), drop the matter because of the persisting public indignation about the destruction of material and the club bar (which is regarded as one of the many ill-advised or outrageous antics of ████████████████████ — he was also something of a cocksman etc.).

3. However, the indictment will be based on the labor contract (conspiracy to defraud). In connection with (2) Mr. ██ has stated verbally that he may (not will) accept the check for $3,800 from the club for the bar; in connection with (3) he seems to feel charges would be too hard to prove. The conspiracy-to-defraud indictment is expected to name Col. ████ (now overseas), Col. ████████, and a Major ██████. Col. Scott believes that Col. ████████'s position will be very bad. Col. █. has a long unsavory record as a confidence man or plain crook in Panama and elsewhere. Gen. Jones feels that the testimony is bound to bring out scandalous wastes and inefficiencies in the former Air Service Command. He is more concerned about this than the direct indictment, which it is believed that Col. ████████ can

more or less meet by claiming that he was only following the direction of the CG, AAF to cut corners and red tape and get the job done without worrying about petty technicalities.

4. It was Gen. Jones' considerate notion, in directing Col. Scott to talk to me at once, that the Chief, OIS. should not be caught with his informational pants down when the newspaper story breaks with a bang, presumably some time next week.

J. G. COZZENS
Major, Air Corps

ADDRESS REPLY TO
COMMANDING GENERAL, ARMY AIR FORCES
WASHINGTON 25, D. C.

HEADQUARTERS, ARMY AIR FORCES
WASHINGTON

11 January 1945

MEMORANDUM FOR THE CHIEF, OFFICE OF INFORMATION SERVICES

Subject: Information from AC/AS Offices.

1. Independent Air Force. (Air Judge Advocate) "There is no
legal requirement that the words 'War Department' appear on the seal
of this Headquarters, nor is there any legal objection to the elim-
ination of the mentioned words from the seal."

2. Beastly Goings-on at Big Spring. (Cont'd.) (Air Inspector)
The AWOL Wac who could not face the moral and physical conditions at
this popular Training Command post (my memo, 14 Dec 44) is one Private
████████████   After questioning at Bolling Field, █████ was returned to Big Spring where she was put under "hospital observation,
and it was concluded that she was suffering from severe emotional
instability and that her complaints were based on either rumor or
imagination, and were without foundation." This, however, is not taken
seriously in the Air Inspector's office. A Major in Col. Scott's
office who attended the Bolling Field questioning thought she was
perfectly rational and almost certainly telling the truth, and that
the quoted pronouncement was a routine bit of whitewashing by the
Training Command █████████, "hospital observation" being the
only available form of confinement for recalcitrant Wacs. The problem of properly disciplining the girls seems to be a difficult one;
but in this connection the Air Wac Officer has coordinated on an AAF
letter prepared by the Air Provost Marshal which lays down procedures.
A copy for the information of the Chief, OIS, is supposed to be in the
mails. The Air Inspector feels that there is some possibility of
unfavorable publicity, sooner or later, in whatever steps may be
taken to enforce discipline (and, off the record, deplores the
inclusion of the former WAAC in the army as an actual military component.)

3. Plan to Save Paper. (Management Control) "In August 1944,
2,056 individual forms were being used throughout Hq. On 1 November
1944, Hq Office Instruction No. 5-12 was released regarding forms,
their use, approval, and procurement, and thus separated forms-pro-
curement from other publications channels and made originating offices
'form conscious'. A survey was made of the 2,056 forms being used,
and the result was that only 825 were found needed for continued use.
As a result of this survey approximately 1,230 plates were released
to be regrained and negatives and stencils destroyed."

4. <u>Continental Air Force Hq. Assignments.</u> (Management Control)
Hq CAF, GO #2, prepared by OPD, will assign to the Hq Staff: Brig.
Gen. Reuben C. Hood, Assistant Chief of Staff, Operations and
Training; Col. Daniel F. Callahan, AC/S, Maintenance & Supply; Col.
Emil H. Molthan, AC/S, Personnel and Administration. Temporary
location of Hq CAF will be in Hq AAF, Room 3A330.

5. <u>Bombs on Japs.</u> (Management Control) Stat Control reports
that during December 1944 the AAF "dropped in theatres opposing the
Japs" a greater tonnage of bombs than in any other month of the war.
Preliminary total was 17,000, as compared to 12,253 in November, and
14,724 in May, the previous high month. Of the December total,
3,100 tons were dropped by VHB.

6. <u>Anti-Aircraft Jet Propelled Guided Missile.</u> (OC&R) "It is
informally understood that Admiral King has placed on an urgent
basis development of an anti-aircraft jet propelled guided missile
for ship-to-air use. Available information indicates that Johns
Hopkins has agreed to undertake the entire project, including introduction into operational use, with a target date of about two years;
and that two to three hundred technicians, and ten to twenty million
dollars, will be devoted to the project. The missile is to weigh
some 2,000 pounds, to range 20 miles with a ceiling in excess of
30,000 feet, to have about 1,800 foot/seconds velocity, and to be
controllable by radar means to the target." (What, no swimming pool?)

In view of the AAF's responsibility for Army development of
aerodynamically sustained guided missiles, and also "in view of our
necessary interest both in the weapon envisaged by the Navy and in
the countermeasures against such a weapon", Col. Giffin of Requirements has requested M&S "to take whatever action necessary to insure
that the AAF is fully cognizant of all efforts devoted to this
project, to the extent, if necessary, of allocating funds and personnel to make this a joint Army-Navy endeavor."

M&S has also been requested "to indicate the action necessary
to re-orient our entire guided missile program along the general lines
of placing development of defensive air-to-air guided missiles in
highest priority" because of "the threat that would be implied against
our own superior air power by the introduction into use of the weapon
described and in view of the increased use of suicide ramming attacks."
(The point would seem to be that it gets more and more likely that for
bombing purposes airplanes carrying crews are going to be obsolete
within the next few years, and the new pitch will be guided missiles
shooting down guided missiles.)

J. G. COZZENS
Major, Air Corps

time, but without realizing what it meant, at least, as it happened—that is, what was bound to follow if such and such was the case). Of course, what it goes to prove is what Smith wants proved, and that boils down to the fact that after the 8 Dec raid on Clark Field we had lost the Philippines, even if Corregidor didn't give up until 6 May next year. We had lost control of the air and we could not get in reinforcements to contest the loss, so it was all up right then. . . .

Saturday 13 January 1945

. . . It developed that Gen Smith, as I feared, was indeed leaving on a particular mission to Kenney, his place to be taken, if probably not filled, by Gen Hood,[54] a mild little BG we had once as Smith's guest to tell about China as he saw it from the ASC [Air Service Command]. Kuter would be better, but Hood would probably be easier to manage, a point I left with George Haddock, who was himself stirring restively over a suggestion of Gen Norstad that he go to Saipan or Guam for a month. Ed Newhouse had a little difficulty yesterday when counter-intelligence turned up the not exactly obscure fact that he used to be a *New Masses* writer and juvenile style Red; and what was he doing here in the high councils of the Air Staff?—the matter came to Gen Smith, and Haddock, perhaps none too easily, turned it off, Smitty, straight West Point on all such matters, being taken aback; but also displaying that quality of temperance or reasonableness which is endearing to those who work with him, by saying finally that if Haddock said it was all right it was; and so dismissing Maj Boberg of counter-intelligence. It had Ed understandably disturbed, his defiant amusement modified by the knowledge that the Army can be stuffy if it wants to; and the fact that he had long ago abandoned his opinions not explaining, from that standpoint, why he had ever had them. [See 1 March 1945.]

Monday 15 January 1945

. . . I was busy getting Smith's stuff on the Philippines together, including a map from Dahlstrom and ten or twelve pages of my ideas on strategy which seemed very lucid and interesting, if only they happen to be true and Smitty likes them. . . .

Tuesday 16 January 1945

. . . I got Smith's piece to him a little after 3 and he read it with approval, Gen Hood being there, apparently taking lessons in how to be an AC/AS. Miss Thompson asked me as I came out if I did not think better of Gen Hood—though I had always thought he was an amiable enough guy, only lacking in Smitty's valuable positive qualities. She is actively concerned since she will carry on as his girl, so I said yes, which seemed tactful and was in fact true—he would be gentle, civil, and easy to manage. To my text Smitty wanted added a few paragraphs to say how we were isolating the Philippine battle field, and so it seemed straight from the horse's mouth that MacArthur was meeting so little opposition not because of some canny plan, but because we were 'interdicting' by air the enemy's routes north and he was not able to bring his forces up to the Agno. It was a pleasant thought, and surely Smitty would not wish to say it unless he knew it was true. I could not think why I felt a sort of persisting doubt, which harassed me while I was providing the necessary text.

Wednesday 17 January 1945

. . . At the conference, which was well attended, Smitty did all right with my short history of the art of war and there were I-could-believe-sincere expressions of regret when he concluded by saying that Gen Hood, who had come in with him, would now carry on. In his office afterwards, where I was persuading him to sign an article Ransom had made out of two of his conference talks on tactical air operations for *Air Force*,[55] Gen Hood, still with him, seemed more at ease and I figured he might be made to do with a little practise; but I doubt if he would ever manage Smitty's nice mixture of dignity and informality—a point pleasantly (I thought) made when he came up before the conference to go in the back door. There was a guard, a private, who, when I said: Here comes the general, came to attention; so I, beyond the jamb, came to attention, too. Smitty gave me a look as he came by, dropped one eyelid, but without otherwise changing his expression, hit me across the stomach with his folded manuscript, at the same time turning to give the guard a nod, and walking on with dignity. . . .

Thursday 18 January 1945

. . . I got around to seeing Gen Hood late in the afternoon with the proposal that we should clear for him and he should use a German analysis of our strategic air operations that the Intelligence Summary published last November. He was plainly nervous about the whole assignment and balked—my own fault, I saw, because I had indicated to him the fact that we might have to work on G-2. Plainly (and with reason) he was none too sure that he was going to fill Smith's boots properly, in this and (probably he was modestly prepared to feel) in any other respect; and I could afterwards see how unlikely he would be to want to begin his career by immediately throwing his weight (that is, using Gen Giles) against G-2. However, it remained important to establish the principle that we, not he, would determine what he took up; so Haddock told me to see what I could do with fighting it out with G-2 myself; and when we knew exactly how we were going to stand, he would then undertake to tell the Gen what he should do. I thought he had a good chance of carrying it, since the same quality of (far from offensive) desire to go along with Smith's customs and theories, at least until he knew where he was, would operate there. . . .

227

ADDRESS REPLY TO
COMMANDING GENERAL, ARMY AIR FORCES
WASHINGTON 25, D. C.

ATTENTION:

HEADQUARTERS, ARMY AIR FORCES
WASHINGTON

17 January 1945

MEMORANDUM FOR THE CHIEF, OFFICE OF INFORMATION SERVICES

Subject: Information from AC/AS Offices.

1. <u>Chaplain Situation</u>. (Air Chaplain) The Miscellaneous Division of the Office of the Chief of Chaplains reports 26 Air Decorations and 23 casualties among AAF chaplains to date.

2. <u>Regular Army Colonels for Overseas Service</u>. (Personnel) A review of Regular Army Colonels who have not served overseas in an active theatre in this war, and who, pursuant to the directive of Gen. Arnold, are to get some of that as soon as possible, shows that there are 247 such. "In addition to these, there is a limited number of lower ranking Regular Army officers who will have to be sent as individuals to an active theatre." This seems to mean that there will be quite an increase in the already over-large theatre staffs.

3. <u>Sleeping with Wacs</u>. (Air Judge Advocate) Case of 2nd Lt. ███████ and 1st Lt. ███████████: "Opinion that the sole action warranted in case of subject male officer who had been acquitted after general court-martial trial of occupying the same bed and sleeping with subject WAC officer, and for whom reclassification proceedings were deemed inappropriate, is punishment for public drunkenness. Further opinion that although evidence indicated WAC officer was guilty" (under AW's 95, 96, Col. Kidner tells me) "of offense of sleeping with man not her husband, and of public drunkenness, and although acquittal of male officer did not prevent her subsequent trial by court-martial for mentioned offenses, in view of the possible failure of proof and all the circumstances, punishment under AW 104 would be a satisfactory solution of the matter." (This may teach them to couple more quietly).

4. <u>B-32 Training</u>. (Training) Gen. Welsh states that "pending completion of tests to determine the operational suitability of the B-32 airplane," the Training Command has been directed to train the necessary instructors and permanent party personnel which will be required for Training Command B-32 transition schools so that they can go into crew production "upon receipt of a notice that a requirement exists for B-32 crews." This somewhat remarkable proceeding was explained to me by Lt. Col. ████ as a move of desperation, due to OC&R declining to state when there would be a requirement, and how much; or even to say when there would be any B-32's available - all this in the face of the CG's flat declaration that 5 groups (my memo, 27 Dec) were going to be converted to B-32's or he would know why. In order that AC/AS, Training may not be caught with its pants down, the Training Command will therefore do what it can (at Fort Worth) to prepare to turn out instructor teams at the rate of

2

10 per month for March, April, May, and June. These instructor
teams would in theory be ready to train transition teams of pilot,
co-pilot, and flight engineer - though nobody yet knows how many
such teams there will be to train, or when there will be B-32's to
fly them in. Fifteen articles had been more or less completed in
December (my memo, 18 Dec) but none was then assigned to the
Training Command.

5. <u>JB-2 Engines</u>. (M&S) Officials of the Ford Motor Company have
informed AAF representative that they can increase production of
JB-2 engines to 100 per day within 60 days. Ford is also working
on an engine for ATSC which is approximately twice the cross section
of the JB-2 engine. Thrust is expected to be at least twice as
great and the efficiency improved. The first unit was tested
early this month and delivery of 3 to ATSC was promised by last Monday. Incidentally, that was the day scheduled for the first live
JB-2 bomb launching at Eglin. All the others had dummy charges.
How this came out is, naturally, not known; since M&S activity reports are back on the old one-or-more-weeks-late schedule.)

6. <u>Unruly Conduct on Troop Train</u>. (Air Inspector) "Investigation
was conducted by the First Air Force of complaint received from
Chief of Transportation that on a movement of enlisted men from
Charleston AAB via the Southern Railway, it was necessary to cut
out the three cars in which the men were travelling at Summerville,
S.C., and return them to Charleston, due to the unruly conduct of
the men. The train commander, Lt. ███████████████████, was
cognizant of the fact that some of the men were drunk, but had
determined that they should make the trip." Investigating officers
recommended disciplinary action against Lt. ██████ which was duly
taken under AW 104 in the form of a reprimand from the First Air
Force Hq. "Although, in the opinion of the Air Judge Advocate, the
railway company could seek damages, information has since been received that the company has waived all charges."

7. <u>Wing Wearing by Parents</u>. (Air Judge Advocate) Col. Patterson
is of the opinion "that although under existing legislation the
wearing of an aviation badge (wings) by the parents of deceased
rated personnel is technically illegal, it is deemed obvious that
there is no likelihood of prosecution therefor." He is of the
further opinion "that new legislation is unnecessary to remedy the
present situation for the reason that the mentioned statutues
empower the Secretary of War by promulgation of appropriate regulations to permit exceptions to their application."

J. G. COZZENS
Major, Air Corps

Friday 19 January 1945

. . . I went down in the morning to see a rather round red Col Louden in G-2, Gilder having talked to him, and I seemed to get a formula in which we could use the material for Hood. He made some round and portentous remarks about the vital importance of covering the sources of our Intelligence material; but, considering the nature of this-to-hand, they did not make too much sense and I could see that, though relatively pleasant, he was not afflicted with the tendency to draw distinctions of the finer sort. . . .

Saturday 20 January 1945

. . . Most of the day went into a struggle with Ransom's text for Smith's *Air Force* article. . . . Gen Hood came around to George Haddock's persuasions and we seemed all set on the topic for Wednesday.

Monday 22 January 1945

. . . I got Hood's stuff shaped up more or less—more, I guess, as it came to quite a lot. . . .

Tuesday 23 January 1945

. . . I got the Gen's stuff into him with Haddock at four—Haddock feeling very bad, but measured and reasonable as ever. The Gen does not promise too well but he was making an effort (though the only comment on the long text that he made seemed to show he was not very bright) and may do better. He was taking it home with him to try out—these things are disarming, and he is a nice guy, really—the sound of it on his wife. Perhaps he will do better when he is up against the necessity of conducting the show; but I could wish he was naturally brighter. In the pm Gerald Carter called me up, this time concerned about his son Martin, who is an ACER cadet, and was instructed to report for duty at Cumberland, Pa on next Monday. However, on Friday he was to graduate from High School and he was also valedictorian of his class. What could I do? I thought nothing; but I called a Major Hale in the Cadet Branch, Personnel, and damned if after a few minutes search of records he didn't say he would, if I liked, issue amended orders, so Martin wouldn't have to go until 12 February. I reported it back to Gerald with some trepidation, since it was certainly well-calculated to make him believe that I indeed run the army.

Wednesday 24 January 1945

. . . Gen Hood did much better than I feared, having obviously really put it to himself—he went too fast, but he took elaborate pains to speak clearly; and, further, quite successful pains to model himself on Smith. It did not come naturally to him, so it rather won me to see him try so hard and do relatively so well. His subject was a great success and there was furious note-taking—so much so, I began to feel somewhat disturbed—that is, over what G-2 would think if, as seemed likely, the German analysis got a big play—still Col Louden had seen the text and didn't squawk.

Thursday 25 January 1945

. . . Whatever happened to all the writing the newspaper people did it was not in any of the papers, so I felt better, figuring that when it turned up later, Col Louden would have forgotten about it. . . . In to see Gen Hedrick, the Air Judge Advocate, pursuing a notion of mine that we could use some such stuff on the conference program. He is a square-faced, mild, intelligent be-spectacled man, not at all averse to the idea (I've never met anyone in high army circles who was; would anyone be?). Haddock had told me to go ahead and sound it out, but I could see afterward it was more to keep me quiet than because he concurred; and I could see, too, how much wiser he was about the management of people than I would ever be. I expect he did not think the idea a good one, because of his temperately collected and accurate newspaper experience; but I was useful and active, and why give me a check first? I could have the fun of my idea and then it could either be eased-out or, supposing I really turned up something, used. In his position, I would know no better than to argue against the thing at the first stage if it did not seem sound to me. This would all be more instinctive than reasoned or conscious—cross bridges only when you come to them. I doubt if he ever read Franklin, but (quite as you would expect) some natural reasonableness puts in practise all the precepts in the autobiography about stating your opinion, and so saying no that the person denied, though he may be disappointed, is never affronted. . . .

Friday 26 January 1945

. . . As I expected, George eased me mildly and lucidly out of the Hedrick business, though that left us with nothing. . . .

Saturday 27 January 1945

. . . Nothing special turned up for the Gen, though there was some agitation over Col Greene's editorial in the *Infantry Journal* suggesting we had too much air force—the best answer seemed to be that only the air force, being a naturally forward-looking group of men, had grasped the scope of this war and planned in the beginning for what they would need—in sharp contrast to the benighted foot army. In town for lunch with Bradshaw and, beyond my memorandum, not very busy, though I went in with Haddock to hear, on Gen Hood's radio, Air Marshal Peck's remarks on the 'birthday' of the 8th Air Force and Giles' response. We were both of the opinion that something would have to be done about Major Preston . . . a tall, dark, born-busybody with no sense.

Monday 29 January 1945

. . . Haddock called off Gen Hood's conference so I found myself in easy circumstances with no more than my memorandum to do. Robert Carson, a motion picture major, turned up at noon to check on the film to be made of Mr A's report and in town with him and George Bradshaw to have lunch. He is a round-headed, rosy-faced, sharp-nosed fellow whom I had heard much of through B&B[56]—pleasant and amusing. . . .

Tuesday 30 January 1945

. . . We had a quiet day—no conference makes all the difference. . . .

Wednesday 31 January 1945

. . . The atmosphere around the Pentagon seemed lively, as to say the Russians were really going somewhere and what with Hitler's speech, something sudden was plainly expected to happen in ETO within a week or so. I daresay they will find themselves fooled again.

Thursday 1 February 1945

. . . I went to the ceremony at which Gen Smith was given the Legion of Merit by Gen Giles; an informal affair in Mr A's conference room, and it was nice to observe how well—by instinct, not by art—Smitty did everything. He laughed a good deal beforehand—there were a dozen mostly minor generals present—colored some, but still was composed, while Giles, who had the normal trouble with the clasp, pinned it on him, standing straight so there was no awkwardness about him and so no possible implication of either real or affected ease or indifference; but nothing suggested that he took himself too seriously, either. Giles made a few foolish remarks, and everybody filed around the table to shake hands with him. When I appeared, bringing up the end, and said that we did not like to see him go, he answered, putting a hand warmly on my shoulder; Jim, I couldn't have done those conferences without you. That was simple truth, but you could see why everyone liked him.

Friday 2 February 1945

. . . We thought we would have Hood speak about the 10th Air Force in connection with opening the Lido Road but we could not get to see him in the morning so it was

HEADQUARTERS, ARMY AIR FORCES
WASHINGTON

2 February 1945

MEMORANDUM FOR CHIEF, OFFICE OF INFORMATION SERVICES

Subject: Information from AC/AS Offices

1. **AAF Examining Boards.** (Personnel) The Adjutant General has submitted a proposal that control of the AAF Examining Boards be transferred to the AAF. Lt Colonel Fitch, Cadet Branch, informs me that this on-the-face-of-it singular and unmilitary willingness to give up something may be ascribed to the Army Service Forces' reluctance to maintain facilities in the nine Service Commands solely for the use and benefit of the AAF. General McCormick immediately non-concurred, and will apparently be successful in reasoning the Adjutant General back into a better appreciation of his duties and responsibilities. (Alternative: the AAF, at its wits' end for personnel already, would have to find men to set up boards of its own all over the country.) General McCormick's arguments: (1) The Secretary of War's directive to the ASF and the AGF to screen all personnel for volunteers for air training means a lot of processing of foot army material which the ASF should clearly do; (2) the imminent necessity for reopening ACER recruiting will require the nationwide facilities of the AGO. (In the General's position is, perhaps, eloquent testimony that the General Council has the AAF by the shortest possible hairs in the manpower matter. If it could by any means be done, it would certainly be in the interests of an 'independent' air force to replace facilities firmly in the grip of the ASF by new ones staffed and controlled by the Air Adjutant General.)

2. **Screening of AAF Colored Personnel.** (Personnel) The screening of negro personnel in the AAF (to be distinguished from the screening of ASF and AGF personnel: see above — my memo, 10 Jan) for pilot training "indicates that out of a total of 7,111 eligible for screening, 902 have volunteered, and 605 have been accepted and sent to an AAF Examining Board for the air crew examination. Due to the lag in receiving reports from the Boards, no definite figure can be given for those passing, although to date 75 candidates have been qualified and assigned to Keesler Field." (The fact of this screening may come in handy sometime. It means that practically every AAF negro has been given a fair and free opportunity to get the same expensive training offered to white personnel.)

3. **Education Program.** (Personnel) "Approximately 1,000,000 soldiers are now participating in the Army Non-military Education program. More than 15,000,000 textbooks have been printed to meet present and future requirements. Another branch of the United States Armed Forces Institute is ready for establishment in Manila to expedite service to military personnel in that area."

4. **Chaplain's Film.** (Air Chaplain) Ch (Col) Gynther Storaasli reports that Ch (Major) Constantine E. Zielinski (hey, wait a minute!) has departed on temporary duty to Culver City, California "for the purpose of reviewing the film 'This is Your Mission' in its final phase."

5. **Air Crew Training Expedient.** (Training) To meet present shortages in enlisted aircrew out-put, AC/AS, Training has hit on the temporary expedient of changing the course at Lowry Field, where about 13,000 air mechanic gunners and armorer gunners are in the works. Leaving out some of the words, the plan is to cut the mechanics course to 6 weeks, and to let the armorers have on-the-job training when they have joined their units (that is, they can get a little instruction by attending courses and demonstrations while the rest of the crew is off flying. All they do when they go along on such training flights is read magazines and pick their noses). Colonel Gardner, Gunnery, feels that this is ok — the air mechanic was of no use anyway, being unable to get out in flight and look at the engines, and being unwilling on the ground to demean himself by getting greasy with the ground crew. Similarly, the armorer got a lot of unnecessary information about types of guns and turrets which he would never use. Lt Colonel Skinner, Tech Training Branch, naturally does not concur; but at any rate the cutting down of this extra training for the categories named means that there will be enough gunners, if in fact little more than career gunners, to meet immediate schedule requirements. This is, of course, as Colonel Skinner says, living on our fat. All indications certainly are that the training program must be enlarged again very soon.

6. **Inclement Weather.** (Training) "Attempt is being made to arrange for use of San Julian, Cuba, for the First Air Force due to weather and six-foot snow drifts at some of the First Air Force air fields."

7. **Literature Production.** (Plans) "Sent comment to Management Control on their proposal to centralize certain literature producing functions at Orlando, recommending that AC/AS, Training, should determine the location of a central control agency for Training Literature, and that a complete plan for publications control should be formulated to incorporate not only Training Literature but all Air Force publications."

8. **Notes from In and Out Log.**
    a. **St Germain signed Spaatz 31 Jan.** Failure of tail pipe flange followed by fire in tail and explosion resulted in loss of P-80 Jan 28. Pending completion of investigation and ground tests, other P-80 is being grounded. Col Price believes trouble is in basic design. Until our complete report is in your hands recommendation is for all aircraft on project MX-409 at home be grounded...

- 2 -

b. <u>USMA London from Dunn 31 Jan.</u> ....Chief, Norwegian Intelligence, Stockholm, reports 2,000 ton U-boat berthed in slipway No. 2 Laksevaag appears being prepared for launching V-1 projectiles. Deck guns have been removed and rails laid ... Norwegian agents watching developments closely...

JAMES G. COZZENS
Major, Air Corps

necessary to come back after I had taken S shopping and Major Preston made himself a great nuisance—I suppose he is bucking for Lt Col and feels that a zealous attention to what is none of his business is better than any quiet or unobtrusive conduct which might be mistaken for (a) indifference (b) ignorance.

Saturday 3 February 1945

. . . Gen Hood had us in to consider some possible material on answering the *Infantry Journal* point about did we build too large an air force and the obvious answer—no, they built too small a foot army. His mind is about as clear as mine, and the conversation was troublesome for Haddock who was often obliged to go through the tediums of respectfully leading him back to the point—the Gen's trouble is that he does not grasp ideas quickly, yet does not want to have that appear, so he answers quickly, soon showing you that the idea he grasped was not the one you were talking about, but another somewhat like it, or in the same vicinity. However, he is civil and agreeable—the virtue, no doubt, of his defect.

Monday 5 February 1945

. . . I spent all day piecing together Hood's piece on Burma, with somewhat too long a time out in the morning being talked to by Dr Learned in Program Control, to whom (in conformity with my fine plan to get some other people to do some work) I had sent a question about whether the AAF was over-strength and then had to hear. He is a round little man with glasses, much given to full explanations—perhaps partly because he is not in a soldier suit. He took care to let me know he had been at the Staff and Command School in some capacity sometime. He is prodigiously insistent and well-informed, but the principal lesson I learned was an old one—you might as well reconcile yourself to the fact that people will think of you whatever they damn please and the notion that if you tell them a few things they will revise their estimate is an illusion.

Tuesday 6 February 1945

. . . Rex Smith and Doulens turned up in the office, back from Europe sometime during the night. They both looked very well, and Smith looked very cocky, as though he had found out a lot of things about a lot of people and meant to make good use of the information. . . . I was busy all day on Hood's stuff, which I got around to him late in the afternoon, somewhat harassed by Preston, whose cordial pushing qualities are hard for me to stomach—and for Miss Thompson, who seemed to think maybe I could do something to him. I did not say what I thought obvious—that he was more likely to be able to do something to me.

Wednesday 7 February 1945

. . . We had some fussing with JCS on piffling points through the morning. The conference, while well attended, seemed something less than a success—Hood was again earnest and anxious, but I had hopefully given him two mild jokes, and what proved to be some bad advice. The jokes were so badly delivered that all he got was stares; and the advice—to interpolate, at various mentionings of points in CBI he knew, material on what he had seen himself—led him to offer half a dozen awkward recounts of boring incidents. His effort and his good temper made it that much more painful, at least to me. I saw that I would have to stop giving him texts really meant for Smith and greatly simplify both words and thoughts to try to capitalize on his earnest, southern-drawl, inarticulate qualities. . . .

Friday 9 February 1945

. . . We had been thinking up some stuff from Hood to try to counter, at a directive from Mr A's sick-bed, the Navy's too proprietory air about Guam—where we were up against the staff decision that BG's would not speculate on post-war matters; and a desired release about the P-80—where we were up against the RAF who seemed resolved to say nothing on the subject of jet propulsion—God alone, or at least not I, could figure out why. It seemed necessary to leave both matters suspended when I went out at noon. . . .

Saturday 10 February 1945

. . . We went ahead with the JP matter and after many conferences and consultations seemed to get a formula clear for Hood to announce the P-80, which somebody has named the Shooting Star. We are getting the motion picture and I keep looking for a jet pilot to add to the show. . . . George Bradshaw who has been some days, even weeks, complaining about his stomach compared notes with George Haddock and decided that he was getting stomach ulcers, which I think is not unlikely as he has not looked well and his cruel regimen of doing nothing all day must tell on you. Though plainly feeling quite ill, the supposition seemed to cheer him as an indication that he might get out, but we could not quite persuade him to go to Walter Reed and see what they thought.

Monday 12 February 1945

. . . The P-80 matter was held up by the intervention of a civilian named Halloway from Lockheed, who did not seem to want us to break the news before the plant paper did—a form of argument I could not follow, but it prevailed; or at any rate Gen Hood made some confused statements on the subject, from which I could not tell what he meant or wanted. Fortunately Haddock was there, so we let it ride. Gen

HEADQUARTERS, ARMY AIR FORCES
WASHINGTON

7 February 1945

MEMORANDUM FOR THE CHIEF, OFFICE OF INFORMATION SERVICES

Subject: Information from AC/AS Offices.

1. JB-2 Bomb Program. (CC&R) The Requirements Division, seemingly unaware of M&S's request to the Chief of Ordnance to rescind previously stated JB-2 requirements (my memo, 5 Feb), has recommended to the Chief of the Air Staff that a program be put into effect which will give the AAF "the capacity of launching 1,000 controlled bombs per month starting 1 January 1946." (Incidentally, the cancellation of the 77,000 project was the subject of an inquiry from SHEAF in the Log. They seemed a little confused. Apparently the last they heard was the suggestion - my memo, 18 Jan - that idle factories in France, Belgium, and Luxembourg might be used to turn out the JB-2's.)

2. Combat Fatigue Nomenclature. (Air Surgeon) At a recent meeting in the office of the Surgeon General, the Surgeon General, the Surgeon General of the Navy, the Medical Director of the Veterans Bureau, the Air Surgeon, and the Civilian Consultant in Psychiatry, got together to consider revision of nomenclature for "the syndrome of symptoms resulting from the stress of military service." The Air Surgeon observes: "Currently there are being used many terms, such as 'combat fatigue', 'operational fatigue', 'tension reaction', etc. The conference tentatively agreed to recommend the term 'anxiety reaction', subclassified as severe, moderate, and mild; and further explained by concomitant findings of stress, predisposition, reactions, and anticipated capacity for military duty."

3. Come-on for AAF Reserve Officers. (Personnel) Gen. McCormick has submitted suggestions to AC/AS, Plans "indicating ways and means of inducing Reserve officers to pursue tours of active duty." He says that incentive to personnel to participate in an officer development program and to pursue tours of active duty may be induced by:
      a. Placing a premium on a college education
      b. Training in grade for Reserve officers
      c. Providing a sufficient number of annual openings in the Regular officer corps for candidates from sources other than the Air Academy.
      d. Bonus at completion of active duty tour for those Reserve officers who fail to attain Regular commissions in each yearly competition.
      e. Favorable exemptions under the income tax law for military personnel on active status, and compensation on inactive status commensurate with duty and study required to maintain proficiency. "It is believed that a plan developed along these lines and correlated with Universal Military Training will produce a satisfactory officer corps for the Air Forces."

4. _Guided Missiles Command Responsibility._ (OC&R) In an effort
to establish the long term responsibilities of the major commands for
the operational employment of guided and controlled missiles, a memorandum has been prepared for Gen. Giles to send to the Chief of Staff.
Responsibility for the development of guided missiles has been established by WD directives; but they fail to state who is going to control
their use. "In view of General Arnold's stated belief that the future
of the AAF lies to a great extent with pilotless aircraft and guided or
controlled missiles, and in view of the confusion that has arisen concerning operational employment of the JB-2 buzz bomb as between the AAF
and the AGF (decision on which assigns responsibility to the AAF), it
is apparent that a firmer policy is required."

The Firmer Policy:

    a. The AAF wants responsibility for all missiles, regardless
of their technical characteristics, which are "capable of complementing
or supplementing the strategic or tactical air effort, with the exception
of those new weapons capable only of complementing, supplementing, or
supplanting close cooperation of air elements with ground elements."
(This can obviously be interpreted to mean any and all missiles that
may be directed at any target pilot-operated planes have ever attacked.)

    b. The AGF may have responsibility for missiles complementing
or supplementing artillery fire "or close coordinating air effort" (but
see above).

    c. The AAF wants responsibility for missiles complementing
or supplementing interceptor fighters "and which are sustained by means
other than the momentum of the missile."

    d. The AGF may have missiles that complement or supplement
antiaircraft fire if they "depend for sustenance (sic) on the momentum
of the missile."

(Incidentally, at a conference 1 Feb an agreement was reached with
the Navy on "under-water propulsion as applied to hydrobombs, torpedoes,
submarine vessels, and assisted take-offs of flying boats." It was
agreed that the Navy would "have primary responsibility, and take the
lead in governing and exploiting these developments, with AAF liaison;
except in the case of the hydrobomb." (This gadget has a 1200 pound
charge and is expected to get "the lethal effect of a large bomb and
eliminate the undesirable features of a conventional torpedo." It has
experimental high-thrust underwater jet propulsion. The United Shoe
Machinery Corp. has the project, under AAF cognizance. The hydrobomb
can be carried internally in the A-26, and should be ready for service
use early this year.)

5. _All Weather Day or Night Fighter._ (OC&R) In discussions with
Mr. Robert Fausel, of Curtiss-Wright, specifications were laid down
for the subject fighter. Mr. Fausel believes Curtiss-Wright can turn
out a twin-engine single seat aircraft with conventional tricycle
landing gear, using for power plants the GE TG-180 or similar gasoline
turbines, which will have a high speed of 600 mph; combat radius, 750
miles; rate of climb, 3,000 ft/minute average to 35,000 feet; armament,
six .60 cal. machine guns, plus rockets.

3

6. <u>Officer Personnel Ratios</u>. (OC&R) Troop Basis has prepared a study on the ratio of officer personnel to enlisted personnel in the AAF, as authorized in the Troop Program, 31 January 1945. There is 1 officer to 6.8 enlisted men in overseas theatres; and 1 to 5.18 in the ZI (1 to 5.91 for the entire AAF). Aggregate AAF strength was 2,302,578: officers, 330,842; enlisted men, 1,956,579. (This would make officers 14.4% of the total.) At the same time, though not in the same connection, Management Control reports that there are 1,839 WAC officers on duty with the AAF, and 35,987 enlisted women, which is an officer-ratio of 1 to 20. (41.7% of total WAC strength is with the AAF.) The fairly high officer-ratio may have something to do with the decision (Commitments Division) to inform the CinC, SWPA, that any further increase in Troop Basis for an A-5 Section for FEAF could not be favorably considered because of the Air Forces have reached the limit of overall officer authorization.

7. <u>Notes for In and Out Log</u>.
    a. <u>COMWESSEAFRON 2 Feb</u>. ...warning when forcing down Jap paper balloon keep well clear as balloon approaches 13,000 ft. altitude. If functioning normally, demolition should occur there or soon thereafter...

    b. <u>US Mil Mis (Moscow) signed Deane 3 Feb</u>. ...Polish partisans Tarnov area...talk freely of probability of fighting Soviets after the war ends and expecting Anglo-American aid...

    c. <u>Wright Field from Carroll 4 Feb</u>. YP-80A airplane subject... in view of extreme pressure on the production program it is not considered advisable to ground any airplanes within the continental limits...ATSC has been operating these airplanes since June 1944 without any serious trouble...

    d. <u>Miami signed Dudley 5 Feb</u>. The first balloon has landed in area under control Eastern Defense Command. As other balloons will probably descend in that area, take necessary steps to insure essential security...

J. G. COZZENS
Major, Air Corps

Norstad talked to the press in the projection room upstairs at 4 and did well—reversing myself, I wished we could have had that. Hood, besides not being good, is probably going to be difficult as he gains assurance, because of his aptness for bum ideas.

Tuesday 13 February 1945

. . . We changed our minds several times on the conference, but finally ended up deciding to do it next Wednesday, a sort of compromise—we agreed not to do it tomorrow; but on the other hand, we did not hold it as long as Lockheed wanted—Hood's own formula. It was an exhausting day.

Wednesday 14 February 1945

. . . In any event, and just as Rex, with an I-thought-somewhat-phoney prescience suggested to Halloway, a signal as they say came back from Air Marshal Portal overriding the local RAF fellow who had agreed to the P-80 thing, so it looked as though we might not even do it next Wednesday. It was hard to think of an occasion when so much work was done to so little purpose.

Thursday 15 February 1945

. . . I was able to catch up with my memoranda, somewhat neglected in the confusion. . . . Everyone decided that whatever happened the war was going on forever.

Friday 16 February 1945

. . . We made some motions about possibly getting some radar stuff cleared for next Wednesday. . . . Up then to see the P-80 film on spin tests, which would be good for our purpose, supposing it comes up again. . . .

Saturday 17 February 1945

. . . Rex decided we could have the P-80 after all, when I found out we could not quite yet use Iwo Jima. He knocked the keys down on his box and told Gen Timberlake and then Gen Hood that he thought so. The key to his character is of course familiarity with the great, or at least powerful, but he adds to it a very important acumen—that is, he knows that they are half-afraid of what he is supposed to know. The ordinary impulse of people who want what he wants is to fawn; he knows better, he faintly threatens.

Sunday 18 February 1945

. . . Down for a minute to the office where Rex was dictating explosive comments to

Spaatz on the Cowan-SHAEF piece about how we were going to do terror bombing, the question being who the hell had taken it on himself to announce it. Since neither he, nor Col Stone, was interested in anything but that, I saw I would learn nothing on the P-80 or Iwo Jima and went home. . . .

Monday 19 February 1945

. . . The answers were coming back, and answers to that going out, on the terror bombing business, which seemed in fact to be the theory of SHAEF's A-2, a British Air Commodore only, and it became (though not certainly) plain that we might be doing that Wednesday. It then developed that weather might keep Gen Hood from getting back from Texas, where he was attending the Mexican fighter squadron nonsense, in time, and would Kuter do it? That would be much better, considering the necessary explanations, which he could certainly manage better than Hood. Rex said; ok, you write it for him, and I'll fix it; which he may no doubt do. The uncertainty and the multiple stops and starts were, however, wearing.

Tuesday 20 February 1945

. . . Until approximately eleven oclock it was supposed that we would have the conference, so I wrote most of it—if you start at 8 before anyone is there, you can get a lot done by 11—it then developed that Smith could not persuade Kuter after all; so we were obliged to abandon it. I felt somewhat annoyed—apparently unable to argue the right way, which would be that at least I need trouble no more. I conclude that I have little patience with work for work's sake. Rex sent me down after lunch to see what I could find out about the rumored notion of Gen Marshall's that the Army should total only 330,000 after the war. Since I am supposed to be the man who knows who to see, I gave it some airs; but, in fact, I only went over to SPD [Special Projects Division] and talked to a Major Johns, who told me it was a squeeze play, the Gen stating that was the best he could do without universal military service. For myself, I am damned if I know whether I think we make the next war less certain, or more, by such measures. Still, it occurs to me that even if it made it more certain, it might delay its onset, and any reasonable delay would be odds against my seeing it—I often detect such signs of what I guess could be called the philosophy of being more than 40.

Wednesday 21 February 1945

. . . We got along quietly while I wrote a memorandum in the morning. . . .

Thursday 22 February 1945

. . . It developed today that the P-80 was being cleared by the RAF—a letter coming from Air Marshal Colyer, so we could probably let it go. Meanwhile, at his conference, Mr Stimson had walked into the terror bombing business saving us that much trouble—by now, I thought it a mistake anyway, since the announcement had, after all, attracted little attention and aroused only a couple of filler editorials; and to deny it would simply focus attention on it. The public attitude is (one judges) not often so naive as we suppose it is—this is war, and while both sides may protest this or that, we are going to do what hurts them and they are going to do what hurts us, and only the relatively feeble-minded ever expected anything else. Why such a devoir of protestations is regularly paid to the feeble-minded would be a nice investigation. Col Harris of the Air Inspector's office had me up late in the afternoon to go over a case of a Pvt Hills who had been slugged a year ago by an MP while in the guard house and got his case to Congress through a Mr Bavin, and apparently scared Mr Stimson to death—he apparently kept mumbling something about a New Patton incident. Harris, while less of a character than Col Scott, is still something; a gray-headed man with the stentorian court-room voice; lucid, energetic, and unmilitary. The War Department was splitting a gut to fix the thing, and it struck me that here again was the same probably unrequired devoir to a supposed soft-headedness which it was always someone else who felt. Pvt Hills had not been seriously damaged; the MP was undoubtedly a Tough Guy, and had no business to do it; but the act of going into the army probably meant to any normal person a perfectly understandable giving-up of ordinary rights, privileges and expectations. The MP was, of course, a son of a bitch; but that was what you had to put up with until the war was over; and so what? . . .

Saturday 24 February 1945

. . . Almost as soon as I got in, Rex asked me to go up and hold Gen Norstad's hand over a speech he was to give at 11.30 to the American Legion committee on universal military training. Reeves had done him something he did not like and it was indeed bad. I don't know how much better what we put together with a secretary was—he did most of it himself, because I soon found that he wanted no truck with simple direct statements—rightly, I think, because his good presence requires from him psychologically a certain number of filler phrases meaning nothing. He went to give it at the Statler, and it then developed from Col Westlake that he was not supposed to mention the subject by Gen Marshall's orders. We got him just before he went on and it was all moderately nerve wracking. As I foresaw, I needed George Haddock there to protect me from that sort of thing.

Monday 26 February 1945

. . . I was busy writing up Hood's stuff on the P-80, which was complicated, as I soon saw even with my limited knowledge that BPR's release (by Major Bacher) had some doubtful statements. Mr Graichen in M&S, a graying fellow with a moustache, agreed when I took it to him. Rex was meanwhile agitated over the release Lockheed was planning to make—characteristically, they had Mr A saying that we had jet supremacy (meaning presumably that the P-80, when we had it, would be better than the German planes). With one angle or another, I was kept busy all day and felt worn by night.

Tuesday 27 February 1945

. . . Gen Hood had me in at 9.30 to add some suggestions of his to the text. While still being a pleasant fellow and easy to get on with his increasing self-confidence is plain—his ideas remain meagre, but he gets more emphatic about them. Lacking George Haddock, all I can or feel inclined to say is: yes sir. At 10.30 we showed him the P-80 film along with Rex and the security officers and Miss Thompson, and that seemed all right; but Col Butler got in to JSC by noon—he had been out ill for a few days; and so we had a hell of an afternoon, JSC insisting that the film should not be shown. I finally dictated to Becky a piece that Rex signed saying the Air Staff thought it should be, and sat over Col Edgerton while he put it through to Gen Surles; but we still had no word when I decided to leave. There were fifty other things—getting a new title for the picture to be made up by OSS [Office of Strategic Services]; discussions with Bacher and Gilder and Edgerton; and phone calls from Butler; and who else, enough to make me at least dead-beat by evening.

Wednesday 28 February 1945

. . . We did not get the film and some parts of Hood's text cleared until almost noon—it was hard to figure what kind of nonsense was going on in Gen Surles' office. The conference was quite crowded and the film seemed to be a success—and it is only fair to say that Gen Hood is getting better—he had to parry a great many questions, and he did it with an increased ease and humor, so they began to laugh. . . .

Thursday 1 March 1945

. . . Ed Newhouse was largely engaged all day in the matter, brought out by the *Times-Herald*, of his one-time Communist connections,[57] and so was George Haddock who spent most of the afternoon with a gang of generals led by Giles talking it all over and not, in the long run, getting much of anywhere—they weren't worried about Ed; but what they could say back to the Congressional committee. Ed supported it about right, concerned but composed; and it seemed likely that, since Mr Lovett was in his patron-of-the-arts mood that George Haddock could fix it.

ADDRESS REPLY TO
COMMANDING GENERAL, ARMY AIR FORCES
WASHINGTON 25, D. C.

ATTENTION:

HEADQUARTERS, ARMY AIR FORCES
WASHINGTON

1 March 1945

SPECIAL MEMORANDUM FOR THE CHIEF, OFFICE OF INFORMATION SERVICES

Subject: Goings-on of Col. ███████, MH, etc.

1. ██████ Army Air Field Bus Contract. Gen. Schneider, Acting the Air Inspector, sent for me this afternoon and suggested that the Chief, OIS, should be briefed on a situation which arose this week at ██████ Field, near ████████████████████. Two men named ████ and ██████ had a contract with the War Department for a bus service between ██████ Field and town. Six of the busses were owned by the government and two by the contractors. In the contract was a clause by which it could be cancelled on ten days notice.

2. Col. ████████████████ Field. Early last week Col. ████ (this is ██████████, with the congressional medal for ████████████ and so on) notified ████ and ██████ that he was cancelling the contract on the grounds that the busses were not properly maintained. The form of the notification appears to have been a telephone call in which the Col. described ████ and ██████ as bastards, said he would put them out of business, and told them to keep their busses the hell off the reservation. ████ and ██████ went to court for a writ to show cause, which was brought out and served on Col. ████ by the sheriff. The Col. took the writ, tore it up, threw it on the floor, and had the sheriff ejected from his office.

3. Senator ██████ of ██████. ████ and ██████ described as 'influential business men' squawked instantly to Senator ██████, who seems to have flown into a rage, summoned Col. Scott and Col. McIntyre, and addressed them on the subject in what Col. Scott described as the most abusive terms he had ever heard. The Senator said that Col. ████ might be a hero; but if he thought the Stateof ████████ would put up with having its courts flouted by any swell-headed army jerk he had another think coming, and furthermore he (the Senator) was going to bring up the whole matter of dictatorial military actions on the Senate floor.

4. Action by the Air Inspector. At Gen. Schneider's request, Gen. Owens got through to Second AF Hq. and had the contract continued for two weeks. Col. Scott, who refers to Col. ████ as "that ape", feels that the 'improper maintenance' charges on the basis of those supplied him (not having maximum weight stencilled on the door; being

improperly lubricated, etc.) are absurd. He had a telephone conversation with Col. ███, and says that the Col. is a type painfully familiar to him -- "no brains, no sense, not worth his weight in chicken s--t outside combat, and maybe not there."

    5. <u>Conclusion</u>. Gen. Schneider and Col. Scott believe that Senator ███ is going to keep his word and make a stink; that Col. ███ s position is largely indefensible; that the fact that he has the congressional medal will assure the widest publicity when Senator ███ sounds off.

                        J. G. COZZENS
                        Major, Air Corps

Friday 2 March 1945

. . . They were concerned about Lt Gen Harmon lost in the Pacific and a great shuffling was going on in the staff—showing me again how little I really know about anything and how poor is my grasp of the principal preoccupations of the top echelon—the point seemed to be, should Gen Hale be put in the Pacific Command. I knew almost nothing about either of them yet it was plainly very important. . . .

Monday 5 March 1945

. . . Up at once to see a Major Brindle in Dr Learned's office on the air crew recruiting matter, and later to Col Thornton in Management Control where he had in his people to fix up something on the recent operations against the Germans for Gen Giles, in theory in person, for Wednesday. What the Gen wanted seemed impossible but Col Thornton, a fleshy pink young man, seemed to think they (his people) could do it, so I left.

Tuesday 6 March 1945

. . . There was nothing coming out of Stat Control until 5 when Col Thornton had me up for another conference and they gave me a fairly good four page summary. . . . Back early and managed to get a rough draft for Giles done by 10.30.

Wednesday 7 March 1945

. . . I got myself up early and to the Pentagon by 7, so I had the text in hand by the time Johnny dutiful came in at 8. Col Clarke and Lt Miller from Stat Control came down to read it as it came off, and they thought it was good and so did I. Apparently they reported upstairs, and I was much propitiated when Col Thornton phoned down to ask if he could see the text after the conference, they said it was so good. I said yes. We then had trouble, first from Col Butler, who squawked about a passage and burned me up a little when, as I started to explain that we had it from the War College, said; Now just a minute, let me talk some. Maybe I did talk too much; but as I get older I get more vengeful; so I took care to let Gen Hood and Col Coe know that I thought Butler was a constant nuisance and a mistake. At nearly noon, Gen Giles decided he would not take it—on the advice of Col Barber, who like Gen Kuter, is clearly on the make in the high command just above our heads. I protested to him while he kept calling me Jim, but of course he did not stir, having whatever ends of his own to serve; but it was amusing to see him faithfully serving them, yet in his well-bred, patient way (unlike Col Butler) figuring that I was easy to handle, and why annoy even me, if all I needed was a soft answer. (A perfect diagnosis.) So Hood took it, and did all right; except that the subject needed somebody quotable like Giles. When I came back from there, a call soon came through which began; Hume

Peabody, Jim. . . . I don't know what is wrong with me—I suppose an inferiority complex; for the same old reason that if, I am inhibited from calling him Hume (as I am), I would rather be called You or Cozzens; and so find myself recoiling, though nothing could have been more gracious—nor, listening to it, a simpler, pleasanter, more winning voice. I gave him back a lot of 'sirs' and 'Generals' but he was undisturbed. I wish I could fit myself better to these awkward relationships.

Thursday 8 March 1945

. . . We early heard a rumor that the 1st Army was across the Rhine south of Cologne and by afternoon it was pretty well backed up, which was a welcome thought. I was busy with my accumulated memoranda but everyone else was idle, speculating on whether the war might not be over pretty soon.

Friday 9 March 1945

. . . Hirsch came up very gloomy about the Rhine bridge-head—it was in the wrong place; the accident of finding the Remagen bridge standing was a German trap, or at any rate they would soon manage to take it out. Haddock told me that Col Whitney, back from Iwo Jima and some talks with MacArthur, told him that they expected the Japs to blow up in 6 months, for reasons which I had long entertained myself, and especially since I saw the Log report on the Jap airfields in Luzon—that they could not take it, in the sense of meeting the organizational and technological demands of waging this kind of war, and soon were in a hopeless muddle from which they could see no way out but suicide—that is, what was mistaken for their fanatical bravery was simply the psychological need to escape from the intolerable mess in which they found themselves floundering. Since this was after all what I would like to believe, I resisted its confirmation a little. . . .

Saturday 10 March 1945

. . . The office was very quiet, with Newhouse in NY and Chamberlin away, and Reeves off by noon (and what a relief; I must be feeling the wear and tear myself; because the time comes, and quite early in the day, when it seems impossible to stand any more—the awful puns, the ridiculous and pompous or self-important conversations on the telephone; the sudden authoritative dissertations on the course of the war (all wrong); the intolerable inquisitiveness which makes him innocently look over the papers on your desk, or come and park himself attentively to hear what George Haddock or anyone else coming in has to say to you. To make it harder, there is the impossibility of telling him off—how could you? He is grotesque with his old square face and goggles and mostly bald head—and he is Jewish, and he is always being overlooked, or neglected, or just forgotten; and he is also amiable and kind-

ADDRESS REPLY TO
COMMANDING GENERAL, ARMY AIR FORCES
WASHINGTON 25, D. C.

ATTENTION:

HEADQUARTERS, ARMY AIR FORCES
WASHINGTON

9 March 1945

MEMORANDUM FOR THE CHIEF, OFFICE OF INFORMATION SERVICES

Subject: Information from AC/AS Offices.

1. <u>P-80 Employment Program</u>. (OC&R) Lt. Col. Holbrook, Requirements Division, has prepared a study for the Chief of the Air Staff which presents a specific program "to obtain maximum benefit from the P-80 aircraft and jet-trained personnel." For the purposes of the study, the estimated operational availability of production P-80's is not expected to amount to enough to equip a fighter group in any theatre before December 1945. Principal points proposed:

 <u>a.</u> The first 30 production P-80's will be held in this country "as the minimum required for essential test, development, and training."

 <u>b.</u> The second 30 will be modified as F-14's for photo-reconnaissance in order to equip 1 squadron at the earliest practicable date (estimated to be November 1945). Decision as to where it will go "will depend on the outlook of the war in Europe on or about 1 August 1945, which is the latest date that definite plans should be crystallized. It was pointed out that there is very little likelihood of employing the P-80 in the war against Germany."

 <u>c.</u> These first 60 planes would absorb all production until approximately the middle of September, 1945. Succeeding production would allow the conversion of about 1 fighter group a month beginning in ~~the~~ December 1945.

 <u>d.</u> <u>The 412th Group</u> will be retained in the Fourth Air Force as a CCTS, and as a training and test unit to furnish cadres of jet trained personnel who can be shipped to the theatres to supervise conversion of fighter and reconnaissance units. It is now anticipated that on or about 1 April <u>1946</u> sufficient trained personnel would become available to release the 412th for deployment against the Japs.

 <u>e.</u> "The entire program will be kept current with the tactical and strategical situation and with revised production estimates as they are received, with the objective of employing this aircraft in combat to our best advantage at the earliest possible date."

2. <u>AAF Manual No. 49</u>. (Air Surgeon) The subject manual, recently published under the cheery title: "Let's Walk" (by the AAF in collaboration with the Institute for the Crippled and Disabled) "is the

only publication of its kind designed to aid the patient in quickly
and simply learning the necessary procedures for walking on crutches
or with an artificial limb. An advance copy of this manual was sent
to General Ent about two weeks ago, and the indication received
yesterday was that he found it of real value."

3. B-29 Bombing. (OC&R) Findings of the AAF Evaluation Board,
POA, in Report No. 4:

    a. "Bombing has not been uniformly good. Current
technique as practiced by the 73rd Bombing Wing is a 12
airplane squadron relying on the lead bombardier to sight, with
all other bombardiers releasing on sight of fall from lead
plane; hence, malfunction or cockpit trouble by lead plane
would cause entire squadron to be abortive."

    b. "Losses of B-29's are low. XXI Bomber Command
losses are less than 4%, which includes those destroyed on
the ground in the Saipan raids. Exclusive of ground
destruction, the loss rate is about 2.5%, with only 6%
lost in combat or over targets. Excessive fuel consumption
or engine failure is the cause of almost 2% of the losses."

    c. "No well organized fighter control or direction
measures appear to have been perfected by the Japanese, and
failure of the enemy to intercept has been frequent. Ramming
tactics at present (15 December 1944) are not considered
intentional, even though such planned tactics have been
experienced against naval craft. It is important to impress
gunners to stick to their guns in defense against ramming,
as the closer the range, the more effective the fire."

4. AWOL Wac. (Air Provost Marshal) "The APMO was informed by
Military Personnel Division that this Hq. had taken steps to transfer
Pvt. ███████████ from Florence Army Air Base, South Carolina, to
Souix City Army Air Base, Iowa. Pvt. ████████ is the member of the
WAC who went AWOL because, being half negress, she preferred an
assignment to a negro WAC unit rather than her current assignment,
which was with a white unit." (The Air Judge Advocate noted on the
same day: "Opinion that there is no legal objection to the transfer, at
her request, of a Wac of Indian-Negro parentage from a white detachment
to a negro detachment.")

5. AAF Casualties. (Personnel) Total casualties, battle and non-
battle, of the AAF overseas between 7 December 1941 and 31 January
1945 amounted to 115,637. Of these, 103,348 (89.4%) were battle
casualties. Of the total battle casualties, 25,443 (24.6%) were
killed; 25,633 (24.8%) were missing; 28,146 (27.3%) are POWs; 6,761
(6.5%) are still in hospitals, wounded; 17,365 (16.8%) have been

returned to duty, or have been repatriated. (Points of interest; there are more POWs than dead, unless it is assumed, as perhaps it should be, that the missing are probably dead. The relatively very low ratio of wounded is something new in warfare. They either get you good or they miss you.)

    6. <u>Resignation for Good of the Service</u>. (Air Judge Advocate) "Opinion where it appears that an officer who is alleged to have committed murder is being held by the state authorities and will be tried for murder by the state authorities, his commanding officer may accept his resignation for the good of the service."

                    JAMES G. COZZENS
                    Major, Air Corps

hearted and sensitive—so you don't know what to do) and Johnny off for the afternoon. Smith was again busy about something, and had no time nor I daresay desire, to tell me what we would do with Gen Anderson next Wednesday, so little was accomplished, and Bradshaw and I sat reading Shakespeare most of the afternoon.

Sunday 11 March 1945

. . . In as duty officer, where I was little disturbed until 11, when Rex showed up with the air of having had a severe night, and some vague remarks about Gen Anderson; and then Haddock and Steve Richards—since they had to spend the afternoon because of some 20th AF operations, I was able to leave by 2. . . .

Monday 12 March 1945

. . . Rex brought me around to see Major Gen Anderson[58] about 10. Though Rex took care once (after Gen Hood came in) to call him Orvil, he was more or less silenced and I was astonished to see that Rex had it right this time (why I should be astonished I don't know; more often than not, he is right, but it is always a surprise). Gen Anderson is thick-featured, nearly white-haired (though he is barely 50, I learned from our files). He stands and moves with a sort of powerful stoop and has remarkably blue eyes, though they look sore, with the eyelids drooping on them. Getting at what he was to do Wednesday, he began to talk more or less at random, but with the greatest vividness and lucidity, ranging around on what was wrong with our air tactics, and why Iwo Jima was a mess, and what he would do, and why the Germans had made fools of themselves. It was all full of sense, and wonderful for our purposes, every word being apt, simple, forceful and full of interest. Hood and Smith pulled out after a while, and he outlined what he wanted to say to me for an hour and a half—he did not want it written, and how rightly; but he was summing up what he meant to say, and it was a pleasure. Like Gen Smith, but more so, you could see some sense in working for him—that is, you can see it's possible to be a soldier and a general and at the same time to be a highly intelligent adult able both to think straight and to speak to the point. I got his points together in a memorandum in the afternoon and fixed some maps for him and felt quite encouraged.

Tuesday 13 March 1945

. . . We had a busy inconsequential day—Col Webster squawked in the morning over the use of the code name (still top secret) Clarion in the memorandum I prepared on Gen Anderson's talk (I thought Rex, who signed them all blithely, might get an administrative reprimand; which would be a poor pay-off; but he fixed it). There was some work to do fixing up notes for Hood, and at 4 we went up to see the

Marine film, *Fury in the Pacific*, which showed the Peleliu landings in some detail; 9 camera men, they said, being killed in the taking. While the shots were very good and real, you can see that art still remains better; because (perhaps a new reason) life is simply too fast. It is simply all over too fast and, except that it was grim, you hardly know what you saw. In many ways the most impressive thing was not the fighting ashore, but the battleships shelling the island—pictures less sketchy and confused.

Wednesday 14 March 1945

. . . In to see Gen Anderson about 10 and he seemed a little below par, having just been down to the dispensary to get something for a cold; but he reacted vigorously to Rex whom I called to come over and give him policy on area bombing in light of the last three 20th AF missions—it is the same; we are not doing it as such. At the conference Gen A began by giving me pause, starting slowly and hesitantly. I found myself feeling a personal responsibility since I had told everyone he was going to be good, and on my say-so I could see it had been passed around, so there was a good crowd, even including Gen Kuter (though I doubt if he was there on my say-so). However, he sure-enough warmed up, presently disconcerting me worse by talking to me, at the corner of the table. At this crisis, it suddenly dawned on me that he had to talk to someone, not just people; so I began guardedly to nod agreement and change my expression to indicate interest and comprehension. This seemed to be just right, because he became immediately at ease, tilting back in his chair, and unearthing his vigorous and effective vocabulary, still talking to me; but with more and more frequent asides to the rest of them. It went on for two hours, but once he was in his stride they naturally listened, and he was very good with the questions— plainly a still more direct and useful stimulus. Afterwards Gen Hood had me in to his office and remarked that it was much too long and wouldn't be that way again; but the degree of resolute control he exercised on what had plainly been a faintly galling over-shadowing impressed me in his favor. He has his limitations, but he tries, which certainly lifts him above a thousand people who don't. Fairly late in the office fixing up odds and ends for Gen Anderson in connection with his forthcoming tour with Rex. . . .

Thursday 15 March 1945

. . . The afternoon went into working out a statement for Hood to make next week on area bombing, the feeling being that if we threw him this preliminary bone he would suffer better Rex's arrangement to have Gen Born steal his party again.

Saturday 17 March 1945

. . . We had an ordinary Saturday with some gestures by Rex toward having Gen

ADDRESS REPLY TO
COMMANDING GENERAL, ARMY AIR FORCES
WASHINGTON 25, D. C.

ATTENTION:

HEADQUARTERS, ARMY AIR FORCES
WASHINGTON

13 March 1945

SPECIAL MEMORANDUM FOR THE CHIEF, OFFICE OF INFORMATION SERVICES

Subject: Pilot and Aircrew Survey Conducted by Special
Service Division in ETO.

1. <u>Nature and Object of the Survey</u>. The Director, Information and Education Division, Headquarters of the Army Service Forces, has forwarded 29 research reports based on a survey conducted last summer (between 11 July and 14 October) at Headquarters, European Theatre of Operations. The object was to analyze "the attitude and general morale" of fighter pilots, medium and light bombardment crews, and heavy bombardment crews.

2. <u>Some Points Common to All Three Categories</u>.
   a. <u>Length of Duty Tours</u>. Everyone was agreed that enough was enough. For Fighter Pilots, too much ("a definite breaking point and measurable impairment of will to fight") came somewhere between 250 and 300 hours of combat flying. Medium Bomber Crews felt they could fly between 50 and 60 missions. Light Bomber (A-20) crews, 40-50. Heavy Bomber Crews, 30-35 (not more than 10 a month). All categories were very anxious to see some system established by which they could know in advance how many missions their tour would consist of. <u>This would appear to be the most important single morale factor</u>.

   b. <u>Pass and Leave Policy</u>. All categories felt that it should be possible to let them know a reasonable time in advance when they would get a pass, or leave. Practice seems to vary greatly from post to post.

   c. <u>Mess</u>. Almost everyone agreed that the messes were not good (which would be normal anywhere); but fighter pilots particularly made the point that no care seemed to be taken about giving them food for breakfast on which a man could fly comfortably.

   d. <u>Stand-downs</u>. All categories felt that notice of stand-downs could easily be given them earlier than it is.

   e. <u>Decorations</u>. All categories felt that they should get the DFC as a matter of course after about 25 missions. The feeling is based on the lavish early policy with ribbons. Now, anyone who doesn't have one feels he is discriminated against.

f. _Training_. All categories feel that their training was deficient in some respects. However, these deficiencies are of a kind that would seem inevitable. In effect, they complain they are put into combat without combat experience. Bomber crews feel that they get too much ETO training along with combat flying, and that they would be better off resting.

g. _Second Tour of Duty_. All categories are "extremely anxious" to know what type of assignment they may expect when they finish their tour of duty (however long it may be). Among fighter pilots, less than 2 in 10 say (the questionnaires were anonymous) that they would "definitely not be willing" to go on a second tour after a furlough (preferably of more than 30 days) in the US. Of Medium Bomber Crews, 4 in 10 are unwilling; Light Bombardment crews, 2 in 10; No similar figure appears for Heavy Bombardment Crews, but about two thirds say "they would probably sign up for combat flying if they were doing it over again."

h. _Live and Learn_. In all categories, "men who have flown relatively few missions are more favorable in their attitude toward combat flying than are men who have flown more."

3. _Fighter Pilots_. 20-30 hours of combat flying a week would be a desirable maximum. 8 out of 10 indicate that they sometimes have doubts about the value of particular strafing and skip-bombing missions. Almost all feel that too-numerous safety restrictions handicap practical and realistic training in the U.S.; but only 3 in 100 rate their training as "poor". Pilots who have flown only one type of plane invariably prefer that type to any other. Of those who have flown the P-47 in combat and are now flying the P-51, 75% prefer the P-51. However, all pilots rate the P-51 "at the bottom of the list in regard to its capacity to take punishment and still get back from a mission." P-38 pilots feel that the combat effectiveness of the plane could be much increased by aileron boosts and dive flaps.

4. _Medium Bombardment Crews_. 6 out of every 10 crew members rate their training as "good" or "very good". 35% think the B-26 is used in combat assignments for which it is not well-suited (night missions; low-level bombing)

5. _Light Bomber Crews_. A significantly larger percentage of light bomber crews (69%) do not feel their type of outfit is "very important" in winning the war. This may be partly corrected by conversion to A-26's. A large proportion of the crews felt that the A-20 needed to be modified, and considering its limitations, was not properly used.

6. <u>Heavy Bombardment Crews.</u> Most officers and men "express strong belief in the overall value of their own part in winning the war". The majority feel that the targets are well selected and that they are doing them serious damage. About half the men say they need more items of equipment - flak helmets, extra heated clothing, oxygen masks, additional parachutes. Of B-17 crews, 92% think they have the best type of plane; of B-24 crews, 76% think they have the best type of plane.

7. <u>Conclusion</u>. The value of this enormous amount of work seems to be very doubtful.

JAMES G. COZZENS
Major, Air Corps

Kenney[59] for Hood's conference, and some conversation with Gen A. E. Jones in M&S on the Cost Plus Fixed Fee contracts and Jo Chamberlin's successful efforts to get himself ordered overseas—a matter I began to feel touched me nearly when George Haddock said that there were inquiries on who in our office hadn't been over, and an apparent staff determination to see that they all did get there (strictly as a reward). . . .

Monday 19 March 1945

. . . We had an upsetting day changing plans about conferences for Kenney, Smith being mostly interested of course in his own jaunt with Gen Anderson. . . .

Tuesday 20 March 1945

. . . On fairly short notice we (or mostly Westlake) decided to put Gen Kenney on at 2.30, and that took some scrambling. He is a little fellow with a ruff of cropped graying hair with very large blue eyes, though pale, and a pointed small but thick face. A shocking scar cuts across his lower right cheek from the corner of his mouth, and probably accounts for his exaggeratedly thick lower lip. He spoke with ease and certain shrewdness, though it was not up to Anderson's; and you could see he had a great weakness for ideas such as his well-delivered account of 'kids' in an outfit of his who had 700 Jap planes, and were upset because the opposition was now so much weaker and poorer that they were afraid they would not get 1,000. He insisted on saying on the record that the Jap air force had ceased to be a threat, and pleased all the newspaper people very much—it was a crowded meeting. His shoulders were so crowded with 3 stars it was hard to figure how he would get a 4th on, if and when they give it to him next week. I judged that like MacArthur, he was that successful thing, a competent romanticist, able somehow to implement the fantasies he was fond of.

Wednesday 21 March 1945

. . . Bob Girvin showed me the proof of a piece for *Impact* on Japan which seemed suitable for working into something for Hood next week, so I was busy on that; though Hirsch soon came in and objected to some parts of the text. It seems that progress is beginning to be made with propaganda to persuade them that they do not all need to go on fighting, though the figures are impressive only in terms of percentages. . . .

Thursday 22 March 1945

. . . in the afternoon Lt Col Headley from the Air Provost Marshal turned up with a major of his to talk over the plans they were making to deal with the AWOL

ADDRESS REPLY TO
COMMANDING GENERAL, ARMY AIR FORCES
WASHINGTON 25, D. C.

ATTENTION:

HEADQUARTERS, ARMY AIR FORCES
WASHINGTON

19 March 1945

SPECIAL MEMORANDUM FOR THE CHIEF, OFFICE OF INFORMATION SERVICES

Subject: P-80 Situation

1. <u>Decision to Ground all P-80's</u>. The decision announced by M&S (my memo, 17 March) was explained in the 15 March activity report (late in getting around, as usual) as due to additional information on the UK 28 January crash. The information: "Due to high humidity (72%) and low temperature (17 F) conditions prevailing at the time of the accident, thrust in excess of design conditions was being obtained from the engine. The tail pipe velocities and tail pipe drag coefficient associated with this additional thrust increased the load on the tail pipe and caused failure of the tail pipe flange, which resulted in the accident." When the suggestion was made from ETO, following the accident, that P-80's be grounded it was argued here that they had been flown for months. However, the fact was that practically all flying had been done under conditions of low humidity and high temperature, and Major Bussey, M&S, tells me that he doubts if one ever had been flown on a damp day with below-freezing temperatures).

2. <u>Changes</u>. The following changes are being made before proceeding with the accelerated service tests:

    a. strengthening of tail pipe flange.
    b. addition of a stainless steel tail pipe shroud.
    c. installation of a fire indicator in the tail.

3. <u>Effect on Production</u>. Major Bussey, in a telephone conversation with Col. Garman, Chief, Fighter Branch, Aircraft Projects, Engineering Division, ATSC, at Wright Field, was assured that these were minor changes and were not expected to delay production. In spite of M&S's announcement last week that service tests would be indefinitely delayed, Col. Garman expects to have the changes completed and the tests started sometime this week. The tail pipe shroud is expected to add 50 pounds to the weight of the tail assembly and this will probably require a corresponding addition of weight to the nose as the balance is very critical.

4. <u>Status of Procurement</u>. "All" the P-80's ordered grounded amounted in fact to 4. Only 1 was a straight production article delivered, as the W-13 schedule provided, in February. Delivery of 2 is scheduled in March and Col. Garman expects to get them all right. 5 will be turned out in April, and 10 in May.

5. <u>Production Difficulties</u>. More precision tooling is required for the P-80 than for any other plane ever built, Major Bussey tells me. Tooling on some items has been changed three times. It is not expected to be completely satisfactory for about two more months - not a matter of great consequence, as the existing engine bottle-neck will not be cleared up until approximately the same time. After that it is felt that they can be turned out very rapidly in almost any desired quantity. The requirements for a PR squadron in November, and for operational combat squadrons beginning in December should be met without difficulty. (Incidentally, Major Bussey, who has just returned from Lockheed, tells me that the most effective piece of employee incentive there was a P-80 nose on which Gen. Arnold, during his visit, wrote: <u>I want a thousand of these right away</u>. That, according to the Major, is the sort of thing that seems to have a real effect.)

JAMES G. COZZENS
Major, Air Corps

problem when the ETO personnel was brought home, given leave, and expected to report back [for] duty in the Orient. His idea was that it might be pointed out to the families of those who deserted that they would regret it all their lives—at first sight, a weak reed; but, allowing for a certain amount of normal simplicity, perhaps as likely to work in a majority of cases as any other argument. . . .

Friday 23 March 1945

. . . There was some stirring around the Pentagon; it being plainly supposed, and perhaps with more reason this time, that the ETO business could not last much longer. Still, the use of various former bursts of optimistic rumor probably lay in the fact that nobody was much inclined to credit it or regard it. . . .

Saturday 24 March 1945

. . . Everything was pulled up sharply in the morning first on Hood's motion—he wanted to talk about ETO operations in connection with the new Rhine crossings, and then by the circumstance that Mr A seemed to decide he would take the Wednesday conference—not a bad idea, if he is reasonably all right, since everyone has undoubtedly wondered about him. However, nothing was settled by evening, so we could expect to work it out tomorrow—the drift or pitch being, of course; We planned it this way. With Ed and Haddock to see Gen Giles make a motion picture piece to tack on the front of a paratrooper film in the air room. His short text was written out for him in big letters on a card, and it seemed simple enough, until he proved incapable of pronouncing the word 'decades' in the dry run. Ed rose in a way I never could have and suggested to Colonel Coe (not very literate either), that the word be changed to years; and then, that no, years was in the line above; what did the Gen think? By that time, it had been pronounced correctly for him over & over; so, revising his own pronunciation, he said he thought decades would do and did it all right for the sound track.

Sunday 25 March 1945

. . . In to the Pentagon by 9.30 but naturally nothing happened and I spent my time sitting on the telephone while Haddock had a long conference with Westlake and Gen Hood on some nonsense about public relations reorganization. The rumors were going around strongly that we were through the German west lines at several points and the armor in the clear on highways east. Similar reports were on the radio in the evening, so it might be true. . . .

Monday 26 March 1945

. . . The matter about Mr A got no clearer because it seemed few people could reach him, but Haddock agreed that an outline I finally figured out about what he should say would be right, so I should go ahead and work on it with the thought that we might put it over. I fixed him a fairly boastful line about how the pay-off in ETO was the way we had planned it—and not untrue—but there is little reason to suppose he would have sense enough to see its advantages.

Tuesday 27 March 1945

. . . I proceeded with the text for Mr A in one of those well-jammed-up days that confuse me all right but that I cannot find it in me to dislike. In the afternoon Spence produced the part about the XXth Air Force on Norstad's behalf, and after Stat Control had argued it out with Intelligence on the figures we finally did get a text to Review by 4. Mr A had meanwhile graciously agreed that he would have it at 1330 tomorrow so the labor did not seem to be entirely lost though there would probably be trouble enough when he saw us, as he said he would at shortly after 8 tomorrow.

Wednesday 28 March 1945

. . . To Mr A's office at 8.30 where Hood, Norstad, General Beebe and Rex went in to see him with the text, Haddock and I being left outside so he would not be excited by a crowd. However, he swore loudly anyway, and in the glimpse I got of him looked like death.[60] We had a flurry of changes, one at least without sense, in the text which he took home with him by 11. I took a low view of the proceedings, but at quarter past 1 he turned up very clean and rosy and in normal fettle—I had some more changed sheets so he said to me; you come in and fix them; so I came in; and presently Hood appeared tip-toeing mousily around the screen—there was something eloquent about it; you could see how he terrified BGs. At the packed conference he seemed to do all right, though with many pauses and a general screwing up of his text—I had forgotten how that exasperated you—reducing statements to a sort of garbled nonsense, taking part and then leaving out the part that made the point, and those mispronunciations (impotent, comparable) but he showed a little fire toward the end on some questions. It seemed pretty plain that at home they had given him some shots of some kind—nothing else could account for the difference between 9 oclock and 1 oclock and the thought was somewhat subduing.

Friday 30 March 1945

. . . Hirsch came in in the morning to say that the General Staff advices were that all the armies were in the clear and Germany was simply being cut to pieces. It was not plain how it could go on much longer. . . .

A Time of War

Saturday 31 March 1945

. . . Somewhat to my disgust, it developed that we were moving to the A ring in much larger quarters, to accommodate the radio people. Haddock told me about it well on in the afternoon, so I went with Johnny and looked at a large barn; but Rex, who seemed in good spirits, said he would have it partitioned up, recognizing that creative writers required privacy and the chance to put their feet on the desk.

Monday 2 April 1945

. . . We got nowhere on the conference Wednesday, many other affairs in connection with our moving being afoot, though we seemed unlikely to do it before Thursday. . . .

Tuesday 3 April 1945

. . . We got nowhere with the press conference until 2, when Haddock and I went down to see Gen Hood. He had a very bad cold, but seemed resolved to go through with it, so pending some material from OSS, we thought we would. He advanced to George some abominably bad notions about things he was going to say to the boys— especially upbraiding them about asking him questions they ought to know better than to ask. George calmly and gently talked him out of it. I suppose Preston put him up to it; and if so, he is a menace; and if not, the Gen needs a nurse. Along about 6 it was plain we would not have the stuff, and George and I had meanwhile seen a film Preston and the Gen thought they wanted to show. It was very dull and bad—they, or one of them, must again be nuts. In the end the conference was called off. . . . It seemed that the Pacific trip was going through with Robert "in charge of it"—his antics were of course insupportable.

Wednesday 4 April 1945

. . . I was busy with a vast counter-intelligence file on the difficulties with the Negro AAF personnel, which, in sum, were not too acute. Most of the trouble came from who-sat-where in southern busses; but there was also an obviously active minor element who (understandably) looked for trouble and found it. I do not see any easy solution, and do what I will, I recognize that my feeling that they are entitled to a fair deal is about skin deep. I just don't like them, and I suppose they would only have to provoke me a little to make me abandon any effort to see their side of it. The fussing about the move and about Robert's trip went on; and maybe (as just stated) my nerves are suffering from the months and now years of this life, but I thought I could hardly stand it.

ADDRESS REPLY TO
COMMANDING GENERAL, ARMY AIR FORCES
WASHINGTON 25, D. C.

ATTENTION:

HEADQUARTERS, ARMY AIR FORCES
WASHINGTON
4 April 1945

SPECIAL MEMORANDUM FOR THE CHIEF, OFFICE OF INFORMATION SERVICES

Subject: Racial Situation Reports.

1. The Consolidated Racial Situation Reports for periods covering December 1944 and January and February 1945, forwarded by Major Bronson W. Griscom, Chief, Evaluation and Coordination Branch, Counter Intelligence Division, seems to indicate that the negro situation in the AAF is not acute anywhere.

2. The biggest single factor, judged by the members of reported rows of incidents, is the application of the segreation policy in busses between southern posts and nearby towns. There are more of these cases than of all others put together.

3. In a large majority of all cases, personnel involved were drunk.

4. Attention is very frequently drawn by the reporting officers to the existence of so-called Bump Clubs - negroes, male and female, who engage with each other to put in a certain number of hour s a week bumping and jostling white people on the street and in stores. However, in point of actual activity, it seems to amount to very little. Presumably they get together and talk and feel good; but then either forget about it, or lose their nerve.

5. The Anti-Segregation Army Regulations seem to be, in general, strictly observed, and what white resistance there is, scattered and passive. As would perhaps naturally be the case, trouble, when there is some, is generally started by negroes - that is, a few spirited or bumptious individuals forcing themselves on whites somewhat beyond the point of mere equal rights. In short, they are looking for trouble.

6. One report (from the ATSC installation at Hill Field, Utah) includes a memo from a CIC undercover agent (a colored man), planted in a NAAC meeting to listen for subversive remarks or plots. Conceivably there is a good deal of this, since the Counter Intelligence Corps is likely to keep its counsel. It is no doubt right and necessary; but probably all interested parties would concur in the desirability of keeping knowledge of the practice from the general public.

JAMES G. COZZENS
Major, Air Corps

Thursday 5 April 1945

. . . To see Gen Hood with Major Ryal on his notion supported by Rex that he would speak next week on redeployment and we seemed to reach an understanding. In the afternoon to see Col Scott, who assisted by Col Outcalt, stated the case on a Lt Shapiro, subject of an editorial in the *Star*.[61] He had pulled a fast one on a court martial by substituting someone else for the defendant in an assault with intent to rape case, and had his phoney identified. It was then declared a mistrial, and they turned on him under AW 96[62] and ran him out. This was proper, and he was unquestionably guilty under the article; but they put it through pretty fast, and you could see that those who put it through . . . were out to get him.

Friday 6 April 1945

. . . We did our moving in the morning, the usual disconsolate confusion and jumble, with stuff stacked around and telephones waiting to be connected. Something told me we would never get our promised walls. However, I was able to get Ryal busy on some copies of a sort of text I worked up, and so left at noon to get the 1 pm to New York.

Monday 9 April 1945

. . . Ryal had duly got the stuff for Hood together so I had it typed up again and took it to him about 4. He seemed content to accept it, which surprised me; but probably he had other worries as it seemed that Eaker[63] was to replace Giles as Chief of the Air Staff and so would probably have his own notions about deputy chiefs. The new office was as dreary as ever and I was glad to get out. At the apartment there was a letter from M enclosing a letter, remarkably elegant and stilted (and yet the internal evidence was of much resource and generosity), from Isabel Taylor to say that my Aunt Ethel (from whom it was being kept) was not the victim of arthritis, as she imagined, but of a cancer of the breast, long past remedy, and could be expected to go out in some discomfort before she reached her 74th year. It works as a kind of reminder that any sense you have (mine is quite acute because it always seemed so to me in my experience—whatever happened to me that was bad or unsatisfactory seemed so clearly my own just desert for having no better sense than to do what I had sense enough to see would bring it about) of order or justice or reaping what you sow is an absurd if salutary illusion, making the Thomist's position on will and reason ludicrous except as a mental exercise with hypotheses and deliberately imagined situations accepted, though contrary to all observed fact, for the sake of the argument. You could say: Be good and you'll be happy—in so far as you have any control over the situation; but that is not far and don't imagine you can strike any bargain with life. What Divine Providence really seems to need is capable PRO personnel.

Tuesday 10 April 1945

. . . Gen Hood eventually got the text to Mr Lovett, but when I saw him about 4 it was plain that he had done little for it. He was very informal and friendly with me and exclaimed several times on Mr Lovett's good sense (which is real and there), but I think the Gen confused it with the Secty's ingratiating affability, faced with a fellow who was without assurance in what he proposed; because he thought (and not wrongly) that discretion was the better part, for him, of explicit recommendation. At any rate, I had it out to Review already, and halting a little, Gen Hood, who seemed to look mostly at a tinted photograph of his I assumed wife and two very-much-like-him young blonde daughters on his desk, said that Mr L did not seem willing to go to bat with Gen Surles, so he supposed, if Gen S squawked, it would be up to him. Though not a great one for management, I saw that I should have gone in with him to see Mr L and presented the case, if not as it is, at least as Rex and Gen Hood see it. I did what I could afterward, representing to JSC and Review that Mr L had felt there was nothing Gen Surles could take exception to, and so, until Gen Surles definitely did, he would not bring the point up. This seemed to work, in the sense that Matthews of BPR telephoned me at 5.30 to say that it was by Surles. Clearly the lesson is that nothing succeeds like assurance—none of them really knows what he thinks anyway, and if you do it respectfully they will thank you for doing it firmly. It was a hard day.

Wednesday 11 April 1945

. . . The conference text, mildly impeded by some reasonless changes which Preston sold the Gen—I was delighted to learn, for the last time; as he is going out with Giles—finally got done. The conference itself was more of a success than I expected in that the news people appeared passionately interested and eagerly took all the generalizations down. The Gen himself gets better in manner, adjusting his emphasis to his text, but I am afraid he gets no better in what might be called readiness, which was what made Smitty so good. If a question put to him is involved, or not perfectly clear, he seems to lack even an ordinary knack for guessing the point and straightening it out. There were a lot of questions on redeployment and demobilization of course, and it was all I could do several times to keep from saying: General, what Mr Moore means is whatever the obvious thing Moore was trying to say might be. I never opened my mouth.

Thursday 12 April 1945

. . . There were some rumors in the afternoon that the President was not well, but I only heard on the radio when I got home in the evening that he had died. The effect of the announcement was certainly dismaying, both because of its overtones of a certain unlife-like melodrama, like a moral lesson about in the midst of life being in death; and the circumstance that would make Mr Truman President (always certainly a possibility, but one which probably nobody in the country—including Truman, would wish to see happen or ever seriously thought possible). S in on the 9.30 train and I was surprised that nobody had told them on the train. . . .

Friday 13 April 1945

. . . I went in early, but it proved that we were not expected to do anything in the way of hurry-up statements. Things were proceeding as usual—the carpenters in, hammering on our partitions—and all comment I heard was indirect. I picked up a QMC major driving in, and he observed that what with the progress in Europe, this would seem to be a pretty full day. I would judge that a probably universal sense of consternation had lasted about a minute, or perhaps at most fifteen. Then the matter seemed to be delivered over to the newspapers and the radio, who came up with a wave of probably not untrue but certainly repellent hog wash which seemed to rule out the possibility of any further personal feeling. . . .

Saturday 14 April 1945

. . . The rumors were very lively that negotiations were going on with Germany or some Germans, or especially von Papen, who seemed to have been picked up by one of the armored sweeps a few days ago; but there was nothing definite, and since everyone was let out because of the President's funeral I was able to get away by two thirty or so. . . .

Monday 16 April 1945

. . . Gen Hood was not in the office so we made a change to the new conference subject and I got people getting together what I could, having my usual row with Marks in Intelligence. As before noted, my nerves must be going. There is something about that beefy, stupified face; that thick slow stirring as he seems to try to understand a simple statement, and then misses it; and then protests with a surly air that you don't tell him what you want—I ended by saying that he would damn well have to give anyway, and he could have his R&R but Haddock, I guess justly, canned the paragraph in which I protested in painfully chosen phrases about our difficulties with the European branch, and asked that he be directed to give us what we wanted. Since we have nothing but ease and good relationships with Lt Col Martin in the Pacific branch I was not ready to admit that it might be my fault.

Tuesday 17 April 1945

. . . In spite of my temperate phrasing and efforts to spell it out for him, I was indeed

ADDRESS REPLY TO
COMMANDING GENERAL, ARMY AIR FORCES
WASHINGTON 25, D. C.

ATTENTION:

HEADQUARTERS, ARMY AIR FORCES
WASHINGTON

14 April 1945

MEMORANDUM FOR THE CHIEF, OFFICE OF INFORMATION SERVICES

Subject: Information from AC/AS Offices.

1. C-46 Squawk in NEWSWEEK. (OC&R) The Requirements Division (Col. Bell) is somewhat upset by a piece in Newsweek 9 April which stated that "the first airborne use of the C-46 proved drastic structural changes were needed for such operations." Specifically, it was represented that the hydraulic system was too easily knocked out by ack-ack, and that the double doors created such a draft that the plane's interior was a very effective fire trap. SHAEF rejoined: that the article was entirely without official basis; that the C-46 was considered a good troop carrier aircraft; that the C-46 was "naturally somewhat more vulnerable than the C-47 due to its being larger and having more area exposed to fire; that any large door whether single or double would admit a certain amount of smoke or flame if the aircraft was on fire; and that the double doors on the C-46 were one of its best features for airborne operations as it permits dropping of two sticks of paratroopers simultaneously." (Undersigned officer was not previously aware that paratroopers came in sticks.) SHAEF conclusion: "this unfortunate and undeserved publicity is most regrettable and is directly contrary to the opinions of this Hq. and the IX Troop Carrier Command regarding the C-46 aircraft." (The 'article' in question was really a note in "The Periscope", a collection of newsy little items about "what's behind Today's News and what's to be expected in Tomorrow's". It said that the C-46 "won't be used in future airborne operations unless and until drastic structural changes are made." Wrong again, apparently.)

2. Post War Air Force. (OC&R) The Troop Basis Division is making a "restudy" of training requirements for the post-war air force. The "basic assumptions" remain what they were (my memo, 24 Feb.) -- 75 groups of 3 squadrons plus 42 separate squadrons with a reserve of effective combat crew members to make up 189 groups of 4 squadrons plus 84 separate squadrons. Twelve months' warning is assumed so that the latter force could be got operational. Effective combat crew status is assumed to last for 6 years after training. "The purpose of this study is to determine the minimum level of training and student capacity which should be met at approximately the time of the defeat of the Last Axis Power. It is felt that the adoption of the post war level of training as a goal will enable maximum release of AAF individuals to civil life prior to the defeat of Japan." (This presumably means that the establishment of the permanent post war training program would more than take care of 'attrition' in the Pacific as long as the war lasts.)

3. **ATC 1946 Pacific Operations.** (OC&R) As of 1 January 1946 the ATC anticipates a requirement of a Troop Basic increase of 17,338. This is based on plans to have in operation 241 four-engine aircraft (36 by Contract Carriers) and estimated ferrying requirements of 1300 tactical aircraft a month (500 B-29's and B-32's; 250 four engine, and 550 two engine). Since there are similar estimated increases for the North Atlantic Division, the China Division, and the ZI, "it is believed that all such estimates will have to be scaled down somewhat."

4. **Freeman Field Situation.** (Air Inspector) The status of the racial difficulty at Freeman Field, Seymour, Indiana, seems now to be roughly this. Mr. Truman Gibson, the Secretary of War's aide, "recommended that the AAF make an inquiry into the entire situation." Gen. Giles instructed the Air Inspector to do this. Col. John B. Harris went out 12 April. The issue will be complicated by the fact of the pending court martial proceedings against the 3 negro officers who "forced their way past an armed Provost Marshal officer." It would be very difficult to explain failure to carry out court martial proceedings on such a charge. The 54 other negro officers who likewise passed the Provost Marshal officer, (but without force; and were released from arrest on recommendation of the Judge Advocate of the First Air Force) would be showing considerably less spirit, or fractiousness, than their conduct to date makes likely if they were to stand by quietly. No very obvious solution exists, since the Army has apparently decided to go along with the great American tradition of making laws and regulations to suit those who holler, and then not-enforcing them, thus suiting the opposite party. The best tactic now would probably be to delay, to play for time, to avoid forcing the issue if it seems probable that the 3 and the 54 will stick together. Mr. Gibson probably feels the same way, because he stated "that a formal investigation would not be required at this time."

JAMES G. COZZENS
Major, Air Corps

enraged to find that Marks, the Jerk, had not given anyone the business of meeting the R&R and so we did not get our stuff until noon, and then due to the efforts of Major Hamblin, a pleasant fellow in the back room. Gen Hood combined his original subject with the new one; so I listened with Col Butler, Gilder, Major Power and Capt Banta to a rendition of the staff presentation by Major Smith, also of AC/AS Intelligence. He is a grizzled, moustached little fellow from the last war, and certainly very good; so I only had to do the part before and the part after (which was plenty). It was a hard day, what with the painters finishing up around and over the desk and the trouble with Marks—but I had to notice, as I have before, that psychologically I seem to thrive on it—the tougher it gets, and the less time there is, and the more people who come in, the better, when it's all over, I feel. It was all over by barely half past five when Johnny typed the last of the Gen's text and I went home, worn out all right, but cheerful and contented.

Wednesday 18 April 1945

. . . Trouble came up on Maj Smith's presentation in the morning and I went in with George Haddock who looked very ill to see Lovett who did not look too well either—the veins prominent at the sides of his forehead, and a sagging under his jaw which I had not noticed the last time I saw him. He made little of Gen Bissell's thoughts that made the trouble, saying God Damn a good many times; whether to put us or himself at ease, I did not know; but he has that reassuring air of intelligence. The conference went off well, after some changes in the text—Gen Hood would not conclude with the line: Air Power makes the difference; so we said instead; Air Power has justified its place in the sun. Still, he steadily improves somewhat in ease, emphasis, and expression; and Maj Smith was brisk and full of fact, like a good college lecturer (which I bet he was). In connection with the morning's matters, Hood brought me in with him to see Gen Kuter, who was sitting with considerable aplomb in Gen Giles' office. Gen Hood said; You know Major Cozzens, sir? and Kuter with an affable air I had to admire, said; Oh yes, the Major and I are old team-mates. The gracious reference, I realized, was to the days early last fall when he had been taking the conferences. Hood was very deferential and a little agitated. I saw that you would have to know a lot about histories going back to West Point to get the relationships straight; but they are a good, if simple, type of human being—Kuter; Hood; most of them.

Thursday 19 April 1945

A quiet day. . . . Much of it went into putting up a 1-250,000 map of Japan on our new wall—quite an undertaking; but we concluded in the end it exceeded anything we had in the old room—as well it might, since it was barely half (the southern half)

HEADQUARTERS, ARMY AIR FORCES
WASHINGTON

19 April 1945

MEMORANDUM FOR THE CHIEF, OFFICE OF INFORMATION SERVICES

Subject: Information from AC/AS Offices.

1. <u>Freeman Field Situation</u>. (Air Inspector) As easily foreseen (my memo, 14 April), the racial difficulty at Freeman Field, Seymour, Indiana, bids fair to be a honey. Now under arrest are a total of 104 colored officers, being held at Goodman Field. The CO of Freeman Field was obliged to close the club 13 April, apparently to avoid having still more under arrest. On 14 April the Deputy, AC/AS, Personnel called the Air Provost Marshal "with reference to the military police battalion stationed at Camp Atterbury, 20 miles north of Seymour, Indiana, in the Fifth Service Command. The Executive Officer has called the Commanding General, Fifth Service Command, and stated that the service command should give assistance prior to any emergency if the AAF deemed it advisable. He also stated that it was felt that the AAF should exhaust all efforts prior to calling on the service command for assistance." The APM adds somewhat glumly: "No further information has been received in this office relative to the situation at Freeman Field." The further information that the APM has not received, is, according to Col. Scott, roughly this: the situation is simply mutiny, and is recognized as such by the Inspector General. It will be treated as such.

This would be serious enough; but the Col. tells me confidentially that a decision has been reached to accept segregation as a War Department policy, and revoke the present regulations. I was interested to learn that Mr. Stimson was never in favor of the AAF's stand, and spoke very sharply to the CG, AAF for exceeding his authority in promulgating the no-segregation directives to the AAF. This is obviously a hell of a mess. I suggested to Col. Scott that surely it would be better at this point to enforce the regulation, no matter how annoyed the southern (and maybe northern) whites might be. He said with some reason, that it was impossible; because (a) we would have a much larger mutiny and one much more serious in its effect on the war effort; (b) the WD, feeling that the AAF had screwed it up, is taking the whole matter over, and will make its own decisions. Be point (b) as it may, the AAF is clearly in for a monumental beating from every liberal element in the country.

2. <u>Post War Flying Training Requirements</u>. (OC&R) Assuming the 75 group peace-time post war air force (my memo, 14 April), the Troop Basis Division believes "the following annual peacetime training levels are indicated as those required to provide a sufficient OR C population of effective combat crew personnel" to meet the wartime

expansion plan (189 groups, plus 34 separate squadrons), and to
maintain a training establishment which could handle the expansion:

Category	NUMBER Per Year
Pilots	8,400
Glider Pilots	1,040
Bom.-Nav.-Radar	5,660
A/C Observer-Flight-Eng.	1,530
Radar Observer	220
Gunners	4,920
POM & Aerial Engineer	1,860

Since these figures are not much below current output in the
principal categories, it follows that a training establishment little
if any smaller than the present one (the AAF will be less inclined
to cut corners and crowd schedules in peace-time) will be permanently
required. Perhaps it would be wise to accustom the public to this
probably now unexpected idea.

3. WAC Fashion Note. (Air WAC Officer) "During the mid-winter
meeting of WAC staff directors at Fort Des Moines, AAF staff directors
recommended that women working at outdoor jobs in the southern part
of the United States be issued class B cotton shirts to wear with
the standard herringbone twill trousers in place of herring bone twill
shirts."

4. JB-2 Progress Report. (OC&R) JB-2 launchings are now resulting
in better than 80% successful flights. 8 launchings from a B-17
have been attempted, 4 of them successful. First tests of the
flash-steam launching equipment will take place this week. The first
multiple cartridge ramp was completed and shipped to Eglin 10 April.
215 JB-2's were accepted in March. Future production is scheduled
at 200 per month on the original order of 2,000. "ATSC is having
trouble placing contracts for the recently authorized procurement of
10,000 due to potential JAC classification in Group 5, and contractor
reluctance because of previous program fluctuations and potential
consumer goods production after V-E Day."

5. Noise Warfare. (OC&R) Major Prout of the Requirements Division
attended a demonstration at Bolling Field of a multiple siren mounted
on a Navy plane. 9 plate shaped sirens are so arranged on the wings
that they can be rotated into the air stream, which then keeps them
spinning. "Several passes varying in altitude from 500 to approximately 10 or 12 feet were made at the spectators. The sirens are
directional and produce an intense noise, and some actual pain, to
persons located along the line of flight.... The demonstration was
arranged through AAF Liaison with NDRC to consider the possibility of
utilizing a terrifying or unnerving noise for psychological effect
in conjunction with tactical operations. At the present time it is
felt that there is no AAF requirement for airborne sound devices for
the persecution of psychological warfare."

3

6. Sex Morality Film. (Air Chaplain) "Conference with Chaplain George Rosso, Bureau of Naval Personnel, regarding material on hand in Air Chaplain Division for a film on sex morality. Chaplain Rosso was promised all available material as well as personal assistance from the Air Chaplain Division in the making of the sex-morality film."

JAMES G. COZZENS
Major, Air Corps

of the islands and there were certainly 40 sheets to adjust and staple on. The Freeman Field difficulty with the Negroes seemed to be getting more acute[64] and Col Scott gave me something on it for a memorandum. Apparently it is impossible not to segregate them; and yet I think he is wrong. We have a regulation and we should enforce it, having made it, not change it—I mean, merely as a matter of policy. . . .

Friday 20 April 1945

. . . The Freeman Field matter seemed to be blowing up a little and I went to see Col Kidner in the AJA's office. He thought I should see Gen Hedrick tomorrow. Meanwhile it was reaching the papers, and the situation was certainly awkward if they were going to take whatever ingenious steps to void AR 210-10 Par 19.[65] I suppose it is a very good sample of the tremendous and, in fact, apparently hopeless, difficulties of attempting to fit practice to theory. You might say; if the majority of officers are white, and the majority does not want colored officers in the club, what are you practising but democracy if you exclude them? The real difficulty would seem to lie in the essentially anomalous position of the army, which is required to be both autocratic and democratic at the same time. The regulation assumes that obedience to orders will be instant and unquestioned (and then there would be no trouble); but it is plain that instant and unquestioned obedience to orders is just what isn't really expected, and it would certainly be absurd and disastrous to try to ignore this realistic circumstance. The only way out is the ordinary way—you do what you can to meet the regulation; and don't do what you can't.

Saturday 21 April 1945

. . . Gen Hedrick, an amiable old fellow, talked to me for one hour and three quarters, principally around the point. The time he was free to take (obviously), and some statements he made, . . . showed that he knew less about the situation than I did because his office was in general by-passed and told nothing. He seemed to believe that they were indeed going to change Par 19, and he did not know what recommendations were being made by Giles thru Gen Owens on behalf of the AAF. He thought it was under debate. I went in town briefly to get my teeth scraped and when I came out, there were two captains from Counter Intelligence who came over in answer to my call to Major Griscom, the racial relations expert, with what dope they had. They thought it mostly poor administration by Col Selway of Freeman Field; but this was not the opinion of Col Harris, the Air Inspector's man who had just come back. I went up then to see Gen Schneider, the Air Inspector in Gen Jones' absence, and he showed me the recommendations that nobody had bothered to show Gen Hedrick. Apparently they are not going to do anything so silly as make an issue—they will do their segregation on a subterfuge, or misinterpretation of the plain meaning of Par 19. Since this was Gen Hedrick's idea too, even if they didn't keep him up-to-date, I had two opportunities to feel that instinctive recoil at the obvious failure to be honest about what you were doing, and two opportunities to see that this was by far the best way of handling it—the price of the self-satisfaction of being honest and forthright was simply too high. This way, a certain numbers of people would call you a hypocrite (and rightly); the other way, you would provoke who-knew-how-many riots and mutinies, with appropriate number of heads bashed in and probably some people killed; circumstances certain to worsen, not better, the situation. It was necessary to leave it at that.

Monday 23 April 1945

. . . We did little but fuss over the Freeman Field affair, which Gen Hunter of the First AF seems determined to screw up by making a statement to the press. Haddock went to New York in the evening to hold him, if anyone could. . . .

Tuesday 24 April 1945

. . . It developed that wiser counsels had prevailed, and Gen Hunter was not to have his conference in NY. Just as good, or better, Gen Eaker, coming in to Giles' place, did not feel ready to see the press tomorrow, so Hood kindly decided we would have no party here. Thus the day was idle, except for the alarms and excursions.

Wednesday 25 April 1945

. . . Haddock was back from NY with a text of Gen Hunter's proposed remarks on Freeman Field. On the E ring everything was much upset with rumors that Eaker would be Deputy CG, but not Chief of Staff (Kuter, presumably); and, even, that there would be a new CG (Spaatz, [66] possibly). I learned from the Manning Section . . . that G-1 [Personnel Section] had this morning informed everybody that it was time the AAF got rid ot its large surplus of officers, and so it might be fairly simple for some of us if things shook down in Europe shortly.

Thursday 26 April 1945

. . . In with Haddock and Delaney to see Lovett about the Freeman Field business where we remained some hour and a half. Lovett, who looked better than when I saw him last, and was as usual temperate, gracious and well-spoken, approved a statement for Col Selway of Freeman Field which would plainly put the burden on the War Dept to give out Circular 20-6, the Command of Negro Troops. I thought that, self-consciously, he was intent only on what anyone would be intent on—clearing yourself of pretending that you were doing one thing while you were in fact doing another and anyone could recognize it and reproach you. Sub-consciously, of

C. H.

ADDRESS REPLY TO
COMMANDING GENERAL, ARMY AIR FORCES
WASHINGTON 25, D. C.

ATTENTION:

HEADQUARTERS, ARMY AIR FORCES
WASHINGTON

23 April 1945

MEMORANDUM FOR THE CHIEF, OFFICE OF INFORMATION SERVICES

Subject: Information from AC/AS Offices

1. <u>Freeman Field Situation</u>. (Air Inspector) For the record,
the recommendations on this matter made by Gen. Giles and approved
by Gen. Marshal are:

    a. Release of the 101 negro officers under arrest, and
        dropping of charges under AW 64 for their refusal to
        sign the read-and-understood blank attached to
        Seymour Field Base Regulation 80-2.

    b. Trial of the remaining three officers (who pushed the
        assistant PM) "if the investigation (by Hq. 1st AF)
        indicates the charges can be sustained."

    c. Transfer of the 477th Bomb Group and its supporting
        units to Godman Field, Kentucky.

    d. Inactivation and demobilization of the units on V-E
        day or R day, whichever is first announced.

(Policy in regard to the officer's club problem in the future will
apparently be guided by Gen. Hedrick's opinion that Par. 19, AR 210-10
"is not interpreted as a requirement that all officers on a base be
permitted to use all clubs. It is the view of this office that
the mentioned regulation was designed to insure every officer the right
to membership in officers' club; but does not prohibit a <u>reasonable
division of club facilities where circumstances make such division
necessary or desirable from a practical, disciplinary, or morale
standpoint.</u>" (This disregards the plain meaning of the paragraph, but
what the hell?)

2. <u>Munition Situation on V-E Day</u>. (OC&R) The Army Service Command
has asked the Chief of the Air Staff about the availability of AAF
units "to help unload ammunition trains if VE Day should be announced
unexpectedly. Because of the tremendous expenditures of bombs and
ammunition in Europe, there are constantly on the rails in the US,
bound for Eastern ports, great quantities of bombs and ammunition.
ASF has determined if the requirement for this flow suddenly ceases
on VE Day, <u>it will be VE plus 210 days</u> before the rails are cleared.
It is obviously dangerous and impractical to leave these explosives
in freight cars in freight yards. ASF requested AAF to designate all
possible units to aid in unloading these cars at various points in
the U.S." (The ASF was notified that the only troops available would
be 2 QM Truck companies - about as much good as nothing.)

3. Embarkation Port Change. (M&S) A shift in the point of shipment of material for the India-China-Burma theatre from Los Angeles to New York is underway. It is expected that by 1 June all shipments for the area would be routed through New York.

4. AAF Losses. (Management Control)
   a. Officer Casualties. "Out of a total of 78,294 officer battle casualties, more than half (53.6%) were suffered by Air Corps officers; 41.2% by Ground officers; 5.2% by ASF officers."

   b. Planes. "As of 31 March 1945, more than half (34,557 out of 64,632) of the AAF combat and transport planes dispatched to all theatres since Pearl Harbor have been lost." (Of the 30,075 remaining; 2,300 have been returned to the U.S., 1,116 transferred to allied air forces, 1,371 are en route; 25,288 are on hand overseas. Of the losses, 865 took place en route.)

5. XB-48. (OC&R) In line with what appears to be OC&R policy to have as many manufacturers as possible have a try at building planes around jet units, Martin is at work on a medium bomber designed XB-48 to be powered by 6 TG-180 units - two nacelles with 3 units in each. The tactical range is estimated at 2,840 miles, the operational ceiling, 35,000 feet, high speed, 534 mph; cruising speed, 440 mph. The maximum bomb load is 22,000 tons and the bomb bay will allow loading one Grand Slam bomb if desirable. "Except for being considerably larger, the airplane is similar in configuration to other B-40 series bombers." However, a new type landing gear is being tried out. This will consist of two main double-wheeled gears fore and aft in the fuselage, with the front gear steerable; and the bomb bay doors will open by retracting into the bomb bay, instead of dropping down. "In accordance with current military characteristics of medium bombers, only two 50 cal. guns, firing from the tail turret, provide armament. The gunner is the co-pilot, sitting behind the pilot and firing the guns by remote control." The planned crew is three, but in view of the range (7 hours), it is felt that another man should be included and possibly more guns. Martin has been asked to "make a study for another man in the nose, to be visual bombardier."

6. Reconnaissance Conference. (OC&R) Representatives of OC&R, M&S, and ATSC were summoned by the Chief of Naval Operations last week for a squawk on subject Subject. "The conference was motivated by a cable from commanders in the Pacific Theatre re the lack of information regarding Japanese installations on Iwo Jima and a request that immediate steps be taken to improve the methods of detecting these installations." Various suggestions were made, most of them, apparently, impractical. "The most useful expedient offered was through low level stereotype photography and visual reconnaissance through high powered (10 power or better) binoculars." (Remaining question in re low level photography and use of binoculars: Who wants to live forever anyway?)

7. <u>XP-86 Designation Change.</u> (M&S) The "Bell-fabricated" fighter, with supersonic (speed in excess of 760 mph) characteristics, now in the works (such as they are) will no longer be known as the XP-86. It will be designated S-1; though at the same time, to make it harder, the term "transonic" is being substituted for "supersonic". Presumably to complete the screwing-up, the designation XP-86 will be given to the new North American one-TG-180-unit job.

8. <u>Notes from In and Out Log.</u>

   a. <u>CINCPOA 17 April.</u> ...The enemy launched heavy air attacks against our forces in and around Okinawa...our planes shot down 62 A/E over Okinawa...67 more were shot down in the Ryukus area... ships anti-aircraft fire off the Okinawa beaches destroyed 38... (How's that about the Jap air force?)

   b. <u>Paris signed Eisenhower 17 April.</u> Practicability of earlier movement of 7 remaining HB groups is subject. One group from Italy available after 15 May...six groups from Eighth AF could be prepared for shipment 30 days notice...

   c. <u>From SHAEF to Gen. Marshal signed Eisenhower 18 April.</u> ...I propose to issue instructions that no soldier is to be sent to the Pacific who has fought in both the North African and the European campaigns...these men will be retained in the theatre for the occupation forces...

                              JAMES G. COZZENS
                              Major, Air Corps

HEADQUARTERS, ARMY AIR FORCES
WASHINGTON

25 April 1945

MEMORANDUM FOR THE CHIEF, OFFICE OF INFORMATION SERVICES

Subject: Information from AC/AS Officer

1. <u>Freeman Field Situation</u>. (Air Provost Marshal) Confirming the opinions expressed by Capt. C. R. Patterson, of Major Griscom's office (Counter-Intelligence), Col. Reynolds reports a visit to First Air Force Hq. "The situation at Freeman Field was discussed at length and a first-hand report of the unsatisfactory conditions existing at that station was submitted verbally by the Provost Marshal of the First Air Force. The officer assigned as ███████████ at that station had very little previous experience and did not carry out his assignment in a proper manner. Guard houses were in very poor condition with an inferior system of guarding the prisoners, discipline was lax, prisoners were not searched at frequent intervals and as a result many dangerous weapons were found when a thorough search was made. Practically every activity in connection with proper security was subject to criticism. The Provost Marshal of the First Air Force immediately arranged for the relief of the officer assigned as ████████████ and arranged for the assignment of a new one. It is expected conditions will immediately improve as the new officer is experienced and has done an excellent job at another field."

(Capt. Patterson's opinion, supported by the evidence in a confidential counter-intelligence report he showed me, was that much of the difficulty arose because the Post Commander, Col. Robert R. Selway, Jr., took the understandable, but Counter-intelligence thought, unwise, course of letting matters slide. ██ Capt. Patterson, who has apparently seen a great deal of this kind of thing, believes that almost all the "racial" trouble on posts results from the old army custom of giving the command of negro troops to officers who had failed to show any marked ability in other jobs. I gathered that he meant primarily, company commanders and so on, and not necessarily post commanders. ████████████████████████████

A point in this connection comes out in another note by Col. Reynolds on his visit to First Air Force Hq. The First Air Force PM "described in detail the methods used in controlling the conduct of colored personnel in Harlem which has a negro population of about 700,000. This area is controlled by a force of 3 officers and 150 military police, all colored. This group has been hand-picked and perform their duty in a superior manner. There has been no trouble to date in this area and it is not anticipated that serious trouble will arise in the future because of the fine quality of the officers and men assigned to this duty."

2. Quick Release Parachutes. (MS) Gen. Kenney's objection in the log to the new parachutes (A-4 and B-9, Drew Pearson type) though distinctly stated to be on the grounds of safety was, according to Major Oakley, "based on the uncomfortable harness arrangement and a minor defect in the release box. No objection to quick release parachutes in principle is involved."

3. Flight Feeding Program. (OC&R) Quite a bunch of general officers were given a demonstration of subject program by the Second Air Force last week. "The entire party was taken aloft in a B-17 and fed a very well cooked luncheon, consisting of soup, meat, potatoes, peas, carrots, beans, cake, and coffee - all served piping hot, having been kept so by the B-2 food warmer. The warmer itself weighs about 40 pounds and contains six food trays, 12 beverage cups, and 6 spoons. The pre-cooked meat and uncooked other food is placed in the food warmer and plugged into the regular electric circuit, which cooks the food and keeps it warm for 18 hours. After this time it is recommended by the Second Air Force that the food be thrown away." A trifle ruefully, Col. Travis adds: "Food warmers are not now in great use in the XXI Bomber Command due to lack of replacement parts and taste imparted the food as a result of the metal trays. Parchment linings are now becoming available, but too late for the present crews of the XXI to overcome their prejudice against these warmers."

4. Air Evacuation of Wounded. (Air Surgeon) The Surgeon, IX Troop Carrier Command, ETO, reports that a total of over 300,000 patients have been evacuated by air by that command. In the first 13 days of April, 34,000 patients were moved. "The bulk of these were from forward air fields in Germany, back to the UK and the Paris area; almost 100% of the wounded coming back from across the Rhine are coming by air."

5. Glider Production. (OC&R) Getting on with a "reexamination" of the glider requirements (my memo, 17 April), another interesting example of somewhat cockeyed planning appears. Somebody decided to check on "the transport aircraft now available and to be made avail-able to CBI and PA." It develops that "neither theatre, or even the two theatres combined, could provide sufficient transport aircraft to effect the number of airborne division lifts proposed by the Supply Supplement to the War Department Troop Deployment Schedule." However, this may be all right because, in any event, "insufficient airborne divisions will be deployed after VE-Day" to utilize the gliders, even if the planes to tow them were available. The Requirements Division

concludes calmly: "Glider shipments to ETO have been cancelled and consequently a large storage problem will be presented by the high monthly production rate."

6. Liaison Aircraft for Combat. (OC&R) Concern seems to have been aroused by the activities of the Marine Corps in fitting up L-5's to fire rockets, and of the Foot Army in trying out at Fort Sill the L-5 as a bomber (2 250 lb. bombs). "Both the Marines and the Ground Forces are obviously interested in exploiting all potentialities of light aircraft. It is apparent that the AAF must be vitally interested in this, as in any other, phase of air fighting." Directives are therefore going out from the Chief of the Air Staff to the AAF Board and the III Tactical Air Command "initiating thorough tests of the combat potentialities of light aircraft, designed to indicate the optimum employment and organization needs of a combat L-5 type. In this connection it was pointed out that while such an airplane could scarcely have been so utilized against the effective defense measures employed by the Germans, Japanese combat area defense against aircraft is primitive at night and not too effective during daylight. It was further suggested that L-5's might well be utilized in a combat capacity by Tactical Air Commands or similar elements without substantial increases in personnel, since maintenance is extremely light and available fighter pilots could run the necessary sorties in many cases."

7. Notes from In and Out Log.

a. USMA Buenos Aires 23 April. ...Great activity over the weekend resulted in hundreds of reported arrests of democratic persons as plotters of counter revolution...

b. To Bret from Marshal 23 April. Consideration by congress of independence for Puerto Rico requires War Dept. view on retention of bases...current military thought here is that War Dept. must point out disadvantages of a change of sovereignty...but the fact remains that purely political arguments may result in independence...

JAMES G. COZZENS
Major, Air Corps

course, this would mean that you wished to pass the buck; (a) either superior authority insisted on the present situation and declared it, so you could say, if you did it, that you were ordered to; or (b) superior authority, subjected to heavy fire, gave way; but still, whatever the unfortunate consequences (if any), that was not your fault. I told Ed about it afterwards, and he, with something of a glitter in his eye, seemed pleased. He would like to have the issue made. Whether because he is ten years younger, or because he has a clearer insight about the brotherhood of man, I could see that he liked the idea of beating-in the heads of the southern officers (stupid little jerks, mostly, it is true) who would not drink their glass of beer with a Negro, while all I wanted was to avoid making them take a stand, so that sooner or later I myself might have to take one—that is; the argument seems to me absurd; how could any sane person object to a Negro officer in an officers club? On the other hand, if there are people who can and do object, as long as they were in the great majority I could not see myself requiring them to accept my attitude on pain of court-martial; or of believing that I would help the situation any, if I did. In fact, I think the present situation, however anomalous should be continued because the people who object are unquestionably losing ground, and might very well continue to lose it until they had none left—an infiltration process is under way and if they aren't provoked to stand and fight soon, they never will be able to. It is not clear to me what will be gained (a) by publishing 20-6 (a very well-phrased and intelligent paper; but still it admits that we will segregate when it seems advisable) and provoking a storm; (b) by, in the face of the storm which is what Ed hopes, changing it to forbid segregation and so consolidating resistance and closing up ranks now very much disorganized, and becoming more and more accustomed to accept what the Negro wants. However, I kept my mouth shut with Lovett because it seemed difficult to oppose a stand so creditable and satisfactory in point of forthrightness, honesty, and self-esteem with the consideration of whether it would or would not be the best thing for the people actually and actively involved. We then checked the release with Gen Hunter in New York (Gen Hood meanwhile retiring himself within himself, with the fairly plain idea of keeping his head down) and it went to the War Department. There (because of prejudice, of course) I think perhaps my practical and ignoble course may prevail. I do not see them publishing 20-6, nor yet rescinding it.

Friday 27 April 1945

. . . There was nothing further on the Freeman Field business, the buck apparently having been indeed neatly passed and the WD was now pondering its position. It seemed confirmed that Mr A would give up his CG job, probably to Spaatz; and that Eaker would be only Deputy CG, not Chief of Staff, and there was some war on about whether Kuter would or would not get that. . . .

A Time of War

Tuesday 1 May 1945

. . . I had a lot of activity reports which I was mostly busy at. In the morning a pleasant partly bald, partly gray-headed Major Talbott came in on a suggestion from Bill Chambers to know if I would like his job—which seemed to be that of a sort of free-lance liaison man for the training command; he went where he liked and asked them how various training bulletins were working out, reporting to Fort Worth, but not having to do anything about it. Since his object was to find a successor so he could get out, which in a way is my own object, it was not for me; but I could see that it was a wonderful set-up for someone.

Wednesday 2 May 1945

. . . We were agitated all day long with rumors—some fairly good, that we were going to need our VE Day announcements. Gen Loutzenheiser, the little merry moustached fellow who looks like a dentist [and] is acting AC/AS Plans in Kuter's place talked to me for awhile in the morning, much interrupted by his box which was expostulating over the probability that Admiral Nimitz might be able to direct some operations of the XXth Air Force, on some stuff we needed for something. I got it late in the afternoon, when things were so hot that Newhouse and Bradshaw and I came back after dinner and sat until 1 am with Haddock, who then stayed all night, but of course nothing happened.

Thursday 3 May 1945

. . . From what could be gathered, it seemed likely that the war in ETO was in fact over, but they were biding their time on the announcement—probably, or perhaps, Sunday sometime, with an eye to when it would cause the least fuss. However, George Bradshaw was to stay all night anyway on Eaker's orders—as was the case last night; it seemed to be a whim of his that someone should stay. Mr A was supposed to be at Rio and we were busy cabling him texts.

Friday 4 May 1945

. . . Off at noon, with nothing further developed, and into the White House with S to meet Jonathan Daniels and his wife, sitting in his sufficiently grand office as Press Secretary; and to lunch, a long delayed affair at the Statler, which seemed to be the only place he could reserve a table—understandable, considering the food. He is pleasant and so is she—he seems glad to be getting out, as he will next week when Truman's new man comes in; and yet I think a little disappointed, having probably reconciled himself to going on with Roosevelt and seeing how that could fit in with some guarded kind of political ambition which I think he feels. His talk was mostly about his writing plans; but I think he could easily transform himself into the senator from North Carolina, and I would even bet, may yet. We came back to find the station wagon which I had parked on the White House drive hemmed in every way by the big black cars of the members of the cabinet who were just leaving a meeting—but it was apparently not about the end of the war.

Saturday 5 May 1945

. . . I spent most of the day fussing with various M&S people on what Lovett might possibly say after VE Day (we had a number of rumors about that, most of them centering on tomorrow) on the production cut-backs and so on. Nothing was accomplished.

Monday 7 May 1945

. . . It seemed clear that the war in ETO was over, and I talked with Haddock, who was in early, about what might be done about getting out. Matters are in some confusion and I said I did not want to get out until he did; but I did not want to stay after he left. He said he would see what he could do. The truth is that, a little prematurely, since I am not out, I found myself with the feeling that there was a kind of dreamlike quality to the whole thing—that is, you can't mistake the fact that it is really you who dreams your own dreams; but all of it, from the night I went down to Washington at the end of July 1942 right through today was a sort of Alice-in-Wonderland mix-up and had little to do with "life," which would be a regular routine of writing in the mornings and working in a garden in the afternoons—perhaps because it was all done without my volition—I just found myself here or there doing this or that as seemed indicated without any logical introduction or any logical conclusion—mixed with that surprise which you never seem to get over when what seems as though it would never end, does end—there you are, and the endless present is all past.

Tuesday 8 May 1945

Rain, beginning about 7.30 (just after I got in) through the morning, putting a probably advantageous stop to some vague nonsense that had been going around about a meeting in the courtyard two hours after the announcement of VE Day—which we listened to over the radio in Brisson's section next door. The whole thing seemed to have been very well calculated and arranged to make it unlikely that anyone would feel an urge to 'celebrate.' I worked on a superfluous statement or two. . . .

Wednesday 9 May 1945

. . . little to do but my memoranda, since things seemed to be in some confusion of policy over what if anything else ought to be stated. The truth is, there seems to be too much stating, but on the other hand, it seems probably a healthy situation when the top military echelon keeps worrying so much about presenting its case to the People—instead of thinking it can just tell them—which, of course, in fact it can; but they are better off not knowing it. I don't suppose anyone in the country has any thought but that we must go on and finish the Japanese war, but the Military all seem to imagine that, if people aren't carefully coaxed, they wouldn't do it.

Thursday 10 May 1945

. . . Our Col Bowman turned up, a fairly pleasant-looking fellow, with a small round dark head and sallow pleasant-looking face. It seemed that Rex was not coming back at all; and, what with the decision by the WD to give out the substance of RR 1-5, I began to realize that some unformed but firm notions I had of getting out were unfounded. The other (RR 1-5) business had come to me early in the week, but I had still imagined Rex could probably by-pass that. I could see that there might be difficulties in implying to Bowman, a regular army man, that I was fed up with the army. I had been meanwhile starting to get some stuff together on the Freeman Field business, borrowing Col Scott's file for the purpose and boldly stealing any papers of which I found more than three copies, vaguely feeling that I might like to do a book around that situation, which seemed to have some analogies with the perhaps more general problem of the compromise in life between what you might like to do, and what circumstances make it sensible to do.[67] It was after that that I saw Bowman, and heard from Haddock the obvious truth that everyone had better lie low for a while—he told me (not without cause) that my memoranda had, perhaps, better be more formal and solemn, until we could size up the Col's attitudes and tastes. I found myself somewhat depressed.

Friday 11 May 1945

. . . Haddock, who had more conversation with Bowman, expressed himself as disgusted, since apparently he was still to run the thing; but everyone else was much relieved. Bowman's idea seemed to be that he would have important work making trips around here and there, and of course he would be glad to get an answer, as he put it, to anything George had trouble in getting an answer to, but George was Deputy and he was here-and-now authorized to run it to suit himself. . . .

Saturday 12 May 1945

. . . We had a long day fixing matters with Gen Norstad who seemed indeed (as AC/AS Plans) to be going to take over Hood's spokesman's job (though nobody had told Hood), and fiddling with details of the 're-organization' and expansion of the office which were part of the things Bowman had left to George. Though nothing was actually done it all seemed exhausting. The day's amusing detail was a piece of paper turned up from the Awards branch asking George to write a citation for the award of the Legion of Merit to Rex; about as good a piece of irony as you could find in a year's looking.

Monday 14 May 1945

. . . We did nothing all day but fuss inconclusively over whether we should or we should not have a conference, supposing we could find anyone to take it. In what was formerly Kuter's office reading the Log, I saw Kuter himself, looking very harried and exhausted with extraordinary circles under his eyes—they went down so much further than you would expect—making some arrangements to get off tomorrow to the Pacific, apparently picking Rex up in California on the way. . . .

Tuesday 15 May 1945

. . . We again had little to do, though Haddock was apparently being sweated. I talked to the Air Chaplain about a sermon which some Jewish personnel had objected to over the loudspeaker, and to the Air Judge Advocate's office about the case of some Lt supposed to be a Communist. I could not help feeling that I would be serving my country as well home and about my own business, but the chances seem to get no better.

Wednesday 16 May 1945

. . . I fretted much of the day getting out of Lt Col Swift in OC&R the details of the mess we are supposed to be making of our guided missiles program—they are all engineers up there, and incredulous or impatient about staff considerations which I find now I can understand so easily; but they also seem candid, sensible, and straight-forward, and maybe the world turned over to them would progress as well. . . .

Thursday 17 May 1945

. . . In town to lunch with Newhouse and George Haddock, who discussed the changes he was busy making, or having made by his Maj Miner. He seemed to feel that he might be able to let some of us out in time—including himself. I keep having the feeling that it is piling up on me—I must get out and get back to my business, but it seems absurd to accept anything so obvious (and unreal-feeling) as the notion that it could all be due to VE day. They had a paper around to check our 'points' and to ask (as they shrewdly phrased it) whether we wanted to get out before the end of the present emergency. You certainly feel a disinclination to say yes; but we all did. In Norstad's office (Kuter left yesterday for the Pacific) I read the Log, elbow to elbow with Gen Roosevelt, the former president's son Elliot who had a large black

ADDRESS REPLY TO
COMMANDING GENERAL, ARMY AIR FORCES
WASHINGTON 25, D. C.

ATTENTION:

HEADQUARTERS, ARMY AIR FORCES
WASHINGTON

14 May 1945

MEMORANDUM FOR THE CHIEF, OFFICE OF INFORMATION SERVICES

Subject: Information from AC/AS Offices.

1. <u>Freeman Field Situation</u>. (Air Judge Advocate) Colonel Kidner expresses the opinion that in the case of 2nd Lts. Robert C. Terry, Marsden A. Thompson, and Shirley F. Clinton: "Lt. Terry should be tried by General Court-Martial under AW 64 for wilful disobedience of the order of the Assistant Provost Marshal not to enter the Officers' Club, and for using violence against mentioned Provost Marshal in obtaining entry into the club. Lts. Thompson and Clinton should be tried under AW 64 for the same offenses; and, in addition, for wilful disobedience of the order of the Officer in Charge of the mentioned club to leave the premises; and also, under AW 68, for refusal to submit to arrest when so ordered by the Assistant Provost Marshal. These charges and specifications are supported by evidence contained in the file."

2. <u>Sergeant Erwin</u> (Air Surgeon) "Sergeant Erwin, recipient of the Congressional Medal of Honor, at Northrington General Hospital, Tuscaloosa, Alabama, a plastic surgical center in the vicinity of his home, is reported to have suffered extensive burns of the right arm and right side of his face; however, it is believed that after skin grafting he will have a good result."

3. <u>Navy Special Weapons Show</u>. (OC&R) Representatives of the Requirements Division attended a show at the Naval Modification Center, Johnsville, Pa., for members of the Guided Missile Committee of the JCS. "The Navy has a hurry-up project to produce within 6 weeks an antiaircraft guided missile to use against Japanese suicide planes to be known as the 'Baby Lark', a tail-first airframe with cruciform sections at nose and tail. Missile to be powered by 8-AS-1000-JATO unit, guided visually with remote radio control, launched from a 20-foot track, mounted on a 5" gun mount, and can be fired in any direction at any elevation."

4. <u>P-82</u> (OC&R) M&S has been requested to mock-up the tenth P-82 (this is the two-P-51's-joined-together which M&S views with little enthusiasm — my memo, 23 February) as a night fighter with either SCR-720 or AN/AOG-1, AI equipment. "The general arrangement of this aircraft will be the same with the pilot occupying the left hand fuselage and the co-pilot radar operator occupying the right hand fuselage. A streamlined

nacelle housing the radar antenna and all associated equipment not required to be accessible in flight is mounted below the wing at the center of the airplane. This nacelle may be quickly detached on the ground or jettisoned in flight, whereupon the airplane becomes a day fighter. As a night fighter, this aircraft should have performance characteristics that exceed those of the P-61. "

5. **Heavy Bombers from ETO.** (OC&R) Disposition of the HB's coming from ETO (my memo, 11 May) has been planned as below:

a. All B-17's prior to G's (50 to 100) and all B-24's prior to L's (1,300 - 1,650) will be disposed of as excess to AAF requirements.

b. All B-17G's (1,500 - 1,800) and all B-24L's and M's (600 - 750) which require more than the number of man hours allowable under AAF Regulation 65-87 to condition for combat use will be declared excess.

c. As many B-17G's and B-24L's and M's as may be required will be allocated to ZI activities to eliminate all 17F's (and earlier) and all 24-H's (and earlier) now operational.

d. Remaining aircraft will be stored by ATSC. "It is believed that not more than 500 B-24's and 1,000 B-17's should be so retained in storage, and that none of them will be required for combat use before January 1946."

6. **Zeke-52 vs P-38, P-47, P-51** (OC&R) The AAF Board Project Report on the Eglin Field tests of a Jap Zeke-52 (picked up on Saipan in first class condition) against a P-38J, P-47N, and P-51D, contained the following conclusions: All three AAF planes are greatly superior to the Zeke in maximum level flight at both 10,000 and 25,000 feet; due to advantages in speed, acceleration, and climb, the AAF planes were able to keep the offensive, or break off at will; the Zeke is greatly superior to all three in radius of turn and general maneuverability at low speeds. Recommendations: Pilots should take advantage of superior speed when engaging Zekes in combat and keep it above 200 IAS; hit and run tactics should be used whenever possible; pilots should avoid following the Zeke through any continued turning maneuvers.

7. **Notes from In and Out Log.**

a. **Paris from ETOUSA, 11 May.....**Extensive but not very advanced developments of proximity fuzes in Germany. Dozen separate developments in as many institutions...probably most advanced is electromagnetic fuze for air to air bombs and rockets...Dr. Salant states there is no cause for panic (sic) as he is confident that the German developments even if transmitted to Japan were not so advanced as to be a danger to us in the Pacific in the near future.....

b. COM Task Force 51, 12 May.....Two Oscars...made suicide dives at NEW MEXICO...second plane hit starboard side at base of stack... extensive damage to AA battery...approximately four 5-inch gun crews wiped out...Preliminary estimate 150 total casualties...uninjured are Admiral Spruance and Chief of Staff...

JAMES G. COZZENS
Major, Air Corps

mourning band, a collection of ribbons and pilot's wings, God knew how got; and dark glasses. . . .

Friday 18 May 1945

. . . I had a busy morning because my eye had early caught an M&S item about Curtiss-Wright, and Gen A. E. Jones up there in a disgruntled, practical-business-man sort of way, headed me back to the Air Inspector, where Lt Col Logan talked to me for an hour and a half, showing me how the screw-up led through both Judge Patterson's and Mr Lovett's office . . . neither of them would touch a nickel in money, or do a faintly dishonest thing; but the problem was one of association and judgment—you trusted the people you knew, and whose abilities you rightly or wrongly respected; you had a lively sense of the immense job to do, and the existence of so many ignorant amateurs trying to do it by rule of thumb. . . . I managed to get off for the 1 pm train, which was a relief.

Sunday 20 May 1945

. . . S seemed to think I might go ahead on my notions about the Freeman Field business in spite of the fact that it was plain that anything, even so remotely connected with the war and the army, when I got it finished, would never sell. It did not make much sense; but I saw that, in psychological self-defense, I would have to start writing or go nuts.

Monday 21 May 1945

. . . I came down on the 8.30 train, somewhat taken aback to read in the papers that my greatly detested Lt Col Marks in Intelligence had expired Sunday morning through asphyxiation in his Bethesda home due to a fire starting downstairs. It gave me a lively turn, since, as Newhouse reminded me as soon as I came in, I had remarked Friday, hearing of some new stupidity of his; it would be nice if he'd just go die. I did not actually have anything quite so drastic in mind, but I could not deny that it was nice to think that you would never have to compete with him again when you were trying to put things together.

Tuesday 22 May 1945

. . . Up with Haddock to see some pictures in the projection room at 9-one, the 14th Air Force China Crisis, which had some good shots; but the truth is that pictures of the air war are much the same and the camera is not the medium—it is fast enough to get the action, and so the action is too fast to register in any real way on a person merely sitting in a projection room or a theatre—I suppose, in fact, it reduces to absurdity the whole "true to life" theory—it reproduces, but it does not interpret.

Col Logan had me up in the afternoon to tell me more about the Curtiss-Wright matter, and it was a busy fairly aimless day, though I did have a try at getting started on some writing, taking care to get in by 7 in the morning. That means you have until about quarter of 9, and I don't know whether you can get anywhere under those circumstances.

Wednesday 23 May 1945

. . . I was busy writing up my papers, except for a visit to Gen Jameson in Plans to find out for Haddock who wanted to know for Gen Hood what the lend-lease policy was in regard to Russia. This did not amount to much, beyond the fact that there would be no Vth Protocol Agreement; but the fact that nobody told Hood anything anymore seemed to indicate clearly that his DC days were numbered. The stress and strain on the staff obviously goes on. My early morning writing plans were somewhat disrupted by the arrival of Reeves at 7.30, fresh from a New York train; and I could not help reflecting with pleasure that he would be gone for some time beginning Saturday.

Thursday 24 May 1945

. . . Did little all day; but because I had begun to fool with my own writing, my morale seemed to improve. In the afternoon Haddock came in to describe the Pacific command which seemed to include Doolittle going to the Pacific with the 8th Air Force reequipped with 29's; Arnold having the command of that and the 20th; and Giles acting as his deputy on the spot. This seemed to mean that Kenney was getting the boot. I could see the machinations, as anyone could guess, were intricate, and full of interest, but I had no way of getting to view them. . . .

Friday 25 May 1945

. . . I was a little delayed in getting off at noon by the need to finish rewriting an OPD version of some remarks of Gen Eaker's to the Woodrum Committee on universal military training—something I still feel will not in the long run prove to be in the air forces' best interest—a year in the army won't train their specialists; but it will do a lot to use up what money Congress will be willing to lay out for military affairs. However, I violently corrected for grammar and emphasis anyway, and was glad to get out, as Robert was having in his writers for the take-off tomorrow, with a preposterous strut and bustle which it is certainly mean to begrudge him, but almost impossible to endure. I exercised my mind as well as I could with an effort to see just why it should annoy you—what is it to you? What can you lose? Why should you care if he sounds like an insufferable little fool? I could get no answer, and though it was plain that Newhouse and Bradshaw were suffering the same way I doubted

ADDRESS REPLY TO
COMMANDING GENERAL, ARMY AIR FORCES
WASHINGTON 25, D. C.

TTENTION:

HEADQUARTERS, ARMY AIR FORCES
WASHINGTON

23 May 1945

MEMORANDUM FOR: Chief, Office of Information Services

Subject: Information from AC/AS Offices.

1. <u>Curtiss-Wright Etc.</u> (Air Inspector) Lt. Colonel Logan, Chief, Contract Inspection Division asked me to come up and look at the piece of paper, prepared by Major Smith of the Office of Legislative Services, which was going to the Mead Committee. It summarizes the Air Inspector's report on Curtiss-Wright and presents all the unfavorable findings with reasonable candor. Presumably the Mead Committee is not going to like what it reads there; but at least the principle that the Air Inspector's confidential records are not at the disposal of congressional committees is preserved. General Schneider, the Colonel tells me, has not yet received any word from Colonel Brownell on Mr. Lovett's reaction to the memo sent in to him last week. At the moment, the situation is therefore this: The Mead Committee will read today or tomorrow that the Air Inspector feels that the fixed price contract figure, to which we are converting, is far too high (it is approximately $170,000 per C-46);

Incidentally, Flying Safety reported that they had been requested to prepare a "study of accidents involving P-47's produced by Curtiss-Wright, Buffalo, as compared with a similar number of aircraft produced at another factory under other ownership." (Lt. Colonel Heath tells me that their accident figures on the P-47, the P-40, and the C-46 will not substantiate any notion the Committee may have that inefficiency and faulty inspection have resulted in an increased accident rate for planes put out by Curtiss-Wright.) Statistical Control has also been asked (19 May) for "statistics" on C-W C-46's and P-40's by OLS.

2. <u>Ground to Air Guided Missile.</u> (OC&R) M&S has sent the Requirements Division a memorandum on the preliminary report on the joint Ordnance-AAF contract with the Bell Telephone Laboratories for a study of the possibilities of designing "a missile that could destroy an aircraft flying at 60,000 feet at 600 mph." The recommended device is "a thin cylindrical body with long tapering sharply pointed nose and flat back for rockets." Length, 19 feet; diameter, 1 foot; fin spread, 4 feet; weight, 1000 pounds, including 300 pounds of fuel. The warhead is detonated by a computer with radar ground sets. The missile is launched vertically. 8 Monsanto booster rockets are supposed to lift it to 1500 feet in 1.8 seconds and then drop

off. The analine-acid rocket motor of 3,000 pounds thrust operates for approximately 22 seconds, increasing the speed to 2,400 feet a second at 46,000 feet. Momentum is then supposed to carry it, at a speed decreasing to 1,150 feet a second, to 95,000 feet. At any point along the way it could be detonated through the ground set computer, and controlled by two X-band gun-laying radars, one following the target, and one the missile. "Bell Telephone Laboratories estimated that 3 years are necessary (2 years for development and 6 months for laboratory systems tests, and 6 months for flight tests). Ordnance has not yet reached a decision as to whether or not they will proceed. ATSC plans to wait for a formal report." (And, Lt. Colonel Fix tells me, to wait, too, perhaps, for results from the Navy's Baby Lark project — my memo, 14 May — which is essentially the same idea, but operating at low altitudes and more modest speeds.)

3. Promotion Policy (Personnel) "Prepared proposed AAF letter for distribution to CG's of Air Forces and Commands quoting the Adjutant General's Letter, dated 10 May 1945, subject: 'Promotions' for their information and guidance. This letter states that it is not the desire of the War Department to generally suspend the promotion of worthy officers and enlisted personnel. It does, however, state that military personnel who will become surplus for any reason, including lack of position vacancy in the new bulk allotment, or who are assigned to units scheduled for inactivation, or who are designated as non-essential, are not eligible for promotion."

4. Army Air Forces Center. (OC&R) Effective 1 June, the AAF Tactical Center will be redesignated at The Army Air Forces Center. The AAF Proving Ground Command will be assigned to the AAF Center. The AAF School of Applied Tactics will be redesignated as the Army Air Forces School. The AAF Board will remain part of the AAF Center.

5. Relief of AAF Officers (Personnel) In re my verbal communication on subject Subject, 1421, 23 May; the pitch for the record is: The Adjutant General has rescinded Section II of Circular 485. Officers are no longer authorized to request relief from active duty when they become surplus, for the good and sufficient reason that nobody will become surplus in the AAF until Lt. Colonel Laking's section has finished the enormous job of assigning "quotas" to all AAF organizations. It is expected that this will require a minimum of 2 months. The quotas will indicate to Chiefs and CO's how many men they will be entitled to let out, supposing they can spare them and wish to let them out. (This seems to leave little lee-way for a decision by the person supposedly best informed on the subject of just how many people he needs to do his work. He cannot let out more than his quota, even if he doesn't need them.) However, officers may continue to request relief in cases of return-to-essential-industry and personal hardship.

6. <u>Moderately Affecting Incident at Andrews Field.</u> (Air Provost Marshal) "The PM of Andrews Field called the APMO regarding the established policy for the housing of a WAC prisoner facing a general court martial. This prisoner is assigned to a squadron at Andrews Field and is charged with harboring an escaped convict because she sheltered, on the field, her husband who is one of ten general prisoners who recently escaped from the train in Alexandria, Virginia."

7. <u>Notes from In and Out Log.</u>

a. <u>Caserta signed Cannon, 21 May.</u> Estimate a total of 1,100 B-24's of which it is estimated 825 can be restored to combat operational use, and 75 B-17's, of which it is estimated 56 can be restored, will be returned to the US.....

b. <u>St. Germain signed Spaatz, 22 May.</u> Volekenrod Braunschweig most lucrative air force target yet uncovered . . . tremendous volume of documents and test data . . . exceptional fundamental wind tunnel data on jet airplanes which Dr. von Karman estimates will advance AAF jet bomber program by eight to ten months if fully exploited and translated . . .

JAMES G. COZZENS
Major, Air Corps

(though I did not ask them) if they would have any answer, either. . . .

Saturday 26 May 1945

. . . I seemed to get out just in time yesterday as Newhouse and Haddock were up most of the night on an estimate of the nature of the next war from Arnold to Marshall for 7.30 this morning. The estimate was indeed chilling for the terrors of the unknown (and perhaps even the timidities that come with getting older) the prospect was plainly appalling, strictly on the basis of what we were sure of as of today. Yet it is hard to imagine how the Russians would come to trust us, or we them; leaving you to judge that the only question was who would think it safest to strike whom first. Miss Johnson got back from her vacation to everyone's relief and pleasure, including perhaps hers, since she was skipping and running around the place all day. I drove Reeves over to the airport after 5 to get his plane to California and found, with the fuss finally all over, that he struck me in parting as much more agreeable and disarming.

Monday 28 May 1945

. . . George Haddock came in to say that he was going to Fort Belvoir hospital for observation, which was understandable, but everyone could see, left us in a very shaky state, the Major Miner who came in with Bowman being left as executive, and knowing nothing about anything; and the Col not purposing to come in until next week (when things would presumably be worse, with no Haddock to guide him). . . .

Tuesday 29 May 1945

. . . There was little to do in the morning as it was deemed advisable not to put through any memoranda for Miner, who seems a harmless graying fellow, not very bright—he responded well to my suggestion that he bounce back to Personnel an R&R asking us to do some indoctrination lecture for them, which was not our business (if we have any) and furthermore was a great bore; but he had passed it in to me anyway and I saw that must stop. After lunch, out to Belvoir with Newhouse. . . . to see Haddock, who was sitting out in the sun between two wings of the incredible hospital—innumerable shacks connected by miles of covered corridors. He seemed gratified by the visit and in better spirits, but clearly not inclined to come back any sooner than he could help, which probably means hard sledding over the next few months.

Wednesday 30 May 1945

. . . I was somewhat surprised about 8.30 by the arrival of Gen Schneider with news of a situation at the Rome Air Depot, where the CIC [Counter-Intelligence Corps] people had planted a microphone in a room used by some fellows attempting to organize a union, concealing it behind an American flag. The organizers tipped off, got some good pictures, which they planned to release if the Col commanding, who did not know the microphone had been put there, would not withdraw charges of trouble-making against a young Negro woman employed at the depot. It seemed important enough to take to Gen Hood, who then found it, I guess you could say, too important; and took it to Gen Eaker; which I don't think was part of Gen Schneider's plan, but he accepted it very well, and I did what I could to conceal my embarrassment, which came from the realization that I was far from an adroit or polished manipulator—little or nothing could be done in any event, but we had a lively day, with all these conferences and a long visit from a couple of counter-intelligence officers who were putting their side of the case to me.

Thursday 31 May 1945

. . . In with Miner to see a fellow from *Look* in Col Brownell's office—he having some fancy notions about an article he thought Mr Lovett had suggested called: Why Not Try the Bombers?—or, in effect, suggesting a revision of JCS plans for Japan. It seemed unlikely, and proved to be; but I could see Miner was far over his depth, and it was up to me to enunciate policy, which I finally did, not knowing how he would like it. I saw then that that was what he had asked me to come along for. . . .

Friday 1 June 1945

. . . As I started to go off at noon Newhouse came back to say that Hood said that Eaker said that Gen Spaatz was going to need a speech to give at Detroit which would involve some statements on a unified War Department and that Hood said he and I were to drop everything and do it. . . . The whole thing seemed to me highly ill-advised but while Hood was talking to us, very cordial, emphatic and imperceptive on the actual issues, Eaker rang in on the box, and Hood said he was even now talking to the 'boys,' and that seemed to confirm the theme. . . .

Saturday 2 June 1945

. . . I was all day on the piece for Spaatz, which Hood received without complaint and took me down to Eaker's place where we waited almost an hour. Eaker, a semi-bald, pursy, red-faced fellow with airs of importance and ruthlessness, had Hood pretty well cowed, and was, you could easily see, a son of a bitch—something I will doubtless find out more about tomorrow when he will have read the speech. . . .

Sunday 3 June 1945

. . . On as duty officer, and after some delay I got to see Eaker, who was a good deal more gracious, allowing me to think that his goings-on yesterday were due to something or other sorely trying him, and it being late in the afternoon. Johnny, who promised to be in, was not and called drowsily at 10.30 to say she just woke up. We had a hell of a time getting the amended speech typed in an hour so Eaker could take it to NY to give to Spaatz when he came in. . . .

Monday 4 June 1945

. . . In the morning it developed that Mr A, talking to Gen Marshall, had been obliged to throw out Gen Eaker's rewritten paragraph on a Dept of National Defence, and Carr who was going with the Gen to Detroit, seemed much agitated, saying that maybe I should go to fix the speech. I could not see it; but he called me back from Philadelphia in the late afternoon and so strongly urged my coming up that I said I would—though without orders. I got the 8 pm train which put me into Philadelphia, where it was drizzling, before 11. The Bellevue-Stratford was full of army, though Gen S and Carr and most people were out on the town. Carr got in in a flurry about 1 and began at once telephoning Detroit (I was sharing a room with him) and anywhere else he could think of, so finally I managed to go to sleep.

Tuesday 5 June 1945

. . . Carr and I had breakfast around 7 with a Gen Doyle, a pursy young BG with a cane and a game leg. Gen Spaatz finally appeared after 8, and we went out with a lot of police and sirens to an airport miles away, off Roosevelt Boulevard, where I found myself packed into the Gen's B-17 with him; Gen Fred Anderson; the General's aide, a sharp faced blonde boy with glasses named Pettinger; and two enlisted men. The 17 was very fancy in wood panels and blue leather seats. The Gen, a wiry grizzled little man with a red blotched complexion, but a manner quite mild and even kindly, settled himself in his own cabin with Gen Anderson, read through the speech while we were taking off, made a couple of changes; and said he would try it for time later. I sat down then with Pettinger and got to see him no more during the flight as he had Anderson send a Sgt for ice and water, and ruminated some over highballs (which somehow shocked me, it seemed so early in the morning). The weather was thick most of the way to Cleveland where it broke a little and over Lake Erie we were joined by some very hot flights of P-47's crowding in, too close for my taste, as escort, and so set down at Detroit about noon. They rushed us to the Book-Cadillac, a pleasing change from the rat's nest of the Bellevue-Stratford, where a leathery-faced little fellow named Thomas, the manager, gave everyone the place, especially Carr and Lt Col Wells who was there in advance with his Lt Elder and some PRO people locally stationed—one of them, a Major Humphrey, proved sensible and amusing. The nonsense was going hard and fast, but I managed to get to go over the speech with the Gen just before his press conference—he still had a glass in his hand, but there was not the faintest sign of any effect; and then we went to the parade, where I could see I was useful to Carr, as I was obliged to dictate on the reviewing stand to a stenographer remarks for the mayor of Detroit introducing Spaatz. We had a lot of planes overhead and the new M-24 tanks underfoot, the chilly afternoon having cleared somewhat. Back at the hotel they had a 'reception' (very lavishly provided drinks) much of which time I spent having the public stenographer do copies for the press of the Gen's remarks, and the agonizingly boring dinner with innumerable speakers, though Spaatz on the radio did all right except for mispronouncing "gigantic," which seems a hard thing to do. Knudsen,[68] in civilian clothes again rambled at length; but the audience, the 100 people who amounted to anything in Detroit, you could see (all men) plainly had a sentimental regard for him. Up to Wells's suite afterwards (very late) with some newspaper men and some girls, who, I gathered, were part of the entertainment, and I was glad to leave at 12 with Humphrey, just about dead on my feet.

Wednesday 6 June 1945

. . . we got off about 10—in the C-54 this time which while not so fancy was in many ways more comfortable than the Gen's plane, and faster, though it did us no good since we had to wait until he landed—we were over Washington by noon. On the ramp in front of the ATC building Gen S posed three times for photographers being embraced by his daughter, a child of 13 or so who rose to the occasion with an older woman's relish—perhaps because she was quite pretty. To the Pentagon with Gen Doyle and his aide. There was little to do, so I presently went out again with Steve Richards to drive down to Ft Belvoir to see Haddock, who looked very well, showing probably that all he needed was a little rest and exercise—probably all I need, too. I felt well worn by evening.

Thursday 7 June 1945

. . . Col Bowman came in to the office at long last and I saw him a few minutes, early, and could not form much of an opinion except that he seemed friendly or amiable and asked me to continue my memoranda, which was all right with me, since I certainly did not want to be left wholly free for the speech nonsense. Getting up one for him took me most of the day. . . .

Friday 8 June 1945

. . . Bowman was in again, but beyond moving Major Miner out of his office, he seemed to do nothing. Downstairs about 10.30 I went to get my shoes shined and found myself next to Gen Hood who stated that he was glad the Col had got in, and

IN   Y REFER TO:

HEADQUARTERS, ARMY AIR FORCES
WASHINGTON

7 June 1945

MEMORANDUM FOR THE CHIEF, OFFICE OF INFORMATION SERVICES

Subject: Information from AC/AS Offices.

1. <u>Status of the B-32</u>. (OC&R) The 22 May decision of the
AAF Requirements Board, approved by Gen. Faker, was to reduce B-32
production as rapidly as possible to a level of 18 aircraft a
month through December 1945. This production will support 1 B-32
group of 3 squadrons at 12 UE and 50% reserve per squadron through
August 1946. The group to be converted is the 312th (FEAF), a
squadron at-a-time in August, September, and October. However, a
memo got up by the AAF Board, ATSC, Proving Ground Command, and
the Training Command, to the Chief of Air Staff recommended that
all B-32 production be terminated at once. "All the above agencies
consider the present B-32 an inferior combat bomber to the B-29, and
none feel that it will ever be a superior weapon to the B-29. Some
feel that the B-32 may become, through development, a satisfactory
bomber, but in its present state of development it is unsatisfactory
for combat service." Points made: B-29 pilots who have flown the
B-32 are unanimous in having no special use for it; a lot of money
will be saved by discontinuing B-32 production; the AAF Board sees no
military requirement for it that cannot be better met by the B-29;
the Training Command "considers the B-32 unnecessary for a postwar
air force." OC&R feels that "cancellation of B-32 production will
accelerate production of the Consolidated XB-36 which has extremely
favorable post-war possibilities." (See below) From a PR standpoint, it is unlikely that the last has been heard of the B-32
program. Advice from technicians that production be abandoned
began to come in at least as early as last summer. Exact figures
on the costs are not available in OC&R: but they are certainly
enormous, and will doubtless be the subject of criticism.

2. <u>B-36 Production</u>. (OC&R) Col. Bailey reports that contracts
have now been let for 102 B-36's. 14 of these are necessary developmental and service test items, and the remaining 88, while unlikely
to see service in this war, "are believed justified in view of the
fact that there is little possibility of any other conventional airplane powered with conventional engines going beyond the drawing board
stage for years to come. Further, the B-36 is considered to be one
of the Air Forces' best bids for national security following the
present conflict because of the extreme range, which is far in excess
of any other developmental bombers, and the very heavy gross bomb
loads." Col. Bailey has a poor opinion of the Mosquito or medium

bomber types, which represent about all the other 'developmental' bombers now in the works, because he thinks them inadequately armed, their ranges are less than a quarter of the B-36 range, and they are all below the 50 ton gross weight category. With Col. Peterson concurring, he says: "It is felt that we must not under any circumstances, permit ourselves to follow completely the present trend of thinking to the extent that our entire future lies in the jet-propelled bomber, as much remains to be done in the improvement of jet engines themselves before the desired ranges and bomb loads are to be realized from this type airplane."

3. WASP Accident Rates. (Management Control) A special report analyzing accidents and accident rates in connection with the WASP program has been completed by Statistical Control. "Fatal accident rates compare favorably with corresponding rates for men. For the period of the entire program the fatal accident rate for WASPS was .060 per 1,000 flying hours, or only one fatal accident for every 16,667 hours flown. The fatal accident rate for men during the same period was .062 per 1,000 hours." (In view of some rumors going around in the last weeks before the WASP program was thrown out by Congress over the CG's objection, this is a very satisfactory finding.)

4. POW's at AAF Bases. (Air Inspector) Gen. Schneider has received reports from a survey of 10 AAF stations where POW's are employed to check on the many allegations of soft treatment. He states that they are handled "strictly in accordance with Army Service Forces instructions. POW rations do not include such items as beef, butter, milk, etc. POW's are not permitted to purchase at station Exchanges, but are permitted to purchase at Exchanges within the POW stockade. These POW Exchanges do not have cigarettes, candy, ice cream, or coca cola type drinks for sale. POW's work from 8 to 12 hours per day, depending upon the type of duty assigned, and normally walk back and forth between stockade and the job in groups under guard. While POW's are treated humanely in that they are not subjected to physical abuse and they are provided with a ration well above starvation level, they are not coddled at the installations visited." (In fact, instances of coddling - the notorious several-hundred-cases of beer for POW's at Orlando - were the result of ASF decisions, and there is no indication that the AAF is involved in any of the criticized practices.)

5. On-the-Deck Training Results. (Flying Safety) The directive, effective 1 March, for low level fighter training, has not yet been continued over a long enough period to give Flying Safety conclusive figures, but Col. Price reports that of the 977 fighter training accidents between 1 January and 30 April, 21 occurred during low

level training. During March the percentage of total accidents that occurred during low-level training was 2.2. April showed a substantially higher, but as yet not finally determined, percentage. (When the decision was made to initiate this training, it was feared that the rate would increase enough to cause a public or congressional reaction. This does not appear to have been the case, and probably no further consideration need be given to the possibility of wide-spread protest.)

6. <u>Labor Difficulties at Bell, Buffalo.</u> (MOS) A sit-down was staged by "scattered groups" of workers at Bell, Buffalo, 28-29 May in protest against the union's attempt to delay lay-off of union officials for 30 days, and a change in the release system of production workers who will be layed off as a result of P-63 cut-backs. The workers were also demanding 48 hours pay for 40 hours work. The plant is being closed for a week "to permit the taking of inventory and the lay-off of 7,000 employees." (These difficulties are routine, and will, of course, continue on an ever-larger scale. In Detroit Tuesday, I was told by officers stationed there that the situation was acute, but not explosive. However, if a practice is made of the fairly plain effort of Bell to get rid of union officials under the guise of a cut-back, it would be well to expect local blow-ups.)

7. <u>Notes from In and Out Log.</u> (Col. Smith arranged for me to read Gen. Fairchild's Log in AC/AS, Plans. These are items appearing in messages of which AFOIS does not receive action or information copies.)

a. <u>CINCPAC 31 May.</u> Total B-29's striking Yokohama 29 May now 459...140 B-29's damaged by flak...

b. <u>Paris 2 June signed Eisenhower.</u> Have in custody over 400 top research developmental personnel of Peenmunde...The research directors and staff realize impossibility for continuation of rocket development in Germany. Most are under 35 and many know no other type of work. They are anxious to carry on their work in whatever country will give them opportunity, preferably U.S., second England, third France...The thinking of the scientific directors of this group is 25 years ahead of U.S....wind tunnel at Peenmunde giving air velocity of ten times speed of sound...Present motor for V-2 realized out of date 3 to 4 years ago. Recent motor designs revolutionary...100 of very best men could be evacuated to U.S. immediately...request early reply...

JAMES G. COZZENS
Major, Air Corps

that he felt that he was very keen and alert—not perhaps the most conclusive testimony in the world. . . .

Saturday 9 June 1945

. . . I drove Maj Miner down in the morning, giving him a briefing on why the Col should reestablish the conferences (the principal reason being the one unspoken—I did not wish to be free for random speech writing) and he said he would certainly take it up. However, I was not able to push him into saying he would take it up today and I got the impression that he was demurely balking against my direction, saying Monday for no better reason. It developed soon after we were in that we had a paper to attend a conference in AC/AS Personnel about why Mr A's scheme for greeting returnees was inept (he wanted a warm personal greeting given to units but they don't come in by units) and Miner suggested I go over there which I did for two hours, hearing six or seven people talk; and stating to the Col that Col Bowman would be glad to advise the Chief of the Air Staff against the project as stated—after all, I was speaking for AFOIS [Air Force Office of Information Services] and thought I might as well speak. It was not yet plain what Bowman had in mind, if anything, so we were all more or less restive in the back room—the consensus being merely that Miner was taking a lot on himself and needed checking.

Monday 11 June 1945

. . . I spent much of my time chasing around after the last word on the Freeman Field matter. This chase took me to a Mr Petersen, a fat blonde fellow who seemed to be an Executive Assistant of Mr Patterson's and wished only to keep clear of the thing; to a Col Gearhart, who was something to Mr McCloy; to a Lt Col Thurman who was Assistant Secretary to the Chief of Staff; to a Mr Ransom, in charge of files; to a Lt Col Jones in G-2, who had the file, where I then saw the recommendations—they added up to amending 20-6 to make it clear that COs at posts like Freeman Field would not be able to keep Negro officers out of any officers club by any dodge. This would keep the War Dept's nose clean, all right, and satisfy Mr Lovett's gentlemanly instincts. All that remains to be seen is whether the Confederates will stand for it; and whether, if they don't, and they are court-martialed, the issue will really become an issue.

Tuesday 12 June 1945

. . . Miner reported that Bowman had arranged to re-establish the conferences with Eaker and asked me to write up a piece of paper on why, which I did; though it presently came back, indicating that I had misunderstood him; and what Bowman wanted was a statement of what we were going to do, rather than an explanation of why we did it—to have got that straight first would have saved a lot of trouble. Newhouse and Bradshaw and I went down to see Haddock after lunch and he did not encourage us too much about his coming back, so it was probably something we would have to fight out for ourselves. What seemed plain was that Miner was going to protect himself with an awful lot of paper work, and Bowman, while not sure of his business, was going along—he seems however an amiable and good-natured man, more anxious to get along with the backroom than not. I think Miner is, too, under the handicaps of his position and a certain native dumbness.

Wednesday 13 June 1945

. . . Miner turned up with a honey (showing how bad it was to get in early) from Spaatz' Pettinger who is a great pal of mine now, except that he has the impression that my name is Joe, and so warmly salutes me, for Gen Anderson at Lockhaven, Pa tomorrow—30 minutes. I got through it somehow in conjunction with conversations with Col Brownell and Gen Hedrick, poor good old man (nobody tells him anything) on the McCloy paper on Freeman Field (I finally worked copies out of Lt Col Jones and brought them around); so we had a busy day. Hedrick's trouble was that the JAG had sent him back his papers with the recommendation that the Negro officers who pushed the Provost Marshal be handled under AW 104.[69] Hedrick said, not without shrewdness, that he doubted if they'd agree anyway; but certainly they were guilty of violating AW 64[70] and should be so charged. I told him I thought so too, and this seemed to fortify him, so he was taking up the telephone to tell the JAG so as I left.

Thursday 14 June 1945

. . . I brought Gen Anderson his remarks by 9.30. He was sitting in Mr A's office, looking a little red and baffled, . . . I could see the returnees were having a hard, if good, time. At any rate, he seemed content, though he remarked that he didn't like to read speeches much—a point I heartily seconded him on, pointing out that the effect was much better when you just got up and spoke. However, Newhouse, who does not leave such things to chance, went in and explained to Bowman that speeches for two star generals were out of order, and Bowman duly wrote a general memo for the staff offices saying that we wrote speeches only for the CG and the Chief of Air Staff, in case anyone wondered. . . .

Friday 15 June 1945

. . . Col Bowman had us in for a staff conference at 9 which he conducted easily, informally, with evidences of good nature and humor. He mentioned a talk he had had with Mr A in Europe in which the CG had said he thought day-to-day PRO

12 June 1945

SPECIAL MEMORANDUM FOR THE CHIEF, OFFICE OF INFORMATION SERVICES

Subject: Freeman Field Situation.

1. Request by Col. Brownell. On 11 June 1945, Col. G. A. Brownell, OAS-A, asked for any information available on the status of the Freeman Field Situation. Inquiries in the offices of the Air Inspector and the Air Judge Advocate were negative, and both Gen. Schneider, Acting the Air Inspector, and Gen. Hedrick, the Air Judge Advocate requested that they be given any information obtained from the Office of the Undersecretary of War on the subject. Gen. Schneider, Gen. Hedrick, and Col. Brownell, were supplied verbally with the following summary of the following decisions, approved by the Secretary of War, and about to be put into effect.

2. Source of the Information. Mr. H. C. Petersen, Executive Assistant to the Under Secretary stated that the matter was one that he had washed his hands of and referred me to Col. H. A. Gerhardt of Mr. McCloy's office. Col. Gerhardt said that action had been taken by Mr. McCloy on the report of a meeting of the Advisory Committee on Special Troop Policies (4 June). Mr. McCloy made certain recommendations which were approved by the Secretary of War. These had been forwarded to Lt. Col. W. E. Thurman, Assistant Secretary of the General Staff. Col. Thurman finally located the file in the office of Col. L. A. Guenther, G-1, where I was able to see the text of the approved recommendations.

3. War Department Recommendations.

a. (Par 2) "The action taken by the CO (Col. Selway, of Freeman Field, at the direction of Gen. Hunter, CG First AF) was within his administrative police powers."

"The Committee does not concur in the finding upholding the basis on which a separation of the Officers Club facilities was made and believes such basis was not in accord with existing AR's and WD policies...Recommend the report be returned to the Inspector General and the non-conformance brought to the attention of the CG, AAF..."

b. (Par 3) Recommends that the trial of the 3 colored officers under arrest for violation of AW 64 be expedited.

c. (Par. 4) Recommends a change in the text of WD Pamphlet 20-6 "Command of Negro Troops". The next text (last paragraph, p. 14) is to read: "Where conditions make it desirable, War Department instructions permit the local commander to provide separate recreational facilities, such as post exchanges, theatres, or sections of theatres for the use of particular military units. However, it is the basic policy of the War Department that provision of such separate facilities does not permit the exclusion on the basis of race or color of any member of the military service from using any and all such facilities established in public buildings. AR 210-10 Par. 19 is explicit in defining the application of this policy to membership in officers' clubs, messes, and similar social organizations."

4. <u>Comment</u>. The distinction in Par. 3a (Par. 2 of the Report) between the approval of Col. Selway's use of his "police powers" and disapproval of the basis on which he made the separation of facilities does not appear justified. Col. Selway could be supposed to be acting on an important line omitted from the new version of the p. 14 paragraph of 20-6. This line was: "The burden of deciding whether or not there shall be some separations in the use of camp facilities is placed on the local command, with the assumption that local conditions will be taken into account." As long as that line was in the text, Col. Selway could hardly be called guilty of "non-conformance" which he would deserve to have brought to the attention of the CG, AAF. If any such action is taken, it is reasonable to suppose, in light of earlier developments, that Gen. Hunter will go to bat for him.

b. The recommendation for expediting the trial of the officers who forced their way past the Provost Marshal into the Club is very desirable from the PR standpoint. The recent flood of questions to the Air Inspector and the Secretary of the Air Staff have been mostly demands to know what was being done about them. However, care should probably be taken to have the court-martial include negro officers, and to admit the public. The defense will undoubtedly raise the issue of discrimination as far as it can.

c. The original purpose of the 20-6 policy was to give the post commander some discretion in establishing segregation if he thought it necessary to preserve order. This discretion is now taken away from him. In one sense, the air is cleared. We will not be doing by various subterfuges what we say we are not doing; but the essential problem will of course remain. Officer personnel from those parts of the country where segregation is ordinarily practiced are not going to like it and the problem of discipline will be a tough one in view of their rooted prejudices and those of their families and home-towns. The Air Inspector tells me confidentially that he foresees a great deal of trouble.

JAMES G. COZZENS
Major, Air Corps

HEADQUARTERS, ARMY AIR FORCES
WASHINGTON

14 June 1945

MEMORANDUM FOR THE CHIEF, OFFICE OF INFORMATION SERVICES

Subject: Information from AC/AS Offices.

1. <u>P-80 Program</u>. (OC&R) Col. Holloway, Requirements Division,
has prepared a program for submission to the Chief of Air Staff
to get P-80's into the Pacific war at the earliest possible date.
The 412th Fighter Group and its supporting 361st Service Group are
given a tentative home station readiness date of 1 December 1945.
An F-5 Photo Recon Squadron, due back from ETO in July, will be
converted to F-14's and trained with the 412th. A total of 10
P-80 groups will be provided for combat duty by May 1946. With
the exception of the 412th, they will be formed by converting
existing fighter groups to P-80's. (I am told that the pressure
behind this program is a concern felt in the Requirements Division
about the possibility of losing the opportunity to get a combat
evaluation of the P-80 if we don't hurry.)

2. <u>AAF Property Donations to Schools</u>. (M&S) Maj. Keane reports
that during April AAF surplus property having a cost-value of almost
four and a half million dollars was donated to educational institutions for use in various courses of instruction. The property
included 9 complete aircraft. During the same month the AAF dropped
accountability on $3,767,940 worth of equipment which had previously
been distributed to schools. (This is a project in which Col. Smith
was much interested. It seems to be a useful if small way of
attacking the surplus; and it can be expected to do the AAF and the
general cause of national air-mindedness a good deal of good. While
the figures are perhaps not yet large enough to warrant calling
attention to the project, it might be worth mentioning in the course
of an indoctrination conference.)

3. <u>Aeronautical Industry Employment Drop</u>. (M&S) The latest
estimates on scheduled cut-backs foresee a drop in airframe contractors'
labor requirements from 679,000 last April to 495,000 in December
(about 25%). Estimated requirements for the industry as a whole
(calculated from the airframe drop) will fall from 1,586,000 in
April to 1,185,000 in December - a decrease of approximately 400,000.

4. <u>Hydrogen Cyanide Spray</u>. (M&S) Lt. Col. L. Smith has received
information from the Chief, Chemical Warfare Service, on some experiments with M-33 70 gallon spray tanks directing hydrogen cyanide
against "caves simulating Japanese fortifications." Result:

"Killing of all animals inside the caves, even though the animals were equipped with the best gas masks available. These American masks are superior to the Japanese in efficiency and duration of protection."

5. <u>B-29 Accident Summary</u>. (Flying Safety) B-29 accidents in May numbered 43, the largest number for any one month since operations began. This brings total B-29 accidents to 346, 100 of them fatal. 646 men have been killed and 184 aircraft wrecked.

6. <u>Freeman Field Situation</u>. (Air Judge Advocate) In connection with the WD recommendations approved by the Secretary of War (my memo, 12 June) Gen. Hedrick, the Air Judge Advocate, called me in to show me the indorsement on file he sent to the Judge Advocate General. This recommended action against the 3 negro officers, held for over-powering the Freeman Field Provost Marshal, under AW 104 instead of trial on charges of violating AW 64 as originally proposed. Gen. Hedrick felt that this was contrary to the recommendation of the Secretary of War, who directed that the "trial" be expedited. He is so representing to the JAG. He and the Air Inspector, and Col. Brownell, Mr. Lovett's Executive, who also talked to me on the subject, agree that the officers should be tried as proposed. However, it seems unlikely in any event that the officers themselves would agree to action under AW 104, since they would then lose their opportunity to make their views on segregation public. If they did not agree, there would be no alternative but to court-martial them. (This whole situation will continue to bear watching. It has died down in the papers; but as soon as the WD decision is announced it is certain to flare up again.)

7. <u>Notes from In and Out Log</u>.
   a. <u>Ft. Shafter 10 June</u>. ...in connection with JCS decision to base Lancasters in the Ryukus the RAF requests authority for Air Vice Marshals Satterly and Sharp to visit our Marianas bases...

   b. <u>Guam from BOMCOM 21</u>. ...an extensive search pushed to southern coast of Honshu has failed to locate survivors from any of 19 planes missing on strike of 25-26 May and it must now be presumed that all aircraft were lost over target...it is interesting to note that of the airplanes painted with jet 622 none were held by search-lights and they suffered no losses...

   c. <u>CINCPAC Adv. Hq. 11 June</u>. Okinawa campaign from 18 March to 9 June...our plane losses total 965 including 312 destroyed on board carriers as a result of damage by enemy or storm...enemy aircraft losses: suicide hits or misses destroyed 216 (this would seem to mean that there were 216 suicide attacks in the period)... total enemy planes destroyed by fleet units 3,736...at one time or another the campaign involved 13 CV's, 7 CVL's, 22 CVE's...total navy planes involved estimated 3,795...

JAMES G. COZZENS
Major, Air Corps

policy was all right, but long-range policy was wanting. It would be a fair guess that neither Mr A nor Col B knew exactly what was meant, and Col B had probably got no farther forward with it since. We broke up after awhile, and he had made a pleasant impression. I went up then to tell Gen Schneider about the proposed steps in regard to Gen Elliott Roosevelt, a piece of information he might not have got until next week otherwise, and he seemed grateful, agreeing that what Gen Eaker had wired Gen Hood who told Col Bowman who told me seemed wise. I was supposed to see Norstad about the conference next week, but he was much delayed. . . .

Saturday 16 June 1945

. . . I got to see Norstad in the morning though not for long as he was due at some meeting Gen Marshall had called, but he seemed more or less agreed that we would take up the AAF angle on universal military training Wednesday, so I went to see Col Moffat, who with a major of his kept me busy from 9.30 until nearly 11. . . . In the afternoon Miner proposed that Bowman should be introduced to the press at the conference and asked for a memorandum on that—a few words would after all do as well. . . .

Monday 18 June 1945

. . . I was busy fussing with what looked like an endless series of conferences—LeMay tomorrow, Norstad Wednesday, Doolittle Thursday—but shortly after Col Bowman (who improves with use) had dictated the story of his life to me for use by Norstad in introducing him Wednesday, he came in to say that we would drop the Wednesday piece and we could just get up LeMay tomorrow. I got to see him with Col Butler and Major Higgins in Norstad's office in the afternoon, which was timed to prevent me from going to Eisenhower's press conference which I had planned to do—I also missed his arrival at the Pentagon in the morning. . . . Every road and all the embankments were then covered with people—in large part WAVES [Women Accepted for Volunteer Emergency Service] and Marine Corps girls from the Navy building on the hill, sitting in rows with, I couldn't help noting, a great show of bare buttock and bottom (such a hot day) as I drove out. They were all gone when I got back—LeMay[71] is stocky, full-faced and dark. He had a dead cigar in his mouth when he came in and he never moved it for three quarters of an hour, though talking around it well enough when occasion arose. The superficial first impression was that he was dumb or gross; but he has one of those faces that grows on you—a real intelligence and even a kind of sweetness—as though he would not do anything mean, or even think anything mean, though he is well known to be a hard man, and you can see that, too—becoming more apparent the longer you look at him. Around the motionless cigar he spoke sensibly. . . .

Tuesday 19 June 1945

. . . We had a wonderful series of alarms and fiascos over the sudden discovery that LeMay would have to make his presentation to the Joint Chiefs of Staff at luncheon, and so the conference could not be at 1.30. I protested to Gen Norstad, who said he could do nothing; and then behind his back to Col Coe in Eaker's office and Col Barber, who also could do nothing. By 10.30 it was apparent the luncheon was coming off so we decided to make the conference tomorrow at 1.30, and then found we couldn't because of something else set up, so shifted it back to 4. I would think, in the course of it all, I made nearly two hundred telephone calls. It did come off duly, and LeMay did very well and even his A-2 [intelligence aide], a young Col Garcia, who made the presentation, did all right. They kept him quite late, so I really felt by the time I got out I had done a day's work—there were all kinds of little extras—like borrowing a WO [warrant officer] from Col Scott to take the transcript, nobody else being available.

Wednesday 20 June 1945

. . . I was busy with my memoranda, and in talking to a Maj of Col Schneider's about the Mitchel Field affair, a medical major Fabbricatore who was supposed to have sold discharges on an ingenious system;[72] and in getting Cpl Anne Poore, Bessie Breuer's daughter, sent to Hawaii in a B-29 to draw pictures—this somewhat surprised me, but showed what could be done if you just told a lot of people authoritatively that you wanted them to do it. In the late afternoon I went up to see Gen Glenn, the Deputy Air Surgeon's executive about the Mitchel Field thing. . . .

Thursday 21 June 1945

. . . I put down all the stuff on Mitchel Field for Col Bowman, who kindly came in to compliment me on it, and took me up with him to talk to Gen Schneider in the afternoon—the talk included a conversation with Gen Hunter at Mitchel on the box, and Bowman admitted afterwards that he had not been able to get a word in edge-wise—the truth is, Gen Hunter, as was the case about Freeman Field, does not seem to realize what he is sitting on. It was a hard telephoning day, what with that; and attempts to get the UMT [Universal Military Training] business set up with Col Moffat's Major Ebey, who took his papers back at the last minute; and conversations with Col Miller in Clemson's office; and at the end, the whole set of answers on the Freeman Field business, brought down by Col Harris—two of them seeming to go a little beyond prudence. Meanwhile I had talked to people at CAF [Continental Air Force] Hq, trying to find out what had been passed on to them about Mitchel Field—they said indignantly nothing, and would I pass on what I knew? I said I did not know whether I could or not; and calls about whether LeMay's

HEADQUARTERS, ARMY AIR FORCES
WASHINGTON

20 June 1945

MEMORANDUM FOR THE CHIEF, OFFICE OF INFORMATION SERVICES

Subject: Information from AC/AS Offices

1. **B-32 Project 98629s.** (OC&R) The Statistical Control Division reported 15 June that two of the B-32's on the combat evaluation project in the Pacific had done some bombing (9 tons each) of gun positions, bridges, caves, and ammunition dumps in Cageyan Valley, Luzon. However, the Requirements Division, OC&R quoted from Lt. Col. S. D. McElroy's first report on the project at length. About everything that could be wrong was wrong with the selected Articles Nos. 58, 59, 62. "Fuel cell leaks, tachometer failures, loading difficulties and other troubles delayed final acceptance of No. 58 until 11 May. No. 58 departed Fort Worth for Mather on 13 May, taking 12 hours to arrive at destination, where emergency procedure was necessary to lower the landing gear. Radar equipment became unserviceable on this flight... in addition, all four tachometers plus various and sundry temperature and pressure gauges failed...No. 59 required an engine change in Hawaii...No. 58 with Lt. Col. McElroy aboard departed Mather Field 17 May...Loran and radar equipment was not operating, ART-13 and radio compass operated only intermittently, and all compasses were from 4 to 14 degrees off resulting in airplane getting 150 miles off course... Departed Kwajalein 22 May for Guam, whereupon oil cooler difficulties necessitated a landing at 111,000 lbs. gross weight. Airplane stalled out at 120 mph., two feet off the ground damaging tail skid...Left Guam 25 May where a near crash was averted on take-off in clearing a hill 300 ft. high two miles from end of 7,400 ft. runway due to possible dead cylinders. Several hours out of Guam a fuel pump seal failed and leaking gasoline presented a serious fire hazard...Checking airplanes (at Clark Field) for combat revealed serious deficiencies - bomb rack salvo switch was improperly wired, making it impossible to salvo; circuit breaker switch for salvo system was wired in backwards; bomb racks in one bomb bay would not fire as the leads to the take-off point had been too short and had never been connected; the azimuth and elevation inputs to the K-15 sight had been reversed in the nose and tail turrets...These deficiencies indicate poor workmanship on the part of Consolidated and either very poor company and Army inspection, or, which is worse, none at all." On the mission reported by Stat Control, "No. 58 nearly cracked up again. No. 1 and No. 3 engines took turns in going overboard to 65" manifold pressure, swerving the airplane across the runway. Inspection revealed that all 4 engines would have gone to 65" or more in a few seconds as all turbo amplifiers had been burnt out...The airplanes have now been assigned to the 312th Bomb Group" (A-20's). (The AAF would certainly seem to be well out of B-32 program).

2. <u>Freeman Field Situation</u>. (Cont.) Mr. Truman Gibson, Office of the Secretary of War, has requested the Motion Picture Services Division to make a spot coverage of Gen. Eaker's visit to Godman Field, Kentucky, tomorrow (21 June). These are the colored officers and men of the 477th Bomb Group, transferred from Freeman Field after the difficulty there. The occasion for the General's visit is the presentation of Col. Davis as the new group commander. The General is giving him a medal, and the Colonel's father, Gen. Davis will be on hand, too. Mr. Gibson tells me that he feels it is desirable to get the material into the newsreels, if possible, and this seems very sensible, if it can be done. I have spoken to Capt. Feuer, of Motion Picture Services, and Mr. Yovin, of BPR, Newsreels, and they will do what they can to get the footage back, and into shape for newsreel use. Whether it is actually used or not is mostly up to Col. Curtis Mitchell, the BPR Motion Picture Chief, and he tells me he will push it, which he may or may not do. However, the War Department has several film projects dealing with negro troops in mind and Mr. Gibson plans to use the stuff that way in any event. Anything of the kind would probably be useful in view of the AAF's uncomfortable situation.

3. <u>XXI Bomber Command Figures</u>. (Stat Control) As of 9 June the XXI Bomber Command had 1,008 combat crews on hand, and as of 11 June, 770 B-29's, 4 TB-29's, 29 F-13's.

4. <u>Okinawa Operations by AAF</u>. (Stat Control) Operations of the AAF against Okinawa (including B-29 raids against the Kyushu airfields) from 18 March through 12 June involved 12,370 sorties, 22,686 tons of bombs dropped; 372 enemy aircraft claimed; 45 AAF aircraft lost.

5. <u>Supersonic Wind Tunnel Restriction</u>. (M&S) Lt. Col. Goodman reports that the Secretaries of State, War and Navy have approved "restriction of visits of British nationals to Supersonic Speed Wind Tunnels so that no classified information will be available to the British except information on developed installations, devices or equipment which may fairly be considered usable in connection with the production of articles which have been developed to such a point that they will be produced for the war against Japan." (This is a development of some importance, in view of the Chicago-Tribune-type squawks about the sinister Britishers outsmarting us all the time. The relationship seems to be reverting to normal.)

6. <u>Notes from In and Out Log</u>.
   a. <u>Paris signed Eisenhower 16 June</u>. ...Included in POW package shipment scheduled to leave 23 June are Heinz Borsdorff and Herbert Pangratz, jet turbine engine aircraft test engineer and test

pilot respectively, formerly at Rechlin. Both needed by Wright
Field for experimental station...(this would seem to indicate that
we are going to follow the suggestion - my memo, 7 June - about
freezing onto the German scientists who are quite ready and willing
to go on with their research for anyone who will give them facilities.
When this leaks out there will probably be a PR problem.)

     b. <u>To Wright Field to Meyers from Phillips 15 June</u>. Direct
you to take action to have all B-29's destined for overseas projects
camouflaged with aircraft enamel jet gloss shade 622 on underside...

     c. <u>Fort Shafter from Richardson 16 June</u>. Operative dates
airfields Okinawa have been considerably advanced over those originally
set up...

                    JAMES G. COZZENS
                    Major, Air Corps

HEADQUARTERS, ARMY AIR FORCES
WASHINGTON

21 June 1945

SPECIAL MEMORANDUM FOR THE CHIEF, OFFICE OF INFORMATION SERVICES

Subject: Mitchell Field Discharge Racket.

1. <u>Origin of the Case</u>. About two weeks ago Gen. Schneider, Acting the Air Inspector, told me for the information of the Chief, OIS, that he had an informal conversation with General Hunter, CG, First Air Force, on what appeared to be a well-organized and lucrative racket operating from the regional hospital at Mitchell Field to sell discharges to enlisted men. Because it was hoped that quiet local investigation might uncover more of it, Gen. Hunter did not ask the Air Inspector to investigate officially. Instead, General Schneider sent up Major J. La Rue Hinson of the Special Investigations Branch on "loan" to Gen. Hunter. Major Hinson has now returned to Washington. Gen. Schneider asked him to tell me what he had found out, feeling that when the whole matter is aired, the AAF is going to have an uncomfortable job of explaining to do.

2. <u>The Alleged Mitchell Field Ring</u>. Key man in the scheme is said to be a Major Fabbricatore, executive officer of the hospital. In some way not yet clear, he established a contact with a civilian (formerly in the service, and perhaps irregularly discharged) named Jimmy Santinillio who owns an undertaking establishment nearby, and seems to be quite a figure in Brooklyn in Italian social, political, and ███████████ circles. Assisting Major Fabbricatore were supposed to be Lts. ████ and ███████ who had charge of detachment of patients, records, cutting orders etc. Associated with Santinillio was a man named ██████ who is already in trouble over the Ratavich case (the officer in CBI who admitted to Col. Cochran that he had taken money to get a couple of men out of the army, and was sent home). The FBI this week began an investigation of Santinillio.

3. <u>Procedure in Arranging Discharges</u>. WD Circular 280, supplemented by a TWX (whose origin is now under investigation in the office of the Air Surgeon) makes it possible for any member of the army to apply for treatment at any army hospital. Thus, a man in an outfit about to be sent overseas, allowed to go home on a final furlough, could go out to Mitchell Field and report himself sick. Major Fabbricatore could then direct Lt. ████ to TWX for the man's papers. Once they had reached Mitchell Field, the man's original outfit ceased to have any record of him. The man, coached presumably by Major Fabbricatore, could then go before a Mitchell Field Board with the symptoms and history of heart trouble, or psycho-neurosis (the favorite complaint, because all boards apparently accept certain

easily put-on symptoms as conclusive) or something, and get a CDD.
Major Fabbricatore would then have Lt. ▮▮▮▮ cut orders sending him
to Dix and he was out, with little trouble, though with some
expense. In fact, a discharge appears to have cost $5,000. However,
if the client was satisfied simply to get out of a hot outfit, part
of the same procedure (sending for papers) could be gone through;
and, for a payment of $1,000 to $2,000 he would find himself ordered
to duty with the 110th AAF Base Unit, Section B, in the permanent
party at Mitchell. This section ran the motor pool, drove ambulances,
etc. Because the paperwork was all in order, Major Hinson had great
difficulty in getting definite proof of irregularities. Close
questioning turned up between 25 and 30 of the Section B personnel
whose presence there was certainly open to suspicion. Capt. Stilphen,
in charge of Section B, felt that there were many more - at one
time the strength of his section was as high as 1,100, far beyond
any requirements; and he had protested to Major Fabbricatore.
Numbers involved in the discharge racket are also difficult to get
at. Discharges averaged 100 a month, but some were certainly legitimate.
Major Hinson estimates, but has no means of proving, that as many
as 500 discharges have been sold since the thing began.

4. Case of Moe Senate. Evidence of a usable sort against the
Major seems to lie mostly in the case of Pfc. Moe Senate, ASF Postal
Battalion in New York. The circumstance that Senate was "hospitalized"
at Mitchell instead of at Ft. Slocum, the ASF hospital, which would
have been more convenient for him, attracted Major Hinson's attention;
and Senate finally told his story. He said that he had been approached
by a man named "Al" (probably Santinillio) who took $2,000 from him
in a cafe, and brought him outside where Major Fabbricatore was
waiting in a car. The Major drove him to the hospital and ordered
him entered as a patient. This was on 11 December 1944. Senate's
papers were sent for; and, on 16 Jan. 1945, an order was cut sending
him to Dix, where he was discharged 19 Jan. 1945. On 20 Jan. 1945,
"Al" met him and received the $3,000 balance. Major Fabbricatore,
who denies any knowledge of anything, is under arrest in quarters -
but not on charges in regard to the discharges. Fabbricatore reported
to Gen. Hunter about two weeks ago that he had something on his
conscience. He told the General that a friend of his who had been
AWOL came to him for help and that, in a moment of weakness or
sympathy, he fixed it for the friend by making a false report that
the friend was hospitalized during that period. Major Hinson believes,
not implausibly, that Fabbricatore had the wind up and imagined he
might somehow beat the other investigation this way.

5. Major Fabbricatore. I went to check with Gen. Glenn, Deputy
the Air Surgeon, on the progress of the investigation in the origin
of the TWX which mysteriously implemented and amplified WD Circular
280, and there talked with Col. ▮▮▮▮▮▮▮ Deputy for Administration.
Col. ▮▮▮▮, I learned, was formerly CO of the Mitchell Field Hospital,

and for that reason much concerned about the whole business - in fact, if Major Hinson's view is correct, some of it must have been going on while Col. ███████ was there. Col. ██████ knew Major Fabbricatore very well, and had a high regard for him. The Major had gone through OCS, and, while ██████ was there, was spending his evenings taking courses at a local high school, to make up credits which he had not had the opportunity to get in his youth. Col. ██████ said the Major was probably the best known, and certainly one of the most popular officers on the post; and that he would do anything for anyone (perhaps an indication of how he came to get into trouble). However, Col. ██████ also said that he had heard from people he knew at Mitchell that since his departure the Major had blossomed out considerably with a new car, a mink coat for his wife, and other evidences of prosperity not usually associated with a major's salary. Fabbricatore ascribed it all to some holdings he had in a winery owned by an aunt. Col. ██████ had met Santinillio, Fabbricatore presenting him as an old friend, and remembered gathering from their remarks that Santinillio was indeed a big shot in Brooklyn Italian circles.

6. _Conclusions._ If the ring operated on the scale that Major Hinson (and Gen. Hunter) believe it did, it is safe to assume that by now thousands of people know, and some of them will sooner or later announce, that money is all you need to get out of the service. The device on which the operation depended - getting the papers sent on to a hospital - is so obvious that it is likely Major Fabbricatore is not the only one who thought of it. This may mean that similar goings-on will be uncovered at other AAF installations. Gen. Glenn is now making inquiries. The status as of today is that no formal action has been taken by the First Air Force to notify the Air Inspector, who is, therefore, officially unaware of the matter, as is Hq. AAF. Gen. Schneider requests that the Chief, OIS, regard this information as confidential pending formal action.

JAMES G. COZZENS
Major, Air Corps

presentation material had really been cleared (an error of Maj Miner's, who can make a million in any given day); and trouble about the distribution of the special issue of *Impact*; and trouble about the pictures for *Look*; and so on and so on.

Friday 22 June 1945

. . . I spent my time clearing up Col Harris' stuff, including long conversations with Gen Hedrick—the alacrity with which he answers, and the length at which he talks, confirms me in my impression that he sits there most of the day waiting for something to do and most of the time it never comes. After talking to Mr McCloy's office, I finally decided that we could amend two of the letters, and let the rest go. . . .

Saturday 23 June 1945

. . . I was on the Freeman Field business with Col Gerhardt and Gen Hedrick thru much of the morning and finally got a memo in to Bowman, who sent it back soon with a buck sheet noted: another excellent piece of investigation; which shows, I suppose, how well he understands the handling of troops, since I found myself speaking very warmly of Bowman's character and intelligence while having a bowl of soup with George Haddock who came in around one, very sunburned and well-looking, with a musette bag over his shoulder. Plainly being and feeling better, he seemed agreed that if they did not discharge him next week, he would come back—very necessary, in view of poor Miner's fantastic entanglements, mostly due to his own laborious slow-wittedness—yet it is plain that he means earnestly and well, and has, though he might well have been provoked to it by now, little or no malice in him—which, as I get older, seems to me quite a lot to be able to say for a person.

Monday 25 June 1945

. . . I got through a version of Norstad's text for Wednesday, though much distracted with interruptions on (a) the Mitchel Field business from Gen Schneider (b) the demand from Lovett's Col Brownell that I come down there to hear the complaint he had from Mylander of *Look* that he had been double-crossed on the radar business by *Life*'s publication of the *Impact* stuff—and so he had been; but nobody had told us or me that the special issue of *Impact* would keep the stuff, or that *Life* would use it. I dictated as much as I could of a draft of Norstad's stuff to Johnny, and kept up as I could with the rest. To Schneider's office with Bowman at 3.30, where Maj Gen S. E. Anderson, the Chief of Staff of the Continental Air Force, finally turned up and we discussed and modified the releases on the Mitchel Field thing—Anderson is a little spry, sandy fellow apparently quite easy to get on with. It was decided to supplement the releases with another one tomorrow explaining why the associated

HEADQUARTERS, ARMY AIR FORCES
WASHINGTON

23 June 1945

MEMORANDUM FOR THE CHIEF, OFFICE OF INFORMATION SERVICES

Subject: Freeman Field Affair.

1.   For the record, the situation as it stands today in regard to the three negro officers still under arrest (Lts. Terry, Thompson, and Clinton) is that the papers on their cases have been forwarded to the First Air Force, with the advice of Gen. Hedrick, the Air Judge Advocate, that the report of the Advisory Committee on Special Troop Policies, approved by Mr. McCloy and Mr. Stimson, directs court martial of these officers on charges of violating AW 64 (Wilful Disobedience etc.).

2.   In so advising, Gen. Hedrick decided to disregard the indorsement of the Judge Advocate General, who had been holding the papers for almost a month. The JAG recommended punishment under AW 104. Gen. Hedrick does not go along, because the recommendation approved by the Secretary of War was "that the _trial_ of the three officers now under arrest...be expedited." Punishment under AW 104 is by definition not a trial, but a waiver of trial. This seems plain enough, but both Lt. Col. E. B. Jones, Secretary of the Advisory Committee, and Col. Gerhardt, Mr. McCloy's executive, stated that the Committee had not in fact recommended charges of violating AW 64 be laid against the officers.

3.   In this case, Gen. Hedrick points out, the nature of the punishment and the procedure is by regulation determined by the Reviewing Officer (who would be Gen. Hunter). Col. Gerhardt notified me this morning that it was definitely not Mr. McCloy's intention to have the term "trial" in the recommendation taken as a _directive_ to the Air Judge Advocate, or anyone else, to hold a court martial unless that was what the Col. described as the "normal procedure". Here, it would, and presumably will, be normal, since the choice of procedure will be up to Gen. Hunter. Col. Gerhardt's point seemed to be that Mr. McCloy would under no circumstances assume responsibility for directing that the punishment of the officers _must_ take the form of court martial.

4.   Gen. Hedrick subsequently called me and said that Col. Gerhardt agreed, in a conversation with him, to send over another paper, explicitly stating that the Secretary of War recommended appropriate punishment, and that he did this understanding that Gen. Hunter would determine the appropriate punishment, and that it would assuredly be charges under AW 64 and court martial.

Immediately after my talk with Gen. Hedrick, Lt. Col. Jones called and read to me over the phone the proposed rephrasing of the paragraph about the trial which he had written at Col. Gerhardt's direction. It directed disciplinary action to be expedited, but added that action, under AW 104 was not therefore precluded. This leaves it up to Gen. Hunter, as indicated above, and the matter may be considered closed as far as this Hq. goes. The court martial will probably be held next week. Gen. Hunter seems to understand the importance of having colored officers on the board. Of the names submitted, at least half were colored.

                                        JAMES G. COZZENS
                                        Major, Air Corps

but previous Radovitch case took so long, which Bowman suggested I might write up (quite reasonably) as he was going off flying tomorrow. Gen Schneider arranged that his man in New York would telephone the stuff in so I only had to figure out how to adjust that, and the composition of a humble-pie letter from Brownell to Mylander, and the inevitable revisions of the text for Gen Norstad could be fitted in. . . .

Tuesday 26 June 1945

. . . Gen Streett called in the morning, very brisk but sufficiently affable on the Mitchel Field matter, and I told him Col Bowman had gone flying (though I was in fact able to reach Bowman at Bolling when they pulled him out of his plane at the head of the runway). He decided he would come over to Gen Hood's office anyway, and directed me and Gen Schneider to be there. He had aged a good deal since I saw him at Colorado Springs nearly two years ago, seeming more subdued and precise; but he was still fond of talking, and about all we got around to was deciding to have Gen Hunter down tomorrow. Meanwhile, I was to draw up a few vague releases. Having also Norstad's stuff underfoot, it was a busy afternoon. I did get to see Norstad in the end, and he, too, is subdued; mild, worried and tired, so we got on well. To dinner at the Chinese Lantern with Bradshaw and Maj Moore and his child wife. The Maj, with whom we discussed flying, insisted that he would take me flying and correct some of my misapprehensions. I was astonished to hear myself agreeing, which made me think I must be tight, though in fact we had few drinks; so in the end I decided I must have a complex on the subject.

Wednesday 27 June 1945

. . . We had a good nerve-wracking day, what with Norstad and his stuff—he had me over to talk to a BG in Tompkins' office by way of additional clearance—they were very glum there about the chances of UMT getting by anyway—and dictating more releases and then the party with Hunter and Streett and Schneider and Hunter's A1 [personnel aide], Col Wold, and Capt Edwards, and Bowman and Hood. This took 2 hours, with Hunter twisting his cavalryman's moustache and exploding in all directions (about 1/4 an act, the rest real and instinctive). We got almost nowhere. Norstad, at the conference, was very good—like Freddy Smith; easy, winning and effective; and I could see that would be all right. Home early and glad to get there.

Thursday 28 June 1945

. . . To see Gen Hedrick about his pronouncement on military justice—it might be well to make some 'undesirable concessions' to Congress in the interests of UMT. He is a nice clean gentle old man and I harried him as little as I could—though certainly he should never have passed out in an unclassified activity report statements so damaging, though true enough. The public certainly feels on the basis of a few publicized cases that military justice isn't justice, and something should be done about it. Col Bowman unloaded on Ed Newhouse a fairly sizeable job—a sort of summary of the bombing of Japan to be presented at the conference next week of the President & Churchill and Stalin. . . .

Friday 29 June 1945

. . . The new Hq Memo 35-6 turned up, promising that anyone over 42 could be released by 30 Sept and this seemed fine to me—but the term was conditional, of course. I spoke to Bowman about it, and he was very agreeable, but sufficiently firm—he could not do without me until he had found a replacement—he hoped we could find one—but when? With some delicacy, I thought, or maybe ingenuity, he said: I know in the regular army we can't expect to get good writers like you; and I'm not holding out for replacements of the same caliber; but I have to get someone who can at least go through the motions. The job is to win the war; I know you feel that as much as I do. As soon as I can find someone to take your place I will be with you 100% in seeing you get out. There was obviously no answer except; For Christ's sake, do you imagine any of this has anything to do with winning any war? It did not seem tactful to make it, so I retired just where I was before, 42 or no 42. . . .

Saturday 30 June 1945

. . . I was busy in the morning talking to Major Heggen, a Negro MP officer in BPR who was going to the Freeman Field court-martial. Not unnaturally, but surprisingly even so, he was very pro-Army and while not anti, at least not pro-Negro. Up then to see Col Scott about Gen Meyers of ATS and formerly the Materiel Command, on rumors that had been passed from newspapers around Wright Field to Westlake to Bowman; and there did indeed seem reason to suppose that they would hear more of Meyers' goings-on.[73] In the afternoon later we were onto the stuff for Mr A, again, Ed very much bound that I was going to be right in it, and I (I fear sulkily) assenting, since it did not seem that he could do it alone, and yet that was just what I had resolved I would not do. Fundamentally it was clear that I acted less through Christian charity than some fear (probably fixed on me at school) that I would lose caste as a good sport if I didn't pitch in and help.

Sunday 1 July 1945

Continued intensely hot; so it was not, in fact, any special hardship to come down to the Pentagon. At noon I went back to bring S down and she stayed until we went to the train. I managed to get the tactical remarks done, though still rebellious. . . .

HEADQUARTERS, ARMY AIR FORCES
WASHINGTON

IN Y REFER TO:

28 June 1945

MEMORANDUM FOR: Chief, Office of Information Services

Subject: Opinions from the Air Judge Advocate

1.   Colonel Kidner of General Hedrick's office reported, 26 June, two opinions of some importance:

a.   <u>Severe Court-Martial Sentences</u>.   A letter has been prepared for the signature of CG, AAF to all commanding officers having general court-martial jurisdiction "directing attention to a number of unnecessarily severe sentences imposed by courts-martial and approved by reviewing authorities in cases involving military personnel with combat records and overseas service.   The purpose of this letter was to point out that although an overseas or combat record does not endow the individual with any special immunity from punishment for offenses committed by him, nevertheless, proper attention must be insured in the cases of mentioned personnel, particularly where it is evident that the offense may have had its inception in a mental or physical condition stemming from combat or operational fatigue."   However, Colonel Frank J. Day, Acting, the Air Provost Marshal, is somewhat restive about what he regards as a "soft" attitude on the part of the Air Judge Advocate.   He reported, also 26 June, that the Air Provost Marshal's office was dissatisfied with the action taken in the case of two officers "who were guilty of personal misconduct reflecting on the military service.   The action did not appear to be sufficiently impressive to restrain the officers concerned on future occasions nor to act as a deterrant upon others.   The report has been studied by the Air Judge Advocate's office and returned through the office of the Air Inspector.   The Air Judge Advocate recommended that no further action be taken.   There have been many similar cases, and it is the opinion of the Air Provost Marshal that an unconsidered attitude of leniency toward offenders, particularly of officers, and more particularly, of officers of field grade, reacts very unfavorably upon discipline generally."   Colonel Day, a fairly tough and salty officer, told me with indignation that the "misconduct" was getting drunk and raising hell and punching policemen or MP's in the nose, and because they were all heroes, they got away with it.   When nothing was done to them, it adversely affected his relations with local civilian police who was accustomed to hand over military personnel to the APM, and he felt that the Air Judge Advocate, if not the immediate commanding officers, should have a better sense of duty and responsibility.

b.   <u>UMT and Military Justice</u>.   While it is considered "practicable" to deal justly and adequately with the disciplinary problem of future

SECT

ADDRESS REPLY TO: COMMANDING GENERAL, ARMY AIR FORCES, WASHINGTON 25, D. C.

trainees under the proposed Universal Military Training program by administratively adjusting the present system of military justice to fit the situation (a similar adjustment is made for the United States Military Academy), General Hedrick feels that "the paramount importance of having the principle of universal military training adopted is such that in order to attain it, undesirable concessions may be necessary. In the event that the opponents of universal military training offer the disciplinary angle as opposition, a detailed plan should be prepared and ready for presentation which will convince Congress that we can do the job justly."

This really extraordinary statement seems to pack about as much dynamite as any two sentences could hold, but General Hedrick tells me that the implied admission that we know we could not hope to impose the rigors of military justice on trainees, and so, reluctantly would make some changes in order to gain our main objective, is simply the way it is. Though wrongly and unfairly (he feels), the public, due to a handful of cases exploited in the newspapers, is convinced that military justice has little or no relation to "real justice."

The concessions would boil down to allowing civil courts to try trainees who committed civil offenses, and this is obviously "undesirable" because the accused is removed for a longer or shorter period from his military station. General Hedrick adds that he thinks it is usually a protection to the soldier to be tried by the military authorities. The civil authorities may be prejudiced against him and their action, at least in less serious cases, will probably be more summary and severe than the military authorities' action. This may perhaps be borne out to some degree by Colonel Day's complaint (a., above). The point about military justice's unacceptability to the public was made in the Minutes of the General Council this week, and the Judge Advocate General prepared a 16-page memorandum in which he also recommended concessions. It would seem that the WD or the AAF or both ought to face up to the much-neglected public relations problem of convincing the country that military trials are fair and that military justice is just.

JAMES G. COZZENS
Major, Air Corps

HEADQUARTERS, ARMY AIR FORCES
WASHINGTON

30 June 1945

MEMORANDUM FOR THE CHIEF, OFFICE OF INFORMATION SERVICES

Subject: Possible Irregularities in Connection with
Curtiss-Wright Stock and Other Matters.

1. Major Mitchell mentioned to me certain inquiries from mid-west newspapers which had been directed to Col. Westlake touching on rumors that an AAF General Officer might have taken advantage of information which his official position made available to him to deal profitably in stock. Inquiries I have made indicate that this is very likely. The officer in question, I am told in confidence by the Air Inspector's Office, has a peculiar history since his first appearance with the Air Service in 1918. He has been working mostly in administrative lines, and is probably the only AAF General Officer whose career goes back as far as that who is neither a command nor a senior pilot. He has been several times investigated for various irregularities. At present he appears to be in possession of more money than his Army earnings or any known private income could account for.

2. Both the former Air Service Command and the former Materiel Command conducted much of their business along lines which brought repeated protests and warnings from the Air Inspector and the Inspector General. This officer appears to have been in the thick of many of the things objected to. Among others associated with him was Col. ▮▮▮▮▮▮▮▮▮▮ and former Brig. Gen. O'Dwyer. Col. Scott tells me confidentially that there is no possible doubt that a great many improper actions and transactions took place, but there is little tangible evidence now available to him - largely because, until the recent change in the ATSC command, the Air Inspector continued to be obstructed at every turn in his efforts to get at facts, or to compel the correction of even grave and obvious abuses.

3. The present CO of the ATSC has the confidence of the Air Inspector's office; but this obviously can't cure what happened in 1943 and 1944. Col. Scott feels that a succession of delayed-explosion scandals, beginning soon and continuing indefinitely, should be expected; and that such attacks, as Drew Pearson's recent innuendo against the CG may increase in number and frequency. The truth is that some people around the CG long pursued a policy of not telling him or showing him things that he might pound the table about unless it was absolutely necessary. It would be better for all concerned if the CG had been kept more fully informed of certain matters for which he will now find himself held responsible.

JAMES G. COZZENS
Major, Air Corps

Monday 2 July 1945

. . . We got to see Norstad with our texts in the afternoon, along with a little buck general named Todd, and Col Stone, and another Col. It was plain that they were not very clear about what Mr A might want, and I could see that I was indeed a fool not to stay clear of such nonsense at any cost since it was now apparently up to me to revise what I had put together along certain uncertain lines.

Tuesday 3 July 1945

. . . What with other things, Gen Norstad seemed to forget his papers from Mr A, so while I had them all done and Ed took them over, we got no more complaints—or attention. . . . in the afternoon with Col Bowman to look at a B-32 at the airport— an ugly brute of a plane with a couple of outsized bombs, one a so-called Tall Boy and one a Grand Slam in its bays. The Col seemed cordially concerned to get on good terms with his staff and I must say he did very well.

Wednesday 4 July 1945

. . .I was busy with the draft of a letter Capt Edwards of CAF Hq sent over on the Negro business—it seemed mostly wrong and bad, and so (showing I never learn) I checked it with the Air Inspector and talked to Bowman, who of course ended by telling me to draw up another one for issue by Hq AAF. This took a long time. Late in the afternoon Major Heggen, back from the Godman Field thing, called me to say that two of the defendants had been acquitted and the other lightly dealt with. This seemed likely to smooth things over for the moment, but you could not help reflecting that it put an unnecessary premium on pushing the Provost Marshal around.

Thursday 5 July 1945

. . . I spent all morning walking my policy letter around, ending in Eaker's office where I found Gen Streett, and Gen Kraus, who kindly remembered me from Ft Worth, waiting outside. Gen S talked a lot in a nervous pleasant way and Gen Eaker, who looks dumpy and sad, said he would look at it later. . . . In the afternoon I was busy with my memoranda. . . .

Friday 6 July 1945

. . . It developed, soon after I was in, that Gen Eaker would not go along with the Policy Letter, Col Bowman said, because he felt that the WD had already stated it; but I think, in fact, because he asked himself the reasonable question; What do we (HqAAF) gain? and the answer was really, nothing. 600-45 is all very well, but if its meaning is not clearly grasped, or if it was deliberately neglected, the results will be

CONFIDENTIAL

HEADQUARTERS, ARMY AIR FORCES
WASHINGTON

3 July 1945

MEMORANDUM FOR THE CHIEF, OFFICE OF INFORMATION SERVICES

Subject: Resume of Freeman Field Situation.

1. **Allocation of Facilities at Freeman Field.** In February 1945 a decision was reached to combine OTU training of the 477th Bombardment Group and the 387th Service Group (both negro) at Freeman Field, Seymour Indiana. Col. Robert R. Selway, Jr., Group Commander of the 477th (a job for which he was selected by Gen. Harper, former AC/AS, Training, as an officer particularly qualified to command negro troops) inspected Freeman Field in February and issued a letter order, effective 1 March, allocating buildings and facilities. The order designated three buildings to be used respectively as an OTU Officers Club, and OTU Officers Mess and an OTU Officers' Recreation room. Another building was designated as Base and Supervisory Officers Mess #2, and certain additional buildings as BOQ's. Col. Selway's action in designating separate club and mess facilities for base and trainee personnel was based on the orders of Gen. Hunter, who ruled that certain supervisory officers all white, "were not assigned to the group to receive training...in other words, they were considered base personnel...This interpretation appears to have been predicated on the assumption that all white officers would be replaced by negro officers before the group departed for overseas." (However, at this period, these white officers were in fact on the T/O of the 477th, not on a Freeman Field permanent party T/O. This is more than a technicality, since it made perfectly clear the fact that the "separation" of facilities was was on the basis of certain buildings being designated for white and colored officers of the same units. This is the weak point in the First Air Force's position as stated by Gen. Hunter. The white officers, though occupying command positions - Squadron Commanders, Squadron Navigators, etc. - were distinctly personnel of the OTU, regardless of whether or not they might later be relieved or replaced.)

2. **Negro Officers Object.** On 9 March, four days after the arrival of the units at Freeman Field, several negro officers raised the question of the legality, in view of AR 210-10 of the separation of base officers' club facilities and trainee officers' facilities. One or two of them attempted to obtain service at the bar of the base officers' club. This was refused. (AR 210-10, 20 December 1940, deals with the administration of Posts, Camps and Stations. Par. 19 states: "No officers' club, mess, or other similar social organization will be permitted by the post commander to occupy any part of any public building...unless such club...extends to all officers on duty at the post the right to full membership...") The incident was reported to

Gen. Hunter who on 10 March sent a secret telegram to Col. Selway "stating that the allocation of separate buildings for clubs..had his personal approval and would be observed by all personnel; that any insubordination should be met by arrest; and that continued insubordination should be met by confinement in the guard house if necessary." On 15 March, all officers of the base were assembled and advised of Gen. Hunter's order, and of his ruling that the white command and supervisory personnel had not been assigned to the group to receive training, and were therefore to be considered as base personnel.

3. The Incidents of 5 April. During the morning Lowell M. Trice, reportedly a representative of the NAACP and reporter for the Indianapolis Record, a negro paper, arrived at the field without clearance and without Col. Selway's knowledge. Learning of his presence in the afternoon, Col. Selway ordered him from the post on the grounds that he had not presented his credentials and applied in a proper manner for admission.

During the afternoon the CCTS unit, approximately 100 officers, arrived from Godman Field. Col. Selway was advised that these officers were planning to descend in groups on the base officers' club that evening and make an issue of the separation policy. The Col. then directed that a Provost Marshal be stationed at the club door with direct orders to exclude any trainee personnel. The officer took his station at 2030, armed and wearing an MP brassard.

Three quarters of an hour later four negro officers presented themselves and were refused admission. They were followed half an hour later by a group of 19 negro officers who attempted to enter. The Provost Marshal blocked the door with his body and outstretched arms. Two of the negro officers (Lts. Thompson and Clinton, defendants in the present action) forcibly pushed the Provost Marshal through the door way. They were met inside by Major A. M. White, the Club Officer, who took their names and ordered them to quarters under arrest. Further groups of negro officers continued to present themselves at intervals, some going away without a fuss, some entering. In one of these groups was Lt. Terry, the third defendant, who also pushed the Provost Marshal aside.

4. Gen. Hunter's Instructions. Informed by telephone of these goings-on, Gen. Hunter directed Col. Selway to assemble all officers and read to them the provisions of the letter order of 1 April. Major Osborne, Legal Officer of the First Air Force, was sent down to assist Col. Selway in drawing up a Base Regulation (85-2) which defined trainee personnel and designated facilities. Gen. Hunter

directed that the requirement be inserted that each officer on duty
would read the regulation and certify that he had done so and
understood it. On 10 April, copies of the regulation were distributed.
The majority of the officer personnel complied with the requirement,
but practically all officers of the CCTS unit refused, stating that
they did not understand the order. With the approval of Gen. Hunter,
Col. Selway then ordered these officers to read the order and merely
certify that they had done so. 101 negro officers still refused.
They were individually offered another opportunity, and AW 64 was
read to them. They were then given a direct order in the presence
of witnesses, and on refusal to obey, were placed in arrest.

5. Action by Hq. AAF. Col. Harris, of the Air Inspector's office
was sent to Freeman Field to make a thorough investigation. On the
basis of his report Gen. Giles recommended (23 April):
    a. Release of the 101 officers with an administrative
reprimand.
      b. Trial of the 3 officers who pushed the Provost Marshal.
      c. Transfer of the 477th to Godman Field.
      d. Inactivation of the units on VE Day or R Day, which
ever was first announced.
Accordingly, the 101 officers were released and given a reprimand.

6. Action by the War Department. The Freeman Field file and a
long recommendation prepared by Gen. Timberlake for Gen. Giles went
to the War Department around 1 May and there the matter remained,
presumably under debate and discussion. On 11 June, Col. G. A.
Brownell, Mr. Lovett's Executive, asked if this office had any further
information. Inquiries in the office of the Under Secretary of War
developed the fact that action had been taken at a meeting of the
Advisory Committee on Special Troop Policies, 4 June, though no
notification of it had been sent to any branch of Hq AAF. Recommendations, made by Mr. McCloy and approved by Mr. Stimson, included the
rewriting of a paragraph (bottom of P-14) in WD Pamphlet 20-6
"Command of Negro Troops". Omitted from the new version was the
highly important line: "The burden of deciding whether or not there
shall be some separation in the use of camp facilities is placed on
the local command, with the assumption that local conditions will be
taken into account."
The recommendation, while approving Col. Selway's use of his
"administrative police powers" stated that the Committee did "not concur
in the finding upholding the basis on which a separation of the
Officers Club facilities was made" and held such basis "not in accord
with existing AR's and WD policies". It was directed that "the non-
conformance be brought to the attention of the CG, AAF." Trial of the
3 officers who pushed the Provost Marshal was to be expedited, but
Col. Gerhardt, Mr. McCloy's executive, refused both to me, and to
Gen. Hedrick, the Air Judge Advocate, to allow that the word "trial"
meant what it means; and answered a request to clarify the War Department's position by retaining the word, but stating that action

under AW 104 (recommended, for some reason, by the Judge Advocate General) was not thereby precluded. On this basis it went to Gen. Hunter, who, as Reviewing Authority, could determine the action to be taken. This was, naturally, court martial on charges of violating AW-64. The court martial opened 2 July.

JAMES G. COZZENS
Major, Air Corps

(a) some local CO will take evasive action and avert trouble (b) some local CO will take evasive action and run into trouble. In the first case, we are that much ahead; in the second case, we can beat on him if it seems advisable. Thus, all an explicit, perfectly clear statement would get us is the loss of any advantages that might accrue under (a). Off at noon to go shopping with S, but by 4 Chamberlin telephoned word to me that Col Bowman was setting up a conference for Mr A Monday and so I came back, concerned to know what it was going to be about. Bowman thought, about the same material we had worked on over last weekend; but Gen Norstad on the telephone rejected that, and suggested the material I had been getting together for him. Ed remarked afterwards, probably not without reason, that it could be figured out easily; the stuff we gave Norstad was not being presented as something from AFOIS, but something Norstad had got up for the overseas party, and it might queer matters if substantially the same stuff turned up for his conference.

Saturday 7 July 1945

. . . We had a hard day, and what with some delays on the material, the text for Mr A was not done. George Haddock came in looking very healthy at noon and confirmed some of our fears—he was not coming back, for which you could hardly blame him; but it seemed to do away with any hope of correcting the errors and extravagances of Miner.

Sunday 8 July 1945

In early, and Johnny not sulking much, came in by 9 and we had the text ready by 11. Over with Bowman to see Mr A then—on the way he remarked somewhat discouragingly that he wished he knew how he could find somebody to let me out; but it wasn't going to be easy. Mr A seemed well and in active spirits, somewhat red-looking, and grumbled, though without ill temper, that they told him he couldn't sound off any more, and so he began to make some changes, toning down the text (which was pretty well toned-down, anyway; but a little was conceded to his usual taste). At about page 6 Gen Eaker came in, so Mr A roared at him, still not seriously angry: well, you better do this, you know what I'm supposed to say. We went into Eaker's office then, and he sat sucking his cigar. It developed that he did not want the Gen to have any text—we would abandon this and give him some topical heads. Gen Norstad, who had been summoned up, concurred—a slight, not unpleasant, but definite change has come over him since he got his second star—it seems to manifest itself mostly by a silent pause before he says anything—he used to be quick and voluble; but I guess he has concluded that is not done. Since, at least, there was no new speech to write, this was not too bad—I thought at first that Eaker, who had not read the text, was going to dream up one of his own. In any event, it made no difference, for I sent Johnny home and went home myself, and within an hour Chamberlin, as duty officer, called to say that the Col instructed him to tell me that the conference was off—perhaps because Mr A had to go to Europe sooner than he thought—something about that seems to have been up over the last couple of days. . . .

Monday 9 July 1945

. . . I spent much of the morning collecting the debris resulting from Mr A's changed plan and doing up a memorandum. . . .

Tuesday 10 July 1945

. . . I found myself hooked by Gen Hood to do him a five minute speech for some bond rally—it seemed to be on the basis of a personal favor, so I had not the character to refuse. The rest of the time I was busy talking to Col Scott and Col Logan in the Air Inspector's office and to a Major Baumann, from Personnel, who came over to see me in the afternoon about the popular misconceptions in regard to the draft—they surprised me, too; it seems we will be taking more, not fewer people over 30 to meet the 100,000 a month figure.

Wednesday 11 July 1945

. . . I wrote Hood's piece in the morning, somewhat plagued by Col Bowman who seemed anxious to insert some AAF stuff in Mr Patterson's conference tomorrow, and the matter of the latest psychological warfare leaflet showing Mr A on one side and a slaughtered Jap family surveyed by a couple of bawling Jap brats on the other. Hirsch brought it up, dubious of its appropriateness—it may be appropriate enough, but it seemed poor policy. In any event, it seemed a little late, since the B-29's were already dropping it—and after all, perhaps rightly. There may be no sense in kidding or trying to kid the people you are killing, and maybe we merely take appropriate measure to kid ourselves, or the portion of the population that you know at first glance would rise against the idea. And still again, we are probably better off for having that naive portion to whom it is important to defer. Late in the afternoon I went down to see Col Beach, a dapper little moustached fellow who was doing the Secty's conference, and went over our difficulties with him. He seemed to have very good sense.

Thursday 12 July 1945

. . . Down to see Col Beach's text at 8.30, but he did not show until nearly nine, a perquisite of his unassigned insigne I suppose—he is a nice smooth mild little man, but he had no extra copy and he made it plain that if Col Bowman wanted to see it,

SECRET

HEADQUARTERS, ARMY AIR FORCES
WASHINGTON

10 July 1945

MEMORANDUM FOR THE CHIEF, OFFICE OF INFORMATION SERVICES

Subject: Information from AC/AS Offices

1. Contract Inspection Division. (Air Inspector) Lt. Col. Logan tells me confidentially that the Office of the Under Secretary of War has strongly recommended that the Air Inspector's Contract Inspection Division be abolished and its work taken over by the Inspector General's Office. Reasons given are an alleged duplication, if not of effort, at least of facilities; and a fine point, or perhaps, scruple, to the effect that contracts as contracts (i.e. pieces of paper) are not materiel or equipment peculiar to the AAF.

██ Examples are the Curtiss-Wright C-46 fixed price contract (my memo, 28 June); and the Douglas C-47 contract, a cost-plus-fixed-fee affair, in which Douglas' estimate, on the basis of which they were paid 4%, was accepted at 170 million dollars, while the actual costs proved to be 97 million. Since Douglas had been making practically the same plane previous to getting the contract, the allowable error in estimate (allowable because operating expenses on plant that had to be built for the purpose could not be exactly predicted) would be between 5% and 10%. ██ While it is true that the Contract Inspection Division did not accomplish its purpose of making certain that the WD and the AAF did not become parties to ill-considered and extravagant contracts, it was through no fault of the Division. Far from abolishing it, the wise course would seem to be to find ways of making its recommendations effective.

2. Discharge-Provision Waiver. (Air Inspector) Separate complaints from several Congressmen (Sullivan, Wigglesworth, Goodwin) deal with a strong-arm maneuver which will probably prove to have been common in ETO. The Field Air Inspector is now at Sioux Falls, S.D. investigating the specific case of the ████████████████████. Preliminary reports definitely establish the fact that the Adjutant, Capt. ███████████████, required enlisted personnel of the squadron to sign the agreement in paragraph 12e, RR 1-1, waiving the discharge provision under the ☐ Readjustment Plan, and so engaging to remain with the squadron until end of the war with Japan. Capt. ████ put

it to them while they were still in Italy with the 15th Air Force,
and told them that if they didn't sign the waiver they would be
left with the Army of Occupation. This practice appears to have
been followed in all squadrons of the 450th. Two of the congressional complaints concerned other outfits still in ETO. The
Air Inspector has forwarded the matter to the appropriate overseas commander for necessary action, and that will probably put a
stop to it now; but it would be well to expect Drew Pearson or someone to come out with the story how the AAF gave its men their "choice."

3. Selective Service Statistics. (Personnel) Major Baumann,
Civilian Personnel Division, feels that the public is under a general
and serious misunderstanding about selective service requirements and
probabilities, and presents some tables to show that the Army's
expressed preference for men under 30 is not being gratified. The
percentage of the total inducted who were 18-25 dropped from 79.5
in January to 52.0 in April; while the 26-29 group rose from 13.2
to 31.9; and the 30-37 group rose from 7.3 to 16.1. Significance:
men over 30, regardless of what the public thinks or the Army wants,
are still very likely to be drafted. It does not seem to be generally
realized that the induction rate is still 1,200,000 a year; that
the principal supply of new material has to come from the 60,000
youths reaching 18 each month, of whom approximately 30,000 can
qualify. This means that every month 70,000 men must be combed out
of the previously much-gone-over older groups, and that inductions
from the 30-37 group, running close to 20,000 a month now, will
markedly increase. Major Baumann believes, I think quite correctly,
that some effort should be made to put the case clearly to the
public. While this is properly a WD matter, it might not be out
of place for the AAF to suggest it to them, since they don't seem
to have thought of it themselves.

4. POW Interrogation Policy. (Air Judge Advocate) Gen. Hedrick
has drafted a memorandum suggesting a revision of WD policy on the
answers POW's may be allowed to give Jap interrogators. He wants to
authorize "the giving of coordinated misinformation in addition to
facts already known to the enemy, as experience has proved that the
Japanese are apparently satisfied with any factual response no
matter how fantastic. They are extremely cruel in the treatment of
those who refuse to answer any questions except those permitted by
present WD directives. As POW reports indicate a definite discrimination against flying personnel, the matter is of vital importance
to this Hq."

3

5. Psychological Warfare Leaflet 2069. Major Hirsch, WDGS, brought me up a note on a new 5" x 7" propaganda leaflet which appears to have been prepared by Col. ███████, Psychological Warfare Officer at Joint Intelligence Center POA. As soon as one is available, he will bring the leaflet itself. "On front, photograph of General Arnold and drawing of landing barges in the lower right corner with bombs dropping on Japan forming the border on the left. On reverse, texts continuing with border designs made up of large bomb on left side; along the bottom, drawing of Japanese family lying crumpled and lifeless while two small, frightened children stand looking at the lifeless bodies." The text quotes Gen. Arnold's statement, "There is no part of the Japanese Empire which is not within the bombing range of our air force etc." (This business of the photograph of the CG coupled with drawings of lifeless Japanese families and small frightened children seems to be about as bum an idea as any those people have had yet. This leaflet is now being dropped by the B-29's, and while it may serve, as intended, "to instill an ever greater fear, and panic, and build up strong antagonism and resentment toward the militarists," I cannot believe that it is in the CG's interests to put out such a thing. It would seem to be a good occasion to bring up again the fact that the AAF has no representative at JICPOA, and clearly, in self-protection, should have.)

JAMES G. COZZENS
Major, Air Corps

Col Bowman would have to come down. In lieu of that, I made a few changes myself and told the Col it was ok. I was then busy with my memoranda, and with checking the B-29 release (tomorrow) and hearing the gossip about the enlisted man who had cut his wrists and throat in the gents room off corridor 1, which we used to use, and so still felt a proprietory interest in. Late in the afternoon, Bowman put in a paper to get George Haddock the Legion of Merit, which seemed to me so just and sound an idea that I abandoned everything else and started to write that up—it has to be pretty fancy, and I did what I could. . . . I had also a note from Robby with dope on John Wagner, and so got Miner to put in for him, and wrote him myself a fawning note to the IX TAC in Germany, urging reasons why he would like to serve here instead of me.

Friday 13 July 1945

. . . I spent much of the morning at Gravelly Point seeing Lt Col Kraft in Awards—an agreeable greying man who suffered from Haddock's complaint, and so felt extra sympathy for him. He made some practical suggestions on changes in phraseology likely to appease the AG. I then saw Lt Col Schuyler in Air Installations on the Davis Field thing, but it was still under debate. In the afternoon I went up to see Col Harris who gave me a shocking letter from a MC [Medical Corps] officer on Davis Field conditions, which I showed to Bowman, who then sent me to take it to Gen Hall in Personnel. Hall, who impresses me pleasantly, swore away a while and I brought it down and wrote a memo for Gen Eaker on the advisability of cutting the losses, which Bowman signed, and which I took up to Coe who seemed of the same opinion and brought it in to the meeting in Eaker's office. A half an hour later Coe called to say Davis Field would be abandoned, as Hall, Bowman, and I wanted. That came through while I was talking to the Col about Haddock's thing, and we were not sure whether or not we ought to credit ourselves with the last straw.

Saturday 14 July 1945

. . . Drew Pearson had a note in his column about officer discharges from Las Vegas on 42 points which I took upstairs to Personnel, and that took some time, a couple of earnest Cols explaining that it was so, but why. When I got down we had a Log message in to say that Reeves had been KIA over Formosa, having got a ride on a B-25 mission and his plane was the one taken out when they went down to shoot up a Jap gun position. We were all considerably taken aback, thinking of the signs undoubtedly given him of what a bore he was and a nuisance in the week before his taking off; and it seemed very hard on the poor little wretch—the only break he had ever got, and yet the best part of it would have been (for him) his coming back to let people (and the prospect was horrible) know about the wars. To NY on the 1 pm train.

Monday 23 July 1945

. . . To Washington on the 8.30 train, . . . and to the office where we were at once embroiled in Eaker's conference for tomorrow. . . . I do not think he has any special mental capacity and what he had was obviously absorbed or even bemused by goings-on at some high level like staff politics or who gets what.

Tuesday 24 July 1945

. . . There was much scrambling around in the morning as Eaker turned up subjects he wanted memos on. Bowman was sympathetic, and said he had persuaded Eaker to direct the staff sections to prepare such memoranda when future conferences were in order. Meanwhile I had a good grip on the bag, and was, in fact, briefing the Gen across Gen Arnold's desk on the last memo when Gen Surles and Bowman arrived to take him to the conference. Here, I must admit, he did much better than I expected. He was contained, but easy and explicit; his somewhat melancholy sharp manner eased to a kind of amiable grumpiness and I soon had to admit that he was putting it over—though partly of course because he had a lot of stuff, and they would not care too much who presented it or how.

Wednesday 25 July 1945

We were all engulfed in the Air Force Day nonsense and I found myself much against my will and grumpily getting out some nonsense for Vandenberg for Los Angeles. Major Moore turned up, sure enough transferred to us, and immediately pinned to the wall above poor Reeves' desk multiple folders showing his pretty wife and daughter. . . .

Thursday 26 July 1945

. . . It seemed there might be a chance of going to NY to attend a conference on the Mitchel Field matter Sat, which was all right with me—while it is not good being here, it is worse getting away—you are distracted when you get back, though in a way new and peculiar to me and not very pleasing, because my theory has always been that if you were not actively uncomfortable, or actively unhappy, or actively bored you must certainly be cultivating an affection if you felt you just couldn't stand it because it didn't happen to be exactly the way you might want it. I seem to see in myself (and with much impatience and disgust) what is really a sort of distraction—I cannot (though more mentally than physically) sit still and be quiet over the kind of reading I always liked, or count on what I am going to like, or feel like, tomorrow or even in a couple of hours. I can see that in the office I am often quite irritable, so that I say things I don't plan to, or even mean—they are not always, or even perhaps often, unpleasant or unwise or injudicious; but, what is to me even less to my liking, unexpected. I mean, it gives me the neurotic feeling (I suppose it is) that I can no longer feel a sort of implicit confidence in sensible self-interest to see me through. In town to have lunch with Jo Chamberlin, who clearly felt much the same way, and so helped me none. . . . After all, relatively, what the hell had you got to complain of?

Friday 27 July 1945

. . . It developed that the NY thing was off, but I thought I would go anyway if I could, S having arranged not to come down. Gen Schneider had some people up on the accident at Florence in which one of our A-26s hit an airlines plane and we had a long session because the southern papers were not, to his mind, or that of a major who was a test pilot working on it, or that of a major from the AJA's outfit, fair to our A-26 pilot. We talked a long time and I agreed. Back then on the Vandenberg business, which had to have changes. . . .

Saturday 28 July 1945

. . . In New York there was infinite excitement over the B-25 hitting the Empire State Building this morning; and, indeed, from our terrace you could see the hole on the south side through which one engine had gone; and S said the flames were impressive at the time.

Sunday 29 July 1945

. . . Though a little ill at ease over being AWOL (though Jo was going to take care of that if need was) it was still pleasant to be out of Washington, though I could see that was no way to handle it unless I was trying to develop my probably imaginary neurosis, bucking for a CDD [Certificate of Disability Discharge]—which would strike even me as phoney.

Monday 30 July 1945

. . . To Washington on the 8.30 train, and somewhat concerned to read on the way that Gen Schneider had been in NY yesterday to present a fawning letter from Gen Eaker (written I learned later by Barber) to Mayor LaGuardia, because I half expected he might have tried to get at Col Bowman through me Saturday. This proved not to be the case and it was plain that the front office never did know I was away. I was immediately busy again with my delayed memoranda (and in better spirits, since I had made little effort to catch up last week). . . .

Tuesday 31 July 1945

. . . I was again busy with a big memoranda and stiffening Col Bowman's resolution that the awful radio piece Mr A wrote for himself—he was back last night—addressed in the first person to the Jap emperor telling him how nasty he was, and what was going to happen to him, ought not to be used. This proved vain, except that it was transferred to the Jap "war lords" but most of the childish taunts were left. To talk to Col Logan about the Contract Division in the morning and to Col Scott about the Empire State matter in the afternoon. . . .

Wednesday 1 August 1945

. . . Mr A's stuff came back early with some additional asinine suggestions. . . . Meanwhile, as soon as he got in (8.35) Gen Schneider sent for me and poured out his tale of the goings-on in New York. He seemed to feel that maybe someone would feel that because he got his name in the papers he was trying to hog the limelight, which was clearly not the case. He suggested that for God's sake Mr A should not go into the matter with Mayor LaGuardia tonight; so I called Bowman on that and he had me relay it to Barber, who made a note. He (Barber) looks more ghastly every day, and was harassed enough over the speech nonsense. We, Jo and I, got another version done; Gen Surles questioned the propriety of it, but it was almost 2 then, and Mr A was leaving, so no one paid any attention. After that I had some calm, with nothing to do but go up and talk to an Airborne major on glider overproduction.

Thursday 2 August 1945

. . . At 2, up with Col Bowman to Gen Schneider's office where (with Price, of Flying Safety; and Kidner of the AJA; and supporting officers) we went over the Florence collision for an hour. . . .

Friday 3 August 1945

. . . S had mentioned to me some rumors Abend brought back about Chennault,[74] and after an absurd and laborious staff meeting in the projection room in which Miner got statements out of several of our new officers, to see Col Scott who amply confirmed the rumors and said he expected in a Col from the 14th in a few days and meanwhile we might do well to plan no special display of the Gen on his return. Taking Col Bowman out into the hall, I relayed it and he seemed grateful; though, at the same time he gave me the word to hop along to a conference going on on the 9th corridor, where I found Col Harris, a Col Howe and a Col Hopper and another old boy from WDGS chewing over a release by Mr May on army brutality, somewhat

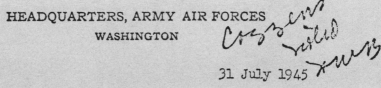

PLY REFER TO:

31 July 1945

MEMORANDUM FOR THE CHIEF, OFFICE OF INFORMATION SERVICES

Subject: Information from AC/AS Offices.

1. Contract Inspection Division. (Air Inspector) I have been
shown confidentially and informally the draft of a memorandum for
the signature of Maj. Gen. Junius Jones to the Chief of Air Staff
on the Contract Inspection Division. It will not be sent until Gen.
Jones, on his return, has seen it and approved it; but it presents
a very full, well-arranged, and lucid argument for resisting the
suggestion of the Under Secretary of War's office (my memo, 10 July)
that the Air Inspector cease to carry out any inspections of AAF contracts. The principal points:

   a. The failure of the Office of the Under Secretary to
   accept the recommendations of the AAF Contract Inspection
   Division has already in several cases left us holding the
   bag on arrangements certain to be criticized if they come out.

   b. The CG/AAF is charged by War Department directives
   with definite responsibilities in procurement of AAF materiel
   and services. A list of not less than 177 specific responsibilities in connection with contracts are expressly imposed on
   him by applicable directives (both the AJA and Budget & Fiscal
   concur). If the inspection of contracts is taken from the Air
   Inspector, the CG, while having the same broad responsibilities
   of command, will be delegating those responsibilities to an
   agency (the Inspector General) over which he has no command
   control.

   c. In the event of a separate Air Force being established
   it might be inconvenient if contracts and procurement of air
   force materiel were at the time, and so as a matter of vested
   interest might be left, in an agency (even if it were a special
   section of a unified Defense Department) outside the Air Force.
The memorandum also contains a list of check points for the inspection
of fixed price and incentive type contracts, which, if applied, would
extend the scope of present inspections to make them more effective
in protecting the AAF interests. I am told confidentially that such
an extension would help a great deal in making it difficult or
impossible (by detailing objections more fully) for the recommendations
to be over-ridden.

2. Florence Field Collision. (Air Inspector) Following the meeting
on this subject which Gen. Schneider asked me to attend last Friday,
and which I reported to you verbally, Col. Scott notes: "Preliminary
report delt with the public hearing connected by the Chief Examiner of
the CAB, which resulted in newspaper releases that carried the inference

that the Army pilot had been buzzing the air liner. Although no
direct evidence was produced to support this inference, evidence
was introduced by airline representatives to the effect that Army
and Navy aircraft frequently buzzed airliners and flew formation
with them. The purpose of the public hearing appeared to be to
present the complaints of EAL concerning interference by military
aircraft with commercial aircraft rather than to determine the real
cause of the subject accident. AAF officers present at the hearing
deemed it undesirable to challenge the methods used by CAB personnel
in the presence of representatives of the press. The AAF expects
to have the opportunity to introduce exhibits and evidence to the CAB
prior to rulings in the case, and the chief examiner has requested
concurrence in conclusions to be determined." (Gen. Schneider's
proposal was that he go over with the Chief, OIS, these exhibits and
details of evidence sometime early this week. The proposed conference
was put off because of Gen. Schneider's trip to New York on the
Empire State matter.)

3. Notes from In and Out Log.

   a. TERMINAL for Eisenhower 25 July. ...no Congressmen will
be permitted to travel in your theatre or from your theatre by air
without payment of fare as presented in Ex Order 9492...charge for
Army water transportation will be limited to subsistence costs only...

   b. TERMINAL for Eisenhower 26 July. ...Unless large
quantities of coal are made available to liberated Europe in forthcoming months...political and economic chaos feared...It is a matter
of great urgency that Germany be made to produce...You are directed
as CG...to take all steps necessary to make available for export out
of production of coal mines in Western Germany a minimum of 10
million tons during remainder of 1945...

   c. St. Germain signed Cannon 28 July. ...add name of Albart
Patin to list of German scientists recommended by this Hq. for
evacuation to US. Patin is outstanding specialist in small poten-
tiometers...(on 29 July, 13 more jet engine people were named. Are
we ready to explain the AAF position?)

   d. CON 3rd Fleet 27 July. ...unfortunately Jap hospital
ship...was mistaken for another gray freighter...before recognized
seen to be down at the stern...

   e. Caserta signed McNarney 29 July. ...proposed unit citation
1st Brazilian Fighter Squadron...I still do not recommend such award.
While the service of this unit was highly creditable, it was not outstanding above comparable American squadrons...

                                        JAMES G. COZZENS
                                        Major, Air Corps

misrepresenting the Lincoln, Nebraska Army Air Base business. All except Col Harris seemed bound that they were going to sock May back; so, somewhat oppressed by the weight, I blocked them as well as I could on behalf of the AAF. My afternoon off proved to be well shot, as Col Hopper was writing up a draft which I had to get back shortly after two to take to Gen Chauncey, who listened amiably while I detailed some of its short-comings. He then sent me over to a new meeting in Gen Persons' office, where Hopper, Hill from BPR, a BG whose name I never got, and some others went over the draft. S was meanwhile waiting downstairs so I saw I was going to have to use force. Gen Persons, a lean headed jumpy fellow who seems to manage the WD liaison with Congress, gave way pretty well and I was able to get Hopper's draft revised so that it made less offensive and childish reading. I took it then with Col Hill to Chauncey, and since my freedom depended on it, told him urgently that he liked it. So he soon agreed. I got out then, close to 4, but was no sooner home shortly after five when Moore from the office began to call—Hopper, perhaps to pay me back, had some wild notions about how we ought to call a Lt Col Sacks in the Training Command, who had reviewed the courts-martial, and warn him that newspaper people might approach him. By 6 I was indeed tired of the whole business.

Saturday 4 August 1945

. . . I felt a certain perverse pleasure in finding that the *Post* made my point of yesterday exactly; and, saying the Army had called May a liar, provided all the incentive he would need to carry on the controversy for a long time. Much of the morning went into my efforts to press Col Goetz in Personnel to demand John Wagner harder from the IX TAC, but I don't think it will come to much, and I would probably do better to cut Bradshaw and Newhouse out on Moore, who seems very keen to understudy and take over my jobs, even if they did see him first. Late in the afternoon Gen Norstad decided he would have a conference next week so we began a last minute scurry to get memos out to the staff sections requiring them to give. Dempsey came over to say Mr A would sign a letter commending Haddock if I would write it, but I was amused to find, on consulting Col Kraft in Awards, that it would hinder rather than help his effort to get George the Legion of Merit, so I told him I would put it off until later next week—the theory seemed to be that if such a thing was on the record they would feel he didn't need the Legion.

Sunday 5 August 1945

. . . Down to the Pentagon in the morning to pass the memos around to the duty officers of the staff sections, which did not take too long and will probably produce little or nothing. . . .

Monday 6 August 1945

. . . About noon Bowman came up with the idea of Mr A's or Gen Marshall's or both that we ought to have a daily press briefing, shaped along the line of the briefing Gen Marshall got every morning. This was so clearly a bad idea, since the press would not want, and certainly wouldn't attend, any such thing, that I was moved to protest; though no one helped me but Lt Col Elliott of Air Forces Group; and Bowman, somewhat cowed by the brass, rode over us and said we must try it. The rest of the day went into a kind of frenzy. . . .

Tuesday 7 August 1945

. . . Late in the morning I managed to get to Bowman again and took the liberty of solemnly warning him that he would be holding the bag if they tried this press conference business and it didn't work. That impressed him, or seemed to, to that point that he fell in with it, and registered a protest to Norstad. In view of the stir over the atomic bomb yesterday[75] the press seemed unlikely to care much what they said anyway; but Norstad agreed to ask them. I got to see him with Major Smith, the moustached little fellow who would do the "briefing," late in the afternoon and the Gen, very jumpy and tapping his feet and shaking papers that he held in his hand, felt, to my relief, that he would not need a text for the whole business, and that he would ask the assembled people what they wanted. Knowing the answer to that, I relaxed a little. A hard day.

Wednesday 8 August 1945

. . . Gen Norstad, though putting his hand on my shoulder, found fault with all the wording (not after all mine) of the Spaatz directive; so we did that over a few times amid an indescribable confusion of detail. At the conference the Gen seemed more composed and did all right, while it was agreed that the briefing would be made part of Gen Kernan's exhibit at 10 downstairs. The strong rumors in the morning that Russia was coming into the Pacific war were confirmed in the afternoon, the air staff obviously regarding it with little enthusiasm.

Thursday 9 August 1945

. . . We began to stir about some stuff for a conference for Arnold next week and I attended Kernan's briefing where Smith did well in front of perhaps 25 correspondents, who however were there because the Secretary was supposed to be having a conference at 10.30. That was called off because he had to go to the White House, which seemed to confirm more rumors that the Japs were folding. Bowman had me in at noon to go over what he thought Mr A should say—in substance what he has been saying, but I did not feel the energy to do more than urge that he also define the status of the atomic bomb—in view of the absurd Jacobson release[76] yesterday and our denial today it seemed likely that it would not be clear. We had the usual run of alarms and complications and I would certainly not be sorry to see the war over.

Friday 10 August 1945

. . . The surrender rumors were very vigorous in the morning, and it did indeed seem that something was cooking but no special reason appeared for thinking it would cook fast. In any event the practical or personal truth seemed to be that the need for Mr A and others to shoot off the mouth would augment rather than otherwise and in our special position the chances of getting out soon might very well be worse rather than better. Though no one would be likely to admit it, you could even imagine that there was a good deal of semi-conscious dismay. Resigned to a long or even endless pull, it couldn't be possible for many people to be settled in their own minds about what they did next, or when or how, and it would indeed be in some ways easier just to go on rather than to face up to a crowd of decisions, none of which there was any sense in making or attempting to make until you had the concrete fact of when you would be out to go on. Off to go shopping with S and back at 3 where I was soon involved in the Empire State press release which George Bailey was screwing up and so had to stay through. There was no more news.

Saturday 11 August 1945

. . . We were hotly engaged with what Mr A would say at a press conference he thought he would hold Wednesday though it seemed a poor time for it considering how unsettled things were. It seemed assumed that Japan was on her last legs and certainly would not last out another week, which was generally regarded as all right but it was certainly viewed on the E ring in the Pentagon with little apparent interest—all minds seemed to be on immediate practical matters.

Sunday 12 August 1945

. . . Bowman had asked me to stand by and called me at 10 to come to the Pentagon where it seemed the conference was going to go ahead, so I spent most of the rest of the day there. . . .

Monday 13 August 1945

. . . We had a restless day over the conference which no one seemed to want to hold except presumably Mr A. I spent some time in the morning with charts on bases and B-29 and B-36 ranges in Gen Todd's office—he is a little bushy-browed red-faced kid who had not impressed me favorably—he seems to be Norstad's messenger boy.

We were waiting for Bowman and it took some time and he was in his remarks so pleasant and if not intelligent, sensible, that I couldn't help wondering if I wasn't developing a kind of habit of taking, on small evidence, a low view of everyone—certainly in my mind I had set him down as a snotty little bastard and he proved to be nothing of the kind. I ran myself ragged all day getting stuff together. . . .

Tuesday 14 August 1945

. . . Mr A's conference was finally called off, to our enormous relief, but since he was going to hold it sometime, we struggled on with the boring material—I was dictating a long stretch of it got from a pleasant Col Bunker in M&S to Johnny, when she remarked (and with how much reason), It seems awfully dull, doesn't it? (It was an outline of the AAF system for research and development.) The message from the Japanese government was duly announced at 7 in the evening, and there was some noise—not too convincing—of automobile horns outside, continuing falteringly for an hour or so; but looking from the windows at people around Parkfairfax, the celebration seemed muted.

Wednesday 15 August 1945

. . . Barber had in 25 or 30 congratulatory messages from the CG to various people to do over, and Bowman decided we might put Mr A on Friday, so it was a hard day. The Pentagon was about half empty, the civilian help all having a holiday, but Bowman kindly said in the afternoon that we could all have two days sooner or later. . . .

Thursday 16 August 1945

. . . The blitz was on early with Mr A's business and though Bowman generously said I could have anyone I needed to help and Moore made himself very useful there were many interruptions, waits, fusses about charts and changes of plans so that Moore and I and the two big Wacs who were doing the typing did not get to leave the office until 10 pm—which was all right with me, since I at least had it safely established for 10.30 tomorrow and so had good hopes of making the 1 pm to New York, but it was a hard day and somehow the war being over did make a difference—it was harder to be patient with the military.

Friday 17 August 1945

. . . We had the usual goings-on before the conference which indeed got off to a bad start when Gen Surles overruled the big map Sealfon's people had so painstakingly made, and we had to put a screen over the Atlantic bases at the last moment. Mr A turned up rosy, and it soon appeared cocky, to a good crowd, deciding not to use his text, and so bumbling along—mostly nonsense, and incidentally caused Bowman acute pain (he turned quite white) and me some embarrassment by failing to use his charts as planned. Bowman, summoned up to explain the area coverage of the planes, could not and was brushed off impatiently; I was invited to point out various transpacific routes a little later and soon stumbled, since the map was overlaid with shaded areas and not designed for the purpose, so he cried out promptly: Doesn't anybody here know any geography? Which I had to admit was merited; and anyway I felt better when Haddock, who had come up, told me that my calm appeared unshaken. . . .

Monday 20 August 1945

. . . Over to TAD in the morning and Gantz seemed to feel he might like to stay in the army and work in Washington so I snapped that up. Afterwards Col Waters went over the roster with me and we picked one or two more names. . . .

Tuesday 21 August 1945

. . .To Washington on the 8.30 and found my absence little regarded—I was stretching the VJ two days a little. I could not help feeling or hoping that quite soon a squawk from Congress would arise about the thousands of HQ officers sitting around on government pay and the chances might get better.

Wednesday 22 August 1945

. . . In to see Gen Norstad in the morning about a conference next week and I had a faint feeling that the end of the war did have its effect. I could not put my finger on it, but a certain authority seemed to have melted from him—he seemed a shade less positive than he became when he got his second star—though perhaps only because he was troubled about something else. At any rate, he seemed more anxious than I had ever heard him before to please and oblige his newspaper audience. In the afternoon, up to look at a technicolor film on Manila and the alleged Jap atrocities—some very bloody shots of dead and battered women and children along with the usual ham—and you could not help wondering if even they were not ham; that is, it is true that perhaps only the Japs would shoot or bayonet a few score, or even hundred, civilians out of spite, and the distinction is important; but the number of thousands of women and children burned to death by the atomic bomb at Nagasaki seemed to make the film's tone of high self-righteousness offensive. The distinction does exist—the bomb does it efficiently and effectively, on a nice impersonal basis, giving the killers no possible personal pleasure in the killing; but the fact remains that the Japs never in the whole course of the war killed as many women and children as we killed in a couple of minutes on that occasion, so it would seem better to reproach them for their barbarity on some other grounds.

Thursday 23 August 1945

. . . We had a busy time scurrying around about the details on the Interim Air Force for Norstad next week and getting through to Col Harris in the Air Inspector's office a request to investigate the fellow who impersonated a British Brigadier and got somebody . . . to fly him and a girl around in an AAF plane. My chances of getting out began to seem a little better when Bowman remarked that he hoped I would stay as long as I "could." The declarations of the past few days and Gen Anderson's remarks last night seemed to indicate that with my 42 years I would be hard to hold, so it occurred to me that I might tomorrow try setting a date. . . .

Friday 24 August 1945

. . . I talked to Col Bowman in the morning and he somewhat guardedly encouraged me in believing I might get out by November. At one of the usual useless staff meetings an hour or so later he appeared for a minute, to say that the critical category had been lifted from our MOSs [Military Occupational Specialty]. In fact, I am afraid his empire will soon disintegrate rapidly simply because the only people who would stay in it would be those with little or no aptitude for anything. That is, there might be men sufficiently able who had a hankering for the military life and so would choose to remain in the army—but nothing about his outfit could gratify that hankering, so he could only hope to get and keep men whose experience convinced them that they would not get far in civil life and would like to hang on to the security of the army pay roll. . . .

Saturday 25 August 1945

. . . I was moving around with animation on Norstad's stuff, taking with me in the morning the Sgt Gross whom I had hired Thursday by telling Miner yes I thought we could use him—it seemed to me he might be good for Chamberlin's report, and why refuse any assistance. He is a round-faced bright-eyed little fellow who had been on some fancy AAF project. In the afternoon to talk at length with Col Kritzer in Plans who said bluntly that strategically we could not justify the old man's 40 groups in the Pacific and that the air force was merely at the old army game of getting all it could when it could. I told him we must justify it, so he said he would give me the facts if I would add the poop, which I felt qualified to do. After that Cannon morosely told me that Norstad had changed his mind about something (from him you cannot tell what, his thought process being complicated and slow) and I could not use the Pacific material on the chart I was having Dahlstrom make. Norstad had gone to play golf so it was too late to find out, and I let it go. Meanwhile John Scott had called me to send up a lean dark shock-headed Texan named Singleton, a Capt who had been a navigator, and before that doing research at the University of Texas. He wanted to stay in the Army and seemed to have the qualifications for this nonsense, so I embraced him at least figuratively, put it up to Col Bowman; and Capt Park, who handles personnel, was busy processing him within fifteen minutes. I took then a brighter view, since I was not merely 42, not merely in a now-again-declared-surplus MOS, but I had found a replacement and could see myself pressing my claims to leave a little more strongly without self-reproach.

Monday 27 August 1945

. . . Our conference arrangements developed under some difficulties as the White House appeared to have been displeased by the Navy's announcement of intentions last week and Surles and his people were quite scared. We went ahead anyway, Norstad, who I managed to catch before 8 oclock, restless and slightly scowling—I begin to realize that this means not that he is mad at you but that he had troubles in the tight little world of air staff politics. . . . We had meanwhile added Gen Schneider (who went through the probably sincere form of balking a little) to our list—that was in addition to Gen Hall and Col Lessig, and I got Dahlstrom going on a chart. It was a hard day.

Tuesday 28 August 1945

. . . We had more trouble and many weary conferences with Plans people over the Norstad stuff. He himself, jerky and jittery with his feet on his desk, went over it at noon with us, and then changed it later. . . . The rest of it was very laborious too, but at least we had a paper back in which Bowman said Chamberlin and I could start trying to get out.

Wednesday 29 August 1945

. . . Norstad stood me up for some time in the morning—I think, the truth is, he finds me a little antipathetic, for reasons I am sure good, but not easy for me to guess. I thought this morning that one element might be that when he changed his mind, he did not like my saying yesir yesir yesir so readily when perhaps it was easy to judge that I did not in fact agree. At 1 oclock, he also stood everyone up—Schneider, Hall, Col Lessig, Bowman, Dahlstrom and me for a half an hour, so we were late in getting started, and things went none too well, as he pointed out that the elaborate charts Dahlstrom had made were full of wrong figures, making a reasonable newspaper man—if there are any—wonder why he was giving them to him. I knew the explanation—that they did not know themselves about the Interim Air Force, but it was clearly a poor excuse. We were all glad to have it over and I could only hope it indicated that my usefulness was about over, too—after all, if he will not take your advice or do what you tell him, why should you be there?

Thursday 30 August 1945

. . . Our chances of getting out seemed to be brightening and a Capt Sioris in Personnel even made it sound quite simple if the Col would just rate the 66-2 forms. We seemed to be getting Gantz and Singleton and John Wagner sooner or later and I found myself beginning to take it seriously, which was not unpleasant. The day went into unprofitable nonsense for Gen Eaker, the Air Force being exercised over Admiral Nimitz' claim that he won the war yesterday. . . .

Friday 31 August 1945

. . . The Col asked me to find out what I could about some trouble at Sioux Falls where personnel about to be demobilized had been held up many weeks, but the Air Inspector had nothing on it, and I was glad to find his interest diverted elsewhere, so I could get off at noon. . . .

Saturday 1 September 1945

. . . The Pentagon seemed somewhat idle and restive, due to the impending afternoon off, and I had little to do but rewrite Moore's part of the speech Bradshaw was doing for Mr A on the formalities supposed to be impending tonight. Meanwhile the corridor outside, which has on it, next to us, the bank, was jammed with mostly Negroes who proved to be busy cashing war bonds which they had no doubt been more or less forced into buying by the office pay-roll plans and certainly could not afford and now (especially with the 40 hour week reduction) had to, or wanted to, get their money back on. . . .

Tuesday 4 September 1945

. . . There was little to do, beyond getting up the forms of discharge papers, unfortunately still lacking Col Bowman's signature on the R&R. He is flying west with Major Moore this week and I thought when he came back something might be done, whether John Wagner had showed up or not. . . . Miss Johnson, incidentally, exposed so long to the sharp retorts and sometimes quite good wise cracks of her business environment, is obviously and rather engagingly developing a knack for the same style conversation herself and can quite often make a remark which she couldn't have made a year ago (and all to the good). . . .

Wednesday 5 September 1945

. . . I was busy in the morning writing up the stuff I got from Col Harris' Col Hogan on the Bogus British Brigadier. . . . In the afternoon we had a conference for the three Doolittle flyers back from the Jap prison camps—two captains (both made so out of hand by Eaker this morning) and a Sgt—Mrs Doolittle, a hardy well-groomed woman, was with them; and they photographed her with the Sgt's arm around her waist. Though very different physically, the three had a curious identical expression of daze around the eyes. However, what they had to say indicated that as always the "atrocity" stories were fantastically exaggerated and Capt Hite so far forgot himself as to say that the Jap doctor who gave him some injections for dysentery saved his life. One of the irksome features of life is that you cannot believe anything that you get through public channels of communication, and very little that you get otherwise, so many observers being so dumb they do not know what they see.

Friday 7 September 1945

. . . My scheme to drive north around noon was threatened early by Maj Miner, who had plainly blundered into something over his depth in regard to a conference Major De Seversky persuaded Miner Judge Patterson wanted held for him. He called me in and asked me if I would be kind enough to set it up for next Tuesday. It seemed to me so unlikely that I took the liberty of calling Barber, who bore me out—then, driven to a fine personal frenzy, since if this nonsense went on I might not get off, I put in to Miss Mundy, Judge Patterson's girl, who soon had me speaking to the Judge. He said no, that was not his idea—maybe when Seversky got back from the Pacific; so I was able (not understating it any, either) to return to Miner and tell him that I had just been talking to the Under Secretary, and it was all a mistake and all off. He looked impressed and agreed. . . .

Monday 10 September 1945

. . . It seemed that Miner had more trouble about Seversky soon after I left Friday—due to his own confusion or irresolution—and kept asking for me, so I was pretty clearly AWOL; but he did not mention the matter when I came in to see him about it this morning and was very friendly in his slightly fawning way, so I could not help wondering if he planned to take it up with the Col, but concluded he would not dare. I fussed with some details on universal military training, prodded by Moore's friend Harrell, a pleasant lanky fighter pilot of his age with a little moustache; and made some motions about a piece for the *Army & Navy Journal* for Lovett's signature. Capt Park developed the fact that Personnel had done nothing until today about re-applying for John Wagner, showing that you should never leave anything you want done to anyone else.

Tuesday 11 September 1945

. . . I was busy tracking down the UMT matter and finally ended with Gen (Fred)

Anderson who told me in a somewhat guarded way—he keeps his rather heavy pleasant face down a little, directing sudden somewhat upward glances at you—that in effect the AAF had gone about (quite rightly and sensibly) and did not want UMT. However, since Gen Marshall did want it for the foot army, and we wanted the unified War Department with co-equal branches which he was fighting the Navy for, the policy was to go along by not opposing it, but not to advocate it any more. In the afternoon I went in to talk to Lovett about his article and he seemed infinitely weary, rubbing his head, but was as usual very gentlemanly so we got it more or less set up. . . .

Wednesday 12 September 1945

. . . I was engaged with Col Kidner of the AJA's office and Col O'Keefe of CAF trying to clear up the Radovich case court-martial reversal and spent a lot of time not getting far. . . .[77]

Thursday 13 September 1945

. . . The Radovich case went on and I spent time talking to Gen Greenbaum in Patterson's office and Mr D'Olier of the Bombing Survey about Drew Pearson's piece on that in the morning. . . .[78]

Friday 14 September 1945

. . . Gen Hall had us up in the morning on an inquiry by the late Capt Colin Kelly's wife on the matter of his Jap battleship, which in retrospect seems most unlikely.[79] It also developed that the Capt, in the recount of surviving crew members, had lost his nerve or something and attempted to bail out of his plane damaged by Jap fighters ahead of his crew. In connection with some cables I had to recount all this to Gen Quesada in the afternoon; and I was impressed or amused when, at this detail, he snapped out of the chair in which he had been lolling and blurted out; Why the dirty son of a bitch!

Saturday 15 September 1945

. . . It was pleasant being off, but on the other hand I find it, for my temperament, not wholly a gain. It somehow seems to me easier, if you have to report for duty, to have to report all the time, 7 days a week. The more they leave you at liberty, the more difficult it seems to support being twitched back Monday. I suppose I never have really been able to believe that I wasn't reporting of my own free-will; and if I failed to, the MPs would pick me up and I would find myself in Leavenworth for a few years. It seems easier to accept the necessity when viewed as something which you have to do because you have agreed to do it; and so it is better to spend all your time at it, with the notion that thus you might get it all over sooner.

ADDRESS REPLY TO
COMMANDING GENERAL, ARMY AIR FORCES
WASHINGTON 25, D. C.

ATTENTION:

HEADQUARTERS, ARMY AIR FORCES
WASHINGTON

11 September 1945

MEMORANDUM FOR THE CHIEF, OFFICE OF INFORMATION SERVICES

Subject: AAF Policy on Universal Military Training

1. <u>Slight Snafu in A-1</u>. Major Harrell, of Col. Thetus C. Odom's
A-1 Policy Planning Division, showed me, on 10 September, an informal
memorandum which he had got up advocating Universal Military Training
by several ingenious indirect means. He was reduced to this activity
because Col. Odom had been instructed that the lid was on UMT. Col.
Odom was not told why, and assumed that it was War Department policy.
Major Harrell was concerned about the matter, feeling rightly that the
whole UMT project was already gravely threatened by the usual post war
reaction; and that, if we wanted UMT, now was surely no time to let it
ride. I told him that I would try to find out informally what the
latest quirk of policy was. The circumstance that the Policy Planning
Division should not have been told seems extraordinary.

2. <u>War Department Policy</u>. In conversations with General Textor,
and Major General Ray Porter, I learned that Col. Odom was mistaken in
supposing that the War Department, or specifically WDSS, SPD, was
imposing any lid on discussion or advocacy of UMT. I checked with Gen.
Davison, who confirmed this, and said that he felt that all possible
steps should be taken to present the AAF case for UMT to the public,
though, probably, care should be used not to give Congress the impression
that the Army was trying to lay down the law. As it developed subsequently, Gen. Davison was in error. By another somewhat extraordinary
lapse in coordination, he had not been told what the definitive AAF
policy was.

3. <u>General Anderson's Statement</u>. In a conversation with Maj. Gen.
Fred Anderson this morning, I learned that the explanation (never given
to Col. Odom's office) for the "lid" was the Air Staff decision that
UMT was not in the best interests of the Air Force. General Anderson told
me that, of course, the Foot Army needed it to survive at all; and since
Gen. Marshall was for it, the AAF could not oppose it. On the other
hand, nothing should be done in the way of arguing for it or advocating
it. That this is the correct view, that UMT could not be of real
advantage to an air force, and indeed, was almost certain to be a real
and definite disadvantage due to the inevitable disinclination of
Congress, after it had appropriated a billion and a half dollars a
year to make America "secure" through UMT, to go on appropriating
further very large sums which would be absolutely necessary to maintain an effective air force, can hardly be doubted. In its very

nature, an effective air force must be composed of volunteers. To maintain it, both officer and enlisted personnel must have long, thorough, and expensive technical training. In General Anderson's clearly-sound view, an Air Force career must be made attractive to volunteers. He has directed A-1 to initiate a study, particularly with a view to the means of providing such a career for enlisted men.

4. <u>Agenda for Consideration</u>. This study will be based on the assumption that the AAF will be co-equal with the Army and Navy under a single Department of War. In the preparation of the study, the following are some of the more important items to which consideration will be given:

    a. An air college for enlisted men as well as officers.
    b. Continued surveys and questionnaires which will keep the AAF Commander in touch with the thinking of enlisted men.
    c. Provision for gradual transition from enlisted technicians to officer technicians, if a suitable plan can be devised.
    d. Such a system of education and training "that will make it possible for a rookie private to develop into an Air Force Commander."
    e. Improvement of military classification and duty assignment system.
    f. Increase of pay scales.
    g. Revision of present ranks and specialist titles and possible abandonment of term "enlisted men".
    h. Revision of T/O&E and manning tables to insure top ranks in all specialties.
(Of course, these are not necessarily changes recommended, but simply things to be considered and discussed. It seems plain, however, that most of them would have to be adopted in one form or another if skilled technicians are to be induced to volunteer. The Air Force will not get the men in peacetime unless it is able to offer pay and opportunities comparable to what a young man could expect in civilian life.

5. <u>Conclusions</u>.
    a. While not opposing UMT in any way, the AAF will do nothing to advocate it, and will be pleased to have the project fail.
    b. The necessity for making an air force career attractive to young men is clearly grasped, and will be implemented in every possible way under a single Department of War, with co-equal Army-Navy-Air Force branches.

J. G. COZZENS
Major, Air Corps

ADDRESS REPLY TO
COMMANDING GENERAL, ARMY AIR FORCES
WASHINGTON 25, D. C.

ATTENTION:

HEADQUARTERS, ARMY AIR FORCES
WASHINGTON

13 September 1945

MEMORANDUM FOR THE CHIEF, OFFICE OF INFORMATION SERVICES

Subject: Status of the Radovich Case

1. <u>Reversal of Radovich's Court Martial</u>. On 1 September
the Board of Review reversed the Mitchel Field court martial which
found Major Walter V. Radovich guilty of accepting $7,000 to keep
two enlisted men from being sent overseas. The court martial
sentence was dishonorable discharge and three years' imprisonment.
The action of the Review Board was reported under such headlines
as (NY Times) "Army Clears Radovich". In fact, the Board held
that the <u>record</u> of the trial was "legally insufficient to support
the findings and the sentence because the lay member of the court
erroneously refused to admit evidence." The undoubted result is
that the public now has the entirely wrong impression that Major
Radovich's trial was unfair and that, in line with popular con-
ceptions of army justice, somebody was trying to pin something on
him.

2. <u>Basis of the Review Board's Action</u>. Col. Kidner, Acting
the Air Judge Advocate, called me on 11 September and told me that
he had a long conversation with Col. O'Keefe, CAF Air Judge Advocate.
The action of the Board resulted from an error on the part of the
Trial Judge Advocate, whose intelligence and knowledge of military
law seem both to have been very limited. The defense entered a
plea to the jurisdiction on the grounds that the appointing authority,
Gen. Hunter, had taken so active a part in the case, that he was,
in effect, the accuser. The TJA most improperly refused to hear
evidence on this plea. The Board of Review was therefor obliged
to reverse the court on the technicality. There was no question
about the "sufficiency" of the evidence showing that Radovich had
accepted the bribe as charged; but this was not made plain in the
ill-considered WD release of 1 September.

3. <u>Present Situation</u>. Both the Air Judge Advocate and Col.
O'Keefe are recommending that a new hearing be ordered. The only
authority competent to order it is the CG/AAF, as CG of the Continental
Air Force. In a conversation with me on 12 September Col. O'Keefe,
asking me to hold his statements in confidence and use them only

for the information of the Chief, OIS, gave me some further
points. Mr. Samuel T. Ansell, counsel for the defense, has made
extremely astute use of the special knowledge of military law which
he got in his army service as Judge Advocate General. His object,
which he has barely missed obtaining, appeared to be to keep an
eye on the statute of limitations (AW 39) and try to delay the
case until it would have to be ruled out. That would be the status
of the case now, and Radovich would go free, if the Board had
taken the usual action in reversing the court martial - that is,
declaring it null and void and ordering a new court martial.
Instead it was found possible to evade AW 39 by simply not making
the null and void declaration. This is a pretty fast one, but
probably necessary ██
Through this technicality, a new hearing can be ordered, although
the 2 year period of AW 39 has actually expired.

4. Conclusions. The high degree of suspicion with which the
public regards court martial procedure and Army justice in general
has not been helped any by the confusing and poorly worded JD
release of 1 September. The most satisfactory course from the PR
standpoint now would be the ordering of a re-hearing by the CG,
and the formal conviction of Major Radovich which must unquestionably
result. This would clear up the misapprehension about the
"insufficiency of evidence". There are two possible objections
to this course and there is some reason to suppose that both will
be made to the CG. First, Mr. Ansell, ████████████████████████████
████████████████, would welcome the opportunity to get himself some
more publicity and free advertising; second, the action of the
Board of Review, while perfectly legal, might be represented by
those interested in embarrassing or discrediting the Army as a
deliberate evasion of the spirit and intent of AW 39. However,
since there is no possible doubt about Major Radovich's guilt, the
importance of establishing it probably ought to outweigh those
objections.

J. G. COZZENS
Major, Air Corps

ADDRESS REPLY TO
"COMMANDING GENERAL, ARMY AIR FORCES
WASHINGTON 25, D. C.

ATTENTION:

$Jw 13$

HEADQUARTERS, ARMY AIR FORCES
WASHINGTON

14 September 1945

MEMORANDUM FOR THE CHIEF, OFFICE OF INFORMATION SERVICES

Subject: Captain Colin Kelly

1. **Mrs. Fedlow's Representations.** Mrs. Fedlow, the former Mrs. Colin Kelly, in a telephone conversation with Gen. Hall 8 September, expressed her concern over the War Department's failure so far to establish the "facts" about her late husband's alleged exploit in sinking the Jap battleship Haruna, 8 December 1941. She had seen in the papers a report that in spite of the Navy's more recent accounting for the Haruna, the hulk of a battleship of that class had been observed about where Kelly was supposed to have bombed it. She had also seen another report that a Jap who had been a crew member on this ship was in our hands as a POW and confirmed the sinking. She pointed out to Gen. Hall that she had never received the Medal of Honor she had understood was to be awarded to Capt. Kelly posthumously. She described some remarkable goings-on on the part of a PRO at Long Beach who retained a package of Capt. Kelly's personal effects for a long time because he said he wanted to give the newspaper he formerly worked for a break on pictures.

2. **General Hall's Memorandum.** Gen. Hall discussed the matter with Mr. Lovett, who "directed that we move in on this affair and get it straightened out in as sensible, dignified, and speedy a manner as possible." Gen. Hall therefore directed Lt. Col. Dunham, Personal Affairs Branch, and Col. Kraft, Awards, to get together what material they could on Capt. Kelly and his 8 September mission. He also directed OIS to be prepared to issue a release when this material has been collected and checked. Major Mitchell turned this directive over to me.

3. **14 September Conference.** Col. Kraft, Lt. Col. Dunham, Major Rider of his office, and myself met in Gen. Hall's office this morning. Col. Kraft presented the file on the Medal of Honor award, which showed that the Secretary of War had answered a congressional recommendation in 1942 by quoting a letter from General MacArthur which stated that the award of the Medal of Honor was not warranted. Capt. Kelly received the DSC instead. The popular misapprehension about it seemed due to a highly colored story first put out by Lowell Thomas and then taken up by the late President and included in a fireside chat. In both versions many of the facts now seem to have been erroneous.

4. _Facts about Capt. Kelly's Mission._ Lt. Col. Dunham had
got together the testimony of surviving members of Capt. Kelly's
crew (a Major Dean, then Kelly's navigator and 3 enlisted men).
They made no claim of sinking anything. They dropped three
bombs on a Jap warship which they thought was a battleship, scoring
two near misses and one hit. The plane carried only three bombs.
The ship was observed to be "smoking and weaving" - probably
attempting evasive action. When nearly back to their base, they
were jumped by 6 zeros, two of whom hit them effectively, killing
one crew member, smashing the instrument panels, and causing one
engine to break into flames. Some understandable confusion followed.
According to the survivors, who however have agreed among themselves
never to mention it publically, Capt. Kelly left his co-pilot at
the controls and attempted to bail out himself before any of the
others went. He was unable to because his parachute pack caught in
the escape hatch and his dead body was found in the crashed plane.
Three crew members and Dean, the navigator, succeeded in getting
clear.

Conclusions. After some discussion, Gen. Hall directed me to have
cables prepared ordering A-2 FEAF to check on the points about the
alleged hulk and the alleged Jap PC. A cable was drafted by Lt.
Col. Cranford, Interrogation, AC/AS-2 and is now waiting on Gen.
Hall's coordination. The General seemed to feel that if this
evidence was forthcoming we would be in a position to give out a
release. For the information of the Chief, OIS, I asked the
General what we would do if no evidence to confirm a sunk battleship appeared. He said that we would be in one hell of a mess.

                                        J. G. COZZENS
                                        Major, Air Corps

Monday 17 September 1945

. . . Everything was quiet and I did what I could to get at Lovett's *Journal* piece, which bored me so intensely that I made little progress. His contention, to support which I had got M&S to give me material through an earnest Major Betts, was that we must have stand-by plants and stock-piled tools for another emergency. Perhaps being an easy victim of the paper reports, I could not see what good they would be with the atomic bomb, so I found it hard to put the case for them, though not impossible, since I seem ready and able to write, with a reasonably attentive eye to the probabilities, whatever I have to write to get myself clear of the obligation. Tom Prideaux came in, very thin but brown, just back. He was at Hiroshima a week ago, and said, speaking of atomic bombs, that it was indeed swept quite clean. He found the Japanese landscape enchanting (presumably with that exception).

Tuesday 18 September 1945

. . . Col Bowman was in early and I had a talk with him—poor wretch—about how I felt I had largely outlived my usefulness. I could see that he had qualities (he is sure to need them in his rash enterprise here) of great patience and fortitude. In the course of almost 3/4 hour of talk while the office gradually opened up, he said it was indeed his business and intention to get me out, described in warm terms the virtues and values of my memoranda (which, of course, he is right about) and got me involved in a discussion of personnel problems of the post-war air force so that when the telephone really began to ring we were able to part, he saying, Thanks very much, with no actual commitments on his part—though I believe that he can and will do what he can for me. I was busy at once on the conference to be held Thursday if Gens Giles, LeMay, and O'Donnell get their 29s in non-stop from Tokyo, or rather northern Hokkaido to Washington tomorrow. It seemed to me they were overplaying it a little, but Mr A wanted it. In the midst of it Rex Smith came in with his new Bronze Star ribbon, bound out himself soon, though he means to have one more trip around the world at the Army's expense. I found myself unexpectedly engaged in persiflage with him, at which Bowman came out and found us, and contributed in the same vein the not unwelcome crack that he was afraid he was going to have to fire me in a few more weeks. As we had word that John Wagner would be in 7 October I could hope that perhaps he would.

Wednesday 19 September 1945

. . . We fussed with the B-29 business tomorrow, which, it seemed to me somewhat injudiciously, they let out to the papers today; and that was eventually borne out by some increasing difficulties with head-winds, making it plain that they were not going to get to Washington non-stop after all. I had meanwhile written

ADDRESS REPLY TO
COMMANDING GENERAL, ARMY AIR FORCES
WASHINGTON 25, D. C.

ATTENTION:

HEADQUARTERS, ARMY AIR FORCES
WASHINGTON

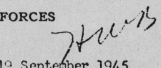

19 September 1945

MEMORANDUM FOR THE CHIEF, OFFICE OF INFORMATION SERVICES

Subject: Misuse of Rescue Boats, ███████████
█████████████.

1. Air Inspector's Investigation. At the direction of the
Adjutant General of the Army, upon the recommendation of the
Inspector General, the Air Inspector ordered Lt. Col. Fred L.
Green and 1st Lt. Arthur C. Eisele (formerly a marine engineer)
"to determine the cause of the unsatisfactory condition of the
P-95, a 104 ft. AAF Rescue Boat, upon the return of this vessel
from the ████████████, 11 April 1945." The P-95, which
cost about a quarter of a million dollars, is now worth as a hulk
about $20,000, Lt. Eisele estimated. This investigation is not
yet completed; but in collecting or attempting to collect the
material he needed, Col. Green came on much evidence in the form
of sworn allegations about the flagrant misuse of the rescue boats
█████████████████████████████. Col. Green's attention
was first attracted to the overall state of the ███████ by
difficulties thrown in his way when he attempted to get the
Mechanical Division records on the P-95. Lt. Gen. ███████████
rejected the formal written request to the Governor ███████████
█, contending, through his Adjutant, Col. ███████, that the
██████████ organization was not under the control of the War
Department (It is, in fact, directly under the Secretary of War,
technically speaking). However, Col. Green "was able to convince
him by a personal interview that the records pertaining to the
P-95 were the only ones he was concerned about." Gen. ██████ then
had those, but no others, made available. The allegations to Col.
Green seem to offer a plausible explanation for Gen. ██████'s
reluctance in the matter.

2. Specific Instances of Misuse.
    a. Gen. ██████'s "Private Yacht". According to the sworn
statement of Major ████████████████, an AUS officer in charge of
the 12th's boats at the time, Gen. ██████ had the P-22, a 72 ft. AAF
rescue boat fitted up for his private use at a cost somewhere between 88 thousand and 225 thousand dollars. These costs were
charged to the Y-37, an Army Tanker, which happened to be in the
Mechanical Division for a major overhaul. Lt. Eisele, who had an
opportunity to see the P-22, noted some of the modifications: a

flying bridge had been added; all gray paint had been scraped
from the superstructure and the natural mahogany varnished;
unfinished bronze fittings were polished to a high lustre and
other iron fittings replaced by polished bronze; "a glance inside
revealed an extremely luxurious interior of bright varnished
mahogany paneling and deep leather cushioned furniture, which
greatly contrasted with a standard AAF 72-foot rescue boat."

b. Gen. ███████'s boat. Major General ████████████ "had
the Q-57, an AAF 60 foot rescue boat converted for his personal
use. Likewise the J-231, and AAF 30 ft. rescue boat was reserved
solely for Gen. ██████'s use. These two boats were assigned to
████████ Field for operation and maintenance. There was one
occasion when a P-38 crashed...Gene ██████'s boats were the only
ones immediately available...Col. Thomas, the Base Commander, sent
these two boats to the rescue. As a result, these boats were
transferred from Col. Thomas's jurisdiction to the Quartermaster
of the Sixth Air Service Command."

c. Gen. ██████████'s Swell Job. Brigadier General ████████
████████ converted for his private use the P-130, a 42-ft. AAF
rescue boat. "One item of expense mentioned was chromium plating
of door knobs, hinges, fittings, etc." The work was done by the
Panama Air Depot at Government Expense. Gen. ██████ got the boat
when Gen. ████████ was transferred ██████████████████.
Incidentally, the Air Inspector has a photostat of an interoffice
slip in which Gen. ████████ directed that the boat should be iced
up and the stove in working order for a fishing party to leave the
████ Dock at exactly 7 o'clock. The Gen. also noted some things
he did not like about previous trips; viz; "that some of the crew
members asked some guests if it would be all right if they had a
glass of beer...that in no single instance has the crew of any
fishing boat brought their lunch with them. He desires that
lunches be furnished the crew tomorrow, and he wishes the crew
to be briefed that they will not ask guests for food or beer."

d. Col. ██████'s boat. Col. ████████████ (since deceased)
had the P-188, an 83-ft. rescue boat, assigned for his personal use.
"It was alleged that this vessel was rebuilt, the dispensary
removed, and a stateroom and bar installed in lieu thereof."

e. Gen. ██████. Brigadier General ████████████ was alleged
to have had a 60 ft. Q rescue boat for his private use but he did
not have it modified. In connection with Col. Green's investigation,
Gen. ██████ said to him that "he was surprised that Washington would
send an investigator for so small a matter as the P-95, when there
were many irregularities of much greater consequence."

3. Conclusions.

a. There seems to be no doubt at all that the goings-on around ████████████ smelled to heaven. There is sworn testimony that Gen. ████ spent over $200,000 in fitting up his "Swoose" an early model B-17; that Gen. ████ converted a C-47 on a similar scale; that the ████ Air Depot was constantly employed in making furniture and gadgets for Generals ████, ████, and ████. Gross misuse of staff cars ("going on dates to visits to houses of prostitution, or use of the car in lieu of"), extraordinary court-martial irregularities, and a general break-down of morale are also alleged. (Civilian employees of the Air Depot went on "strike" and cancelled their war bonds).

b. The Air Inspector is sending the file to the Adjutant General for whatever action he deems necessary, with the note: "Although many of these irregularities affect the AAF and AAF personnel, Hq AAF does not have direct responsibility in these matters, nor jurisdiction over the command involved."

J. G. COZZENS
Major, Air Corps

some bombastic stuff for Mr A, which was plainly going to need revision; but by 7 pm nothing seemed certain, so I left it. . . .

Thursday 20 September 1945

. . . We had a really frenzied time with the conference which had to be moved down to the Ordnance conference room at 1D444. Here eventually Gens Giles, LeMay, and O'Donnell turned up, followed by Mr A who rambled a lot before leaving, again neglecting his text and the map Dahlstrom had prepared. However, before he came, Gen LeMay instructed me in command procedure by suddenly turning on me as I showed them their seats and more or less backing me against the wall, snarling out that this was another PR mess (which it was) and what was he supposed to say and why hadn't he been briefed? I did not know, and said I was sorry; in fact, it was not well managed and since he saw it and guessed I knew it, I could see that the brow-beating was probably an old and useful device with him— make me or someone do better next time. I judged that he probably reserved it for moments when he really did have a complaint. After that things went better than planned, LeMay contenting himself with gazing morosely at Miss Johnson's legs and exploding some good newspaper opinions that the Japs would have been licked in time maybe without the atomic bomb.

Friday 21 September 1945

. . . In the morning I went up to Col Odom's office for a conference on what they thought they could do to incite enlisted men to enlist. Col Odom is a West Pointer of pleasant manner and slow thought, so it was long; but I had what I could see really might become the satisfaction of finally prevailing, even though the point was so obvious you could not see why there should be a struggle or argument; viz, should we or should we not put out a piece of paper promising people things which we would like to give them but did not know we could? Out for a couple of hours to go shopping with S, and back to see Col Gann in the Air Surgeon's office over whether or not there had been a great swiping of morphine syrettes from first aid kits. They said not; but Col Reynolds, the Air Provost Marshal, told me on the phone that there certainly had been. . . . About Chennault, I forgot to note that yesterday afternoon Gen Schneider sent me out to see a Col Hare just back from China . . . and largely confirmed, though he said he could not prove, the grosser Chennault rumors. I reported the matter verbally to Bowman, and we agreed that the best thing to do at the moment was undoubtedly nothing.

Monday 24 September 1945

. . . I finally got myself down to Mr Lovett's piece[80] and managed to bring it over to Miss O'Day in the afternoon. Shortly after lunch Gerald Carter called me. He had a sad, very literate letter from Martin who had just been washed out at Tuskeegee in Basic; and much evidence—prizes in war bonds he had received and his papers for primary and to appoint him a cadet officer—seeming to show he had done all right up till then. His own story was that he had been brushed off, which I thought was probably true, what with our pilot surplus, and our even narrower need for Negro pilots. However, I took the stuff to Dempsey, who had his disgruntled expression and his feet on the desk, and his plans to get out soon. In a curious indirect way I could not help feeling that that played some part—pleasing me might do him in civilian life some good (how wrong of him) and could never do him any harm (quite right)—so after some drawing and filling, he dictated a hot R&R to Training saying that Gen Arnold wanted all the facts on the thing by telephone not later than tomorrow and a complete file by next week. It will not help Martin, but might hold Gerald; and, I suppose, gratified Dempsey and me with a sense of power.

Tuesday 25 September 1945

. . . Gerald kept calling to hear the news, but I missed much of it, being over at Gravelly Point to see Col Kraft about Haddock's Legion of Merit, which I found I had screwed up fine, in that as of 19 Sept Kraft became able to give them himself, while the bounce-back from the AGO made it necessary to put in there again if we did. After lunch Gerald got me and showed up, though I sent Johnny down to give him his papers, not being equal to it. . . . Major Reed of Personal Affairs had meanwhile come over on the Colin Kelly matter, and I finally got him to call Capt Bean, Kelly's navigator at McDill Field in Florida. Bean said that no such thing as the alleged bad conduct on Kelly's part ever took place. . . . so I trotted around to correct the story for Gen Hall and Gen Quesada.

Wednesday 26 September 1945

. . . I spent a long time in the morning with a Lt Col Welter in Gen Schneider's office on the AAF separation plans which were well screwed up, in that nobody around Hq told anybody else what was planned or ordered, a symptom, I suppose of the general disintegration, few of the AUS [Army of the United States] people who did most of the work being interested any longer in anything but getting out—it would certainly be true of me. I have the greatest difficulty in keeping my attention on this nonsense.

Thursday 27 September 1945

. . . Gen Quesada had me over in the morning to ask some more questions about Kelly—he was as agreeable as possible, taking me by surprise by his desire to shake my hand and I am sure I was doing him wrong in my private feelings of pleasure—something about his handsome high color, and apparently overflowing gleefulness, taken with the designation AC/AS Intelligence makes you think, or try to. . . .

Monday 1 October 1945

. . . Little was going on, though Gerald had been calling me and I picked up the file on Martin from Dempsey's office. It seemed to show that Martin had been washed out for sufficient cause, or at least his flying progress report seemed to show a detailed lack of aptitude. When Gerald called again I did what I could to show him this was no disgrace. . . .

Tuesday 2 October 1945

. . . there was no special work, though I went up and had a long talk with Gen Schneider on AAF contracts with the idea of giving Bowman a summary of some possible hot spots he might look for after (I hoped) I was long gone. In the afternoon Gerald called me again, having been upset by a letter from 4 of Martin's classmates saying he had a raw deal. I did what I could with that, disconcerted somewhat by Gerald's bursting not merely into tears, but into disturbing vaguely animal-like howls of pain and sorrow in recognition of what you could see was, however fatuous, a terrible disappointment. He recovered himself and said he was sorry and I said whatever I could think of.

Wednesday 3 October 1945

. . . We had little to do. Col Bowman came in to say he was flying to New York with Moore to report to Mitchel Field hospital where they were apparently to determine his physical fitness for service—he has been showing more and more these uncontrollable skakings of his head and hands, apparently not associated with any mental jitters, and the Air Surgeon was clearly concerned about him. This gave us pause, as getting out was more or less a gentleman's agreement with him, and if they did not let him come back, what? . . .

Monday 8 October 1945

. . . Maj Reed called to say that Gen Witsell had answered a Florida congressman out of turn on the Colin Kelly matter, so I did a lot of telephoning about that. . . .

Tuesday 9 October 1945

. . . I spent much of the day on the telephone with a variety of buck generals over a fresh flare-up on the Mitchel Field discharge racket and Major Fabbricatore who had got his complaints to the papers over some five months in custody with no trial. I talked to Gen Schneider and Gen Greenbaum and Gen McIntyre and Col Wilber and Col O'Keefe and Col Hogan and got nowhere.

Wednesday 10 October 1945

. . . I went up to talk to Lt Col Martin in the AI's office about AAF contracts which seemed on the whole in better shape than we supposed. Moore flew up to NY to pick up Col Bowman who was apparently going on many weeks sick leave so we set to work on our papers hoping he might sign them tomorrow. . . .

Thursday 11 October 1945

. . . Col Bowman did not get in but there was a hard day's work in writing and rewriting the papers and trying to shake loose Capt Singleton, whom AC/AS 3 was difficult about. I finally brought it to Gen Hood whom I had not seen for many weeks. He is much less mousey as Eaker's one deputy, but I could judge that he was making the same mistakes in judgment, only with more assurance. . . .

Friday 12 October 1945

. . . Bowman came in briefly at 11, looking better, and told Wilkins to sign my papers, which he did; so I could, though somewhat incredulously, see myself perhaps getting out a week from Monday. They were having a conference for Kenney and some of the Pacific generals; but I painstakingly took no part in it, anxious to show my non-essentiality. . . .

Monday 15 October 1945

. . . I went over to Gravelly Point to see Capt Sioris in Unit Personnel and found to my surprise that things were fairly uncomplicated. They seemed to think Wilkins' paper was good and I soon found myself fixed up for Andrews Field Thursday; and the Air Adjutant General, as promised, gave me my orders before the afternoon was over, so I could begin to believe that this was really it. Gantz came in late in the afternoon, so everything seemed to be going all right. To dinner with George Bradshaw—who is, I could not help reflecting, the only person around here I would especially miss—and maybe Miss Johnson, for an agreeable youthfulness, and what are probably considerable qualities of character, or of essential simplicity and niceness in striking some balance between being everyone's pet and yet never taking the least advantage of it—always equally ready to be teased or kidded or to buckle right down and work as hard as necessary.

Tuesday 16 October 1945

. . . I passed much of the time taking Gantz around to introduce him to personages on the Air Staff, and was somewhat taken aback, though certainly not displeased, by the many kind expressions about my leaving. I began to feel that really we must have been all buddies. . . .

Wednesday 17 October 1945

. . . I took Gantz around some more and in to have luncheon with George Haddock and Bradshaw and out to cancel my Parkfairfax lease. I did not find that doing these things for the last time was as sad as I read everything done for the last time is.

Thursday 18 October 1945

. . . Out to Andrews Field early, as was suggested, but found I had merely to wait on the steps of the Separations shed until 8. The Lt inside said then it could not be done in one day; but I recollected my earlier experiences in the training command field, which the lay-out at Andrews made me think of, and went to see the Lt Col commanding, telling him I had a job to do with Gen Norstad tomorrow (take Gantz to see him) and so. He immediately telephoned everyone and after much hanging around in line over the physical examination—an affair which, while long, was so perfunctory there was little or no sense in it—a medical major went around the 22 nude discharges with a stethoscope, transferring it from beneath one left pap to another as fast as he could move; and then again, poking for hernia, and requesting those who were not circumcised to pull the foreskin back—and so I did get out. . . .
To supper with George Bradshaw at his place where he cooked quite a good chicken. I know he is the only one met in my military career that I would ever care to see again, and so was easily persuaded that he felt the same way. . . .

Friday 19 October 1945

. . . I went down to the Pentagon infinitely relieved to be clear of it, thinking I would take Gantz to see Norstad, as I said yesterday; but Norstad was busy, and anyway, Gantz did not show up until I was leaving at 11 to see about the movers. Bradshaw brought in a somewhat expensive bauble we had joined in getting prepared for Johnny, and she seemed affected by the receipt of it, asking me also for a letter of recommendation, which I made a good one. It seemed clear that she quietly planned to seek work among the arts. . . .

Saturday 20 October 1945

. . . We got off about 10, when the junk dealer came in to take the rest of the stuff, and drove by the New Castle ferry to Pennington. A little less had been done on the house than I hoped, but the country looked wonderful. . . .

APPENDIX

Speeches and Public Statements
Drafted by James Gould Cozzens

Statement for General Arnold on the Wright Brothers
(see 15 November 1943)

The really great moments in the story of human endeavor are almost all lost in the past. Nobody knows who first learned to make and use fire, who invented the wheel, or who reduced spoken sounds to writing. It seems fantastic when we realize that one such moment occurred—not back beyond recollection somewhere in the haze of history—but only yesterday, a mere forty years ago when, by means of the Wright Brothers' bicycle shop contraption, man first flew.

All momentous inventions, because they enormously extend human capabilities, have in them potential harm and potential good. Today we see the harm. Our enemies turned the airplane to uses of attack and destruction and tried to teach us its terrible powers. We have been obliged to read the lesson back to them. We hope and believe that when we have finished they will never forget it.

When that day comes, and the world is free to turn to the good we will see great things. We know already what the airplane can do to shrink the world and bring nations together. We look forward to a resulting community of interest and growth of mutual understanding when men of good will make ever increasing use of the great gift of flight. Only then can we justly evaluate it, or understand how much we owe to the intelligence and skill, the courage and determination of the Wright Brothers, the men in our generation who conquered the air and in that act remade the whole shape of human affairs and gave us a new world.

(Cozzens Papers, Princeton University Library)

Christmas Message for General Arnold
(see 15 November 1943)

Last year at Christmas we began to see light after the long darkness of the war's early months. Thanks to your enormous efforts as individuals and as a united body, I felt that we could expect with assurance a new year that would be a bright year and a proud year. I think we in the air force have found it so. The hopes we held were abundantly realized, the confidence we felt proved to be well-founded.

This Christmas we have all that to be thankful for and our hopes for the future are very high. In the consciousness of hard jobs well done, I think every man and woman in the air force will have at heart a merry Christmas even in surroundings that must be strange and sad.

Christmas eve, and Christmas day some of you may find yourselves engaged in deadly combat. Many of you will be suffering hardships and dangers in situations unlike any you ever imagined. Very few of you will be able to spend Christmas as we would all wish to spend it. That must wait for those Christmases to come when we have finished the job.

With these thoughts in my mind I send my Christmas greeting to every one of you, wherever you are. Your courage and endurance, your devotion and your labor have carried us strong and safe, one year nearer victory.

May God bless and keep you all.

(Cozzens Papers, Princeton University Library)

Speech for General Arnold, Los Angeles Coliseum (see 30 December 1943)

We are getting a lot of good news these days. I have just given the Secretary of War a report covering the work of the Army Air Forces during two years of war. It was the plain record of how the men of the Army Air Forces had done a tough, nearly impossible job. We built the biggest air force in the world. I think it is the best air force in the world, and any of our enemies who are honest with themselves have probably come to about the same conclusion. I don't have to tell you that without the work done in the great plants of this Los Angeles area it wouldn't have been possible.

I'm proud of you and you should be proud of yourselves. But having said that, I also want to say here and now, that *we* haven't done enough, and *you* haven't done enough. If we make any mistake about that, all our recent good news is really bad news—bad for me, bad for you, and worse than bad—deathly, fatal for our sons overseas.

This is because the tempo of a successful war is progressive. We have to do all we can and then immediately double it. The enemy can stand the kind of blows that we gave him last year even though they were heavy and though they hurt him. What he cannot stand and what we can and must give him are those redoubled blows. It was right there that the Germans failed against England. It is sometimes suggested that bombing won't work because the brave and resolute English took all the Germans could give them and still were not beaten. Mark that. All the Germans *could* give them. I don't believe any people—German, English, American, Japanese—I don't care who—will be able to take what we plan to give them. It isn't just a matter of courage or endurance. You can't fight a war with sticks or stones or your bare hands. What we mean to do is hit their war industry so hard, so often, and on such a scale that sticks and stones will be about all they can get in the way of military equipment.

I say this is what we plan. I have been looking at a list of the War Department contracts being filled here in Southern California. It takes three closely typed pages. Those of you who actually make airplanes can see where *you* come in, all right. A few more planes—or even one more plane in some cases—may make a real difference in the outcome of a mission.

It is a little harder, if you spend all day making turnbuckles or valves or rheostats. I can only tell you that we have got to have them, as many as you can make, as fast as you can make them. That is your part and I know you are going to do it.

The other part, the part of the fighting men in our air forces, fills the newspapers. You may believe what they tell you about our missions. We do not follow the German and Japanese custom of reporting imaginary victories or scaling down our losses to what we wish they were. I know you realize that as we go on these losses will continue. You will hear about them fully. Most of our bombers come back safe from their missions, but when ten, twenty, thirty, do not come back I think we all can feel something of the desolation laid on a hundred homes. It is the price we pay, and we are going to have to keep on paying it every day the war lasts. You can do something about that. You make enough of the stuff, and the Air Forces will deliver it to the right address and that will be the end of the war. We have the men to do it.

I want to tell you now about one heavy bombardment crew. I am not naming names, because the point is that we have thousands of men who would do the same, or more—whatever they must do to do their duty.

This was a heavy bomber returning from a mission. They'd got out of the target area all right but on the way home they ran into flak and enemy fighters. They took a rocket shell and then a hit from a 20 mm. cannon in the cockpit. They got some more in the bomb bay, the rudder, and the No. 1 engine. The cockpit was bad. The pilot had been hit in the face, leg, and neck but he managed to motion to the co-pilot to take over. The co-pilot did. He simply asked the navigator to see if he could do anything about the pilot. There wasn't much to do. The navigator looked at the co-pilot then. The co-pilot had been hit in the right arm, the right side, the leg and knees. But he was still flying the ship. The bombardier and the engineer came up and they got the pilot out of his seat and into the nose. He died there. The navigator went back then to the pilot's seat. He had held the controls a few times, and before he went into the army he had had a few hours in a puddlejumper back home—not much of a preparation for taking over a crippled B-17. He did what he could and the co-pilot, when he was conscious, tried to help him. The gunners fought off the attacking fighters until they quit. They kept flying. They found their base. The co-pilot could not speak, but he could make signs—shake or nod his head, try to help yank the stick back. I don't know how they did it. I would say it was impossible. They put that plane down on the runway all in one piece—unless you count a hundred and thirty odd holes.

That's all there was to it. There are more spectacular stories. Our men have done almost incredibly heroic things. But that homeward bound, fearfully damaged plane with the navigator who had the nerve to try, with the badly wounded co-pilot slumped beside him, and the pilot lying dead in the nose, sticks in my mind. I hope it will stick in yours. Those are the kind of men who are fighting for you in the Army Air Forces. I think you are the kind of people who will see that they never lack anything your utmost effort can give them to bring them home safe and soon.

(Cozzens Papers, Princeton University Library)

Letter to President Roosevelt
(see 5 January 1944)

The President,
The White House.

Dear Mr. President:

During our recent journey to Cairo and Teheran I described to you the work being done by a Committee of Historians then engaged at Army Air Force Headquarters in a study of the German war potential. It was a project in which I was much interested, and which I thought would also interest you.

Our idea was to turn over, under suitable conditions of security, the secret and confidential intelligence files on the subject to a group of eminent American historians. Their special training in evaluating scientifically the raw materials of history seemed to promise a type of report that would be very valuable to us, whether it conflicted with, or confirmed intelligence findings prepared in the usual way. It would allow us to bring to bear on the important job of understanding the enemy's situation the best American brains, whether civil or military. This work has been completed and I am sending you the report.

The committee was asked also to draw up, from the historian's standpoint, a study of possible parallels between 1918 and 1944. Their highly interesting conclusions are appended. I was, of course, pleased to see that in their view our essential thesis of air power is sound, and that the conclusions tend to confirm our intelligence findings. I concur with the committee's opinion that successful invasion must involve the destruction of most of the German air force, and that when the Army Air Force and Royal Air Force bombing missions can no longer be strongly opposed the end of the war will come quickly.

Respectfully yours,

H. H. Arnold,
General, U. S. Army,
Commanding General, Army Air Forces.

Incl.
Report

(Cozzens Papers, Princeton University Library)

Speech for General Arnold, National Geographic Society (see 15 January 1944)

The War in the Air

The real mission of the Army Air Forces in this war can be stated very simply. We fly airplanes to selected important enemy targets and drop on these targets a sufficient weight of explosives to destroy them. We do this because we know that if we make even a percentage of these targets useless to the enemy we will seriously impair the production and servicing facilities of his military organization. This makes him less and less able to stand up to our attacks. In the end he must go down under them.

Much everyday argument and popular difference of opinion among both amateur and professional disputants arises from the initial failure to make clear points on which all agree, as well as points on which all do not agree. No one denies that explosives explode. No one denies that a heavy enough explosion in the right place will obliterate any human construction. The question is, how to get that explosion to the right place.

In the Army Air Forces we advocate flying it there. Under some conditions there is plainly no other possible way of doing it. The choice is between bombing the enemy from the air or leaving him undisturbed. We don't deny the difficulties of bombing him fully and effectively. We do say that on the basis of past experiment and experience we have great confidence in our ability to deliver explosives by air and to hurt the enemy mortally that way.

This confidence of ours does not rest entirely on the showings of our own reconnaissance and intelligence. The enemy eloquently supports our belief that we are hurting him by the frenzy of his attempts to stop us. Of course, his version of what we are doing and ours often conflict. We don't argue with him. Who is right, who is telling the truth and who isn't, will come out in the histories written after the war. We only say now that he does not act as though our missions were the failures, to him harmless, to us ruinously expensive, that he describes. Men who flew with the great mission of January eleventh and saw the fantastic array of aircraft that tried to keep us off the vital targets of Oschersleben, Halberstadt and Brunswick believe the enemy must have been desperate. He put up everything, good, bad or indifferent, that could fly. He guessed what we were out to do. We have this evidence that he believed, as we did, that if we did it, literally hundreds of the fighter planes he showed he needed badly right then—and which he was certainly going to need worse later—would never reach his flying fields. This was the job he could not keep us from doing on January eleventh.

That is what we mean when we say that our losses were not excessive. That is the sense in which we mean that we can afford them. That is why we say, in light of accumulating experience, that our strategy of air power has proved sound. We think it works out in action as efficiently and economically as anything connected with the great wastage of war can. Of the men as individuals, of the men who died in our lost bombers, we say this: they went to do with skill and courage what must be done. We remember them feelingly and with pride. We hold them in lasting honor. They gave all they had; and that is what our country may require at any time of any one of us.

This evening I have with me five Army Air Forces films which are being shown to the public for the first time. In them you will see what this air war is like. You will see planes shot down and planes crashing and the camera will show you unsparingly the ruin and destruction brought about by air attack. All these things are real and true, not the arrangements and effects of peace time moving pictures. They will tell you better than any words of mine that this is a tough war, a grim war, a war to our enemies' death or ours.

However, I'm not showing them to you because I imagine you haven't grasped such elemental truths. I never put much stock in the notion that the American people are so unrealistic that they think the war is about over. I don't think they need to be scared into sense, any more than I think they need doses of optimistic pap to keep their hearts up. I think both their sense and their hearts are all right, and that all they want to know is the facts, and from the facts they can tell without help from anyone what the score really is.

These films are full of facts, the plain fact of the thing actually happening before your eyes. You will see us devastating the Japanese air bases in the South Pacific, you will see us over Germany, you will see us cleaning up North Africa, and reducing Pantelleria—the actual action of our missions.

Before you look at these pictures I think it would help you to understand the always fast and often furious action, the skies dotted with bomber formations, the bursting flak, the attacking fighters, the falling planes, if I were to show you how we plan and conduct such missions and where each bit of quick or [confusing] action fits into the simple and logical general plan of action.

To illustrate, I have prepared several plans showing the various stages of action in the course of the mission of October 14th when we hit the ball bearing plants at Schweinfurt, deep in Germany.

I. A brief summary of the purpose of the mission, its importance, the composition of the attacking forces, the losses on both sides, and an estimate of the results.

II. Six of the more important diagrams presented one after another, with an explanation of the meaning of the markings, analyzing the developments in terms of football tactics, or other simple analogies.

(ALTERNATE)

What you will see only indirectly, and by implication in the overseas setting and the foreign countryside, is an equally important fact about this war. That is the vast influence of geography on its conduct and progress. When you watch our planes take off from the landing strips in New Guinea or Africa or England it may seem so much a matter of course that you do not ask yourselves how they got there, or for that matter, how the landing strips got there. The literally titanic job the Air Forces had to do before they could even begin their real mission of delivering explosives the members and friends of the National Geographic Society can appreciate better than anyone else. In places that few or none of you have ever seen outside the pages of the National Geographic Magazine we have set up bases big enough to handle the whole fleets of planes that make up a modern air force. We have them equipped and operating in the deserts and the ice fields, in almost uncharted mountains, and on islands that once went years without seeing a ship. . . . .

(Cozzens Papers, Princeton University Library)

Appendix

Draft of Foreword to *25 Missions*
(see 7 February 1944)

You are about to watch the Eighth Bomber Command fly a deep penetration daylight mission into Germany. You will see most of it from a special vantage point—over the shoulders of the men in the Memphis Belle, making their twenty-fifth trip.

It was a momentous day, because this was to be the Memphis Belle's last trip. She had a distinguished record and a crack crew. She had been picked to go home to show the Training Command posts and the Operational Training Units what team work was and what a crew should be.

In other theaters, under other conditions, many bombers and many crews have completed more missions, but never tougher or more nerve-wracking ones. The Memphis Belle and her crew started in the early days when we hadn't the swarms of bombers we have now. Often we hadn't enough fighters to escort them at all. We never had enough to escort them properly. It was rugged.

It is still rugged. Those of you who have been there know. Those of you who haven't been there can look and learn. This is a tough war, and it is going to take all we've got, and the best we've got, to bring that day when every bomber and every crew can head home in triumph.

(Cozzens Papers, Princeton University Library)

Second Anniversary of the Army Air Forces
(see 7 March 1944)

Two years ago the Army Air Forces organization was set up in its present form and I think we have a good deal to celebrate on this anniversary. Two years ago our situation was pretty grim. It is still pretty grim, make no mistake about that; but it is a situation that the enemy find about ten times as grim as we do and to date the Army Air Forces have had a foremost part in making it look that way to him.

I don't have to tell you that this shift in —shall we say—emphasis, from what he was

374

doing to us to what we are doing to him was no easy job. Having to fight at the same time that we were building up the means to fight kept us pretty busy. That is why I haven't until now even met many of you who have been working long, faithfully, and well, right up stairs, or down the next corridor, from my office. That is why most of you haven't even known by sight the men who run those air forces and commands whose work and problems you handle every day.

We have many of those men here now and I want you to meet them and look them over. I think you'll be proud of them, as I'm proud of them; and as I'm proud of you. In days to come, when we have the job finished, I think all of us will look back on these days as good days in our lives, days when we did the biggest job in the world, and did it all right, and did it together.

(Cozzens Papers, Princeton University Library)

Draft of Proposed Remarks for Delivery by General Arnold, at *Memphis Belle* Premiere (see 21 March 1944)

You are about to see, over the shoulders of the crew of one of our heavy bombers, what the air war in Europe is like for the people fighting it. The men and their actions will speak for themselves; but before you look at the actual scenes of this new kind of warfare I would like to tell you something about its plan and purpose. The crew of the Memphis Belle is one of thousands of crews; the flight you will watch is one of thousands of flights. Taken altogether, the picture they make up is so enormous and complex that it is not always easy to grasp the part of the individual crew or the single flight in the general plan. This plan is simply to destroy Germany's ability to make war.

The Memphis Belle and the thousands of other heavy bombers are instruments for putting this plan into effect. Each mission is a step toward its accomplishment. It is a big job and we must do it in a big way. The missions we send out are not to be confused with what used to be called air raids. A raid was a hit-and-run affair peculiar to the early days of air warfare. With the planes and equipment then in use the only practicable technique was quick—really, sneak—blows with the hope of a few lucky hits. We don't do it that way any more. A great mission of today is a planned battle. We try to take the enemy by surprise, to go by a route he doesn't expect, to feint him out of position, and if possible to make him uncover the point where we mean to slug him. This is simply a matter of tactics. The strategic point is that we have pre-determined objectives and enemy action has never yet been able to force us to turn back without hitting our objective. We go where we have reason to believe we can do the most, at any given moment, to carry out our general plan, and we are prepared to fight our way there.

In the film you will see what this means. Of course, not every plane on every mission is going to have quite such a rugged time. On the other hand, there are planes on almost every mission making a one way trip. We have been getting great results from what is, statistically, a very economical expenditure of lives and equipment; but we don't get them free. The price of victory is what it always was, the lives of brave men. The men in the planes that don't come back are the ones who buy it for us and the ones who pay for it.

You will understand, then, that our missions are by no means merely 'preliminaries' to invasion. They *are* invasion. No one who has ever watched one of these great expeditions start against Germany will doubt it. The imagination can hardly grasp that skyful of planes, twenty miles across the front, a hundred miles deep; formation after formation of our heavy bombers, under the swarming cover of our fighter escort. We are invading, and not at some remote beach head. We are hitting the enemy where he lives. He knows that if he cannot stop us he is licked.

Here is the crux of our air strategy, and here we have been able to face the enemy squarely with a desperate dilemma. The only way he can fight back against these air attacks is by putting up strong forces of fighter planes. He has no fighter planes to spare. He knows that when we come ashore in the west he is going to need those planes desperately. Oughtn't he to save them?

He can't save them. Our bombing missions are headed right for the real source of all his air power, the plane factories, the ball-bearing plants, the vital installations. Without those he will be driven from the air in a week. He must put his fighters up and try to exchange them for enough of our bombers to cushion, though he cannot avert, the stunning blow. He is now in the fix that he had the Royal Air Force in during the Battle of Britain, but with a difference deadly to him. The German Air Force then had this same opportunity, but they were not ready for it. Hitler missed the boat because his bombers were too small, too few, and, being unarmored and almost unarmed, too nearly helpless when attacked. We have not repeated his mistakes.

Here surely is one of the great ironies of history. The men who planned this war, the men who thought themselves masters of the air, who believed in air power and were going to show the world how to use it, find that the wheel is come full circle. They thought right; but it is on them, on their airdromes, their factories and their cities that the proof is falling and will continue to fall until they can fight no longer. This is the meaning of the mission of the Memphis Belle. This is the meaning of the air war we are waging in every theater.

(Cozzens Papers, Princeton University Library)

Draft of speech for: Brigadier General T. D. White,
AC/AS, Intelligence
(see 26 March 1944)

Gentlemen:

Now that you have successfully completed the Air Forces staff course, I feel sure that you all know what staff work is, and what a staff officer is expected to be and to do. You have, of course, mastered the principles of the employment of air forces in general, the structure and function of strategic air forces, and the organization and composition of tactical air forces. There is, you may have noticed, some discussion in the newspapers and elsewhere about the command and employment of air power; but you have that straight, and can quickly set right anyone who hasn't got it straight.

Naturally you know all about radar, and flight communications, navigational equipment, bombs and bombing techniques. The procedures of air intelligence—a field in which I take a good deal of interest—are perfectly clear to you. You understand how to plan air operations, and how to conduct all necessary briefing, interrogation and reporting. AAF medical problems and equipment have been described to you, and I daresay in a pinch you could help out the Air Surgeon. If you are assigned to a fighter group headquarters, the instruction you have received in tactics and technique should enable you to advise the CO, if he seems at a loss, on the proper use of fighter planes as escort and cover, in interception, on sweeps, and in the sometimes intricate night fighter problems, both with airborne radar equipment and in conjunction with searchlights. The AAAIS Board and the AAA Operations Room are an old story to you, and if help should be needed in setting them up, I am sure you will be invaluable.

You will have no trouble in elucidating the principle, and when necessary correcting the practice, of air-ground cooperation, and we can count on you to resolve any difficulties in connection with Troop Carrier Aviation.

Maybe some of you feel that you are still less than experts on one or two of these subjects. It wouldn't surprise me if your feeling were correct; yet I believe—indeed, I know—that you are going to be good staff officers. We have taught you what we could in the time available. We have tried to make staff duties clear to you, at least in outline. We have tried to cram a great deal into a short course—not with the notion that you would know everything when we finished—but in the belief that you will at least know how much there is to know. If you have grasped this, you are well-equipped to understand the vital function you are going to perform and the heavy responsibility it lays on you.

The real job of a staff is getting complete, accurate and fast information to the Commanding Officer, so he can draw conclusions and come to sound military decisions.

Whatever your specific job, your duty boils down to this. In your field you are the Commanding Officer's eyes and ears. You are expected to see and hear everything that HE would see or hear if he could split himself into twenty people and be at twenty points simultaneously. He must be sure that you have not, through inattention, overlooked anything, or through ignorance failed to recognize anything, or through plain dumbness reported the wrong things. In short, he must rely on your informed alertness, the high quality and quickness of your intelligence, and—perhaps most of all—on your fundamental good judgment and good sense.

This is why I say that I know you are going to be good staff officers. You are the pick of a pretty special crop. Men who lacked the right qualities and abilities were screened out of the applicants for the Leavenworth course. These graduates were screened again, and you who were accepted for the AAF Staff Course satisfied our experts that we could use you in higher staff jobs.

If you are worried about whether or not you really have the abilities that you know by now are going to be required of you—stop worrying! We did that worrying for you, and you wouldn't be here this morning if we didn't know you could do it. What you have been taught is important; but much more important is your demonstrated capacity to learn. You can and you will catch on fast.

I think you will catch on fast, not only in the sense of grasping your duties and learning to do them right when you reach the posts to which you will be assigned, but in the sense of understanding that vital function I spoke of, and accepting fully that heavy responsibility. Among you are men of various backgrounds—some of you have had combat experience, some are on flying status, some are regular Army officers, and some had no military background but simply in civilian life showed qualities and abilities that we badly needed.

Those of you who have been in action, and those of you who are flyers are especially likely to have a feeling that your new jobs represent a kind of come-down. You are going to have to spend a lot more time at a desk, and I think there is an instinct in every man which keeps telling him that desk-sitting is a hell of a way to fight a war. You are going to have a lot of paper work, and we all know about paper work—make seventeen copies of everything; arrange these lists alphabetically and burn them. Of course, somebody has to do it; we often just wonder why we have to be the ones.

In your case, the answer to that is easy. You have to be the ones because a staff must have the best men in point of intelligence and ability that the Army Air Forces can supply. We conducted a careful search for such men, and—here you are. You're elected.

The qualities that made you eligible for the certificates we are about to award are the qualities that fit you for the staff job you will shortly fill. These jobs probably won't be exciting, or glamorous, or ever likely to put you in the public eye. You will work like a dog, and you will have heavy and wearing responsibilities. When you make a mistake you'll hear about it fast enough; when you do well the chances are it will be just taken for granted and nobody will thank you.

What you will have, however, is the satisfaction in the simple knowledge that you are doing your best, where your particular best is vital. When we have won this war and they ask you what you did, you may not have as much material for shooting the breeze as some; but, inside, as long as you live, I think that fine and proud sense of good service gladly and intelligently given will be yours. I don't know what more a man could want.

(Cozzens Papers, Princeton University Library)

General Arnold's Appeal for Blood Donors
(see 6 April 1944)

In wars of the past the state of the wounded was generally desperate. This war is different. Today a wounded man is almost sure to recover if we can get medical help to him in time.

Many new techniques and treatments contribute to the remarkable record, but certainly the one thing that must have chief credit for saving thousands of lives is blood plasma.

Ways have been found to prepare plasma in a powdered form that keeps indefinitely and can be made ready for instant use, regardless of blood type, by simply adding distilled water. In the Army Air Forces we see that this powdered plasma gets where it is needed, and that everyone knows how to use it. It has even been administered to wounded crew members on our bombers in flight, and men who would have died on the way home did not die.

The only source of plasma is blood. Whether or not our wounded get enough of it depends on how many of us give blood. The quick and painless process is simple. Because it is simple we sometimes forget that it is vital. If we put off, or neglect to make, our donation we may be literally exposing some soldier to death. Let us remember that the need continues and increases. Let us, each of us, make sure that no wounded man anywhere will be denied his chance of life.

(Cozzens Papers, Princeton University Library)

Draft
Speech by: Major General L. S. Kuter
To: American Society of Newspaper Editors
(see 18 April 1944)

I have just returned from a trip. It took forty-six days and covered thirty-eight thousand miles. I went at General Arnold's direction to acquaint some of our commands with the views and plans of the Air Staff. This gave me a very good chance to see what our Army Air Forces are actually doing.

Yesterday you heard from General Arnold about the great operations over Europe. I would like to tell you a little about what I have just seen in the Southwest Pacific and the Far East. My trip took me into India and Ceylon, to Chunking and the advance bases in China, to Australia and New Guinea and many of the Pacific Islands. What especially impressed me, and I feel sure, would impress anyone who could see it, was, first, the progress we are making in cleaning up the Pacific, and second, the remarkable work of General Chennault's forces in China. The situation on these two air fronts is different in every respect but one. What they show in common is consistent and decisive defeat of Japan in the air.

The accomplishment of General Kenney's Southwest Pacific forces can, I think, fairly be called phenomenal. If you think back to our first landing on Guadalcanal, and the slow and desperate struggle to seize and hold it, you will recall talk about what was called "island-hopping." Much of the public, and many newspaper writers seemed to feel (with understandable concern) that if we were going to Tokyo an island at a time we might join the Japs in planning, as they say they do, on a hundred years war.

Of course this was not our idea at all, and we don't plan on a hundred years war. Furthermore, if the Japs really do figure that way they are quite wrong. Except perhaps for home consumption, I don't think they really do. What has happened in the last year is as obvious to them as it is to us. They are quite intelligent enough to recognize the tactical pattern in General Kenney's clean-up program.

Like all good tactics, those of our South Pacific war in the air are simple. We establish what might be called an air line of battle. Its location is determined by our bases and the enemy's bases. A year ago this line of battle might be considered half way between our base at Port Moresby and the Japanese bases on the north shore of New Guinea. The truth was, it was a little closer to Port Moresby, because we hadn't the numerical strength to match them. It was simply a slug fest. If we hit them, they could hit us right back—and did. We then had nothing in our favor but the quality of our planes and pilots. We were entirely engaged in stopping the Japanese air offensive.

As soon as we had the strength, our first step was to advance an air line of battle. It meant seizing or making untenable the Japanese bases. We did this, mostly by air, across the mountains. The signal instance was the operation by which the Markham Valley was seized. Here we set up our new base, and began to strike the more distant points to which the Japanese had been obliged to withdraw. General Kenney neutralized the advance Japanese fighter strips. With the enemy fighters grounded and destroyed, the attacks were then directed at cutting off supplies and wrecking ground defenses. In this way we could push out new bases of our own, and advance our line of battle again.

Perhaps this sounds like another tedious, step-by-step clean-up. I don't think the Japanese regard it that way. I was at our great Markham Valley base three weeks ago. From it we had just pulverized the enemy forces that had been desperately got together at Hollandia. For this kind of war is cumulative. We have the Japs off balance; they can no longer trade blows with us, and so while they hurt us less and less, we hurt them more and more. In two days at Hollandia we ended their chance of a comeback in New Guinea. We destroyed over two hundred of their planes on the ground or in the air. We lost one P-38.

In attacks perfectly coordinated with the navy this same general plan has been followed in the archipelagos north and east. The point is that the Japs may hold any number of islands, but, in this modern war, islands have no value except as they serve as bases for air or naval forces. Our giant four or five hundred mile strides, taking us over and past them, make them useless to Japan. Our planes have swept them clean of Japanese air power. The Japanese navy now knows that any attempt under the shadow of our air fleets to supply these bases means throwing away whatever number of ships or planes they chose to venture. In short, we are cleaning up the Pacific and we are cleaning it up by thousands of square miles at a crack.

Now, in case this picture, while arousing just pride in your fighters and flyers, encourages you to any degree of complacency, or gives you the feeling that the war is as good as over, I would like you to look at the situation in China. That is the crucial point, for we are not going to win this war by merely recovering, no matter how swiftly or brilliantly, the outposts Japan overran in the Pacific. We are going to have to hit Japan at home as we are now hitting Germany at home, and that means Chinese bases.

In China the situation somewhat resembles that in New Guinea back before we were strong enough to take the offensive. We are short on air power in China, and though we enjoy there the same superiority, pilot for pilot and plane for plane, that we have always had, and hence can deal the Japanese repeated telling blows, our operations add up to little more than an efficient and aggressively conducted holding action. We cannot now practise our South Pacific tactics in China because of the difficulties of supply.

As you know, every gallon of gas, every ton of bombs, and round of ammunition, used by General Chennault has to be flown in over the so-called Hump, the very difficult and dangerous mountains. We are putting through a road as fast as we can. Even that won't be adequate for large scale supply, but the desperate effort the Japanese are now making to reach a point where they can interrupt the line in India, shows well enough the importance to them of keeping the Fourteenth Air Force on short rations.

I saw the operational bases in China where these supplies are so badly needed if we are to advance our air battle line and extend our action. A revealing comment on that was General Chennault's rejoinder when he was notified that our party—two general officers, six colonels, and a Navy captain—was coming in. His answering message ran: SEND GENERALS ALONG. WOULD SWAP COLONELS FOR WEIGHT IN GAS. WHATS A SAILOR GOING TO DO HERE?

We had, I'm glad to say, a big plane, so we were able to use our own gas in and out, and leave him a thousand precious gallons as a sort of house present.

As the case often is when outfits are short handed and undersupplied, and every man knows he must do a little more than he possibly can with a little less than he has to have, the morale of the Fourteenth is very high. Their quarters are bamboo huts; there are no officers clubs or Coca Cola machines. Except for coffee and a small square of butter for breakfast, they are living off the land so that no vital cargo space will be used for fancy chow. The life is Spartan, but in the course of four months this short-handed, undersupplied force destroyed well over 200,000 tons of Japan's dwindling supply of shipping off the China coast. It is heartening to see so much accomplished with so little, but don't let's imagine that we have done more than make a beginning on a very big and very tough job.

This is, of course, where you come in. We have made our plans, and events have proved them good. The shifts on the map of the Pacific show you how they work. You have seen many such changes during the past months and you will see more. The effect of these operations is cumulative. They will pay off increasingly; but they must be pressed and pushed by a fighting spirit no less stern and stubborn here at home than on the advance air strips of the Orient.

The Japanese have no hope left but that you will tire. I do not think you will. Our men can do the fighting and flying to clear the Pacific and win the struggle to pour in those supplies that General Chennault now waits on. What they want from you is the firm backing of your determination. Give them that, and you may be sure the great day is coming soon when our air line of battle will move in thunder relentlessly across the Chinese provinces, across the Yellow Sea and the Sea of Japan, and fix itself in consuming flame squarely over our enemies' home islands. There is the Japs' last ditch, and there we will finish them.

(Cozzens Papers, Princeton University Library)

Draft of Script for: General H. H. Arnold,
Fourth Anniversary, RAAF Participation in
Empire Air Training Scheme
(see 25 April 1944)

As Commanding General of the United States Army Air Forces it is a pleasure and an honor to greet our fellow flyers and fighters of the Royal Australian Air Force on the important occasion of the Fourth Anniversary of their participation in the Empire Air Training Scheme.

At the beginning of the war the Royal Australian Air Force had about three hundred officers and three thousand men. They were faced with the same tremendous problem that faced us in this country. The courage and resolution with which they solved it deserves and has our highest admiration. They met their high quota in the scheme fully and unfailingly. I know the people of Australia will just as fully and unfailingly support them in the work that remains.

The work already done has forged a strong bond between the Royal Australian Air Force and the United States Army Air Forces. Australian Air Crews turned out by the Empire Air Training Scheme have flown thousands of sorties with the Royal Air Force in our great joint operation to break German air power in Europe.

With our Fifth Air Force under General Kenney in the South Pacific, Australian units have taken a first part in bringing about great successes against the Japanese. We will not soon forget their achievements in the Bismarck Sea Battle and at Milne Bay. Often our flyers and theirs worked so closely together that it is hard to differentiate figures or establish just who did what. I can only say that what we and they did, we did as one, united in resolution, united in action.

May we continue so to fight and fly together. May the Royal Australian Air Force, with the vital support of the Empire Air Training Scheme, go from strength to strength; while, as we surely will, we go together from victory to victory.

(Cozzens Papers, Princeton University Library)

Remarks For: General H. H. Arnold,
Conference of Commissions for Inter-American Development,
Waldorf Astoria Hotel, New York, N.Y.
(see 3 May 1944)

I am glad to be here tonight with the members of the Inter-American Development Commissions. I am glad of the chance to look with you to the future. Those of us who have heavy responsibilities for the day to day operation of our vast war effort often find ourselves with little time for anything but the present. We must concentrate on one thought; we must drive toward one goal—quick and complete military victory over enemies whose terrible threat to us was that we would have no future except as slave units in a world organized for exploitation. They would take care of what plans and developments there were. We wouldn't have to bother.

Well, that isn't the way it's going to be. It is safe to guess that, in both Germany and Japan, postwar planners and those who look ahead are glum about the prospects. During the last few months the Army Air Forces, in hearty cooperation with the Royal Air Force, have done much to make the present an overmastering preoccupation with the Germans. So far this year, more than a hundred German cities have felt our bombs. We have plastered 48 aircraft factories, many of them repeatedly, as the enemy has tried to rebuild. In April we knocked down 1,140 German fighters and destroyed 177 more on the ground. The U. S. Army Air Forces that one month flew 66,000 sorties over Hitler's Europe, and dropped 57,000 tons of bombs—more than in the whole year of 1943. We are continuing this treatment; and the Japanese, for their part, may rest assured that it is only a matter of time before we apply it to them.

Because we are able now to deal blows like these, we can confidently say that the postwar world in this hemisphere is not going to be our enemies' world. Plans and developments will be up to us. It is a job for all the Americas, and now is none too soon to start it. The presence here of so many able men seriously engaged in practical and realistic consideration of ways and means for the intelligent development of our resources and the continued valuable cooperation between the American Republics is most reassuring. None of us knows when the war will end; but by such means as this conference, we can at least take care that the end does not, like the beginning, find us far from ready.

The job is big, and much certainly remains to do, yet I think we may properly congratulate ourselves on what has already been done. An important—and we will agree, I am sure—very good and fortunate, result of our common effort to win the war is a great strengthening of the good relationship between republics of the Western Hemisphere. War has shown us how interdependent we are. Common interest binds us in a cooperative alliance. In short, we do not have to ask what sort of post-war relationship would mutually benefit us. We know already. All we have to do is find the practical means to continue and extend this relationship.

That "all" is, of course, plenty. The end of the war will bring grave economic problems. I think none of them is insoluble. We have proved, and are proving daily, that our economies can support and complement each other. We have joined in what is certainly the greatest cooperative enterprise the world has ever seen—the winning of this war. It is sometimes suggested that winning the peace may be harder. I take it that those who say so mean just this—that we will fall out; that the hard-learned lessons of mutual dependence and effective cooperation will be forgotten; that our interests will necessarily conflict; and that we will have neither the good sense nor the good will to harmonize them.

I don't believe it, and I see no reason why any thoughtful person should believe it. Speaking for myself—and yet also as an American, reasonably well aware of American thought and sentiment—I think the lesson will stick. As a member of the Joint Chiefs of Staff I can say that, without the cooperation of the other Americas our position, once grave enough, would have been, frankly, desperate. I know that without it we could not now be standing where we do stand—everywhere on the offensive, everywhere in full command of the initiative, everywhere sure sooner or later to be victorious. This isn't the sort of thing you forget. For reasons of military security, I can not mention many specific contributions that made great and successful operations possible, but I would like to remind you of some important general measures taken by the American nations together.

Without stint or hesitation, the republics of Central and South America joined in the defense of the Western Hemisphere by giving us key bases to cover the approaches of the Panama canal. Colombia was vigilant in watching against the possibility of enemy air fields in the vast savannah country. Venezuela greatly eased our problems with her petroleum products which supplied us with aviation fuel along our southern route. We have also important refining facilities in Peru. Ecuador placed at our disposal the vital Galapagos Islands. Immediately on breaking relations with our enemies, Chile organized patrols and convoys and arranged air protection for her nitrate fields and copper mines. Uruguay has done us great service as headquarters for the Committee for Political Defense of the Western Hemisphere. Brazil, Mexico, Cuba and the Caribbean nations were quick to offer naval and air forces for the campaign that cleared American waters of the submarine wolf packs.

Brazil's contribution, which includes forces even now preparing to join us in the assault on Europe, was still more important. I cannot imagine how we could have flown equipment to General Chennault, or bombers and transports with personnel and supplies for far flung battle fronts, or as a specific instance, the ammunition that enabled General Montgomery in 1943 to turn the tide of the war in the African desert, without Brazilian bases.

Appendix

I have stressed the aviation factors of our common effort because it is plain that aviation will continue to play a greater and greater part in the economy of the post-war Americas. Air transport will affect almost every project by which this conference may seek to continue and advance our economic cooperation.

The mountains of Central America, for example, and the Andes of the southern continent, can be crossed by air in a matter of hours, bringing together cities and peoples otherwise days or even weeks apart. With great modern planes like the C-54 and the Constellation we can now fly from the United States to any point in the other Americas in two days. When facilities for night flying are available we will be able to do it in one day. Experience gained during the war will, moreover, work directly to bring about the widest possible use of aviation. Techniques that we learned in flying over the "hump" to China can be adapted for the greater safety of pilots and planes crossing the Andes. Our extensive experiments with jungle flying and glider landings will certainly stand post-war aviation in good stead in the tropical regions of this hemisphere. You can easily see what the aviation of tomorrow must mean to Inter-American unity and development.

Because you are practical and realistic men, you see too, I feel sure, a point sometimes glossed over in predictions of this kind about progress in mutual understanding as the airplane diminishes distances and draws the world closer together. Air transport does, and to a greater and greater degree will continue to do, exactly that; but air transport is certainly not going to unify the world by itself. The fact that those of us who are geographically most distant from each other can be brought by air to meet face to face within a day isn't going to end human differences. As a matter of fact, meeting face to face is sometimes a pretty good way to start a quarrel.

What we are going to have to do is meet in the same spirit that we meet now—the spirit that has carried us thus far through a desperate war together, and must carry us to victory. Who, looking around here tonight, can doubt that we have that spirit? I think we can always work together for a postwar world, just and prosperous, strong and happy.

(Cozzens Papers, Princeton University Library)

Remarks for Major General Henry C. Pratt,
Lake Charles Refinery Dedication,
Lake Charles, La.
(see 24 May 1944)

All of us here must feel great pride and pleasure in seeing the Lake Charles refinery ready to go. For me, there is a special satisfaction in it. My air force service dates back a long time. When I was with the Materiel Command at Wright Field after the last war, we worked and worried a lot, seeing what we could do with better fuels for the old Liberty engines. New fuels not only made possible amazing improvements in performance; they actually made possible new engines, which in turn made possible modern flying and today's planes. To anyone who remembers the early days, a plant like this is something to see. We know exactly what it means in terms of making our planes fly faster, go farther, and hit harder.

This faster flying, harder hitting air force, created in this country since the war started, is the mightiest in the world. Building the thousands of planes and training the hundreds of thousands of men was a gigantic job and every American can be proud of it. In bitter fighting on fronts around the world the merit of our planes and the valor of our flyers have proved to be all we hoped for, all we knew they would be, and more. This is a good place and time to remember that what they do depends on what you do. On you rests the heavy responsibility.

This is true of all war jobs, but in many of them it isn't easy to see the direct connection between the work in front of you and the battle half way around the world. Here it is easy. Nothing could be plainer or more direct. All of you, laborers, steam fitters, welders, operators, chemists, engineers can see where you come in. Without fuel, not a plane is going to leave the ground—no gas, no go. Anyone who has a hand anywhere here in making sure that, without hitch or let-up, we get every day every drop of the hundred octane gasoline that this plant was built to give us, is not merely backing the attack. He is, literally, powering it.

This full effort is what the Army Air Forces, the men who are flying and fighting, expect of you; and I know you expect no less of yourselves. I say it with confidence, for it seems to me that this enormous plant has a meaning even more important than the vitally needed thousands of barrels of fuel it will add to our supply. This is the first of the new plants, new from the ground up, embodying the last word in efficient processes and improved techniques. It is the visible, tangible response of American ingenuity, American brains, and American determination, to what was perhaps the deadliest danger this nation

387

ever faced. Around us here we have the living, the operating and producing, proof that, whatever our enemies thought, the American people can and will meet every demand, every danger, and every difficulty. The common effort, well-planned, ably directed, and steadfastly carried out, which created the Lake Charles refinery where two years ago there was nothing, tells us all we need to know. The spirit with which we built is the spirit with which we will work, and, you may be absolutely sure, the spirit with which we will win.

(Cozzens Papers, Princeton University Library)

Remarks for Major General Robert W. Harper,
Harvard Business School Alumni Association Conference,
Soldiers' Field, Boston, Mass.
(see 30 May 1944)

I am very glad of the opportunity to attend this conference of the Harvard Business School Alumni Association as the representative of the Commanding General of the Army Air Forces. Although the Army Air Forces have one first, all-absorbing job, which is to win this war—a job which you in essential New England industries play, and must go on playing, a large part—we, too, have faced great problems in adjusting what might be called our military economy to the vast emergency of this war. We, too, are very conscious of post-war problems which are bound to face us as soon as we win.

I don't hesitate to say 'as soon as we win,' not 'If we win.' Because we have done so much, and done it so quickly, and with steadily increasing signs of success, some of us may let ourselves believe that we really have won already, and it is all over but the shouting. In fact, we have already won, in the sense that our enemies lost when they didn't succeed in overwhelming us right away. That failure was fatal to them, but I don't think anyone here makes the mistake of imagining it is all over. What we need to win is not shouting, but unceasing work, unrelaxed determination, and the continued willingness to make great sacrifices and to bear great strains.

If this is what we need to win, it is also what we are going to need to make the adjustments and meet the problems that will come with victory. We have what we need to do both. The definite plain proof is in the job already done. How we did it seems to me to bear on all plans for the future. The post-war problem resembles the war problem. In the

Air Forces we had two immediate needs. First, to create, both by conversion and by new construction, what amounted to whole new industries employing hundreds of thousands of men. Second, to train two and a half million experts in what was, for most of them, entirely new jobs. What we are going to have to do, once the war is over, will be very much the same thing. We did it for war. I see no reason why we can't do it for peace.

My special job and my special interest has been in the vast training job, and I would like to tell you something about what we had to do, and what we did, and how we did it.

General Arnold, in his 1944 report to the Secretary of War—which I hope many of you had a chance to read—remarked that just before the war we ranked about seventh among the nations of the world in military aircraft—*but not in plans and ideas*.

I want to stress that point, because that vital form of preparedness was really what saved us in our hour of greatest danger. We knew, because we had given it close study and careful thought, what we would have to do. We had figured out ways of doing it. The treacherous first blow of the war surprised us, and did us great damage; but it did not confuse us. We had foreseen the need for the great air force we have today. An air force about twenty-five times as big as the air force of 1941. This means that twenty-four out of every twenty-five of our men were given their training during the last two and a half years. To organize such a program would have been hard enough, even if we had been free to devote all our time and attention to it.

As it was, we had to fight in the air on many fronts. Our production facilities, still far from ready or complete, had to supply as well as they could, our own fighting air forces overseas; the air forces which had to be held to meet the acute danger of direct attack on this continent, our commitments to our allies, and the expanding, absolutely essential needs of the training program—absolutely essential, because our chance of ever fighting more than a defensive war in the air, and even of fighting that defensive war effectively, depended on trained men.

It is no good building planes if there aren't pilots to fly them. Furthermore, the kind of air force we had to have to win was an offensive air force. The backbone of an offensive air force is the heavy, long-range bombers that bring the war to the enemy's air fields and assembly lines. Minimum training for pilots of such planes takes one hundred weeks—almost two years from the day the man reports for training to the day he can fly out on a mission.

Those who must fly with him—bombardiers, navigators, engineers, radio operators, gunners—can be turned out in a shorter time. So can the equally essential ground crews without whose very hard and exacting work no planes are going to fly at all. But every job is a job for a trained man, and somewhere, somehow, every man must get his training.

Just in terms of physical layout and equipment this meant covering the country with air fields and bases—really, an enormous network of technical schools with complicated and elaborate equipment to teach literally hundreds of special skills. The Air Forces did not have ready even a fraction of such fields and bases; it didn't begin to have men enough even to act as instructors. We were certainly faced with a problem as bitter and difficult as any that can face us with the coming of peace.

It was solved by energy, ingenuity, and common sense. The first step in the longest and hardest job—training pilots—was taken with the decision to use civilian flying schools to teach air cadets. Just plain flying, taking up a light plane and getting it down again, had to come before military flying or any training for combat. While thousands of cadets were thus getting into the air for the first time, we had a few precious weeks to get basic and advanced fields ready and to set up the facilities to give the unit training that would turn out the combat teams that fly the heavy bombers. To house the men in training we built what we could, and we rented what we could—over five-hundred hotels at one time. To get ground staffs, we commissioned and trained nearly 18,000 qualified men from civilian life, and established almost overnight the great officer candidate schools to make available for command and direction the special abilities of men in the ranks.

You must remember that all this was going on at once. Posts were being built, runways were being laid down, training equipment was being installed, even while new classes were arriving at gunnery or navigation or bombardier schools. New and necessary types of training were set up two jumps ahead of the men who were preparing to take it. It wasn't merely a matter of training men and sending them to groups already operational. Dozens and dozens of entirely new groups had to be formed with skeleton staffs trained as rapidly as possible by men with actual combat experience—mostly at the AAF School of Applied Tactics at Orlando. On the face of it, it seemed impossible; but the fact, seen plainly in the sky over every fighting front, is that it wasn't impossible, because we did it.

It is this record of practical energy, ingenuity and common sense that fills me—and, I hope, fills you—with confidence about the future. Granted that generalizations on energy and ingenuity and common sense are not going to solve specific tough problems of jobs for returned men, and conversion of war industries. We must have definite plans for peace, plans as definite as the plans we had for war. But in making those plans we certainly can count on the fact that, as a nation, energy, ingenuity and common sense worked for us in a great emergency. In simple logic, they can and will work for us again.

In the air forces particularly, we can feel that the training job has not been thrown away, in the sense of contributing nothing to the problems of peace. True, the end of the war is going to find us with many more trained pilots than jobs for pilots; and many more airplanes—including types whose only use is military—than we immediately need; and enormous production facilities that must be shut down and converted.

But almost all of the two and a half million air force men have special training, and on top of that, the hardest and most exacting sort of practical experience in a great variety of mechanical and technical jobs. It is no mere guess, or wish, to say that, whatever the future brings, it will offer vastly enlarged fields for men with such training and such skills. It is clear that aviation is going to play a larger and larger part in the economy of the future.

Because we know our problems now, because we can give them our earnest thought and prepare to meet them with practical plans, I think we can lick them. No one who saw, as I saw, fully and from the inside, the building of American air power, will feel dismay. We *have* done it before. We—you, I, all of us—can do it again. Let us, with good heart and high confidence, get on with the job of this war, and with the job of that peace.

(Cozzens Papers, Princeton University Library)

Proposed Remarks for General Arnold, Business Advisory Council Dinner, Mayflower Hotel, Washington, D.C. (see 24 June 1944)

Gentlemen:

In the armed services we are well aware of the importance of the practical work of the public spirited members of this council in meeting the great problems of the war production. Both strategically and tactically we are limited in any proposed plan or operation to what can be accomplished with the available supplies and weapons. When we get them, how good they are, and how many we have, determine what we can do and what we can't. At every step in the long course of production that lies between the raw material and the finished airplanes that our fine young flyers take into battle the knowledge and experience of men successful in the conduct of business affairs has been vitally necessary. With the workers and the fighters they make possible what might be called the total teamwork—the combined contribution of skills and knowledges of all our people—that in turn makes possible the conduct of modern war, and that is going to win this one for us.

I have stressed this matter of teamwork and the vital part played by the knowledge and experience you have so fully and freely placed at the nation's disposal because I am going to tell you about some factors in the air war that, at first glance, seem to involve only the men who are flying and fighting and the thousands more who service and maintain the planes that fly and fight. Their skill and ingenuity is extraordinary and their courage and devotion beyond praise; but, because the dangers and hardships are all theirs, do not imagine that the job is all theirs. You are not merely admiring spectators of heroic but remote actions. Your obligation is great and your responsibility is heavy. We have to have your knowledge and experience. You are part of the team.

During the last few weeks we have seen some remarkably instructive instances of the effective uses of air power in carefully coordinated operations with land and sea forces. The complete and detailed evaluation of them is not possible now, partly because we are not going to give our enemies information that would help them to meet our constantly heavier and more frequent blows, and partly because our enemies are, naturally, in a position to conceal from us certain effects of these blows. However, we know enough to be sure that what they are concealing will normally be damage greater and more serious than our observation and reconnaissance let us see.

Within these limitations we can consider, first, an example of relatively short range coordinated bombing of a number of targets—the operations of the Fifteenth Air Force against the north Italian railroads on May 13th; second an example of very long range smash at a vital industry which in any former war—and, indeed, even a year ago in this war—would have been completely safe from attack—the 20th Air Force's bombing of the Japanese Imperial Steel Works at Tawana on June 00; and third, the still undetermined, but certainly most suggestive and significant and I think closely related question, which I know you must all have asked yourselves; Where is the German Air Force?

As you doubtless know, it is very difficult to put a railroad out of commission by bombing it. Breaks that halt traffic are easily made, but they are also quickly and easily repaired. To do an effective job it is necessary to multiply the breaks and especially to hit the yards at those points from which wrecking crews would normally go out with the heavy equipment needed if the damaged line is to be cleared and repaired rapidly.

On May 13th last the Fifteenth Air Force put up almost eight hundred heavy bombers and a fighter escort with the object of crippling German railroad traffic in the Po valley. Practically simultaneous bombings of thirteen points on the Brenner Pass line carrying the principal load of traffic from Germany and on the Po valley line from Piacenza to Cesena on which the German forces then attempting to defend Rome largely depended, took place. These operations cost us one bomber. The effect was this. We had for some time been taking care of the railroads south of Rome but it was still possible, if difficult, for the Germans to get the minimum amount of supplies they needed by truck from points on the Piacenza-Cesena line. We simply arranged it so that no supplies would reach those points for a number of days. We figured that, in the face of the furious assaults of General Clark's forces, the Germans could not possibly hold if even for a limited period, they got no food, and particularly if they got no ammunition which they were expending in enormous quantities. We knew they could have little or no reserve in Rome because we had for weeks made rail traffic impossible by unceasing air attack. Without it there was no way to build a reserve up. The result was, of course, the fall of Rome, and a perfect demonstration of proper cooperation between ground forces, and air forces. I have just seen the following message from General Alexander to the Commanding General of our Air Forces in Italy: ON THE BRILLIANT VICTORY JUST GAINED BY OUR COMBINED ARMS, I TAKE THIS OPPORTUNITY OF EXTENDING TO ALL RANKS OF THE TWO AIR FORCES MY DEEP GRATITUDE, THANKS, AND CONGRATULATIONS FOR THE SIGNAL SERVICE YOU HAVE RENDERED TO THE TROOPS UNDER MY COMMAND. WITHOUT YOU WE COULD NOT HAVE DONE IT. WITH YOU WE WILL GO FORWARD TO STILL GREATER SUCCESS.

Let us consider now the bombing of the Japanese steel works at Yawata by our new B-29's—the Superfortresses. We have here what appears to be, and at this stage, is, a purely air action. We developed planes of great range and large bomb capacity and from distant bases delivered a blow at a selected target—selected because we, of course, know where we should hit to hurt Japan's war potential most. I say that this *appears* a purely air action, but that is because the preliminary blows in any coordinated effort of air, land, and sea forces are the logical and natural province of the air forces. We do not expect the B-29's to win the war by themselves. What we do expect is that, by giving us greater range and harder hitting power, we can step up the normal progression of the air-land-sea assault. What we did at Yawata, and what our new Twentieth Air Force is going to do elsewhere to the war plant in Japan's home islands, has a direct and obvious connection with any sea and land operations we may contemplate. The steel that Yawata isn't going to make will turn up missing at some point very critical for the Japanese, just as the supplies that came to a halt in the Po valley due to our air action, turned up missing when the Germans had to have them if they were to keep us out of Rome.

With these two examples of effective blows from the air in mind we can approach the mystery, agreeable and interesting to us, of the vanishing Luftwaffe. First, we know where it isn't. It isn't over our Norman beach heads. It did not come to meet us when we made the greatest landing in history. To explain this amazing fact several theories may be advanced. In the order of their probability, I would arrange them about as follows: (1) The Germans have decided to reserve the Luftwaffe and have powerful air forces carefully hidden on secret fields awaiting some decisive moment, perhaps to be identified by Hitler's celebrated intuition. (2) In order to give all their fronts a necessary minimum of air power, it was necessary to avoid heavy losses over the invasion beaches. By taking this prudent course, the Germans have, therefore preserved their air force in being. (3) There isn't any Luftwaffe left in the meaning of an effective modern air force with its thousands of highly trained airmen, its vast replacement depots of planes and parts, and its highly geared smoothly functioningaircraft production industry. This is not to say that the Germans haven't many formidable planes and many excellent and determined pilots. It is to say that they haven't enough of either to offer effective opposition to the enormous Allied air fleets, and by effective, I mean not only in terms of numbers and firepower, but probably most important, in terms of morale. Brave and tough men will take great chances and face long odds, but I don't envy the German pilots who day after day after day are expected to take off into the sky full of hell awaiting their outnumbered forces.

To the theory that the Germans are holding out on us, common sense makes several objections. From the standpoint of an airman, the Germans have been offered during the last few weeks what were certainly the best and most tempting targets of all time. Imagine what we would have done to German ports, crowded like the English ports with shipping for the invasion! After that, there was the gigantic, you might say, unmissable, sea full of ships moving across the channel. After that, there was the target of the beaches where we swarmed ashore piling our vital supplies and material up around us with no room to dodge or duck and no place to go but back into the deep sea. I can't believe that even Hitler's intuition would advise him to wait for better chances to use what air power he had.

It is true that the Royal Air Force, back in the days when the shoe was on the other foot, did follow the strategically shrewd and sound plan of refusing to expend its fighters by attempting to hold off all the bombers, then making what the Germans have since decided to call "Terror Raids," on England. The case is not the same. The British faced a possible sea-land invasion. The right time to hit any invasion is before it gets a foothold and if the Germans had ever started across the channel you may be sure the RAF would not have waited for a more "strategic" moment. That would have been it—the thing the reserves had been kept for.

We can't, of course, know the full story until after the war. Did our great bombing missions, resolutely and relentlessly continued for so long, cripple German aircraft production? Maybe they didn't; but right now, it certainly looks as if they did. Did our hammering of the German airfields and the transportation lines make it impossible for the German high command to get up the forces to throw us back into the sea while we still held no adequate port and had to struggle with very bad weather to land the absolutely indispensable supplies and reenforcements? We don't know—yet; but you can be sure we would not be in Cherbourg if the Germans had been able to find any way to keep us out.

In short, it is difficult for me to believe that the German Air Force is in reserve, or that it is prudently distributed on some principle certainly heretofore unknown to the art of war. I believe that our strategical plans were sound. I believe that our operations, carried out with skill, courage, and determination by our airmen in following these plans, have enabled the Air Forces to do their proper part in the great coordinated effort of all our arms. This is what we are going to continue to do. The heroic work of our sea and land forces leaves no doubt that they are also going to do theirs. United, we are going to win, and I don't think there's much our enemies can do about that.

(Cozzens Papers, Princeton University Library)

A Message from the Commanding General
(see 3 August 1944)

As we draw closer to the day of victory in Europe and Asia the Army Air Forces must undertake a new job. In vital importance it is second only to winning the war. We all know that a sound, prosperous, and lasting peace will not automatically follow victory. We must bring it about with the same single-minded determination that is bringing victory to our armed forces. We are starting on this job now, and you are one of the officers we have picked to do it.

The job is to settle the hundreds of claims arising from termination of our procurement contracts and to assist in the disposal of excess property resulting. Enormous sums of money and the livelihood of millions of workers are involved. To meet our war needs, we created an aircraft industry which is now the biggest single industry in this country;—in fact, the biggest single industry the world has ever seen. What happens to it when we no longer require production at present levels gravely concerns us all. If cut-backs and reconversion are mishandled, the impact on our whole economy will be disastrous. It will also greatly jeopardize our national security, which is bound to depend more and more on a sound and vital aircraft industry, able to lead the world in the design and construction of tomorrow's planes.

Plainly, this is not a job that just anyone can do. Intricate business problems must be grasped clearly and solved quickly. The prime requisite is good business judgment. We need the experience which only years of service in responsible executive positions can instill. That is why we have picked you.

I know that you realize that this will probably be your last army assignment. Perhaps you hoped, before the end, to get a post that would give you a chance for real fighting. I know that many of you are anxious to return to civilian life as soon as the war is over, and I am going to do everything in my power to see that you get out as promptly as possible. From checks we have made, we know that we will have enough civilian workers and officers who wish to remain in the service to wind up what business is left if you go about the job with energy and efficiency. Meanwhile, I assure you that those qualities—energy and efficiency—will continue to be the basis for promotion.

Your new job requires close and patient application; but it should be interesting and stimulating. You will deal with matters of high importance, in direct personal contact with men of great abilities, men who built the biggest industrial enterprise of our time, and who will be leaders in the peacetime development to come.

I know that the services you can give are absolutely necessary, and I consider the AAF fortunate in having them available. Yet I think you are fortunate, too. However heavy the responsibilities this assignment places on you, whatever the personal sacrifices it may require from some of you, you have now, and always will have the deeply satisfying knowledge that you freely and fully gave what only you could give when we most needed it.

(Cozzens Papers, Princeton University Library)

Draft of Article for the Honorable
Robert A. Lovett,
Assistant Secretary of War for Air
For: *Army and Navy Journal*
(see 1 September 1944)

The Way to Win a War

On August 22nd, 1944, a very welcome tribute was paid the air forces of the United Nations. We are indebted to Lieutenant General Kurt Dittmar, the Nazi commentator, for his free and frank acknowledgment of what we have been accomplishing in Europe. Explaining the ruinous break-through in Normandy, he observed grimly that "the tremendous air superiority of the enemy is in a position to hamper every movement. One cannot doubt that here lies the basic cause for all our difficulties."

"Difficulties" puts it mildly. This war's great lesson is teamwork—the coordinated efforts of land, sea, and air forces bring victory. When control of the air is lost, troops on the ground may still fight on, often desperately and well, but the odds against them become immediately enormous, out of all proportion to any actual discrepancy in numbers and equipment between them and the enemy's ground forces. This modern military truth—perhaps new to the Germans, though they got a taste of it in Africa—we understand perfectly. We learned it the hard way during the dark and bitter first months of our war in the Pacific. I hope and believe that we as a nation will never forget what it was like when the Japanese held the air over the Philippines and we could oppose them with no more than a handful of fliers in half a dozen makeshift planes. That handful of fliers did wonders, but wonders on that scale couldn't keep Bataan or save Corregidor. If things had been different, if air superiority had been ours, who can doubt that the Japanese, far from being able to inflict on us the most humiliating defeat in our military history, could hardly have established, and certainly could not have long held, even the smallest beachhead on Luzon?

The unhappy lesson was resumed when we sent what pitiful air forces we had left to try to help the Dutch in Java and Sumatra. We got more of it when we came so frighteningly close to losing New Guinea and were not even sure that Australia could be saved. That isn't a part of the war that we like to dwell on, but we must not, now or ever, put it out of mind. We must not, now or ever, run any risk of having to face an enemy at the disadvantage so deadly to us in 1942 and so deadly to the Germans in 1944.

We know why we were at that disadvantage. Surprised by a treacherous attack, we had too little air power in the Philippines to defend our position. This is an explanation. It will not serve as an excuse because there can be no excuses for any act or policy that may endanger our national existence. It simply says why we were thrown out of the Philippines. We are going back because we have now what we needed then.

We also know why the Germans found themselves in the position that General Dittmar, with so much reason, deplored. Our air forces and the Royal Air Force heavily and systematically—and at no small cost—attacked for months the sources of German air power. We planned with care and worked with determination to bring about exactly that tremendous air superiority which covered the landings in France and brought to nothing every German effort to contain us.

A principal factor was, of course, the courage and resolution of our air crews who faithfully carried out our plans regardless of danger and regardless of loss. But let us remember that the men who fought for us while we were losing in the Philippines and the South Pacific had no less courage and resolution. What they did not have was the necessary equipment. Courage and resolution are things we can always count on the spirit of our people to give us, but we did not bomb Germany's air force to pieces by courage and resolution alone. Without the finest airplanes in the world we could have accomplished little or nothing. If we had given our men bombers like those the Germans sent against England—so many sitting ducks for the RAF—we would have succeeded no better than the Germans. Without the fastest and hardest-hitting fighters in the world to escort our bombers we could not have long supported our losses.

This is another lesson that I hope and believe we have learned. If our planes are not as good as the enemy's planes, we have, actually, no air power at all. If they are not better than the enemy's planes, we cannot hope for national security. As we draw closer to victory in Europe and Asia we must make vital decisions on exactly this point. At the war's end we will have planes by the thousand, many of them brand new, all of them very expensive. We are going to have to face the fact that the greater part of them are not worth keeping. There is no longer any military secret, except in technical details, about the jet propulsion planes. In numbers too few to affect the issue in Europe both we and the Germans have them. By the time the war ends, we will undoubtedly have a good many of them. The P-38's, the P-47's, even our incomparable P-51's, all planes of brilliant record and brilliant accomplishment, little later than tomorrow are going to have the military value of so much junk. We must handle them accordingly.

Of course that is not the end. The best we can now do with the new principle of propulsion will seem poor and crude when compared to the developments of the near future. We must make sure that we—our air force, our aircraft industry—lead in these developments. This means maintaining a vital and adequate air force, and an industry with the technical facilities to design and build planes which will continue to be the best in the world. In our plans for the future we must provide the essentials—the great bases, the trained men, all the materiel—for such an air force. We must manage our reconversion program so that our aircraft manufacturers remain sound and solvent. We must keep our commercial air lines second to none. We have learned how to win a war in this air age. Our best hope for a long and secure peace lies in remembering what we have learned.

(Cozzens Papers, Princeton University Library.
Rewritten as "Air Lessons for the Future,"
Army & Navy Journal
[Special Numbers for 1943-1944], 22, 162.)

NOTES

[1]The Air Force Training Aids Division (TAD), 1 Park Avenue, New York City.

[2]A projected Air Force magazine.

[3]An Air Force magazine.

[4]Cozzens was collaborating on "The Air Force Training Program," *Fortune*, XXX (February 1944), 147-152, 174, 176, 178, 180, 183-184, 186, 189-190, 193-194.

[5]Cozzen's wife, Bernice Baumgarten, was a prominent New York literary agent. She had dropped her first name, Sylvia, but he referred to her as "S" in his diaries. While Cozzens was serving at the Pentagon she visited him almost every weekend.

[6]Service rating form.

[7]An office in the C ring of the Pentagon.

[8]Jo H. Chamberlin, magazine writer and editor.

[9]Robert Reeves, author of *Dead and Done For* (1939), *No Love Lost* (1941), and *Cellini Smith, Detective* (1943).

[10]Edward Newhouse, novelist and short story writer, author of *You Can't Sleep Here* (1934), *This Is Your Day* (1937), and *Anything Can Happen* (1941).

[11]Vogel was the *Fortune* writer assigned to "The Air Force Training Program"; Paine and Furth were *Fortune* editors.

[12]Apartment complex in Alexandria, Virginia.

[13]Cozzens had been stationed at Gravelly Point, Washington, D.C., in 1942.

[14]A civilian at the Civil Aeronautics Administration with whom Cozzens had collaborated on the handbook *Airways Flying* (Training Aids Division, 1943) and "Airways Flying," *Air Transport*, I (September 1943), 39-42.

[15]George Haddock was a former Washington newspaper editor. He provided a partial model for Capt. Collins in *Guard of Honor*.

[16]Gen. George S. Patton, Jr., had slapped a soldier suffering from battle fatigue.

Notes

[17]For achievement in aeronautics.

[18]Maj. Gen. Clayton L. Bissell, Assistant Chief of Air Staff, Intelligence.

[19]Henry L. Stimson, Secretary of War.

[20]New York: Aerosphere, 1944, p. xcvii.

[21]Oveta Culp Hobby, commanding colonel of the Women's Army Corps (WAC).

[22]Robert P. Patterson, Undersecretary of War.

[23]"Arnold Reports Production Wiped Out in Triple Target," *Washington Post* (13 January 1944), 1-2; statement on bombing of factories at Oschersleben, Halberstadt, and Brunswick.

[24]19 January 1944, 18: "It seems quite clear that oratory, even General Arnold's, does not win battles. . . ."

[25]Hollywood director William Wyler.

[26]Cozzens's mother, Bertha Wood Cozzens.

[27]Warner Brothers, 1945. Screenplay by Ranald MacDougall and Lester Cole from an original screen story by Alvah Bessie.

[28]Robert A. Lovett, Assistant Secretary of War for Air. Cozzens later commented on Lovett: ". . . he could handle, really master, in a way no one but George Marshall matched a man, say, vain or perfidious often like FDR; a table-pounding roaring Hap Arnold, a braggart & poser like MacArthur. He was so quiet you'd say he never could until, incredulous (and I'll bet they were too) you saw he'd not a hair turned, gone and done it" (to MJB, 28 February 1976). Lovett served as Secretary of Defense during the Korean War.

[29]Burton K. Wheeler, Democratic Senator from Montana.

[30]Bradshaw, a 1930 Princeton graduate, was the author of short stories and cookbooks.

[31]Maj. Gen. Lawrence S. Kuter, Assistant Chief of Air Staff, Plans.

[32]Col. John Allison maintained flying control during the Burma campaign and protected the river crossing near the Bhama Road. As a fighter pilot he became a double ace in the CBI theatre.

[33]Special House Committee chaired by Representative Robert Ramspeck of Georgia.

[34]*The Pointer*, XXII (20 October 1944), 1.

[35]A mock-up of a cockpit for instrument training.

[36]Fleet-Admiral Chester W. Nimitz, senior American admiral of the Pacific theatre.

[37]*A Walk in the Sun* (New York: Knopf, 1944).

[38]Financier Floyd Odlum.

[39]*The Harvard Advocate*, to which Cozzens had contributed as an undergraduate.
[40]Gold braid.

[41]Col. Philip C. Cochran, air commander in Burma; he provided a model for Flip Corkin in the comic strip "Terry and the Pirates."

[42]Lt. Gen. Barney M. Giles, Chief of Air Staff and Deputy Commanding General, AAF.

[43]Deputy Chief of Air Staff and Chief of Staff, Twentieth Air Force; Norstad became Supreme Allied Commander Europe SHAPE (1956-1963).

[44]The Reverend Richard M. Doubs.

[45]Frances Perkins.

[46]Cozzens had worked with Harris at *Fortune*; Harris's wife, a feminist, retained her maiden name.

[47]Brig. Gen. Frederic H. Smith, Jr., Deputy Chief of Air Staff. In 1961 he became Vice Chief of Staff of the Air Force.

[48]"U.S. Reported Working on Atomic Bomb," *Washington Post* (26 October 1944), 13.

Verbatim Transcript of Army Air Force Press Conference Conducted by Brig. Gen. Frederic H. Smith, Jr., Deputy Chief of the Air Staff, 25 October 1944

The first Question:
"There has been renewed speculation, especially from overseas points such as Stockholm, of new German secret weapons, including a 40-ft. rocket bomb with atomic explosive features. Do our technicians look upon these ideas as within the realm of possibility or is it to be considered entirely in the field of psychological warfare?"

I would like to answer that by stating that, of course, nearly anything is in the realm of possibility these days. Technological development under the impetus of war has produced so many fabulously or fabulous weapons, as well as application of electronics, and so forth, that almost anything is possible. There are technical difficulties, however, in launching enormous robots, and the preparation for the launching of these tremendous rockets is extensive. The elaborate platforms on the invasion coast are typical of the installation, storage, or launching which must go along with any effective bombardment by such weapons. As for the bomb-carrying capacity of robots, there is no certainty that the Germans, who have been forced back, can greatly increase the efficiency of the V-2 by just enlarging the size. In other words, in going back further, their launching sites being farther from the target—assuming it's London—they must incorporate fuel carrying in the increase in size so that the war head, itself, doesn't increase proportionately with the rocket, itself, due to the increase in range problem. It is safe to say that every country is working on large, destructive missiles which will go a long way. And no doubt the Germans are use—working on the use of atomic explosive power. They'd be foolish if they weren't working on such a project. I am not enough long-haired man to know just how far along we are in this country on controlling atomic power. (Cozzens Papers, Princeton University Library)

It was deemed necessary for Cozzens to be briefed on the atomic bomb to prevent inadvertent leaks. See *Morning Noon and Night* (New York: Harcourt Brace & World, 1968):

A couple of days before, it seemed, the officer in the writing section of OIS who prepared remarks for a Deputy Chief of Air Staff chosen to meet the press regularly on the C.G.'s behalf had with utmost inadvertence among answers to questions submitted by newspapermen put in the Deputy Chief's mouth a statement about the atomic bomb. Since the writer had no actual information on the subject the answer was hardly informative. Neither the writer nor the Deputy Chief, a personable young brigadier general who had the assignment because he was liked by the press, saw anything in the few sentences but standard operating procedure—that harmless unsignifying polite brush-off routinely used when you had no answer to give. Glancing at the prepared note sheets lying before him on the conference table the Deputy Chief read off the question. Well, like all the belligerents, he informed the gathering, we were deeply interested in such a bomb's possibilities. You could be sure we had our people working on it.

Consternation in high quarters when this 'harmless' comment credited (horrors!) to an Air Staff spokesman of rank came out in a newspaper was understandable—though maybe high quarters might have reflected that the perfection of their security measures was demonstrated about to the hilt when an Air Staff general officer surely on the Top Secret list could give this innocent proof that he hadn't ever been allowed to know the atomic-bomb project existed. But now plainly demonstrated, too, was an overlooked danger in such effective absolute security. It was judged to be essential for a selected few persons—one having connection with OIS—to be told that not only were we 'working on it,' but also we had got so far that our having it was certain. Under absolutely no circumstances was a remotest reference to be made to the work (pp. 305-306).

[49]Special Senate Committee investigating the defense program, chaired by James Mead of New York—formerly the Truman Committee.

[50]Admiral Marc A. Mitscher, task force commander in the Pacific.

[51]*Tactics and Technique of Air Fighting.* Cozzens had tried to revise this manual in 1943 with Capt. Reade Tilley.

[52]James V. Piersol, "New Air Force to Guard U.S., Relieving AAF," 13.

[53]On 12 January 1947 Cozzens wrote to his mother predicting an eventual attack on the U.S. by Russia: "My information on this point is, I think, good because it comes from reading everyday for a year and a half the secret messages of the AAFHq In and Out Log which left little doubt that the Russian government mortally feared and hated us—even to the point of having tipped off the Germans who came over the Russian fields the night after the only really large 'shuttle' raid and destroyed most of the bombers we had put down there" (Cozzens Papers, Princeton University Library).

DeWitt S. Copp, *Forged in Fire: Strategy and Decisions in the Air War over Europe 1940-45* (Garden City: Doubleday, 1982), pp. 468-469:

It was a plan to establish fields and facilities in the Ukraine so that long-range missions could be conducted without the return flight. Code name FRANTIC had been under preparation since the Tehran Conference.

....

In all, six FRANTIC missions were flown, and the first one carried out by the Eighth Air Force, on June 21, brought a staggering result, the Eighth suffering one of the heaviest losses of the war. Not in the air but on the ground. A German reconnaissance plane had tracked the force to Poltava after it attacked targets in Poland. That night the German bombers came. Russian antiaircraft was incapable of harming them. When the smoke cleared, forty-three of the 114 Forts were finished. So were fifteen Mustangs, and another twenty-six aircraft were damaged. Fortunately, there was only one American fatality.

See Edmund Hicks, "Soviet Sojourn," *Airpower Historian*, XI (January 1964), 1-5; Russell Bradshaw, "To Russia: One Way," *Aerospace Historian*, XXV (December 1978), 198-205.

Morning Noon and Night (pp. 390-391):
. . . 'Mr. A.' stormed impulsively around. He was, I learned from the Secretary's Executive Officer, in one of his regular high rages about the administration's continuing to indulge the Russians in their stubborn refusal to let us set up air bases behind their lines—we had, ready and waiting, everything to do it—and thus conduct a 'transit' bombing of German targets. This would probably cut at least in half Eighth Bomber Command losses, a great part of which resulted from the B-17's having to turn back to England against defense elements fully alerted along the way. It was too goddam unreasonable. We'd need only a month or so to do the whole job; all we wanted from the Russians was a few square miles of ground, and nothing would cost them a cent, and lives of 'his' men were at stake, and he wasn't going to stand for it any longer.

(I confess I would be interested to know just how the Secretary contrived—as he always did—to cope with this. Hard fact of the matter, reported by our Intelligence, was that the Communist rulers would remain obdurate and absolute in rejecting every proposal of the kind. Their compelling reason was that they simply didn't dare let the subject Russian masses catch even a glimpse of our military way of life, our wealth of equipment, and most particularly, the routine lavishing of comforts and conveniences on our servicemen. The old Comintern-line myth, still forcibly fed by the Kremlin to its dupes, about miseries of 'the people' under 'capitalistic enslavement' exploded before their eyes—well, comes now, Stalin can bet, the real revolution!)

[54]Brig. Gen. Reuben C. Hood, Jr., Deputy Chief of Air Staff.

[55]"Isolating the Battlefield," *Air Force*, XXVIII (March 1945), 8-9, 36.

[56]Brandt & Brandt literary agency, where Bernice Cozzens worked.

[57]Willard Edwards, "Survey Disproves Army Denial That Reds Get Commissions," *Washington Times-Herald* (1 March 1945), 1-2. This article cited Newhouse as a former staff member of the *Daily Worker* who "has openly admitted in his writings that he was a member of the Communist Party." Newhouse observes, "As luck would have it, I was too shy, too detached, and much too lazy to act out my teenage political enthusiasms; and so, the late *Times-Herald* to the contrary notwithstanding, I never did join the Communist Party" (to MJB, 24 March 1982). See James Thurber, *The Years with Ross* (Boston: Little, Brown, 1959), p. 167.

[58]Deputy Commander for Operations, Eighth Air Force. In May 1945 he became Senior Military Advisor, U.S. Strategic Bombing Survey.

Notes

[59]Lt. Gen. George Kenney, Commanding General, Far Eastern Air Forces.

[60]Gen. Arnold was recovering from a heart attack.

[61]"Army Injustice," *Washington Evening Star* (5 April 1945), A-10; "The Army's Error" (9 April 1945), A-9. At 12:40 p.m. on 3 September 1943 Lt. Sidney Shapiro was charged under Articles of War 96; at 2 p.m. he was tried; at 5:30 he was found guilty and dismissed from the service.

[62]Articles of War 96: "Though not mentioned in these articles, all disorders and neglects to the prejudice of good order and military discipline, all conduct of a nature to bring discredit upon the military service, and all crimes or offenses not capital, of which persons subject to military law may be guilty, shall be taken cognizance of by a general or special or summary court-martial, according to the nature and degree of the offense, and punished at the discretion of such court."

[63]Lt. Gen. Ira Eaker, former Commander in Chief of the Mediterranean Allied Air Forces, replaced Gen. Giles as Army Air Forces Chief of Staff on 30 April 1945.

[64]*Indianapolis News*: "3 Negro Officers Held for 'Jostling' Provost Marshal" (12 April 1945), 8; "100 Freeman Field Officers Are Held in Club Dispute" (20 April 1945), 16. *Indianapolis Times*: "Freeman Field Row is Probed" (20 April 1945), 6. *Indianapolis Recorder*: "Arrest 60 Air Officers; 3 Held" (14 April 1945), 1; "Arrest 101 Air Officers of 477th" (21 April 1945), 1; "Plan Changes to Aid Airmen" (28 April 1945), 1; "477th Officers Held Under Armed Guard" (26 May 1945), 1. *New York Times*: "104 Negro Officers Held" (21 April 1945), 15; "Negro Colonel Heads Unit After Race Row" (22 June 1945), 5. *New York Post*: "Negro Officers Face Trial—Protested Ban" (11 April 1945), 5; "F.D.R. Gets Plea to Free Negro Officers in Bias Case" (12 April 1945), 10; Paul Sann, "Army Probes Jim Crowism in Camp, Bars New Arrests" (16 April 1945), 14; Sann, "Army Veils Jim Crow Probe" (17 April 1945), 8; Sann, "May Transfer Colonel From 'Jim Crow' Field" (19 April 1945), 4; "Negro Fliers Cleared in Camp Probe" (26 April 1945), 7.

See Earl D. Lyon, "The Training of Negro Combat Units by the First Air Force" (Albert F. Simpson Historical Research Center); Alan Gropman, "The Air Force Integrates: Blacks in the Air Force from 1945 to 1965" (Tufts University dissertation, 1975); Alan M. Osur, *Blacks in the Army Air Forces During World War II: The Problems of Race Relations* (Washington: Office of Air Force History, [1977]).

[65]AR 210-10, paragraph 19: ". . . membership or admission to an officers club shall be denied no officer on duty at that post."

On 23 April 1945 Cozzens wrote his mother about the Freeman Field situation: "My own impulse would be to enforce the regulations which prohibited segregation. I can see that it is not practical. Failing that, my next impulse would be the clarify the matter by admitting that we were going to practise segregation. This, too, is wrong, because we then define the issue. For every purpose except that of enjoying a personal sense of virtuous candor, the right policy is to evade the issue, because though slowly and laboriously, the problem is working itself out—there are plenty of AAF fields where colored officers are perfectly free to come into the club and there has been no trouble of any kind. If we point the issue, either by enforcing the regulation and so provoking riot and mutiny at one field, or by changing the regulation to conform to the practise we are in fact allowing, everyone is going to have to take sides. If a thousand white officers are arrested and court-martialled because they do not want to drink beer with negroes we are not going to improve the relations between the races. I find such problems wearing, but I had to see that Gen Hedrick, the Air Judge Advocate, with whom I was discussing it Saturday, is right. Hypocrisy is an essential ingredient in human relationships"(Cozzens Papers, Princeton University Library).

[66]Former Commanding General of the Eighth Air Force, Commanding General of the Army Air Forces in the European Theatre of Operations and Commanding General of the Northwest African Air Force; in July 1945 he became Commanding General of the U.S. Strategic Air Forces in the Pacific. Spaatz became Commanding General of the Army Air Forces in 1946 and the first Chief of Staff of the United States Air Force in 1947, when the Air Force became a separate branch of the military service.

[67]This note marks the inception of *Guard of Honor.*

[68]Lt. Gen. William Knudsen, former president of General Motors corporation, was director of industrial production during World War II.

[69]Articles of War 104: "Disciplinary powers of commanding officers. Under such regulations as the President may prescribe, the commanding officer of any detachment, company, or higher command, may, for minor offenses, impose disciplinary punishments upon persons of his command without the intervention of a court-martial, unless the accused demands trial by court-martial."

[70]Articles of War 64: "Assaulting or wilfully disobeying superior officer. Any person subject to military law who, on any pretense whatsoever, strikes his superior officer or draws or lifts up any weapon or offers any violence against him, being in the execution of his office, or wilfully disobeys any lawful command of his superior officer, shall suffer death or such other punishment as a court-martial may direct."

[71]Maj. Gen. Curtis E. LeMay was Commanding General of the Twenty-first Bomber Command in the Marianas and planned the B-29 raids on Japan. He later became Commanding General of the Strategic Air Command and the Air Force Chief of Staff.

[72]"M'Arthur Doctor Defends Major," *New York Times* (13 December 1945), 19; "Major Fabbricatore Convicted; Gets 3 Years for Army Frauds," *New York Times* (22 December 1945), 1. Fabbricatore was found guilty of seventeen of nineteen specifications; he was sentenced to dismissal from the service, forfeiture of pay and allowances, and three years at hard labor.

[73]In 1947 Maj. Gen. Bennett E. Meyers, retired, former Deputy Chief of Procurement for the Air Forces, testified before the Senate War Investigating Committee on his financial dealings with Howard Hughes. It was also charged that Meyers was the hidden owner of the Aviation Electric Corporation of Dayton, Ohio, for which he solicited wartime subcontracts as an officer. On 12 March 1948 the Federal District Court in Washington found Meyers guilty of three counts of persuading a witness to commit perjury before the Senate War Investigating Committee; he was sentenced to a twenty-month-to-five-year prison term (*New York Times* [13 March 1948], 1, 16).

[74]Maj. Gen. Claire L. Chennault, leader of the Flying Tigers and subsequently commander of the Fourteenth Air Force in China. He resigned on 14 July 1945, making it clear that he felt Washington was not giving Chiang Kai-shek sufficient support.

[75]The first atomic bomb had been dropped on Hiroshima.

[76]Dr. Harold Jacobson had informed the newspapers that the atomic bomb would leave behind killing radioactivity for seventy years.

[77]On 29 June 1945 Radovich was convicted by a general court martial on all four counts of violating two articles of war; he was dismissed from the service and sentenced to three years at hard labor (*New York Times* [30 June 1945], 19). Radovich and Samuel and Elias Bayer were indicted for conspiracy on 12 July 1945 (*New York Times* [13 July 1945], 13). The court-martial conviction was reversed on 1 September 1945 by a board of review because the trial record was "legally insufficient to support the findings and the sentence because the lay member of the court erroneously refused to admit evidence" (*New York Times* [2 September 1945], 21). Radovich and the Bayers were found guilty of conspiracy on 23 October 1945 (*New York Times* [24 October 1945], 4); but the convictions were set aside by the U.S. Circuit Court of Appeals on 15 August 1946 (*New York Times* [16 August 1946], 4). The Supreme Court upheld the conviction of Radovich and the Bayers on 9 June 1947 (*New York Times* [10 June 1947], 11).

[78]"The Washington Merry-Go-Round," *Washington Post* (13 September 1945), 7B. Pearson described the strategic-bombing survey as "one of the Army's best boondoggling projects."

[79]Kelly was credited by Gen. Douglas MacArthur with having piloted the bomber that sank the battleship *Haruna* north of Luzon on 9 December 1941.

Wesley Frank Croven and James Lea Cate's, *The Army Air Forces in World War II* (Chicago: University of Chicago Press, 1948) provides the report of the Office of Air Force History:

Capt. Colin Kelly in the fifth bomber had been directed to locate and if possible sink an aircraft carrier previously reported along the northern Luzon coast. After a search of the target area he found no sign of a carrier, but Lt. Joe M. Bean, his navigator, had spotted a large Japanese warship which the aircrew took for a battleship. Indeed, early reports of the ensuing action placed the ship in either the *Haruna* or the *Yamishiro* class. Actually, it is now known that no Japanese battleship participated in the initial invasion of the Philippines, and that the *Haruna*, the favored choice in subsequent reports, was engaged until 18 December in support of the Malayan campaign. . . . At any rate, Navy PBY's claimed on the following day to have hit a ship of the *Haruna* class in this same general area. Japanese sources indicate that the ship picked out by Lieutenant Bean was in fact the heavy cruiser *Ashigara*, flagship of the Third Fleet in its current operation. As it moved slowly on the outskirts of the enemy convoy it made a good target, and the bombardier, Sgt. Meyer S. Levin, released in train the entire load of three 600-lb. bombs from 22,000 feet. Although the Japanese assert that no hits were made, the bombs scored near misses and to Kelly's crew it appeared that one of them had struck squarely amidship. When the B-17 turned back toward its base, the warship appeared to have been stopped with black smoke pouring from it. All gunners held their stations during the return flight except the radio operator, who served also as lower-turret gunner, and who left that post to receive landing instructions from Clark Field. Suddenly, as the plane neared the field, two enemy fighters attacked from the rear of and below the plane in an approach which probably would have been observed sooner had the lower turret been manned. Bullets riddled the big bomber. "The commander's dome flew off," the instrument panel seemed to disintegrate, a machine-gun burst penetrated the left rear gunner's post killing T/Sgt. William J. Delehanty, the low-pressure oxygen tanks in the radio compartment exploded, and the empty bomb bay burst into flames. When the flames spread, Kelly ordered the crew to bail out. S/Sgt. James E. Hokyard, Pfc Robert A. Altman, and Pfc Williard L. Money dropped out of the rear compartment; Bean and Levin tumbled out of the escape hatch; and Kelly and co-pilot Lt. Donald D. Robins prepared to follow. The latter succeeded in pulling the rip cord of his parachute after being thrown clear of the plane by a tremendous explosion, and all those who previously had bailed out of the plane reached ground safely. But Kelly's body was later found near the wreckage of his plane (Vol. I, pp. 216-217).

Col. E. L. Eubank's 19 February 1942 narrative report of the flight notes: "It is not known exactly how Captain KELLY met his death. He may have been rendered unconscious by enemy action (Lt. Bean having observed that the B-17 was attacked by the second enemy pursuit plane just before it exploded), he may have been killed as a result the explosion, or he may have been struck by some part of the plane as he attempted to jump" ("History of the Fifth Air Force and its Predecessors," Part I, Appendix II, Document 25).

A North American Newspaper Alliance dispatch based on interviews with his "closest brother officers" reported that "Captain Kelly was still able to open the sliding door in the roof, climbed out of his seat and jumped, but the plane took a bounce and he was thrown aside and hit the leading edge of the ship's tail, stunning him and possibly killing him. He was unable, of course, to open his parachute" ("New Yorker Bags 4 Enemy Planes Out of 8 Downed in Luzon," *New York Times* [24 December 1941], 9).

Lt. Donald Robins, the co-pilot, wrote an account of the mission for the United Press which provides no details about Kelly's final actions: "The rest of the story is vague. . . . I believe I was thrown out of the plane by an explosion, and through no volition of my own" ("How Capt. Kelly Sank Battleship," *New York Times* [7 March 1942], 3).

See Carroll S. Shershun's "The Man Who Downed Colin Kelly" (*Aerospace Historian*, XIII [Winter 1966], 149-152) for an interview with Zero pilot Saburo Sakai.

When the radioman, Pfc. Robert Altman, was relased from Japanese captivity in 1945, he told the press that Kelly's B-17 had scored a direct hit on the *Haruna*, but he provided no details about the circumstances of Kelly's death (Elgar Brown, "How Colin Kelly Died Revealed by Plane Mate," *New York Herald Tribune* [31 August 1945], 3).

Although it was generally believed that Kelly was awarded the Congressional Medal of Honor, he was awarded the Distinguished Service Cross on 21 December 1941 by Command of Gen. MacArthur.

[80]"Miracles Take Time," *Army & Navy Journal* [Special Numbers for 1944-1945], 28, 214.